German Romanticism
and Science

Routledge Studies in Romanticism

1. **Keats's Boyish Imagination**
Richard Marggraf Turley

2. **Leigh Hunt**
Life, Poetics, Politics
Edited by Nicholas Roe

3. **Leigh Hunt and the London Literary Scene**
A Reception History of his Major Works, 1805–1828
Michael Eberle-Sinatra

4. **Tracing Women's Romanticism**
Gender, History and Transcendence
Kari E. Lokke

5. **Metaphysical Hazlitt**
Bicentenary Essays
Uttara Natarajan, Tom Paulin and Duncan Wu

6. **Romantic Genius and the Literary Magazine**
Biography, Celebrity, Politics
David Higgins

7. **Romantic Representations of British India**
Edited by Michael Franklin

8. **Sympathy and the State in the Romantic Era**
Systems, State Finance, and the Shadows of Futurity
Robert Mitchell

9. **Thomas De Quincey**
New Theoretical and Critical Directions
Edited by Robert Morrison and Daniel Sanjiv Roberts

10. **Romanticism and Visuality**
Fragments, History, Spectacle
Sophie Thomas

11. **Romanticism, History, Historicism**
Essays on an Orthodoxy
Edited by Damian Walford Davies

12. **The Meaning of "Life" in Romantic Poetry and Poetics**
Edited by Ross Wilson

13. **German Romanticism and Science**
The Procreative Poetics of Goethe, Novalis, and Ritter
Jocelyn Holland

German Romanticism and Science
The Procreative Poetics of Goethe, Novalis, and Ritter

Jocelyn Holland

Routledge
Taylor & Francis Group
New York   London

First published 2009
by Routledge
711 Third Avenue, New York, NY 10017

Simultaneously published in the UK
by Routledge
2 Park Square, Milton Park, Abingdon, Oxon OX14 4RN

Psychology Press is an imprint of the Taylor & Francis Group, an informa business
First published in paperback 2012
© 2009 Taylor & Francis

Typeset in Sabon by IBT Global.

All rights reserved. No part of this book may be reprinted or reproduced or utilised in any form or by any electronic, mechanical, or other means, now known or hereafter invented, including photocopying and recording, or in any information storage or retrieval system, without permission in writing from the publishers.

Trademark Notice: Product or corporate names may be trademarks or registered trademarks, and are used only for identification and explanation without intent to infringe.

Library of Congress Cataloging in Publication Data
Holland, Jocelyn, 1973–
 German romanticism and science : the procreative poetics of Goethe, Novalis, and Ritter / Jocelyn Holland.
  p. cm. — (Routledge studies in romanticism ; 13)
 Includes bibliographical references and index.
 1. Goethe, Johann Wolfgang von, 1749–1832—Criticism and interpretation. 2. Novalis, 1772–1801—Criticism and interpretation. 3. Ritter, Johann Wilhelm, 1776–1810—Criticism and interpretation. 4. German literature—18th century—History and criticism. 5. Romanticism—Germany. 6. Human reproduction in literature. 7. Literature and science. I. Title.
 PT2213.H65 2009
 830.9'145—dc22
 2008044843

Chapter 2 contains an extensively revised version of "*Eine Art Wahnsinn*: Intellektuelle Anschauung und Goethes Schriften zur Metamorphose" in *Intellektuelle Anschauung— unmögliche Evidenz*, edited by Sibylle Peters and Martin Schäfer (Bielefeld: *transcript*, 2006), 79–92. Reprinted with the permission of *transcript*. Part of Chapter 4 was published as "The Poet as Artisan. Novalis' *Werkzeug* and the Making of Romanticism" in *German MLN* 121, no. 3 (2006): 617–630. © The Johns Hopkins University Press. Reprinted with permission of The Johns Hopkins University Press

ISBN13: 978-0-415-99326-5 (hbk)
ISBN13: 978-0-203-87901-6 (ebk)
ISBN13: 978-0-415-65496-8 (pbk)

Bianca Theisen, in memoriam

Contents

Acknowledgments   ix

1   Introduction   1

2   Poetic Procreation and Goethe's Theory of Metamorphosis   19

3   Friedrich von Hardenberg and the Discourse of Procreation   56

4   The Poet as Artisan and the Instruments of Procreation   85

5   Johann Wilhelm Ritter and the Writing of Life   113

6   Procreative Thinking—Scientific Projects   134

Conclusion   157

Notes   165
Bibliography   209
Index   219

Acknowledgments

I cannot express the extent of my gratitude to those who helped me complete this manuscript. To my parents, John and Jeanne Holland; to my dissertation advisors, Rüdiger Campe and Bianca Theisen; to my colleagues at UCSB, to my friends, and to Gil: thank you!

1 Introduction

> If we return to the field of philosophy and consider evolution and epigenesis once more, then these seem to be words with which we only hinder ourselves.
>
> (Johann Wolfgang von Goethe, MA 12:101)[1]

> Everything indicates that the essence of procreation is absolutely to be sought more deeply than in the mere laws of matter.
>
> (Johann Wilhelm Ritter, *Fragmente*, n. 504)[2]

According to Karl Ernst von Baer, it was a combination of luck and scientific practice that led him to identify the mammalian ovum in 1826, an important step in unveiling the secret of human procreation:

> Sonderbar! dachte ich, was muss das seyn? Ich öffnete ein Bläschen und hob vorsichtig das Fleckchen mit dem Messer in ein mit Wasser gefülltes Uhrglas, das ich unter das Mikroskop brachte. Als ich in dieses einen Blick geworfen hatte, fuhr ich, wie vom Blitze getroffen, zurück, denn ich sah deutlich eine sehr kleine, scharf ausgebildete gelbe Dotterkugel. Ich musste mich erholen, ehe ich den Muth hatte, wieder hinzusehen, da ich besorgte, ein Phantom habe mich betrogen. Es scheint sonderbar, dass ein Anblick, den man erwartet und ersehnt hat, erschrecken kann, wenn er da ist. (Von Baer, *Selbstbiographie*, 311)

> Strange! I thought, what must that be? I opened a vesicle and carefully lifted that little fleck with the knife into a watch glass filled with water, which I then brought under the microscope. As I took a look at it I jumped back as if struck by lightning, for I clearly saw a very small, precisely formed yellow yolk orb. I had to recover before I had the courage to look again, for I was worried that a phantom might have deceived me. It seems strange that the sight of something which one has expected and longed for can cause a fright when it is finally there.

This passage in von Baer's autobiography moderates the thrill of an electrically-charged epiphany with a healthy dose of skepticism. Is the vision which causes him to leap back from the microscope a mere trick of the light or a legitimate scientific discovery? Fortunately, the latter: the "phantom" of the mammalian ovum, which had long haunted theories of procreation without being confirmed, was no ghost. Von Baer, with a nod to the earlier observations of William Cruikshank and others, can take his credit for revealing the "discovery of the true state of the generation of mammals, including humans."[3]

The state of the unknown can be as thrilling as the moment of revelation, often more so. Towards the end of the eighteenth century, despite an abundance of theoretical explanations and empirical data, the mystery of procreation remained unsolved and European fascination with the topic had reached a peak. If the physiologist Johann Friedrich Blumenbach is to be believed, procreation was *the* secret of the day, "the most basic object of research for inquiring minds."[4] He speaks for the masses with his delicately posed question, "What goes on inside one creature when it has given itself over to the sweetest of all impulses and now, made fecund by another, should give life to a third?"[5] Blumenbach's question, which governs his treatise *On the Formative Drive and the Process of Procreation*,[6] captures the fundamental enigma which had preoccupied mankind ever since the first procreating pair stared in astonishment at its own offspring like a second divine creation.[7] His conviction that procreation was one of the most important unsolved questions of his time was echoed by many of his contemporaries, including Franz von Baader, Lorenz Oken, and Wilhelm von Humboldt, who, much like the original man and woman in Blumenbach's mythological account, marveled at the ability of human birth to approximate the divine. For Humboldt, the emergence of life, though relying on material which is already there, nonetheless remains "ein unergründliches Geheimnis" (an unfathomable secret).[8] Any initial appearance of gender neutrality is deceptive. Humboldt differentiates very clearly between male and female roles in the process of procreation.[9] Both he, Blumenbach, and their contemporaries were well aware that a significant portion of procreation's mystique derives from the "secrets of the females," a subject which for Blumenbach spanned the classical Greek philosophy, the "carnal" books that heated the theological debates of the Middle Ages, and later debates.[10] Or, in Kant's laconic formulation, "man is easy to investigate, woman does not reveal her secret."[11]

Not only in science is procreation a matter of inquiry around 1800. Literature has its own penchant for secrets, and the writers of German Romanticism conduct their own investigations. Johann Wilhelm Ritter muses in his fragment collection that "everything indicates that the essence of procreation is absolutely to be sought more deeply than in the mere laws of matter,"[12] and Friedrich von Hardenberg, writing under the pen name Novalis, speculates on the "mysticism of this operation" between body and soul.[13] My study poses questions about procreation as basic as Blumenbach's. How do we account for procreation as a discursive phenomenon? What patterns, tendencies, and distinctive rhetorical features characterize this discourse? Is there a particular perspective or literary response to this scientific and cultural enigma which could be described as a poetics of procreation?[14] Implicit in these questions is the assumption that the study of the literary text, not bound to any single line of inquiry, is uniquely situated to assess the interdisciplinarity of the phenomenon. 'Procreation' around 1800 extends beyond a narrow set of physiological questions to include all processes of generation. I have therefore chosen as case studies three authors whose literary writing is shaped by diverse scientific interests which, taken together, are as far-reaching as the problem of procreation itself: Johann Wolfgang von Goethe, Friedrich von Hardenberg, and Johann Wilhelm Ritter. In each case, the writing on procreation is determined by the scientific knowledge of the individual in question. No matter how far afield they export procreation from the original context of species generation, there are certain narrative challenges inherent to writing about it. My study is therefore concerned with a very basic problem: how literary genres integrate processes of generation into narrative form. The questions which arise as Goethe, Hardenberg, and Ritter address this problem relate to the accuracy of theoretical language in relationship to the mutability of a living organism, the temporality of generation, and the narration of life (i.e., narrating the processes of evolution and emergence). These case studies are by no means homogeneous: they do not subscribe to a particular theory of procreation, nor do they emerge from a unified philosophical system or scientific agenda. This diversity of background allows a study of procreation to contribute to an understanding of how scientific theorems are received in literary texts around 1800. I pursue this line of inquiry in the following study by demonstrating how the three writers all engage procreation as a narrative and linguistic phenomenon.

The discourse on procreation around 1800 unites theoretical models with phenomena far removed from the physiologists' dissecting tables, and integrates them into dramatically different contexts. For example, scholars have shown how the language of procreation was appropriated into theories of creative genius current in this period. Wilhelm von Humboldt equated genius with "the intellectual force of procreation."[15] Even Fichte's subject philosophy, usually associated with an absolute, self-positing ego, is cast in a new light when early Romanticism visualizes its dialectical reasoning as a dynamic, gendered process. Goethe, Novalis and Ritter stand out for extending the reach of what one might call "procreative language" into new, unforeseen directions. They use it to describe natural and artificially induced phenomena ranging from galvanism and chemical combustion to magnetism and planetary motion. Seventeen years before Mary Shelley completed her novel about a human body electrified into life, Ritter already fantasized that if animal magnetism "is merely a play of procreative forces, then they must, collected with batteries, work wonders, for example really fertilize through mere touch."[16] Hardenberg speculates that the galvanic chain is a model for how body and soul connect in the procreative act. In Goethe's poetic vision, the fundamental scientific practice of observing the living phenomena of nature is reconceptualized as procreative. Just as species generation relies naturally on the human body

4 *German Romanticism and Science*

for the labor of reproduction, so, for the Romantics, the 'tools' of the human senses and intellect are consciously wielded for a procreative act, the production of ideas.

INTERDISCIPLINARY PROCREATION

The widespread attention granted to procreation can be connected to a general historical trend in the development of the sciences. It is well-documented that in Britain, Germany, and on the European continent as a whole around 1800, those fields of study which today we think of as the natural sciences were rapidly diversifying.[17] New areas of chemical and electrical research began to emerge within the universal science of physics, and biology as a field of inquiry was introduced around this time, but they would only be codified into discrete disciplines after the turn of the century. Before then, the boundaries between different fields of scientific thought were remarkably porous, in the sense that techniques of experimentation and scientific terminology had not yet reached the point of specialization which would preclude the wide dissemination of ideas. The same is true for rigorous distinctions between literary and scientific writing. The secret of procreation not only fueled scientific programs and intense scholarly rivalry, it is also central to Romantic literature's fascination with scientific topics. Dietrich Engelhardt comments that those who study this era of scientific history will always be led towards "general reflections" "on the essence and operation of the natural sciences, on the responsibility of the natural scientist (*Naturforscher*) toward nature and society, over the relations of the natural sciences to art, theology, and philosophy."[18] In the writing on procreation, the interests of literature and science coincide with the greatest intensity.

The early "interdisciplinarity" of the language of organic generation, its pervasiveness in the arts and sciences around 1800, seems to be anticipated by those same physiological theories which raised the burning question in the first place. These theories conceptualized procreation as the most general force of living organisms. For both Blumenbach and his student Carl Friedrich Kielmeyer, a single supreme force in living organisms was responsible for procreation and growth and even had the ability to replace damaged limbs. This "force of reproduction" as described by Kielmeyer was "the most general force and the one spent on organisms to the greatest degree."[19] In the 1793 work which established his reputation as a physiologist, titled *Ueber die Verhältnisse der organischen Kräfte unter einander [. . .]* (*On the Relations of the Organic Forces amongst Each Other*), Kielmeyer also expresses his astonishment over the "wealth of shapes" which the force of reproduction acquires under the hands of nature: "Here it comes to light in an immense volume of the body, there in little points which our eye can scarcely still touch and distinguish with light, here it appears eternally uniform, there in the shape of a changeable fairy."[20] Kielmeyer's description plays with the notion of a reproductive force that hovers at the intersection of the seen and the invisible, the empirically graspable and the fantastic. Drawing upon Herder's *Ideen für die Philosophie der Menschengeschichte* (*Ideas for the Philosophy of History of Humanity*, 1784–91), Kielmeyer also connects physical procreation to the realm of ideas. He observes an inverse relation between the procreation and the force of sensibility. Whereas less developed organisms tend to have larger numbers of offspring, man, as the most developed species, is distinguished by few offspring but an abundance of "intellectual" progeny: his ideas (*Vorstellungen*). From the sense of wonder Kielmeyer expresses at the force of reproduction as a protean creature at work throughout the entire organism, it is a small step to the analogical thinking of German Romanticism, which expands the conceptual reach of procreation even further. Just as for Kielmeyer and others the force of reproduction is central to all organic processes of the body, a more generalized understanding of procreation is central to an early Romantic interest in connecting different branches of scientific thought and considering them in relation to the poetic. Just as procreation is *the* mystery of the day for the scientific community, it also enables the Romantics to test and expand their analogical thinking and study of the arts and sciences.

THE SCIENTIFIC DEBATE

Throughout the eighteenth century, the secret of procreation was embedded within a tangle of scientific observations, religious doctrine, and superstition. Blumenbach, writing in 1791, laments that after centuries of research, the question of human procreation has led to more false paths than any other field of the natural sciences: "even *Boerhaave's* teacher, *Drellincourt*, has alone collected 262 groundless hypotheses on the process of procreation from the writings of his predecessors,—and nothing is more certain than that his own system is the 263rd."[21] The labyrinth of false paths can ultimately be reduced to the "two main roads" of epigenesis and evolution (today more commonly referred to as preformation), described by Blumenbach as follows:

> Entweder nemlich man nimmt an, dass der reife, übrigens aber rohe ungeformte Zeugungsstoff der Eltern, wenn er zu seiner Zeit und unter den erforderlichen Umständen an den Ort seiner Bestimmung gelangt, dann zum neuen Geschöpfe allmälig ausgebildet werde. Diess [sic] lehrt die Epigenese.
> Oder aber man verwirft alle Zeugung in der Welt, und glaubt dagegen, dass zu allen Menschen und Thieren und Pflanzen, die je gelebt haben und noch leben werden, *die Keime* gleich bey der ersten Schöpfung

erschaffen worden, so dass sich nun eine Generation nach der anderen blos zu *entwickeln* braucht. Deshalb heisst diess die Lehre der Evolution. (Blumenbach, *Bildungstrieb*, 13–14)

> Namely, one either assumes that the mature, but otherwise rough and unformed procreative matter of the parents, when it arrives at its time and under the right circumstances at the place of its determination, is then gradually formed (*ausgebildet*) into a new creature. The theory of epigenesis teaches this.
>
> Or one dispenses with all procreation in the world and believes on the contrary that for all humans and animals and plants which have ever lived and will yet live, *the seeds* have been made already at the first creation, so that now one generation after the other merely needs to *develop* itself (*sich . . . entwickeln*). Thus it is called the theory of evolution.

Whereas epigenetic theory tried to account for reproduction as a complex of organic processes, including growth and nutrition, advocates of preformation downplayed their role. They postulated the formation of progeny before conception (i.e., 'pre-formed' in the egg or sperm) and, in their most extreme arguments, preformationists also believed that *all* generations of man were created with Eve and stored in her ovaries to be passed down over time.[22] Though not always a supporter of epigenesis, Blumenbach had adopted this position by 1791, and the biases of his descriptions are doubly instructive. He portrays epigenesis as the emergence of form out of formlessness, leaving the more controversial question of agency carefully out of the picture. The question of what, if any, "vital forces" controlled the patterns and progress of organic growth was a contested point.[23] Blumenbach's short summary also omits another contested aspect of epigenesis theory, which posited not only an increased responsibility of both parents in the process of conception (rather than the simple awakening of a preformed creature), but also the virtual "self-formation" of the newly created progeny after conception had taken place. He then proceeds with some disingenuous rhetoric by imputing that preformationist theory dispenses with "all procreation" and speaks for "all" living creatures, past and present. One would not guess it from Blumenbach's description, but such a hardline position was not characteristic of preformationist theory as a whole. As Stephen J. Gould writes, "the imagination of a few peripheral figures must not be taken as the belief of an entire school."[24]

The respective histories of these two theories have been described in detail, and it suffices to emphasize just a few aspects relevant to the current study. In the debate between epigenesis and preformation, it is generally accepted that epigenesis triumphed. The course of events leading up to this point of view is convoluted, the two theories are historically intertwined more than such a reductive one-sentence statement would suggest. The concept of epigenesis can be traced back to Aristotle's *On the Generation of Animals*. In this treatise, Aristotle describes the human embryo arising from the male semen (understood as a "secretion" from all parts of the male body) and female menstrual blood. Though on the one hand his model appears to posit a male impulse which transforms inert female matter, Aristotle also emphasizes that both participate in the creation of the embryo.[25] Already in the second book of *On the Generation of Animals*, he puts his finger on the issue integral to the later debate, namely the tension between the emergence of "new" structures as opposed to the unfolding of "pre-formed" ones.[26] Jumping ahead to the eighteenth century, even a cursory glance reveals that the battle lines were not as clearly drawn as one might think. Nor is it particularly easy to narrate the history of the debate, due to the fact that many of its chief proponents shifted their positions over time or modified their points of view so as to become less extreme. For example, Albrecht Haller and Christian Wolff are positioned against each other in this narrative such that the preformative belief that "nil noviter generari" (nothing new is created) of the former clashes with the doctrine of complete formation advocated by the latter.[27] Haller, however, was not always such a staunch advocate of preformation. As Shirley Roe has demonstrated, he shifted his viewpoint in 1757, in part after encountering Buffon's *Natural History*.[28] Buffon, in turn, when he writes a brief history of the embryological question at the beginning of his *Natural History*, rejects the potential radicalism of the preformationist model,[29] and sees advantages to both theories: "An embryo was preformed in its germ because all the parts of the germ were each a model of the animal as a whole, but it was also formed by epigenesis because, the sexual organs being first formed, all the rest arose entirely by a succession of new origins."[30]

Buffon was not the only one to admit the potential for a middle ground between the two extreme points of view, whether out of open-mindedness or strategic neutrality. The refinement of preformationist theory occurred hand in hand with advances in observational techniques and improved apparatuses. Until von Baer identified the mammalian ovum, the new observations did not necessarily occur to the detriment of preformationism. The realization that there are innumerable microscopic organisms invisible to the naked eye—some of them distinctly human-shaped—made it plausible that these tiny, pre-formed creatures were simply waiting to be born, but not all preformationists cared to go so far.[31] In a study which carefully reconsiders the contributions and nuances of preformation theory, Clara Pinto-Correia revisits the work of Charles Bonnet:

> By proposing that the 'germ' is not a fully preformed creature, but rather a loose sum of all the 'fundamental parts' of the future individual, he dispensed with the idea of minuscule men or minuscule horses that sooner or later would doom the entire theory to ridicule. By admitting that all generations were not precisely encased—much as he liked the

concept—but that beyond a certain level of smallness they could just float around awaiting their moment, he shaped the concept of 'infinite smallness' into a much more credible version. (Pinto-Correia, "Ovary of Eve," 58–59)

Even if, for a variety of reasons, epigenesis became the dominant mode of explanation by the beginning of the nineteenth century, one needs to be careful when examining the larger picture. This holds true both for our current perspective and for the earlier epoch. Although it may appear in hindsight that epigenesis emerged as the victor, the truth lies somewhere in between the two theories.[32] No one would claim that the human ovum contains completely pre-formed life, but with the discovery of genetic coding it is equally inaccurate to say that life emerges in the womb through a chemical reaction of completely "unformed" substances. Stephen J. Gould comments that this debate, like many others, has been resolved "at Aristotle's golden mean": the epigeneticists were correct in that "organs differentiate sequentially from simpler rudiments during embryological development," but the preformationists are also correct to assert "that complexity cannot arise from formless raw material."[33] A prescient tendency to mediate between the extremes can be found as far back as the eighteenth century and is also evident in von Baer's 1826 autobiography (cited previously). In it von Baer stakes out a middle ground between Christian Wolff's epigenetic theory and the preformationist theory of his opponents: The development of the embryo is not a "new formation" (*Neubildung*) but a "re-formation" (*Umbildung*).[34] Von Baer's concern with finding proper language to describe the phenomenon is evident when he wonders whether the words *Evolution*, *Ausbildung*, and *Entwicklung* might not be more appropriate than either *Präformation* or *Epigenese*.[35] This attention to the language of generation finds its strongest exposition in the writings of German Romanticism.

An additional concern of the present study is to discuss how, at least in the cases of Goethe, Novalis and Ritter, literature around 1800 defines its own middle ground as far as the procreative themes are concerned. There is evidence that each author was familiar with the theories of epigenesis and preformation. Goethe read Wolff and Blumenbach, Novalis cites Kielmeyer, and Ritter spent his years at Jena conducting physiological research and in contact with the leading scientists of his day. Given their close contacts to a scientific community preoccupied with this very problem, it is surprising to witness the skepticism (as voiced, for example, in the Goethe quotation of the epigraph) or silence (Novalis and Ritter) with regard to epigenetic and preformationist theory. In the case of Novalis and Ritter, one does not find a clear reception of either theory—the word "epigenesis" does not appear once in Novalis' encyclopedia project. At the same time, however, the texts of all three writers considered in this study are saturated by the scientific vocabulary, theories, and motifs of generation and reproduction without employing the terms "epigenesis" and "preformation." The conclusion can be drawn that their poetics of procreation does not rely upon a strong preference for one theory or another; nor does one find traces of a gradual acceptance of epigenesis at the expense of preformation. In an attempt to remain attuned to the many topics woven into the Romantic discourse on procreation, the arguments put forth in the following chapters do not purport to trace a teleological narrative or to evaluate a project in terms of success or failure. Instead, they consider the procreation in Romantic-era literature with a focus on different analogical couplings and seek out moments of affinity in the individual responses to a historical phenomenon.

The existing scholarship on biological generation around 1800 has tended to be more partisan in its approach, favoring the more successful theory of epigenesis. This is the case with the central study in this field, *Self-Generation*, by Helmut Müller-Sievers.[36] The title is programmatic. Müller-Sievers argues that epigenetic thinking is the dominant model not only for early 'biological' discussions around 1800, but also for the philosophy of Kant and Fichte, and for language theories.[37] One of the book's central theses, put forth in the introduction, is that "the genealogy and function of epigenesis . . . provides an altogether unique means by which to understand the momentous and irrevocable changes in philosophy, language philosophy, and literature at the end of the eighteenth and the beginning of the nineteenth century. . .".[38] In Müller-Sievers' reading, epigenesis becomes a polemicized concept because, as he writes,

> epigenesis allows philosophical and literary discourses to account for their own origin without recourse to extraneous causes. Epigenesis is thus the condition of the possibility of any claim to absoluteness, be this a philosophical or literary absolute. The only form under which the absolute can be said to exist is the organism, since only organically can the interminable chain of causes and effects be bent back onto its own origin, and only as organic can a discourse claim to contain all the reasons for its own form and existence. This means that the discourses of epigenesis have a tendency to close themselves off against specific criticism and 'objective' presentation. (Müller-Sievers, *Self-generation*, 4)

One of the consequences of this line of argumentation is that epigenesis writes the story of its own success. The "obliteration" of preformation is relegated to the status of a (epigenetically performed) "textual event." This is a strong statement, which could be mitigated by scientific discoveries that also made the case for epigenesis.[39] In general, Müller-Sievers' theses are heavily invested in thinking through the social and political consequences of developments in reproductive theory around 1800. To pursue this line of inquiry, preformation and epigenesis are strongly dichotomized and, despite references to a "philosophical or literary absolute," the literature of the period receives comparatively little attention. The present study, which focuses on the contribution made by the literary text to the discourse on procreation, can be said to exist in productive tension with *Self-Generation*. Starting out from the premise that literary texts offer a point of departure that permits a more nuanced inquiry, the present study will argue for a weaker polarity between the theories of epigenesis and preformation. Any account of Romanticism's engagement with procreation must be able to shift as productively between points of view as Goethe and the Romantics do themselves. This observation is central to the analysis in each of the individual chapters as well as to the overall question guiding the study, how a poetics of procreation positions itself with regard to scientific theory.

SPEAKING OF PROCREATION

The fanfare surrounding the great mystery of procreation might seem exaggerated in light of Michel Foucault's research on the history of sexuality: "what is peculiar to modern societies, in fact, is not that they consigned sex to a shadow existence, but that they dedicated themselves to speaking of it *ad infinitum*, while exploiting it as *the* secret."[40] Foucault's argument that there was an increasing "institutional incitement" to speak about sex during the eighteenth and nineteenth centuries, as well as a growing number of fields (ranging from biology and medicine, to psychiatry and pedagogy) which were preoccupied with sex, has long since become a cornerstone of the broader archaeology of sciences.[41] The statements by Blumenbach and Humboldt on the mystery of procreation cited previously, as well as the proliferation of theories on the issue debated during the eighteenth century, might be read to support Foucault's main contention, but they are not the precise target of his study. "Sex" for Foucault usually refers to the medical discourse on the practices and pathologies of human sexuality. He distinguishes between "the physiology of plant and animal" reproduction and "the discourses on human sexuality"[42]—between "a biology of reproduction, which developed continuously according to a general scientific normativity, and a medicine of sex conforming to quite different rules of formation" which becomes more apparent in the nineteenth century.[43] Whereas studies of plant and animal physiology exhibit, according to Foucault, a general "will to knowledge," the discourses on human sexuality are distinguished by a just as persistent "will to non-knowledge" and "systematic blindness."[44]

Where does the Romantic understanding of procreation fit in with regard to this model? There are studies of human physiology which embody the greatest examples of scientific normativity around 1800. Yet, the "systematic blindness" which, according to Foucault, haunts the discourse of sexuality is at work here, too. The microscope proved to be an instrument for expanding the scope of empirical observations, but it is also true that observations are subjective. Thus they can be manipulated to validate a theory whose success is also an affirmation of religious and political authority.

The years following the refinement of the microscope in the seventeenth century were filled with observations of homunculi and animalcules which, conveniently, seemed to validate the theory of preformation: Hartsoeker, Leeuwenhoek, and others thought they saw little fully-formed organisms in sperm or eggs of humans and other species, which seemed to confirm that all human and animal generations were originally created by God.[45] Romantic writing on procreation around 1800, in which a marveling at the mysterious in scientific writing coincides with a reception of scientific details in literary texts, does not display a well-developed awareness of the distinction between the "will to knowledge" and the "will to non-knowledge."[46] The pleasures and prohibitions of sexuality are never too far removed from the rationalism of scientific pursuits on the issue of procreation. One need only refer to the 1791 edition of Blumenbach's treatise, which contains two illustrations. The first is an image of a brooding hen next to the inscription *Veneri Caelesti Genetrici* (to the heavenly and maternal Venus). The hen cocks her head directly toward the observer with an inscrutable gaze. The volume concludes with another exchange of gazes: an emblem of two snakes head-to-head, lovingly entwined, and the comment: "a proper and yet, as experts of nature know, very significant image of the pleasure which is a consequence of the formative drive."[47] This second illustration excludes the gaze of the outside observer. The arrangement of emblems is counter-intuitive. One would expect pleasure to come before responsibility, rather than having a feathered embodiment of the maternal Venus give way to a spectacle enacted by the chief symbol of Christian sin. Yet as Blumenbach attests, the "product" of the formative drive need not be limited to progeny. It can feed back and reinforce the desires of the procreators. German Romanticism will take this idea in creative new directions.

PROCREATION AND GENDER

This study is concerned with questions of gender to the degree that they are context-generated. Goethe, Novalis, and Ritter each mobilize a different vocabulary when writing about themes of procreation, and the ways in which the categories of the masculine and the feminine fit into broader theoretical orientation of these writers are not necessarily identical. The following readings do not attempt to advance the broad argument that the discourse on procreation is symptomatic of a major change in the way questions of gender are treated in literary texts around 1800. Nor do these readings claim that procreation is (deliberately) instrumentalized in an attempt to reconfigure questions of gender. Such claims would not be justified, since the writers in question tend to envision "procreative" scenarios in contexts removed or abstracted from the human body. In other words, there is a site-specific tension between the process in question (for example, the laws of nature governing the production of electricity, or the consumption of oxygen) and the gender categories mobilized in the individual attempt to bring this process into narrative form. My chief interest is to expose in detail the complexity of the discourse on procreation around 1800, to treat it as a narrative problem, and then to consider the ways in which the results of these readings might refine or even revise established points of view on gender categories in Romanticism. There are a number of theoretical approaches that the field of gender studies has either established, appropriated, or critiqued in order to conduct research which concentrates—more than the present study does—on the representation of woman (or man) in the literary text and related questions. They include discussions of gender with regard to the material–social situation of men and women (Duden, Jordanova[48]) and the special role played by 'woman' at the locus of discursive production (F. Kittler[49]) or in the dichotomous thinking inherent to Romantic aesthetics (Menninghaus[50]). More recent work by Alice Kuzniar and Martha Helfer, among others, has also revisited claims made about the role of women in Romantic literature proposed by the earlier scholarship.

Before putting these different approaches in perspective, the problem of *Geschlecht* needs to be considered in its historical (etymological) context. Today, *Geschlecht* can be used as an approximation for the English word "gender" (in both the social and grammatical senses), but *Geschlecht* is not sharply distinguished by sex except through specific usage. Through the end of the eighteenth century, however, the word's additional meaning of family lineage was dominant. Ute Frevert has tracked the significations of *Geschlecht* at different stages of its history. She notes that one of the standard lexica, by Johann Heinrich Zedler,[51] uses *Geschlecht* "to differentiate between man and woman on the basis of morality"[52] in the 1739 edition, whereas later editions focus on anatomical difference or "special articles like 'bones, muscles, nerves, temperaments,' on the basis of which the differences between male and female *Geschlecht* are observed more precisely."[53] Frevert also discusses the changing definitions of 'man' and 'woman' in relation to the shift of emphasis in *Geschlecht* from a question of social lineage to one of anatomy. She observes that eighteenth-century encyclopedias devote much more space to their definitions of *Frau* than to those of *Mann*, whereby the latter gradually disappears: "already in 1747, woman is apparently more of a puzzle than man; it is, at least in the imagination of the lexicon authors, more present, requires definitions, parameters, discursive canvassing."[54] This assessment conforms both to the general cultural interest in the secret of procreation described previously and to what Claudia Honegger has described as "the elevation of the man (*Mann*) to the norm of human being (*Menschen*) in the sciences and the assignation of a special status to the woman, who thus becomes the object."[55]

The prior scholarship on Romanticism has acknowledged the centrality of woman (*Frau*) without necessarily agreeing on how she should be read. In her role as mother (with emphasis on the "mother–child" couple) she has been the ultimate condition for discursive production since Friedrich Kittler's *Aufschreibesysteme*. In her role as woman (with emphasis on the "woman–man" couple) she has been confined as the plant to man's animal, the nature to his art, the object to his subject, the *you* to his *I*. These dichotomies have not remained uncontested. Ludmilla Jordanova, in a study which focuses on the material culture of the eighteenth century, has argued that in cases such as man/woman, nature/culture there can in fact exist a "dialectical relationship between the members of each pair"[56] and that such contrasts are not always as distinct as they are described: "This is partly because social and conceptual changes take place slowly, erratically, and in piecemeal and fragmented ways. It is also because the polarities themselves were riddled with tensions, contradictions and paradoxes."[57] Granted, Jordanova does not base this claim on the highly stylized gender roles which emerge in early German Romantic literature. Her views are derived from the late-eighteenth century discourses on medicine and labor and apply primarily to British Romanticism. A similar line of questioning can also be discerned, however, in the work of scholars who focus more closely on the authors treated in my project. Astrida Tantillo, in her reading of Goethe's botanical studies, makes a case for interpreting gender categories as "complex and not strictly hierarchical."[58] An earlier essay by Alice Kuzniar has already shown how in the case of Friedrich von Hardenberg the presence of female characters can "undermine binary oppositions."[59] Her reading of *Heinrich von Ofterdingen* (posth. 1802) shows how even if "a woman's voice that issues from a male body cannot refer to a real femaleness grounded in experience," a male writer can "like a female writer—design interventionary constructs based on the assumption of woman's specificity or difference" and that "unique female paradigms in canonical male-authored works may challenge the dominant androcentric model."[60] Kuzniar's interpretation has been received and expanded upon by Martha Helfer, who suggests that we consider not only representations of female voices by male authors, but also other ways in which the female voice can be "programmed throughout the text."[61] In this reading, the male does not "usurp" the female voice (for example, of the mother). Instead, "Novalis as male author writes woman's originary poetic voice *as mediated by man, as ultimately necessary to man.*"[62] There will be an occasion to revisit each of these arguments in the following chapters.

POETIC PROCREATION

Despite the consensus in recent years that scientific investigations are integral to what was formerly perceived in a narrow sense as the "literary" movement of German Romanticism, the relation between literature and science remains a contentious topic. Müller-Sievers is among the most vehement when decrying readings of literary texts which challenge the discursive divide between science and literature: "Unless the analysis can show how science *informs* the literary text, unless it raises science from the unfathomable depth of the content to the surface of writing, unless the writing of science crosses over into the science of writing, the relationship between literature and science will always remain anecdotal at best."[63] Other scholars have navigated this question from different perspectives, often avoiding the claim of "literature as science" or "science as literature" altogether. Astrida Tantillo's recent book on Goethe, which readdresses his work as it relates to a philosophy of nature, illustrates how poetry and science for Goethe respond to the same creative activities of nature.[64] Robert J. Richards has observed that the conjunction between science and art in Romanticism is "easy to misinterpret" and prefers to speak of the relation between subjective acts and the objective principles of nature as "isomorphic" in reference to Schelling's philosophy of nature.[65] The question of what might emerge from a productive coupling of literature and science runs through the present study, from the first chapter on Goethe's theory of metamorphosis to the final chapter on Ritter's fragment project. It argues that, as is the case with the rival theories of epigenesis and preformation, the middle ground is the most fertile.

Although each facet of my study connects procreation to the relation of literature and science, the discussion of Goethe's botanical studies does so most directly. The critical scholarship of the past years has reaffirmed Goethe's contributions to the natural sciences (Amrine[66]) and the philosophy of nature (Tantillo), and has also kept Goethe's work center stage in the debate on literature and science around 1800. Re-reading Goethe with a focus on procreation can advance the discussion even further. Metamorphosis, which Goethe defines through the related activities of growth and reproduction, *is* a prolonged process of procreation. In his poem on the metamorphosis of plants, Goethe embeds the scientific activities of observation and experimentation within a procreative context. In a letter that refers to the same poem, he also posits the question directly, whether a poet can advance the cause of science.[67] My reading focuses the poem as a vehicle for discussing procreation in the broader context of Goethe's scientific work and for raising questions pertinent to the study as a whole. These include the relationship between physiological change, the productive observation of the natural world, and the acquisition of knowledge.

Another aspect to procreation that this study explores is the tension between organic and mechanical language and processes. In part at the urging of Romantics themselves, organicism has long been understood as the quintessence of their poesy, a point of view which remains rooted in the scholarship even today. The question has been raised, however, as to the role of mechanistic thinking in Romantic poetics. Timothy Lenoir, in his work on the research programs which dominated the life sciences from the 1790s through the 1850s, has discussed a confluence in "teleological and mechanical frameworks of explanation." [68] The "teleo-mechanism," according to

Lenoir, derives its impetus from Kant's discussion of teleological judgment in *The Third Critique* and Blumenbach's concept of the "formative drive" (*nisus formativus*): both Kant and Blumenbach believed that mechanical explanations are necessary, if insufficient, to describe the organic realm. Though Lenoir's research has become a cornerstone for the history of science, his observations could be integrated much more into discussions of Romantic literature.

One of the arguments taken up by my study is that in discussions of procreation, "mechanical" thinking plays an important role in conjunction with organic teleology. Apart from *The Third Critique*, an important precedent can also be found in the *Groundwork of the Metaphysics of Morals* (1785) where Kant defines marriage as "the union of two persons of different sexes for lifelong possession of each other's sexual attributes (*Geschlechtseigenschaften.*)"[69] Kant notes that this exchange, however pleasurable it may be for a human being, risks contravening "the right of humanity in his own person" insofar as "a human being makes himself into a thing (*Sache*)."[70] The threatened contravention is resolved insofar as the exchange is mutual and goes beyond mere instrumentality: "while one person is acquired by the other *as if it were a thing*, the one who is acquired acquires the other in turn; for in this way each reclaims itself and restores its personality."[71] My study discusses how the permitted "use" of the other as tool or instrument for the purpose of procreation takes on new dimensions in Romantic thinking, particularly in the novels and aphorisms of Novalis. An important aspect to this problem is the relation of parents to progeny, of the artist and craftsman to the product. Kant writes that it is impossible for us to have a concept of bringing forth a new life in all its freedom yet without its consent.[72] Romantic procreation is equally concerned with the question of progeny, if for different reasons. The "product" of procreation is a stop-gap which can take a number of forms in addition to that of the child. These include the self (in autoproductive contexts), the work of art, and even, in a kind of procreative feedback loop, the process of procreation itself. For literary poetics, this experimenting with mechanistic and organic processes raises questions regarding the manner in which narration is allowed to unfold, the relationship between procreation and self-generation, and, more generally, the ways in which Romantic literature develops genres which can account for these different modes of production.

The part of my study which focuses on the work of Friedrich von Hardenberg is the one most engaged with the relation of mechanical and organic motifs in the Romantic poetics. One objective is to introduce the reader to the full range of the discourse of procreation in his work. Conventional interpretations have tended to view the procreative themes of his writing as more or less thinly veiled gestures of self-reflection: Novalis is the poet who looks into the eyes of the beloved only to see himself. I begin by reconsidering his engagement with the philosopher Johann Gottlieb Fichte in the "Fichte Studies" before turning to his later work. My reading then shows how his thinking about procreation cannot be easily assimilated into the available biological models of epigenesis and preformation, although it plays with structural components familiar to both. Hardenberg also develops his ideas about procreation by connecting it to processes of chemical combustion and galvanic chains.

Much like Goethe's concept of metamorphosis, procreation is a protean creature for Hardenberg: it perpetually reinvents itself to try out new and unusual couplings. It inscribes itself within large-scale narratives which transcend any single episteme to encompass the life sciences, philosophical activity, and historical models. The next section, which bridges between Hardenberg's aphoristic work and his two novels, *Heinrich von Ofterdingen* (posth. 1802) and *The Apprentices of Sais* (posth. 1802) argues that the key to navigating the manifold of metaphors, figures, and scientific ideas intersecting within the discourse of procreation in Hardenberg's work lies in the concept of the instrument (*Werkzeug*). Hardenberg makes use of a wide arsenal of instruments in his writing with which he hammers and files everything from poetic inscriptions to battleships. He also reflects upon the instrument's mediating function between the organic and inorganic realms, as well as between science and literature. I relate the instrument's contribution to the discussion of procreation in Hardenberg's work to questions concerning the conceptualization of the human in late-eighteenth century anthropology. After giving a cursory of overview of the functions of the instrument in the aphoristic writings, I discuss it in greater detail through a reading of *The Apprentices of Sais*. The many voices of this text articulate competing theories of man's relation to nature while keeping the focus on physiological and psychological formation. I show how Hardenberg's unfinished novel uses the instrument both to relate scientific and philosophical ideas concerning man's relation to nature and as a strategy for connecting these ideas. The principle of an organic, productive instrument allows Hardenberg to maintain order within a text that articulates a multitude of potentially contradictory points of view.

Wilhelm von Humboldt reminds us that the mystery of procreation lies concealed behind the interstice of past and future: "One knows what precedes procreation and sees the being which results from it; How both are connected? is enveloped by an impenetrable veil."[73] The Romantic fascination with temporal processes, and the relations of repetition, continuity and rupture which inform their thinking on the past, present and future finds direct expression in the ephemeral present moment of procreation. In *The Order of Things*, Foucault writes that "a profound historicity penetrates into the heart of things, isolates and defines them in their own coherence, imposes upon them forms of order implied by the continuity of time" and cites as an example how the "study of the organism takes precedence over taxonomic characteristics." Kielmeyer marvels at the ability of the reproductive force to manifest itself not only in the smallest discernable points of life and the most immense bodies, but also at the fact that it can linger unused for centuries and then act in the passing of a moment (*Zeitfluxion*).[74] Ritter imagines gargantuan narratives of procreation which stretch across the epochs of human history. Humboldt's insistence on the "impenetrable veil" indicates a reluctance to impose a particular "form of order" or a single temporal framework on the process of procreation. However, the eighteenth century is not monolithic. In *The Problem 'Time' in German Romanticism*, Manfred Frank sees the relation of spatial and temporal frameworks in a fundamentally different light. He argues that within the Romantic project, for example, Novalis' Fichte reception, lies the "program for a genesis of space from time." Frank advances this claim with direct reference to procreation, stating that space in Novalis' philosophical thinking is "generated" by time. Mediating between Foucault's "temporalization" of objects, on the one hand, and Frank's derivation of space from temporality, on the other, my study shows that the inherent fluidity of procreation's temporality resists categorization while also revealing a consistent set of concerns.

Time, as a categorical problem, is so intrinsic to the discussion of procreation that each chapter engages it on some level, through the cycles and deviations of organic life and as a manifold of chemical and physical and intellectual processes. As Wolf Lepenies has pointed out in his discussion of natural history in the eighteenth century, "the historicizing of nature is internally connected with the historicizing of the knowledge of nature. Identity and difference, extraction and contraction, metamorphosis and intensification are valid in nature as in individual life and society."[75] One of the functions of the discourse of procreation touched upon in this study is the ability to move fluidly across scales. It bridges the micro-processes of the living organism, the span of a life, and the epochs of human history. The final sections of my study concentrate on the work of Johann Wilhelm Ritter as a scientist and Romantic, for whom temporal processes are of central importance with regard to procreation. The focus is on Ritter's two-volume fragment project published just before his death in 1810 and misleadingly titled *Fragments from the Estate of a Young Physicist*. I first connect procreative and epistemological motifs of the prologue to the fragments, a "self-biography" written with thinly concealed anonymity under the guise of a fiction. Ritter claims to have written the prologue for those who wish to make of themselves physicists and experimentalists, and my reading will argue that the process of becoming a scientist occurs not through imitation but through the act of deciphering. Ritter has created a puzzle of his life by appropriating his mother's birth- and deathdates as his own, and he couples these dates with the genesis of the fragment project and the prologue. Throughout the text, two competing structures can be observed: one ontological, the other concerned with the acquisition of knowledge. Both are connected to writing and scientific research, and to how these activities invoke procreation. The reader of the prologue, as the decoder of the life, is drawn into the physicist's most intimate space—his "secret workshop"—and finally (not without voyeuristic thrill) into the privacy of the domestic sphere. The prologue connects the exchange of chronological narrative for spaces of knowledge and procreation to the construction of a living monument. The reader, as builder, will collect the fragments as if they were the "scattered limbs" of the physicist, make them into a "temple," and thereby project the ideas of the physicist into the future.

The final section of the book discusses how procreation acts as a bridge between different areas of Ritter's scientific research. I analyze the numerous contributions he made to the discourse of procreation while attempting to unify the scientific study of chemical, magnetic and electrical phenomena through the discovery of one single principle, valid in both the organic and the inorganic realm. My readings focus on three closely connected topics to demonstrate how ingrained the language of procreation is in Ritter's scientific program. First I show how Ritter aligns the concept of indifference with the female body, the process of procreation, and a range of scientific phenomena. The second, related topic is the apparatus of the pile, which Ritter also understands in terms of difference and indifference. Shortly after Volta developed the pile around the turn of the century, it was used to refine the process of water electrolysis, an area of research to which Ritter also made tangible contributions. On the basis of examples drawn from Ritter's scientific essays and fragments, I discuss how the pile provides Ritter with a model which facilitates his thinking about procreation across micro- and macroscopic scales of time and space. The third topic marks a return to the study's point of departure—Goethe's theory of metamorphosis—to argue that Ritter's references to Goethe require a reading of the pile's procreative potential in a new light. This reading underscores an argument that runs throughout the book as a whole: that for the Romantics, the language of procreation has its own formative power. When one observes how Ritter returns multiple times to processes of procreation in different contexts (as does Hardenberg), it becomes evident that they mutually inform each other, but also that a tension exists between these specific contexts and a more generalized narrative of procreation. Given that procreative language is exported beyond its home discourse of physiology to the degree visible in Ritter's work, the coherence of the procreative narrative can no longer be taken for granted. The way Ritter brings together the realms of nature and culture around one term allows him to unify these realms conceptually: the logic of physiological procreation informs scientific discourse, and these discourses imprint themselves upon procreative models.

2 Poetic Procreation and Goethe's Theory of Metamorphosis

> Vor einiger Zeit kam ich auf den Gedanken die Idee von Metamorphose der Pflanzen, durch dichterischen Vortrag, noch weiter zu verbreiten und ich lege hier den Versuch bey. Linné war liberal genug um den Dichter unter denjenigen zu nennen welche der Wissenschaft förderlich seyn könnte, ich wünsche daß mir diese gute Absicht nicht ganz mißlungen seyn möge. (WA 4, 13:272)[1]

> Some time ago I had the thought to disperse the idea of plant metamorphosis even further through a poetic exposition and I include the attempt here. Linné was generous enough also to name the poet among those who could be beneficial to science. I hope that this good intention may not have entirely failed me.

What does it mean for a poet, or for literature itself, to be "beneficial" to science, and why does Goethe find that plant metamorphosis can accomplish the task? This chapter will argue that the answers to these questions lie at the heart of Goethe's contribution to the discourse of procreation around 1800. Readers have observed numerous intersections between his scientific and literary endeavors, whether in the chemical couplings of *Elective Affinities* or the alchemical and physical speculations of *Faust*. A literature informed by the language and tropes of science is nevertheless not the same as one which engages in, contributes to, or is in some way beneficial to scientific thinking. Goethe's elegy, "The Metamorphosis of Plants" (1798), is unique in this regard. It offers the opportunity to imagine what form literature's contribution to science might take, not only by integrating the concepts central to Goethe's earlier scientific study of metamorphosis, but by casting them in a new light. The study of plant physiology had already proven fertile ground for unexpected couplings between literature and science, as Goethe's journals and correspondence during the 1780s attest. A good example is his quest for the fabulous *Urpflanze* (primal plant) on Italian soil. After all, an understanding of the *Urpflanze* was supposed to provide a "key" to creating new plants, as Goethe mused in a letter to Charlotte von Stein dating from 1787:

> Mit diesem Modell und dem Schlüssel dazu, kann man alsdann noch Planzen ins Unendliche erfinden, die konsequent sein müssen, das heißt: die, wenn sie auch nicht existieren, doch existieren könnten und nicht etwa malerische oder dichterische Schatten und Scheine sind, sondern eine innerliche Wahrheit und Notwendigkeit haben. (LA II 9A: 365)

With this model and the key to it, one can thereupon invent plants into the infinite which must be consequent, that means: which, even if they do not exist, still could exist and are not just painterly or poetic shadows and illusions, but rather have an internal truth and necessity.[2]

The *Urpflanze* has the ability to interface between the scientific and the poetic: it is more than illusory, if less than alive. It invites the possibility for an imagined plant, if conceived according to the correct model of generation and organization, to have the same "truth" and "necessity" as a living one. If that were the case, such a plant could escape the illusion of literature, participate within a scientific theory, and help develop theories of living organisms. It remains to be seen whether Goethe's poem might be able to substantiate the loftiness, even audacity, of such a claim—that the representation of an imaginary plant might have a role to play in scientific discourse.

It is well-documented that Goethe's speculations about possible intersections of art and nature (or art and science) received an additional spur from Kant's *Critique of Judgment* (1790).[3] A letter from the jurist and writer Gottfried Körner to Friedrich Schiller dated October 6th, 1790, relates how he and Goethe found unexpected "points of contact" in Kant's critique of teleological judgment and used their common interest in Kant not just to philosophize on nature, but also to discuss art.[4] Goethe's essays "Anschauende Urteilskraft" (Intuiting Judgment) and "Einwirkung der neueren Philosophie" (Effect of Recent Philosophy) are further evidence of his efforts to link scientific and aesthetic theories of nature.[5] In these short works, Goethe reflects upon how his reception of Kant, and the proposition that aesthetic and teleological judgments may be linked to one and the same faculty of judgment, confirmed a prior interest in considering art and nature jointly. Goethe's thoughts about points of contact between the realms of art and science should not be limited to his reading of Kant, however, and nowhere does the *Third Critique* incite literary authors to take up scientific problems. Rather, the broad spectrum of Goethe's study of nature—including the first notes on plant physiology which pre-date his voyage to Italy and have usually been overlooked by the critical scholarship—needs to be taken into consideration in order to address the question of literature's engagement with science as raised by the poem on plant metamorphosis.

An entry in Goethe's journal dated June 18th, 1798, makes reference to the poem and records an evening spent with Friedrich Schiller, where they discussed "the possibility of a portrayal of the theory of nature by a poet."[6] The "theory of nature" had undergone substantial changes since the publication of the essay on plant metamorphosis in 1790. During that time, Goethe developed new ideas concerning human relations to nature. He contemplated the activities of seeing [*sehen*] and intuiting [*anschauen*] natural phenomena, developed his understanding of scientific method, and—as is evident in the *Wilhelm Meister* project—devoted himself to the problem of *Bildung* as a process of joint physical and intellectual formation. Given that numerous aspects in Goethe's literary and scientific thinking during the 1790s can be connected to a theory of nature, the poem arguably does more than transpose the earlier concept of plant metamorphosis into an aesthetic form.[7] In light of Goethe's suggestion that the poet might have something to contribute to science, the question arises, to what extent the poem responds to the new developments in Goethe's thinking about organic phenomena and expands the theory of metamorphosis.

At first glance, the poem on plant metamorphosis appears to be an exercise in "poetic procreation" far removed from conventional notions of scientific thinking or experimentation. It tells of two lovers in a garden: a man, who narrates the poem and possesses the secret of plant metamorphosis, and a woman who remains confused by the multitude of organic forms around her and by the strange language of botany. Step by step, the narrator guides his beloved through the stages of plant metamorphosis. He describes the unfamiliar processes of organic procreation through anthropomorphic metaphors of the human couple's anticipated union, such that the practice of observation staged by the poem doubles as a sexual courtship. "The Metamorphosis of Plants" could be read as a love poem whose flowery language merely mirrors the garden setting; Goethe's intension to "disperse" [*verbreiten*] the idea of metamorphosis would thus be understood as a marketing strategy to introduce a scientific concept to a broader, female readership.[8] The early publication history of the poem supports this idea: It was first published in Schiller's *Musen-Almanach* of 1799 and unofficially dedicated to the "actual beloved," Goethe's common-law wife Christiane Vulpius, who aided Goethe during his botanical research.[9] The poem was published in several subsequent editions of Goethe's work, including a collection of his scientific studies. In that edition, Goethe inserts the poem as part of a brief essay describing the fate of the 1790 essay on metamorphosis. Goethe comments that female friends had been scared away by his "abstract gardening" and the "ghostlike schemata [*Schemen*]" which displaced the sensual pleasure generated by living plants: "Then I tried to entice these well-meaning souls into participation, through an elegy which shall be permitted a place here, where it, in connection with scientific portrayal [*Darstellung*], ought to be more comprehensible than if it were integrated in a series of tender and passionate poesies."[10] Goethe's remark that the poem is more comprehensible in a scientific, as opposed to a poetic, context, leaves open various ways in which its contribution might take place. Literature can certainly disseminate new scientific ideas by bringing them to a wider (female) audience, but Goethe appears to be suggesting something more, which gives rise to at least two possibilities: that literature can incorporate scientific ideas in an interesting way (as many of Goethe's texts do), and that literature can in fact be "beneficial" to science by accomplishing something that science cannot.

The set-up of the poem is intricate enough to preclude an easy answer. As passionately as the narrator addresses his beloved in anticipation of their union, he also formulates the love poem as a strict pedagogical exercise: an incitement for the woman in the poem and the reader to visualize the stages of plant development and to share in the intuition of the phenomenon, in tandem with the idealized union of the male and female observers.[11] The feminine addressee of the poem complicates an established scientific model of observation by introducing an intimate relation between the seeing subject and the observed phenomenon. The poem effectively presents us with two observers (man and woman) and two phenomena (woman and plant); in this constellation, the woman becomes both the spectator and spectacle of metamorphosis, equally aligned with mankind and with nature. I will return to these couplings of poetry and science, man and woman, nature study and anthropology throughout the chapter to show how they lead to a more complex representation of metamorphosis than in the botanical work alone.

The critical literature on the poem has tended not to take it seriously as a vehicle for scientific thought.[12] Yet there are compelling reasons for rethinking Goethe's proposition that the poem can in fact be conducive to science. The first concerns the role of figurative language. The anthropomorphic language which might appear to signal "poetic" as opposed to "scientific" writing can be found both in Goethe's earlier work on metamorphosis as well as in the contemporary scientific literature. The question concerning the role of metaphor and figurative language in Goethe's descriptions of natural phenomena will require even further precision, because his criteria evolve (significantly) over time. Just as relevant for this study is the way in which Goethe's early thinking about the language of scientific writing develops in tandem with his ideas on scientific observation and the intuition of the phenomenon. My reading advances the argument that the poem constitutes an experiment in communication whereby the narrator attempts to convey an active intuition of the phenomenon (the living plant) fundamental to Goethe's theory of metamorphosis. These lines of inquiry ultimately lead to procreation. Metamorphosis is a subject linked to sexuality, and the act of visualizing the phenomenon is an inherently productive activity for Goethe. Not only does he define the life cycle of the plant through the moments of procreation and birth, he connects these concepts directly to the cognitive activity of the observer. Finding an adequate language to describe living phenomena in a state of change and to communicate his intuition of them proved more difficult than Goethe had first imagined. Already the first notes on metamorphosis, which date from the time of Goethe's optimistic letter to Charlotte von Stein, are marked by intense self-questioning concerning both the gendered language of procreation and a proper description of the process. It is Goethe's quest for the best way of seeing and "speaking" nature—of representing growth and reproduction *and* the observer's relation to these processes—which leads to procreation as a basis for his contribution to both literature and science.

BOTANICS AND 'BILDUNG' (1): BEGINNING POINTS

When Goethe first began the scientific study of plants in the early 1780s, he entered a field which had a tradition of practicing self-censorship with regard to the appropriate use of language. For one, there were concerns about decency. It was no secret that plants were sexual organisms, but to find an appropriate language of description was another matter. The sexuality of plants was not, however, something which could be kept under wraps. The theories of classification developed by Nehemiah Grew and Charles Linné used variations in the "genitalia" of plants as the basis for differentiating between species.[13] Linné's *Praeludia Sponsaliorum Plantarum* (1729), an elaborate, highly anthropomorphized model of plant anatomy published some fifty years after Nehemiah Grew's initial treatise, covered new ground in plant sexuality. He observed "male" and "female" flowers on separate plants as well as the more common case of the "hermaphrodites" (the primary object of observation in Goethe's botanical studies as well) where both reproductive parts are found on the same plant. Linné drew his terminology from the Greek words *andria* ("man": stamen) and *gynia* ("woman": pistil), and in the *Systema Naturae* (1737), he displays the various "marriages of plants" in tabular form. His detailed observations depict testes, vulva and vagina among the plants' sexual organs.[14] Linné categorized differences between plants on the basis of their number of stamens, whether the marriages are "public" or "private," and whether the "husband" and "wife" share the same bed.[15]

During the eighteenth century, theories of plant procreation became increasingly popular, and questions of moral language remained as much of a concern as accuracy.[16] The sexual metaphors of Goethe's poem, with its "marriage" and discrete coupling, acknowledge the historical tradition from which they derive and in which they still participate to some degree. That said, the poem is by no means a simple homage to the *philosophicus botanicus*. As much as Goethe admired Linné's achievements, the poem opens as a polemic against the challenges of the Linnaean terminology:

> Dich verwirret, Geliebte, die tausendfältige Mischung
> Dieses Blumengewühls über dem Garten umher;
> Viele Namen hörest du an und immer verdränget,
> Mit barbarischem Klang, einer den andern im Ohr.[17]
> (V.1-4, MA 12:75)

> Overwhelming, beloved, you find all this mixture of thousands,
> Riot of flowers let loose over the garden's expanse;
> Many names you take in, and always the last to be spoken
> Drives out the one heard before, barbarous both to your ear.

The ears of the narrator's companion are under assault by a foreign horde of indistinguishable names, as the onomatopoetic origins of "barbaric" might suggest. Amidst the onslaught, articulating the theory of metamorphosis becomes an act of resistance. Goethe advocates a similar rejection of Linné's "sweeping" theory of the sexes in favor of a more general approach in a conversation, recorded by Eckermann, from February 1st, 1827: "I still remember very well that with the formation of the sexes the theory became too sweeping for me than I had courage to grasp. That propelled me to follow the matter in my own way and to find that which would be common to all plants without distinction, and thus I discovered the law of metamorphosis."[19] In addition to questions concerning the use of comparisons and metaphor, Goethe's argument with Linné evolves out of a basic difference in perspective concerning the botanist's relation to empirical evidence.[20] Whereas Linné's analytic method drove him towards increasing detail, Goethe's impulse was to "unite" and reduce difference to a single form.[21] Goethe's tendency to move from the particular to the general, from an impression of the parts to one of the whole, needs to be considered in tandem with his changing views on the use of figurative language in scientific descriptions. The same impulse, which encourages him to emphasize transitions as opposed to specific forms, will eventually lead him to focus on processes, rather than momentary stages in development.

Goethe's concern with the use of comparisons in descriptions of metamorphosis is linked to the problem that objects change over time, but an object in metamorphosis goes through different stages which are nonetheless linked—as Goethe would say—by a common transcendental form. He came to believe that a successful comparison would need to fulfill certain requirements. For example, a metaphor comparing a plant to another object or organism would need to convey the plant's mutability. In other words, not only should it capture an essential kinship, it should have a predictive power as well. One text which couples the lives of humans and plants was arguably essential for Goethe's first writings on metamorphosis: beginning in 1783, he participated in the development of Johann Gottfried Herder's multivolume *Ideen zur Philosophie der Geschichte der Menschheit* (*Ideas on a Philosophy of the History of Mankind*, 1784–1791). The scope of Herder's work is immense. It begins with the earth as a "star among stars" and—after following the course of human and natural history—ends with a discussion of European man in the eighteenth century. In the first volume of the *Ideas* one also finds elaborate comparisons between humans and plants, in which a chapter titled "The Realm of Plants of our Earth in Relation to Human History" discusses the similarities between the life-cycles of humans and plants.[22] On the one hand, plants are like humans: "a plant has a kind of life and age, it has sexes [*Geschlechter*] and fertilization, birth and death."[23] On the other hand, Herder also claims that human life, as "vegetation," logically shares the "destiny of plants"—"like plants, man and animal are born from one seed, which also, as embryo of a future tree, supplies a protective covering. The seed's first structure develops plant-like in the womb. . . . Our life-spans are the life-spans of plants; we arise, grow, bloom, fade, and die."[24] There are echoes of Herder's "first structure" [erstes Gebilde] in Goethe's poem where the plant/child, called by the same name, transforms through the various stages of development:

> Aber einfach bleibt die Gestalt der ersten Erscheinung
> Und so bezeichnet sich auch unter den Pflanzen das Kind.
> Gleich darauf ein folgender Trieb, sich erhebend, erneuet,
> Knoten auf Knoten getürmt, immer das erste Gebild
> (v. 21–24, MA 12:75)

> Single, simple, however, remains the first visible structure;
> So that what first appears, even in plants, is the child.
> Following, rising at once, with one nodule piled on another,
> Always the second renews only the shape of the first.

Intrinsic to Herder's ruminations on the humanness of plants or on the vegetative traits of humankind is his attention to functional similarities between the two groups. However, after the initial comparison between seed and womb, he eschews morphological characteristics. Instead, he defines the parallels between the life cycles of humans and plants in terms of processes. The initial structural similarity gives way to comparable phases of change over time articulated through verbs such as "arise," "grow," and "bloom." The comparison maintains its predictive potential by subjecting the first form to a series of parallel transformations, without trying to cling to morphological similarities.

Herder's lengthy comparison changes dramatically when he arrives at the stage of procreation. He uses vocabulary similar to Linné's without citing him directly: "the blossom, we know, is the time of love for the plants. The sepal is the bed, the corona its curtains, the other parts of the flower are instruments [Werkzeuge] of propagation which nature has displayed openly on these innocent creatures and decorated with all glory."[25] The increased focus on details interrupts the flow of metamorphic change. Through a static description the flower acquires contour: Its space becomes more complex, attracting the observer's gaze. Our attention is drawn to the center of the plant's reproductive activity—and then diverted. Although the instruments are apparent, the act of procreation remains hidden. The bed is cloaked by the curtains that surround it. When Herder's narrative transitions from the elaborate description of procreation's "tools" to their function, simple declarative statements give way to a subjunctive: "[Nature's] great purpose should be reached." This purpose is then qualified as *propagation, maintenance of the species*."[26] The rest of the chapter leaves little doubt that such a goal is endlessly attained—the subjunctive "should" simply acknowledges that procreation is the hinge upon which the survival of the species turns. Ultimately, nature produces a multitude of seeds, far more than can survive in any single generation. As a result, procreation is paired with death, and the life of the species comes at the expense of the individual. There are a few points to keep in mind from Herder's account of procreation in metamorphosis, and all of them have to do with narrating the "mystery" of procreation. The first is the balance struck between descriptions of processes and states of existence—the tendency to circumscribe the non-narratable moment of procreation with an abundance of descriptive details. The second is the "grammar" of procreation. If there is such a thing, its preferred mood is the subjunctive, required for hypothetical situations. This too relates back to the "mystery" of procreation. Finally, the coupling of procreation and death (as its structural opposite, but also physiological commonplace with regard to nature's surplus of seeds) is a constellation which Goethe will consider as well, together with the contingency of procreative success, in his later work on metamorphosis.

If a theory of metamorphosis lies at the heart of Goethe's botanical studies, it is safe to say that procreation, as the regeneration of the living organism, is central to Goethe's study of metamorphosis from the inception. His early botanical studies reveal a joint concern with the observation and description of the phenomenon, as well as the uncertainty of how best to describe either the organs involved or the process of procreation itself. Before the 1790 essay on metamorphosis, before setting foot in Italy, and before ever jotting down the laconic phrase "Alles ist Blatt" (everything is leaf), which would come to define his botanical project,[27] Goethe had observed the growth of various young plants—dates, palms, and beans. The notes on these observations, which date from the time of his collaboration with Herder, already reveal an interest in comparing human and plant organs. One group of notes, in which Goethe considers the comparison between the organs of humans and plants, has been grouped under a heading called "On the Cotyledons."[28] As the first seed leaf (or pair of leaves) sprouted by a plant, the cotyledon was often associated with the "birth" of the new organism. When sketching out ideas for the essay, Goethe proposed to test these physiognomic comparisons for their validity. A list titled "for a theory of the cotyledons" contains the following notes:

10) die Spur der Placenta die an den Palmen so sichtbar ist zu verfolgen.
11) die Idee daß der untere Cotiledon nicht die Placenta sondern der Uterus gravidus sey an welchen die Placenta befestigt ist zu verfolgen. (LA II 9A: 31)
10) the trace of the placenta which is so visible on the palms to be pursued.

11) the idea that the lower cotyledon would be not the placenta but rather the Uterus gravidus upon which the placenta is attached to be pursued.

In this list and in other drafts Goethe accepts the authority of tradition when comparing the cotyledon with the placenta. Their superficial similarity is hinted at by their approximate semantic congruity (the Greek etymology of "cotyledon" is a cup-shaped hollow, a "placenta" in Latin refers to a round flat cake[29]). Elsewhere, Goethe describes the cotyledons as "true leaves" which do not look particularly leaf-like (though perhaps more like placentas). They are "swollen, unshapely, unformed and filled with a simple material . . . without vessels being particularly noticeable."[30] As he progresses in his studies Goethe becomes increasingly skeptical about the validity of a comparison between the first leaves of the plant and the reproductive organs of animals. He warns about the "danger of comparisons" noting that they are "even in Linné's work only [the] cover of the undiscovered."[31] Goethe emphasizes that comparisons "of various hulls of the seed with the little skin of animal births are only illusory and all the more dangerous, since one is kept from getting to know the nature and quality of such parts."[32] Instead, he suggests that we shift our attention to the common tendency of species to regenerate: "Since all creatures which we call living are equal in that they have the force to produce their own, thus we are correct to look for the organs of procreation, *just as* through all the species of animals, *also* in the realm of plants."[33] General comparisons remain fruitful only as long as they are not pursued in excessive detail. One can look for joint manifestations of a force—since all living organisms have the "force to produce their own" and compare functional similarities (how animals procreate, how plants reproduce), but it can be dangerous to push comparisons too far. Goethe does not suggest that scientists abandon metaphor and figurative language. If anything, his comments indicate a profound respect for metaphor's predictive power in a biological context. Goethe's real issue is with those who use such language "incorrectly," so as to create a division between the observation and the description of the phenomenon.[34] The analogy of the cotyledon and the placenta posits a (formal) similarity, which, however, contributes little to an understanding of these organs' structure or function.

It would be an oversimplification to characterize Goethe's early botanical work as a wholesale exchange of morphological for functional comparisons. Goethe's first observations of plants are of a heuristic kind and cannot immediately be subsumed under a single method of observation and description. During the 1780s, he was just as intrigued by the image of a young bean plant emerging from the *uterus gravidus* of a lower cotyledon as he was by the idea of rejecting the material substratum of the metaphor altogether and imagining the plant as a cluster of points. For Goethe, the "root point," "naval point," and "heart point" could also comprise "the various points of the plant's beginning."[35] Here, too, one can observe Goethe seeking a more flexible language. For the purposes of comparison, the difference between designating a plant's *heart* or a *heart point* is significant. A point, according to Euclid, "is that which has no part."[36] Without divisibility, a point is something which we can only imagine. When the incentive to identify morphological similarities is downplayed by emphasizing the organ as "point," the structure of the heart as organ is no longer called into question—it is reduced to pure function. The concept of the "point" entered the discourse on organic reproduction long before Goethe. One need only recall Harvey's embryological observations in *De Motu Cordis* (1628) and *De generatione* (1651). In his study on the chick embryo, Harvey identifies the *punctum saliens* as the first indication of automotive blood that appears in the embryonic fluid.[37] Goethe's description of the plant as a nexus of beginning points robs any single one of its claim to be the origin.[38] The holistic vision of a plant as a cluster of mobile points emphasizes process over static shape and proposes a language of comparison concerned with the plant as a growing, metamorphosing organism. Such an interpretation of the plant also takes a creative turn away from a linear description of plant growth and reproduction and suggests that Goethe is less interested in constructing a narrative that would define an absolute "beginning" or "end" to the plant cycle than in creating a productive and composite image of the whole. We can think of the "point" comparisons as an intermediary phase between morphologically based metaphors and ones which focus solely on process, and as an important stage in the theory of observation Goethe develops in the decade prior to the 1798 poem on plant metamorphosis.

Goethe relates his early meditations on plant points directly to the process of procreation through the concept of a node, or *Knoten*. The node can be thought of as the three-dimensional analog of the point, mediating between abstraction and the physicality of procreation. The first node—equated with the "umbilical point"—takes in nutrients through the root, processes them, and forms vessels.[39] It has the ability to generate new roots and leaves. It can produce other nodes above it, or towards the side. Ultimately Goethe's description of the node closely resembles his later characterization of the leaf: "the entire plant is a frequent repetition and extenuation [*Ausbildung*] of the first node in its various multiplicity [*Mannichfaltigkeit*].[40] He describes the process of growth and generation governed by the node as a "kind of procreation": "since in all this a kind of procreation seems to occur, and not merely a kind of development and separation, then the question arises, to what extent such a procreation, if one could and should assume it, would have a similarity with the one which occurs through pollen. Should be investigated most precisely, and its trails to be avidly pursued, let the result be what it will." [41] Procreation, in this way of interpreting at the plant, is not just one activity, but rather the governing *"Zeugungstrieb"* which governs the entire organism. Without Goethe's knowledge, this point of view is very close to Blumenbach's notion of a formative drive or *Bildungstrieb*.[42]

BOTANICS AND 'BILDUNG' (2): APHORISTIC PROCREATION

The previous section discussed Goethe's increasing attention to the language of botany as it relates to the narration of metamorphosis and procreation. Another aspect to Goethe's early botanical studies, which also concerns the narration of organic processes, has to do with the question of genre constraints. Goethe's first attempts to organize his thoughts on the theory of plant metamorphosis were neither poems nor essays. They are the scrawled notes of a scientist: isolated words, lists, questions, corrections, as well as excerpts. Goethe's scientific notes take the form of fleeting observations and brief aphoristic statements which are only later incorporated into a more discursive science and poetry of metamorphosis. Since aphoristic writing has an important role to play in the scientific discourse around 1800—and comprises an important point of overlap with Hardenberg and Ritter, who made use of aphorisms to capture their most peculiar thoughts about procreation—the following pages will broaden the discussion of observing and narrating procreation in Goethe's early botanical work to include the question of genre.

The tradition of recording scientific observations in aphoristic form can be traced back as far as Hippocrates. While the scholarship on the aphorism is generally at a loss as to the precise criteria with which to define it as a literary genre (for example, whether the sentences are complete or incomplete, long or short), there is general agreement on the trends it has followed since antiquity. Once used exclusively for scientific and medical purposes, aphoristic writing gradually migrated into the fields of moral philosophy and anthropology after the Renaissance, before being claimed as a literary genre in the eighteenth century.[43] Gerhard Neumann has observed that the aphorism first gains popularity in Germany around 1800, precisely at the moment when the natural sciences came to the attention of those literary authors with which this study is concerned: in addition to Lichtenberg, he mentions Hardenberg, Ritter and Goethe.[44] The explanation Neumann offers is that literature and science around 1800 show an inability to bridge the gap between sensual experience and the objective reflection to which it is submitted.[45] The aphorism was a testing ground where the records of individual experiences were tried, and in some cases, contradicted by theoretical contemplations. Goethe's aphorisms on procreation describe empirical phenomena and, as does the poem on plant metamorphosis, deliberately embed the scientist as observer in the process of observation and notation. They are an attempt to work through the very general questions about how to observe, describe, and conceptualize living organisms in a state of change. At stake is not just a description of plant metamorphosis, but also a mode of representation which expresses both the phenomenon and the observer's relation to it. The correlation in Goethe's notes between aphoristic writing and physiological processes also receives special significance in light of what Neumann refers to as the aphorism's "organic moment."[46] Neumann describes Herder's "phenomenology" of the aphorism as one which rests in part on the conjoining of word and flower (as in the *pensée*) derived from the Gnomic tradition.[47]

In a notebook he carried on his voyage to Italy in 1787, Goethe jotted down a group of twelve aphorisms, or *Lehrsätze*,[48] which number among the first in his oeuvre. He was in Rome at the time, and had recently made the acquaintance of Karl Philip von Moritz, with whom he conversed on a number of subjects, including aesthetics and botany.[49] The aphorisms can be divided into three groups of four. They begin with a meditation on what is common to all living things, continue with a focus on procreation and birth, and conclude with observations directed towards the plant kingdom. As far as Goethe's thinking of metamorphosis is concerned, the aphorisms comprise a middle ground somewhere in between the reams of notes and excerpts which comprise his early research and the more formal essay from 1790, with its one hundred and twenty-three paragraphs, title headings, and footnotes. In a peculiar way, they even seem to contemplate a scenario where the phenomenon requires the presence of the observer for procreation and birth to occur, which indicates that Goethe's ideas about plant procreation are developing in tandem with a theory of observation. Written prior to Goethe's 1790 essay on plant metamorphosis as well as the essay in which he formulated his methodology of experimentation, *The Experiment as Mediator between Subject and Object* (Der Versuch als Vermittler zwischen Subjekt und Objekt, 1792; published 1823), these aphorisms are an important early record of Goethe's methodology. The first four aphorisms are directed towards the definition of a general force shared by all living things:

> An allen Körpern die wir lebendig nennen bemercken wir die Kraft ihres gleichen hervorzubringen.
>
> Wenn wir diese Kraft getheilt gewahr werden bezeichnen wir sie unter dem Nahmen der beyden Geschlechter.
>
> Diese Kraft ist diejenige welche alle lebendige Körper mit einander gemein haben, da sonst ihre Art zu seyn sehr verschieden ist.
>
> Die Ausübung dieser Kraft nennen wir das Hervorbringen.
> (FA 1:13, 179)

> On all bodies which we call living, we notice the force to bring forth their own.

When we perceive this force divided we define it under the name of the two sexes.

This force is the one which all living bodies have in common with each other, since otherwise their way of being is very different.

The practice of this force we call bringing forth.

The rhetorical structure of these aphorisms follows that of an initial scientific proposition—the first aphorism is the only one which can truly stand alone—followed by three statements whose function it is to explicate, expound upon and ultimately to circle back to the original claim. Goethe does not define the force in question more precisely, but he does suggest it is something which can be symptomatically observed. Although the general activity of the force is to be considered pure "producing," when perceived to be divided it can be characterized as two sexes.[50] The presence of the scientist under whose purview the phenomenon is both observed and named is crucial to the persuasiveness of these aphorisms. It is in those entities which we name living beings that we see the power of self-generation. When we perceive division, we characterize it under the labels of the two sexes. The aphorisms remind us that concepts such as production, division and sexuality are constructs which we create for ourselves to organize our perception of the phenomenon into logical patterns and forms. They insist upon the connection between generation and observation as a productive state of existence.

Even when the aphorisms depart from their initial emphasis on a general force, they remain a tightly woven chain of inter-referential observations and theoretical statements: each aphorism points back to the one before. The next four aphorisms distinguish the individual moments of procreation and birth:

> Wenn wir an dieser Ausübung zwei Momente unterscheiden können nennen wir den ersten das Zeugen, den zweyten das Gebähren.
>
> Dies Gebähren ist der Ackt wenn der gleiche Körper sich vom Gleichen absondert.
>
> Den abgesonderten Körper nennen wir in dem ersten Augenblicke da wir ihn abgesondert gewahr werden die Geburt.
>
> Das Gezeugte und Gebohrne schreitet unaufhaltsam fort wieder zu zeugen und zu gebähren, und verändert sich in jedem Augenblick.
> (FA 1:13, 179–180)

> When we can distinguish two moments in this process [*Ausübung*[51]] we call the first procreating, the second giving birth.
>
> This giving birth is the act when the same body divides itself from the same.

The disassociated body we name, in the first moment when we perceive it as divided, the birth.

The created and newborn [organism] moves onward inexorably to procreate and give birth again and alters itself in every moment.

Again, the relationship which informs the aphorisms is that between the force of reproduction, its symptomatic appearance in the organism, and the observer who identifies the changes and names them—the three activities of observation, naming and reproduction occur simultaneously. The observer perceives the cycle of generation as an endless sequence of two moments, procreation and birth. The aphorisms define the act of giving birth both from the perspective of the observer (who sees it as a separation of fruit from plant) and from the position of the observed entity (for which it is an act of self-division). They lack a comparable description of procreation. Though named, it is neither defined nor narrated. Instead, the narrative of the plant's life-cycle skips from general production or growth to birth. This omission is consistent with a repeated emphasis on division over joining: a rhetoric of division, connected to the kind of observation Goethe describes in the aphorisms, far outweighs that of union. Division begins with the divided force manifest as two sexes, continues with the two differentiated moments of procreation and birth,[52] and is carried further through the "doubled" divisions in the process of birth as described in terms of the observer and the phenomenon. In the 1790s, beginning with the essay on plant metamorphosis, Goethe will introduce the concept of anastomosis as an act of growing together, which in turn will prove essential for his views on plant, procreation, and the activity of observation. In this earlier group of aphorisms, however, he edits the activity of conjoining, essential through it may be to the procreative process, in favor of a discussion on division which links the cognitive process of the observer with the physiological process of the phenomenon. The final four aphorisms pursue the concepts of procreation and birth further as Goethe shifts his focus towards plants.

Da wir uns hier nur auf die Betrachtung der Pflanzen einschräncken sey es an diesen allgemeinen Betrachtungen genug. Die folgenden widmen wir den Pflanzen ins besondere.

Vom Zeugen und Gebähren zum Zeugen und Gebähren vollendet die Natur den Kreislauf des Lebens einer Pflanze.

Wir müssen uns nicht irre machen lassen wenn wir bemercken daß einige Pflanzen nachdem sie sich ihres Gleichen hervorgebracht noch ferner bestehen. Wir betrachten die Pflanze nur in dem Kreise der einmal durchlaufen sich immer wiederholt. Es wird die nähere Bestimmung dieses Verhältnisses im folgenden nicht fehlen.

Wenn wir die Pflanze als gebohren zuerst gewahr werden das nennen wir die Frucht. (FA 1:13, 180)

Since we limit ourselves here only to the observation of plants, these general observations should suffice. The following we dedicate to plants in particular.

From procreating and giving birth to procreating and giving birth nature completes the life-cycle of a plant.

We must not confuse ourselves when we observe that some plants after they have brought forth their own kind still further exist. We observe the plant only in the circle which, once passed through, always repeats itself. The closer definition of this relation will not be absent in the following pages.

When we first perceive the plant as born we call it the fruit.

Herder's *Ideas* emphasized the correlation between procreation and death as a way of circumscribing the single life-cycle of the plant against the continuum of the species. Goethe's description allows the observer an analogous role (i.e., to create a separation, albeit it one recast as productive) by isolating a single cycle of growth and procreation within a context of further development. The connections the aphorisms make between the observer and the phenomenon have a strong resonance in Goethe's further work on metamorphosis. They articulate a starting point for thinking about observation and description as creative—even poetic—activities and it will be shown that the observation of the organic world thematized in Goethe's poem on plant metamorphosis has its basis in scientific practice.

METAMORPHOSIS AND THE WORD

Goethe's essay, *The Metamorphosis of Plants* (1790), followed from the "discovery" of the *Urpflanze*. This was not a single species of plant, as Goethe had once hoped, but rather a general "type" which could model plant development. The theory of metamorphosis Goethe developed from his meditations on the chimerical *Urpflanze* has sparked widely divergent reactions, from the time of its publication through the present day.[53] Yet the essay where Goethe formally introduces "the greatest conception of the post-Baconian age," as Gottfried Benn has called it, is at least at first glance relatively modest in its claims. Goethe clearly defines the parameters in the 1790 essay: his intention is to describe a pattern of plant growth and reproduction applicable for only a certain subset of all vegetation—flowering annuals—and to limit himself to a particular kind of metamorphosis, the so-called "regular" or "progressive" metamorphosis that describes the growth of the plant from seed leaf to fruit as the "transformation of one shape [*Gestalt*] into another" climbing "as if on a spiritual ladder, to that pinnacle of nature, the propagation through

34 *German Romanticism and Science*

two sexes."[54] Though Goethe crafted the essay from his own empirical observations, many of the concepts and observations were not new to the scientific community.[55] There is nevertheless more to the concept of metamorphosis than its somewhat humble trappings, as Gottfried Benn's rapturous description would also suggest:

> Sie umschloß die Identität und war gleichzeitig das naturwissenschaftliche Prinzip der Gestaltung; sie war Kontinuität, aber eine, die sich im Individuum unterbrach; sie war Monismus, aber sie hatte Nuance: Ausdehnung und Zusammenziehen, sie hatte Stil: Eile und Erschlaffen, sie hatte Mittel: Äußern und Verbergen; sie war eine Interpretation der Welt aus sich selber, aber sie umschloß die ruhelose Dialektik des *en kai pan*, ein Begriff, der vermittelte zwischen der Gesetzlichkeit ewiger Formen und der schöpferischen Freiheit des Lebens. (Benn, *Goethe und die Naturwissenschaften*, 175–176.)
>
> It encompassed identity, and was at the same time the natural-scientific principle of shape [*Gestaltung*]; it was continuity, but one that interrupted itself in the individual; it was monism, but it had nuance: expansion and contraction; it had style: haste and laxity; it had means: exposition and concealment; it was an interpretation of the world from itself, but it encompassed the tireless dialectic of the *en kai pan*, a concept which mediated between the lawfulness [*Gesetzlichkeit*] of eternal forms and the creative freedom of life.

Benn's description of Goethian metamorphosis as both a scientific principle and aesthetic concept, with echoes of philosophical traditions reaching back to Leibniz and the pre-Socratics, captures its essential hybridism. There is an aesthetic sensibility underlying Goethe's concept of metamorphosis which anticipates the poem of 1798. Both can be read as Goethe's coming to terms with Linnaean vocabulary, and both tell the story of the plant's life-cycle by generalizing an individual who can stand in for the whole. Above all, both the essay and the poem are shaped by a desire to communicate the organic law governing the metamorphosis of plants.

As in the aphorisms discussed previously, Goethe's essay is an attempt to tell one chapter (or cycle) in the story of plant life in such a way that it can then adequately account for infinite sequels of procreation and birth. It is a story Goethe can tell all the more easily because in the very beginning he cordons off those kinds of metamorphoses whose histories cannot facilitate our understanding of predictable patterns of change. He prefers to focus on "regular" and "irregular" over "chance" metamorphoses. Whereas the irregularities of the second category can facilitate our understanding of normal patterns of change exhibited in the first, Goethe asks his readers to avert their attention from the third kind, which includes changes caused by contingencies: unexpected circumstances in the environment relating to weather, insects, etc. He does hint that this might be a topic for future scientific study, and the problematic role of contingency in otherwise predictable metamorphosis will be taken up during the discussion of the poem in the next section. Despite Goethe's avowed decision—both as a scientist and as a narrator—to take the "regular" route in his experiments and in his essay on metamorphosis, a question arises at the end of the text which is troubling enough to cast a shadow over the success of the narrative as a whole.

In the penultimate paragraph of the essay, after a lengthy discussion of plant metamorphosis in terms of a single organ, a transcendental leaf which transitions through various stages, Goethe points out that something is missing. What we lack, he claims, is a word to encompass all aspects of the organ in its metamorphoses. "It goes without saying that we must have a general term with which we could indicate this variously metamorphosed organ and compare all manifestations of its form."[56] Goethe does not specify what kind of "word" he is searching for. In the prior paragraph (§119) he already established the use of "leaf" to designate the various manifestations of the organ,[57] but he nonetheless believes it self-evident that we need something else.[58] He complains that defining contiguous organs in terms of one another leads to tautological statements: "For we can just as well say that a stamen is a contracted petal, as we can say of a petal that it is a stamen in a state of expansion."[59] What Goethe requires is a word which can act as a reference point for all manifestations of the changing organ, a word both separate from the phenomenon and yet logically connected to it at the same time. A closer look at the content of Goethe's essay will shed light on what kind of "word" he means and lead back to the problem of procreation. This discussion will lay the groundwork for the subsequent reading of the poem on the metamorphosis of plants from 1798, which can be seen as a poetic response to the lingering question of the "word."

Like other theories of metamorphosis which came before, Goethe's was designed to reduce a manifold of empirical phenomena to a number of principles which, taken together, would be sufficient to explain the development of plants. Goethe, as did other botanists, organized discrete observations by positing the existence of a single organ whose transformations comprise the various stages of metamorphosis. Goethe's theory differs from the preceding ones, though, in relating these different stages of plant growth to a single, pulsating force which he describes in terms of an alternating expansion and contraction. This force can be observed already in the seed leaves, to which Goethe devotes the first section of the essay: these are the first "organs" [*Werkzeuge*] that emerge from the seed in its initial stage of growth.[60] Goethe understands their development within the movements of expansion [*Ausdehnung*] and contraction [*Zusammenziehung*] that govern the growth of the plant, and describes six of these pulsating shifts. The seed's expansion to the stem leaf [*Stengelblatt*] leads to an eventual contraction into the sepal [*Kelch*].[61] A second phase of expansion to the blossom leaf [*Blütenblatt*] follows, which then gives way to the second contraction into the sexual organs of anthers [*Staubgefäße*] and pistil [*Griffel*]. A third expansion forms the fruit before the final contraction to the seed begins the cycle anew.[62] The essay is structured chronologically: each stage of plant growth is related both to the abstract notion of "leaf" and the force of reproduction which propels the plant from one stage of growth to the next. Goethe pays particular attention to the stage of procreation, where the sequential nature of plant growth acquires greater complexity as the plant divides into two sexes.

GROWTH, REPRODUCTION, AND ANASTOMOSIS

Goethe's 1790 essay on the metamorphosis of plants can be read as a synthesis and further development of his earlier thinking about procreation as discussed in his aphoristic work. He continues to define the individual stages of plant metamorphosis in terms of growth and reproduction and includes the concept of anastomosis.[63] Instead of insisting primarily on spatiality (and in particular, separation, which played a fundamental role in the twelve aphorisms cited previously as a problem of both development and observation), Goethe turns his attention to the temporality of metamorphosis. The question is no longer simply what changes the plant undergoes, but also the rate at which these changes occur relative to each other. In §113 Goethe summarizes his views on procreation and describes this transition in detail:

> Betrachten wir eine Pflanze in sofern sie ihre Lebenskraft äußert, so sehen wir dieses auf eine doppelte Art geschehen, zuerst durch das *Wachstum*, indem sie Stengel und Blätter hervorbringt, und sodann durch die *Fortpflanzung*, welche in dem Blüten- und Fruchtbau vollendet wird. Beschauen wir das Wachstum näher, so sehen wir, daß, indem die Pflanze sich von Knoten zu Knoten, von Blatt zu Blatt fortsetzt, indem sie sproßt, gleichfalls eine Fortpflanzung geschehe, die sich von der Fortpflanzung durch Blüte und Frucht, welche *auf einmal* geschieht, darin unterscheidet, daß sie *sukzessiv* ist, daß sie sich in einer Folge einzelner Entwickelungen zeigt. (§113, MA 12:65–66)

> If we observe a plant as it externalizes its life force, then we see this occur in two ways, first of all through *growth*, in that [the plant] produces stem and leaves, and then through *reproduction*, which completes itself in the formation of blossoms and fruit. If we inspect growth more closely, we see that, as the plant reproduces itself from node to node and from leaf to leaf, as it vegetates, a reproduction may also be said to take place that distinguishes itself from the reproduction through the

flower and fruit, which happens *all at once*, because it is *successive*, and that it shows itself in a sequence of individual developments.[64]

Goethe extends the meaning of the term 'reproduction' to encompass the plant's production of itself and the production of the fruit, defining two aspects of plant generation in terms of reproduction (*Fortpflanzung*). The first, as growth (*Wachstum*), occurs successively along the vertical axis of the plant stem. The second aspect, which is the actual reproduction, describes a cluster of simultaneous changes which occur during the stages of sexual development where the plant blossoms and bears fruit. The changes lead to the division of the heretofore asexual plant into two sexes; the anther and pistil develop contiguously and contemporaneously to one another before joining in the production of the fruit. Already in the observations from 1788, collected under the title "Laws of Plant Formation," Goethe connected the concepts of growth and reproduction in order to emphasize their common goal, the plant's "production of its own kind": "On those bodies which we call plants, we notice the doubled force of producing its own: on the one hand without the visible effect of the sexes, and on the other through their visible effect."[65] With respect to the troublesome "word" whose absence Goethe laments at the end of the essay, it is possible to see how the stage of sexual reproduction presents an additional challenge for anyone who would try to narrate the stages of plant growth as a sequence of emerging parts. The appearance of the two sexes disturbs the linearity of plant development and makes a linguistic demand on the observer to account for things which occur both sequentially and simultaneously.

Plant procreation heralds a shift in the uniformity of plant growth where the linear sequencing that captured the manifestation of the metamorphosing "leaf" gradually gives way to a simultaneous appearance of the sexual organs, stamen and pistil. At the point when the growing plant divides into its reproductive organs—when a more complex form emerges—Goethe integrates the concept of anastomosis into his narrative:

> Kaum daß noch die feinen Häutchen der Staubbeutel gebildet werden, zwischen welchen sich die höchst zarten Gefäße nunmehr endigen. Wenn wir nun annehmen, daß hier eben jene Gefäße, welche sich sonst verlängerten, ausbreiteten und sich einander wieder aufsuchten, gegenwärtig in einem höchst zusammengezogenen Zustande sind; wenn wir aus ihnen nunmehr den höchst ausgebildeten Samenstaub hervordringen sehen, welcher das durch seine Tätigkeit ersetzt, was den Gefäßen, die ihn hervorbringen, an Ausbreitung entzogen ist; wenn er nunmehr losgelöst die weiblichen Teile aufsucht, welche den Staubgefäßen durch gleiche Wirkung der Natur entgegen gewachsen sind; wenn er sich fest an sie anhängt, und seine Einflüsse ihnen mitteilt: so sind wir nicht abgeneigt, die Verbindung der beiden Geschlechter eine geistige Anastomose zu nennen, und glauben wenigstens einen

Augenblick die Begriffe von Wachstum und Zeugung einander näher gerückt zu haben. (§ 63, MA 12:48)

The delicate membranes of the anther, between which the excessively tender vessels come to an end, are scarcely able to develop. If we now admit that at this stage those very vessels, which would otherwise have elongated, broadened, and again sought one another out, are at present in an extremely contracted condition; if we now see the highly elaborated pollen proceed from them, which compensates through its activity for what the vessels which produce it have lost in expansion; if it is at last set free and seeks out the female organ, which, through a natural correlation, occurs in the neighborhood of the stamens; if it firmly adheres to this organ and communicates its influence to it: there is nothing then to prevent our calling the union of the two sexes an immaterial anastomosis, and believing that, at least for a moment, we have brought closer together the concepts of growth and of reproduction.[66]

Through a series of propositions, Goethe couples observation and hypothesis to explain the union of the stamen and pistil. He imagines a scenario where the stages of plant procreation move one after the other in front of his mind's eye. Finally Goethe posits an anastomosis which has both physical and intellectual overtones. Anastomosis, which derives from the Greek word for "mouth," refers to the growing together or conjoining of two distinct organic parts. Goethe uses the term to distinguish his own theory from earlier ones which saw metamorphosis as a process of diminution since the organs of the plant become smaller.[67] Anastomosis denotes both a communication and a coupling between the physical and intellectual. What Wolff, for example, saw as a "weakening" is for Goethe a turn towards refinement which culminates in the "immaterial anastomosis," the almost imperceptible transfer of pollen from stamen to the pistil, where it is then absorbed.[68] The essay also argues for the importance of anastomosis as a bridge to explain sexual union in the plant. Neither pistil nor stamen forms an individual organ, "and when the precise relation between it (the feminine part) and the masculine part really becomes clear for us, we find the thought of calling the copulation an anastomosis more appropriate and illuminating."[69] The importance of anastomosis at this point in Goethe's essay cannot be overstated: it anchors his theory that each stage of plant development is the transformation of a single organ while conforming to the procreative structure of the unification of pairs.[70] By uniting the concepts of growth and reproduction, the sequential and the simultaneous, it is also the physical process that aligns most closely with Goethe's specific requirements for the observation of the living, metamorphosing organism.

The question of language remains a concern for Goethe in those concepts which underlie his interpretation of the natural world. Given the importance of the concepts of "expansion" and "contraction" for his views of nature in general, it is surprising that he had expressed dissatisfaction with these notions already two years prior to the essay:

> In the progressive modification of the plant's parts a force takes effect which I can only call by approximation expansion and contraction. It would be better to give it an x or y in algebraic fashion, because the words expansion and contraction do not express this effect to its complete extent. It draws together, expands, forms, re-forms, combines, divides, colors, loses color, spreads, lengthens, weakens, grows harder, distributes and withdraws.[71]

The problem which Goethe's earlier work already touches upon, and which receives full attention in the 1790 essay, is that in order to describe plant metamorphosis adequately and convey a correct image of it, one must communicate both synchronic and diachronic changes. Goethe's discontent with the words "expansion" and "contraction" has less to do with those two concepts in particular than with discursive language in general. He suggests that we would be better served by treating our language as an algebraic one of x's and y's which could overcome the limits of discursive speech and, as variables, could symbolically represent a multitude of activities. Goethe also lists knowledge of algebra among the prerequisites for understanding metamorphosis in the botanical essay (§ 102).

OBSERVATION AND EXPERIMENT

The relationship between the viewer and the phenomenon is fundamental to Goethe's studies of plant metamorphosis. The 1790 essay and the 1798 poem emphasize different aspects of this relationship's potential which, in turn, are closely related to developments in Goethe's thinking about scientific experimentation during the 1790s. The concept of metamorphosis Goethe had established by the time of the essay required that the mind's eye and the corporeal eye move between the empirical phenomenon and the intuited *Urphänomen*.[72] This occurs when the observer recalls the manifestations of the phenomenon like a film. The observer can replay this film both backwards and forwards, and, in the act of beholding, he or she can grasp the phenomenon as a whole. Eckart Förster describes two requirements of intuition. The first is to "arrive at a sequence of observations that can be seen to form a whole, and amount to (as it were) one single experiment, a single piece of empirical evidence presented in its most manifold aspects."[73] The second, more challenging requirement is to reproduce the phenomenon in the mind: "I thus have to be in thought everywhere at once, at all places at the same time: in other words, the thought has to be intuitive, not just discursive."[74] This kind of seeing becomes possible when one also imagines the transition between two subsequent stages of plant development, which cannot be observed in real time.[75]

In the metamorphosis essay, the kind of seeing described previously facilitates the transition from empirical observation to theoretical claims. Several of the examples Goethe chooses in order to prove his point are oddities of plant growth—such as the "proliferated" (*durchgewachsen*: literally "grown through") rose and carnation—where two contiguous stages appear together and can really be seen as well as intuited. In the case of the proliferated rose, the sepal and crown leaves, instead of contracting into the reproductive organs of stamen and pistil, grow further along the stem: prolonged successive growth replaces the expected simultaneous development of the sexual organs. The newest crown leaves show traces of the anthers. They visually confirm the theory that both anther and crown derive from the same abstract notion of leaf. To support the argument of the essay, Goethe then frames these transitory moments between phases of plant development within the overarching narrative of cyclical plant life. If for Goethe the corporeal eyes divide by perceiving differences in the phenomenal world, the eyes of the mind unite sense impressions into concepts. As we have seen in Goethe's aphorisms on plant formation, when he relates birth to the faculty of human perception (i.e., "The disassociated body we name, in the first moment when we perceive it as divided, the birth," FA 1:13, 179), he superimposes the event of recognition (as a cognitive event) over the organic process. Although he does not by any means suggest that the process of reproduction depends on the presence of an observer, his words underscore a human tendency to relate natural phenomena to the limits of perception.[76] Through division, human intellectual activity overlaps with biological processes. Within the framework of the experiment, and within the fields of morphology and physiology, Goethe understands human observations as activities of division and combination:

> Der Mensch kann ohne diese nur das was gesondert ist erkennen, eben darum weil es gesondert ist. Er muß um zu erkennen, dasjenige sondern, was nicht gesondert werden sollte; und hier ist kein ander Mittel als das, was die Natur gesondert unserer Erkenntniß vorgelegt hat, wieder zu verbinden, wieder zu Einem zu machen. (LA 10:58)
>
> One can anyway only recognize what is divided, because it is divided. One must, in order to recognize, divide what is not supposed to be divided; and here is no other means than to reconstruct that what nature has shown to our faculty of reason as divided, to make one again.[77]

Goethe seems to present us with a paradox: man can only comprehend and gain knowledge from what is divided, precisely because it is already divided—the act of recognition implies a cognitive division. At the same time, man has also been granted the ability to recognize this state of affairs and reconstitute artificially that which should not have been divided in the first place in order to aid his understanding of the natural world. With these words, Goethe affirms that humans have the ability to replicate the organic processes of procreation and birth as intellectual operations.[78] Although relevant to Goethe's botanical work as a whole, the activities of separating and merging first unite in the process of anastomosis, where the physical and intellectual bridging of divided parts goes hand-in-hand.

Goethe's ideas about the role of seeing in scientific experiments, though central to an understanding of the essay on metamorphosis, continued to develop at the time of its publication. In a short essay published three years afterwards he devotes himself exclusively to this problem in the fullest sense as it relates to the method of scientific experimentation. With specific reference to the fields of botany and optics, "The Experiment as Mediator between Subject and Object," first drafted in 1792,[79] approaches the fundamental problem of how to think of an active, seeing subject in conjunction with the object of scientific experimentation. The essay addresses the difficulty of observing natural objects either by themselves or in relation to one another, without inclination—a botanist, for example, should be influenced neither by the beauty nor the usefulness of the plant. One can compare this statement to Kant's "disinterested" observer of art and nature in the *Third Critique*.

Goethe defines an experiment as the repetition of experiences.[80] The essay claims that the value of any single experiment lies primarily in its iterability, and that this also holds true when the scientist integrates a single experiment into a series. Goethe states repeatedly that scientists need to pay careful attention not to assume a similarity between phenomena or experiments too quickly; no single experiment proves an assumption, or confirms a theory. He warns that many scientists make mistakes during the transition from cognition to application and recommends an immediate investigation after each successful experiment to see what might follow it. Rather than constructing a relation between two discrete attempts, Goethe suggests that the "multiplication" [*Vermannigfaltigung*] of every single experiment" produces the best results.[81] He champions the idea of a composite experiment, incorporating "series" of smaller ones, because "it presents the formula under which countless individual examples of calculation are expressed."[82] Goethe moves towards a notion of mathematical knowledge as the highest kind and the one most suitable for expressing experimental results,[83] and he understands the discursive function of mathematical proofs as detailed elaborations of an existing intuition. We can compare this idea to the comment that knowledge of algebra is helpful for understanding plant metamorphosis. The "formula" which indexes a manifold of experiments is analogous to the x or y which would express several words at once. His description of the experiment, where the proof is a discursive mirror of the complete intuition of the whole, is also compatible with an understanding of metamorphosis which is intuited from the composite view of the phenomenon. Both the experiment and the intuition of metamorphosis rely upon the unity between the whole and its parts, and the necessity of repetition by no means detracts from this relationship.[84] Rather, repetition (re)produces the phenomenon in the mind of the observer and assures the correctness of the intuition.[85] That Goethe was still thinking about his work on the experiment when, five years later, he wrote his poem on plant metamorphosis, is certain. In 1798 he revisited the essay on the experiment and sent it to Schiller for comments, giving rise to a lengthy correspondence about what Goethe referred to as the "Precautions of the Observer" (Kautelen des Beobachters).[86]

LITERATURE IN THE SERVICE OF SCIENCE: "THE METAMORPHOSIS OF PLANTS" (1798)

Readers of Goethe's poem on the metamorphosis of plants, while emphasizing different aspects of it, have tended to concur with the three-tiered scheme that Astrida Tantillo proposes in *The Will to Create*. Tantillo suggests that the poem is written "to explain plant metamorphosis to women," "as a metaphor of [Goethe's] own relationship to his lover, Christiane" and "to argue that poetry and science, like the divided and initially unequal lovers, may be united as equals."[87] There is ample evidence to support these. Not only was the poem—which Goethe refers to as both an elegy and a didactic poem—first published in a women's journal with a dedication to the "actual beloved" (Christiane Vulpius[88]), but furthermore its metaphors of marriage and union leave little doubt that the scientific principle of metamorphosis has met its match in amorous poesy. Whether or not the union is one of equals depends on how one chooses to balance the metaphors of the poem against the gender roles performed by the narrator and his beloved. Most readings of the poem fall within Tantillo's description, some with greater emphasis on potential sources of influence.[89] There is one notable exception which offers perhaps the most exhaustive reading of the poem in the context of Goethe's poetic work. Günter Peters makes the bold claim that the idylls and elegies Goethe wrote during the 1790s can be read as "stations in the quest" for a particular understanding of language, a quest which the poem on plant metamorphosis demonstrates "programmatically."[90] Peters' reading of the poem is ground-breaking in its thoroughness. Though focused on Goethe's poetic work of the 1790s, he also discusses the poem's relation to scientific thinking. I will take up various points of Peters' argumentation while adding to his and Tantillo's readings something essential they leave unexplored, namely the possibility of its contribution to science—the possibility suggested by Goethe himself in the letter to Neuenhahn. Both Peters and Tantillo, in order to discuss the encounter of poetry and science, instead cite another text by Goethe, "Fate of the Printed Work." In this short text, Goethe discusses the fate of his essay on metamorphosis after its initial publication, and includes a copy of the poem on plant metamorphosis with the following rationale: "One forgot that science had developed from poetry, one did not consider that after a reversal over time, both could once again meet each other amicably, to mutual advantage, at a higher level."[91] Procreative language notwithstanding, the poem proposes more than a "friendly meeting," and that the encounter between literature and science it stages might be produced in ways that the secondary literature has not conceived. The following pages will consider to what degree the "poetic" qualities of the poem, rather than just "uniting" it with science in friendship or love, are also engaged in the advancement of scientific thinking.

The elegy couples two kinds of productivity, the life-cycle of the plant and human intellectual activity.[92] The narrator of the elegy gives his mute companion a command to "observe" [*betrachte*]. In an ambiguous turn of phrase which designates both the woman's incipient "growth" as well as the plant's ceaseless change, he incites her to envision the development of the plant through an entire cycle:

Werdend betrachte sie nun, wie nach und nach sich die Pflanze,
Stufenweise geführt, bildet zu Blüten und Frucht.
(v. 9–10, MA 12:75)

Growing consider the plant and see how by gradual phases,
Slowly evolved, it forms, rises to blossom and fruit.[93]

The narrator asks the woman to focus her attention and select an individual plant from the confusing morass. Yet the "plant" to which he refers does not belong only to the empirical confusion. Rather than enjoining his companion to seek out one plant among the many, his words implicitly demand that she envision *the* plant typical for the growth of all plants so that she may learn for herself the secret unity behind the seemingly endless plurality. Each subsequent verse explains a new stage of growth in the plant as it unfolds in the minds of the two observers and maintains the duality of the empirical phenomenon and the abstract idea. On the one hand, the narrator's description of plant metamorphosis extracts the narrative of the growing plant into an atemporal realm, completely dissociated from the historical life-cycle of the plant. On the other hand, from its first verse, "Overwhelming, beloved, you find all this mixture of thousands" (Dich verwirret, Geliebte, die tausendfältige Mischung, v. 1), the elegy claims the status of a spoken narrative, and its narrator uses deictic references to convey a sense of locality to the otherwise intangible garden. He speaks of "this riot of flowers" (dieses Blumengewühls, v. 2), and, when his companion finally acquires the concept of metamorphosis, she learns to decipher the confusion "here," in the garden (Aber entzifferst du hier, v. 67). Through the deictic markers, the elegy establishes a link between the empirical plant and the imagined one. The narrator puts to the test the proposition Goethe made in the letter to Charlotte von Stein that an imagined plant can have as much validity as a real one. Towards the end of the poem, the narrator requests that his companion return her gaze to the "teeming of so many colors" (bunten Gewimmel, v. 63) so that she can now apply her newly gained knowledge to decipher the "holy letters" (heilige Lettern, v. 76) around her.[94]

The elegy reaffirms the (literally) "poetic" qualities of experimentation through the deliberate conjuring of the plant, and thereby plays with the limits of experimentation itself. As in the "Experiment as Mediator" essay, iterability—and the notion of singularity against which it positions itself—plays an important role in the poem. The narrator tests the iterability of metamorphosis: both through the repetition of certain phrases familiar to readers of the metamorphosis essay, and through the repetition of seeing itself. The elegy is also invested in the subjective experience of seeing as a process of transformation that mirrors organic reproduction. In the very moment when the narrator encourages his female companion to observe a single, empirical flower, subject–object relationships in the poem double. While the woman gazes upon the plant, the narrator observes both the plant and the woman. His gaze—both the eyes of the body and the eyes of the mind—splits between the two objects. The multiple pairings and polarizations—of woman and nature, man and woman—suggest that the relationship between the human couple relies upon a visual logic (i.e., one predicated on the shared experience of seeing) as well as an organic one. The narrator and his beloved are thus manifestations of the same principle that the initial pair of the cotyledon leaves at the beginning of the plant's growth cycle embodied.

The problem of iterability also highlights gender differences in terms of the respective roles played by the man and the woman in the elegy. When writing on the experiment, Goethe states that "every experience is actually an isolated part of our knowledge, through frequent repetition we bring this isolated knowledge to certainty."[95] The intuition of the *Urphänomen* constitutes a repetition and confirmation of knowledge for the narrator, but for his companion it is a first. Her initiation confirms his knowledge. The narrator enjoins her to envision a plant within its entire cycle of change, yet in order to accomplish this, he must extract this plant from its continuum, and create the fiction of a beginning. As in the aphorisms which locate the "birth" of the plant in the visual experience of the beholder, here too seeing becomes a creative act. The singularity of the woman's experience coincides with the atemporal "first": "the first visible structure" (die Gestalt der ersten Erscheinung) and the first "shape" that designate the metaphorical plant-child. The plant cycle she observes becomes suggestive of her intellectual experience and of the transformation it implies. For both the narrator and his beloved, personal *Bildung* is at stake. If the woman were to fail, the status of narrator's own knowledge could be compromised, since her intellectual activity confirms his. The status of the poem as experiment therefore complicates the established gender hierarchy, given that the role of the woman effectively doubles. She is both a student and, to the degree that she shares in the active observation of the plant, a scientific colleague. The success of this collaboration remains uncertain.

FROM ESSAY TO ELEGY

The narrator of the elegy, fluent in both scientific and poetic discourse, "translates" the concept of plant metamorphosis for his beloved with the exception of a single "word."[96] His description of plant metamorphosis alone does not suffice to impart "the word that unlocks" (das lösende Wort, v. 8), because the woman must learn to see and intuit the phenomenon for herself. Only then will she understand the "secret law" (geheimes Gesetz, v. 6) of metamorphosis. Nonetheless, the poetic "translation" remains surprisingly true to scientific language. The narrator weaves descriptions of the developing plant together with those of human intimacy so as to connect his and his companion's transformation to that of the plant they mutually envision. In the process, a new figural language emerges which draws its inspiration from the scientific essay. For example, in the essay, the "masculine part of the plant" turns towards the feminine in order to "communicate" his "influences" (§ 63) through anastomosis. In the poem, the exchange of "influences" connotes communication. Both the essay and elegy on metamorphosis share an emphasis on the emergence of sexual organs as the most important stage of plant development. At the same moment where Goethe's botanical essay invokes anastomosis, the elegy's metaphors become fantastic: a marriage ceremony, witnessed by the Greek god Hymen, takes place in the innermost circle of the plant's crown. Its secrecy recalls the chorus at the opening of the poem that proclaimed a secret law governing all plants.[97] The innumerable pairs of stamen and pistil that participate in the ceremony are a poetic exaggeration (exceeding even Linné's wildest schemes). Yet the "magnificent aromas" (herrliche Düfte, v. 55) that the poetic plant exudes connect it once again to empirical experience. Just as in the poem the scent signals Hymen's presence and the completion of marriage, in the empirical world the aroma of plants betokens the presence of pollen through which the stamen fertilizes the pistils. In addition to the "word that unlocks" the moment of procreation itself remains uncommented, undescribed, and uncommunicated. There is an implicit tension between the inevitability of the natural process (which, through the metaphors of the poem, is strongly coupled to human love) and the contingency of human understanding. Niklas Luhmann writes that the eighteenth century heralds the "discovery of incommunicability." With this discovery come, according to Luhmann, questions which shaped aesthetic dicussions in the second half of the century, such as the possibility or impossibility of communicating "authentic" experience in a work of art, be it on the stage or in the literary text.[98] Goethe's poem is aware of the incommunicable in one regard, as a "word" which the narrator cannot say and attempts to circumvent. Whether one interprets this "word" as an expression of love or of a scientific law, one tendency of the poem is to grant the success of the narrator's project the inevitability of a metamorphosis in action. Yet there is a counter-tendency as well, or at least one too enigmatic to be fully understood. It is the silent female in the center, who is observed by the narrator but whose own observations and understanding are kept silent. The poem therefore leaves open a small gap, within which lies the measure of the narrator's success or failure.

The elegy also integrates specific concepts central to Goethe's botanical discourse: expansion, contraction, and anastomosis and interweaves these concepts in ways designed to be agreeable to the female public. If Linné's language is barbaric, Goethe's is seductive. Consider, for example, how the word *Ausgedehnter*—extended—appears in the elegy to describe the manifold apparitions of the plant's first structure:

> Ausgebildet, du sieht's, immer das folgende Blatt,
> Ausgedehnter, gekerbter, getrennter in Spitzen und Teile.
> (v.26–27, MA 12:75)
>
> Mutably fashioned each leaf after the last one unfolds,
> More extended, spikier, split into lances or segments.

The poem incorporates the movement of extension—*Ausdehnung*—central to Goethe's understanding of natural processes as rhythms of expansion and contraction. The extension is performed through a series of compatible adjectives which suggest the unfolding of the leaf in the mind's eye. Contraction—as *Zusammenziehung* and *Zusammendrängung*—also weaves through the narrative of plant development. The narrator refers to them with regard to the plant's reproductive stage—first, when the sepal's petals appears crowded around the stem, and subsequently when the blossom emerges:

> Ja, das farbige Blatt fühlt die göttliche Hand.
> Und zusammen zieht es sich schnell; die zärtesten Formen,
> Zwiefach streben sie vor, sich zu vereinen bestimmt.
> (v. 50–52, MA 12:76)
>
> Yes, to the hand that's divine colorful leaves will respond.
> And it quickly furls, contracts; the most delicate structures
> Twofold venture forth, destined to meet and unite.

Once again, the poem deploys rhetorical devices of repetition and familiarization in order to persuade and instruct. These verses enact the very activity of "Zusammenziehen" by enclosing it within a row of sibilant words. In particular, the second and third verses play with the alliterative coupling of "s" and "z" (zusammen zieht es sich schnell...Zwiefach streben sie vor...) so as to glide more smoothly to the end of the highly anthropomorphic drama, the plant's sexual union.

The concept of anastomosis, ranked highly in the 1790 essay on plant metamorphosis next to growth and reproduction, has an equally important role to play in the poem. Only if the narrator's companion learns the concept of metamorphosis well enough to see the same pattern everywhere throughout nature can the pair successfully realize their own "immaterial anastomosis":[99]

> Freue dich auch des heutigen Tags! Die heilige Liebe
> Strebt zu der höchsten Frucht gleicher Gesinnungen auf,
> Gleicher Ansicht der Dinge damit in harmonischem Anschaun
> Sich verbinde das Paar, finde die höhere Welt.
> (v. 77–80, MA 12:77)

> Rejoice too in the present day! Holy love
> Strives to the greatest fruit of like minds,
> To like perspective of things so that in harmonious intuition
> The pair may join, may find the higher world.[100]

Against the grain of a poetic tradition in which lovers gaze longingly into each other's eyes—that is, a tradition which privileges the reciprocity of the gaze—the final verses of Goethe's elegy suggest that the pair may well achieve their desired unity through "harmonious intuition" of a third. Strictly speaking, access to the "union world" depends upon the pedagogical success of the narrator. According to the logic of the poem, the human pair—who are increasingly embedded in botanical metaphors—can only "transform" (i.e., procreate, and come to intellectual fruition) if they are of "like mind." The poem thereby subordinates the natural teleology which the pair itself is embodying to their intellectual activity.

Most readers of the elegy accept the union of the pair as a given. Astrida Tantillo balances the successful union of the two lovers in the poem against Goethe's personal frustrations in the attempt to unite poetry and science.[101] Matthew Bell claims the views of the two lovers are "united by the power of love and the force of the metamorphic process of growth."[102] Adolf Portmann argues that the "union of the sexes as a hidden anastomosis" signifies for Goethe a true "monandria monogynia" in the Linnaean sense of pairing a single male with a single female element rather than the vulgar harem of male partners surrounding the solitary female in the center. The hidden anastomosis also signifies the highest concentration in space, the closest one can come to the transcendence of space and time, a spiritual event, even a symbol of the union of God and man.[103]

A destabilizing element, even for readings less hypertrophic than Portmann's, is the elegy's use of the subjunctive mood in the same verse that speaks of a possible union. Though it was not unusual in Goethe's time to employ the subjunctive after the conjunction *damit*, its usage introduces a hortative gesture—a "should" in place of a "will"—in the logic of the couple's union. The grammatical contingency in the elegy, which competes with the propositions of "truth" and "necessity," can be attributed to the possibility of human fallibility (for example, the case where the woman fails to see "the open secret"). More generally, it introduces a tendency that seems contrary to Goethe's theory of metamorphosis as it has been discussed thus far. In fact, such a counter-tendency is not unique to the elegy, but can already be found in the 1790 essay, in Goethe's third category of metamorphosis. As mentioned during the discussion of the essay, Goethe designates this third kind as "contingent" [*zufällig*] and within it he collects cases of metamorphosis caused other factors which are foreign to the idea of metamorphosis as it relates to the empirical phenomenon of plant metamorphosis.[104] Without going so far as to claim that Goethe's poem really entertains the possibility that this kind of contingent metamorphosis, decisively marginalized in the earlier essay, might intrude, it is nevertheless striking that both models of plant metamorphosis leave room for a logic of contingency. In both cases, if for different reasons, what the concept of metamorphosis posits as necessary in fact might not occur. What is more, Goethe's essay on the spiral tendency will reveal a renewed interest in the problem of the contingent—as that which is not "lawfully" necessary—in an otherwise predictable plant development.

ELEGIAC "ABSENCE" AND UNITY

Goethe's decision to refer to the poem as an elegy (as well as a teaching poem) raises a basic question—i.e., how the genre-defining characteristics of the elegy might function in the scientific discourse on metamorphosis—which an analysis of content cannot answer. A closer look at what an elegy is (by late-eighteenth century standards) and how Goethe's responds to certain generic expectations will also shed more light on the troubling notion of the contingent. Goethe composed the poem in antique elegiac form, in distichs of alternating hexameter and pentameter. He had already worked with this meter in the *Roman Elegies*, a poetic cycle written and revised in the decade prior. More relevant even than purely formal considerations is a contemporary theory of the elegy with which Goethe was intimately familiar. Schiller's poetological essay, *On Naive and Sentimental Poetry* (1975), disregards purely formal definitions and places the elegy in the category of "sentimental" poetry (that is, poetry that conveys the poet's reflection upon an object rather than conveying feeling through the immediacy of representation).[105] According to Schiller, elegiac poetry manifests a tendency towards an ideal.[106] The elegiac poet sets nature in opposition to art, and the ideal in opposition to reality, so that the representations of nature and the ideal triumph, along with the pleasure derived from them. When nature and the ideal are inaccessible—the first "lost" and the second "unreached"—then the poet finds himself within the genre of the elegy (as opposed to the idyll, where both nature and the ideal are attainable): "the elegiac poet seeks nature, but as an idea and in a totality in which it has never existed, even as he laments [nature] as something that once was there and now is lost."[107]

Read against the backdrop of Schiller's programmatic definition, Goethe's designation of his poem as an elegy appears problematic, since the text does not seem to embody any significant absence (the use of deixis described previously contributes to this impression). Goethe's scientific writings also do not permit even an imagined separation of empirical phenomenon and idea.[108] Rather, the idea of the plant remains connected to the empirical world through active contemplation, which discourages a reading where the envisioned plant would constitute an "elegiac" lack or absence for the two observers. We have already seen, however, that there is a "missing" element of the poem: the "word that unlocks" (das lösende Wort, v. 8). If the narrator were to impart this "word" to his companion at the beginning of the poem, then the mystery of plant metamorphosis could be explained without her personal observation of the phenomena, and there would be no need for the poem at all. But the narrator circumvents the "word"—perhaps out of sheer didactic enthusiasm, as some interpretations have claimed,[109] or perhaps because the word around which the elegy constitutes itself (and which would act de facto as the elegy's *telos*, as its cognitive goal) does not exist.[110] The conditions for its possibility cannot be met in discursive language: to communicate the intuition of plant metamorphosis, one would need a language that functioned more like an algebraic x and could represent sequence and simultaneity at the same time.

As mentioned previously, the notion of a missing word has a precedent in §120 of the metamorphosis essay, where Goethe laments the lack of a word to encompass all aspects of the organ in its metamorphoses ("It goes without saying that we must have a general word [*ein allgemeines Wort*] to indicate this variously metamorphosed organ, and to use in comparing the manifestations of its form"). Goethe's makeshift solution of "leaf" ultimately called attention to the fact that there is no available word—indeed, no available language—with which to capture the complexity of the plant's growth and reproduction. This, in turn, had led Goethe to the unsatisfactory possibility of tautological definitions whereby he identifies contiguous organs in terms of one another. In the elegy, the problem of "the word that unlocks" functions both pedagogically and poetologically. It is a pedagogical problem because the woman must learn how to see the natural world with the eyes of the body and the eyes of the mind. She must acquire the intuition that the narrator wishes to communicate to her discursively. The "word" is also a poetological problem because it informs the absence associated with the genre of the elegy. One of the ironies of the poem is that it engages in the same problem articulated in the scientific essay, and even reframes it in the context of a scientific experiment, but is not able to guarantee a solution.

CONCLUSION: THE SPIRAL TENDENCY

Almost forty years after the publication of his essay on plant metamorphosis, a new theory in the field of botany encouraged Goethe to review his earlier work and to take an active role in its development. The theory centered around the spiral vessels of plants, and claimed that these spiral vessels belong to a larger tendency which induces the various organs of a plant to develop in a spiral around a vertical axis. One of the first to present the theory to the scientific community was Carl Friedrich von Martius, a professor of botany and curator of the royal botanical gardens in Munich. Martius revealed his observations in lectures held in Berlin and in Munich for the Isis society, where the minutes were published as a two-part article in 1828 and 1829. A letter from Goethe to Martius dating from March 28th, 1829, makes the earliest (though fleeting) reference to the Martius' discovery. The following three years, up until the week before Goethe's death in March 1832, witnessed an increasing flurry of activity on Goethe's side. His correspondence, numerous notes and journal entries, in addition to the publication of the essay "On the Spiral Tendency" (1831) all testify to Goethe's continued fascination. In a letter to Ernst Heinrich Friedrich Meyer he expresses his own amazement at the turn of events: "That I, close to the end of my life, should still be caught up in the whirlpool of the spiral tendency was also a strange fate."[111]

Goethe was not indifferent to the fact that the spiral tendency conformed for the most part to his own view of metamorphosis.[112] Martius also emphasizes this correlation and cites Goethe by name in the 1829 speech,[113] where he takes Goethe's notion of metamorphosis and ascribes a (symbolic) mathematical order to it. Martius then designates the organic "movements" of the leaves to form the blossom as circular rotations (*Umläufe*) and orders them according to their number and size. Goethe, in his essay from 1831, refers to the spiral tendency as that which "forms" and "determines" blossom and fruit and summarizes Martius' position: "The construction of a blossom relates to a position and order of a certain number of metamorphosed leaves which is unique for each species."[114] Consequently, Martius dares "to undertake a symbolic representation for the individuals and to construct a new system thereupon."[115] He preserves Goethe's notion of the *Urphänomen* central to the theory of metamorphosis, but his insistence on the spiral infuses botanical discourse with a figure whose legacy cannot be overlooked.

In Goethe's writings alone, the spiral has a considerable pre-history outside of the field of botany. In inorganic realms it can function as a mechanical explanation and describe mineral formations.[116] Goethe describes the motion of the earth as a "living spiral" and "animated screw without end."[117] In addition, the spiral as a geognosic or astronomical figure also plays a role in Goethe's literary poetics. In the novel *Wilhelm Meister's Journeyman Years*, Makarie "orbits" the sun in a spiral trajectory that is "always removing itself from the middle-point and circling away towards the outer regions."[118] In fact, Goethe claims that it is the way of all "spiritual beings" to strive in increasing spirals towards the periphery.[119] At the same time, his notion of the spiral carries a gesture of return: the orbit towards the periphery constantly returns to familiar ground before extending its reach even further. A similar pattern is also described in the introduction to the *Theory of Colors*, where Goethe suggests that human progress spirals insofar as it inevitably repeats its mistakes while rediscovering true insights.[120]

Goethe's essay "On the Spiral Tendency" both calls attention to these familiar concepts and poses a new problem. With reference to his 1790 essay (§61), Goethe reminds his readers that the existence of "spiral vessels"—now claimed as the smallest elements of the spiral tendency—should already be familiar to them. In two different passages, he compares the spiral vessels to Anaxagoras' notion of homoiomeries in order to assess the relation of the spiral vessels to the whole plant: "We consider them as the smallest parts, which are entirely like the whole to which they belong . . . they share their specifications with [the whole] and in return receive specification and determination from it."[121] The comparison hints at a claim Goethe will make in the following passage that the spiral vessels are not limited to the reproductive organs of the plant (the focus of Martius' study), but can be found throughout the whole. Goethe reminds us that the "stuff" of Anaxagoras' cosmology was "continuous," not "particulate," which meant that every thing also contained a portion or share of every other thing.[122] Yet whereas the early Greek philosopher, limited by his own premises, had no choice but to arrive at the conclusions he did, Goethe, from a later standpoint, can use the same concept productively. Even if Anaxagoras only used the homoiomeries to describe "very elementary phenomena," writes Goethe, "here, however, we have really discovered on a higher level that spiral organs permeate the plant to the utmost degree, and we are at the same time certain of a spiral tendency, whereby the plant completes the course of its life and finally arrives at the end and perfection."[123] In the name of Anaxagoras, Goethe also allows his thinking to trace a spiral figure of progression through return. Because the concept of metamorphosis is central to the theory of the spiral tendency, it is inevitable that this late scientific project—by revisiting the earlier one—should assume the same contours of the very figure it proposes to investigate.[124] Given that the theory of the spiral tendency depends upon the same intuition fundamental to Goethe's earlier works, one would expect Goethe to have adapted to it without difficulty. Not only do Goethe's notes and letters attest to the contrary, he admits in a short essay published in 1820 with a collection of morphological writings that he never found intuitive thinking particularly easy:

> Die Schwierigkeit Idee und Erfahrung miteinander zu verbinden erscheint sehr hinderlich bei aller Naturforschung: die Idee ist unabhängig von Raum und Zeit, die Naturforschung ist in Raum und Zeit beschränkt, daher ist in der Idee Simultanes und Sukzessives innigst verbunden, auf dem Standpunkt der Erfahrung hingegen immer getrennt, und eine Naturwirkung, die wir der Idee gemäß als simultan und sukzessiv zugleich denken sollen, scheint uns in eine Art Wahnsinn zu versetzen. (MA 12:99–100)

> The difficulty of combining idea and experience with each other seems obstructive in all study of nature: the idea is independent of space and time, the study of nature is limited in space and time, thus in the idea, the simultaneous and successive is intimately linked, from the point of view of experience, however, always separated, and a natural process, which we in accordance with the idea have to think of simultaneously and successively, seems to put us in a kind of madness.

The same kind of thinking which requires an oscillation between idea and experience, and also describes the simultaneous and successive growth of the plant, provokes a kind of madness which returns when Goethe is confronted with the task of imagining the vertical and spiral tendencies in tandem with one another. Goethe sets the spiral tendency in opposition to the vertical tendency; together, they replace the functions of "growth" and "reproduction," or "successivity" and "simultaneity" elaborated in the 1790 essay. One important distinction is that whereas the earlier work tended towards a logic of alternation, the essay on the spiral tendency prefers to speak of one "prevailing" over, or "overpowering" the other even though they both are present throughout the stages of plant development.[125] Goethe admits that he finds it difficult—even "impossible"—to conjure the joint functioning of the vertical and spiral tendencies as an intellectual intuition.[126] In the following passage from a letter, which also appears in the essay on the spiral tendency, Goethe resorts to a parable (*Gleichniß*):

> Man trete zur Sommerzeit vor eine im Gartenboden eingesteckte Stange, an welcher eine Winde von unten an sich fortschlägelnd in die Höhe steigt, sich festanschließend ihren lebendigen Wachsthum verfolgt. Man denke sich nun Convolvel und Stange, beide gleich lebendig, aus einer Wurzel aufsteigend, sich wechselsweise hervorbringend und so unaufhaltsam fortschreitend. Wer sich diesen Anblick in ein inneres Anschauen verwandeln kann, der wird sich den Begriff sehr erleichtert haben. (WA II 7:54)

> Let somebody, in the summertime, position himself in front of a stake planted in the garden on which a vine climbs, snaking upward from the bottom, [and] fastening itself tightly [to the stake], pursues its living growth. One should now envision convolvel and stake as if both were equally living, climbing from one root, producing each other in alternation and thus striding relentlessly forward. Whoever can transform this sight into an inner intuition, will have made the concept much easier for himself.

The comparison Goethe suggests requires at least three intellectual moves: first, one must imagine that the garden stake is a living being. Then, one must imagine the development of the stake and the vine before, finally, one transposes this image into an intellectual intuition identical to that of the *Urpflanze*. Even then, the comparison does not entirely work.[127] The questions which arise—why an intuition of the vertical and spiral tendencies proved difficult for Goethe, why he resorted to a comparison that "does not entirely work," and why he feared that problem of spiraling is more of a "gordian knot" than an "affectionate tangle" for generations to come—are best addressed through a closer look at Goethe's return to plant metamorphosis through the phenomenon of the spiral tendency.[128]

Just as he did in the 1790 essay, Goethe uses gendered language to describe plant growth and sexuality to describe the vertical and spiral tendencies. The vertical tendency, which "externalizes itself from the very beginning of the seed growth onward," is "lasting" and "persisting."[129] It structures the axis of the plant, "produces continuity," and comprises "the masculine supporting principle."[130] The spiral tendency, by contrast is "the real producing life-principle," and "directed to the periphery."[131] Goethe describes the spiral tendency furthermore as "that which continues, increases and as such passes by, isolating itself from [the vertical tendency]" and—in a surprising move—as "concluding, demanding the conclusion."[132]

Goethe detaches notions of "masculinity" and "femininity" from their specific references to the sexual organs, and broadens these two metaphors so that they range freely through all stages of plant development. The essay on the spiral tendency describes the water plant *Valisneria*, where male and female reproductive organs comprise separate plants. This example permits Goethe to move from the specific to the general and incites the most pronounced use of gendered language:

> Kehren wir nun ins Allgemeinste zurück und erinnern an das was wir gleich anfangs aufstellten: das vertikal- so wie das spiralstrebende System sei in der lebendigen Pflanze aufs innigste verbunden; sehen wir nun hier jenes als entschieden männlich, dieses als entschieden weiblich sich erweisen: so können wir uns die ganze Vegetation von der Wurzel auf androgynisch ingeheim verbunden vorstellen, worauf denn, in Verfolg der Wandlungen des Wachstums die beiden Systeme sich

im offenbaren Gegensatz auseinander sondern, und sich entschieden gegeneinander überstellen, um sich in einem höhern Sinne wieder zu vereinigen. (LA I 10:362)

If we return to the most general stage and remember that which we put forward right at the beginning: the vertical- just like the spiral-striving system is most intimately joined in the living plant; we now see here this one proves itself decisively masculine, that one decisively feminine: thus we can imagine all vegetation from the root onward as secretly androgynically combined; upon which subsequently in the process of the changes of growth the two systems divide from each other in an apparent opposition, and decisively position themselves across from one another, in order to join again in a higher sense.

The last sentence recalls the final verse of the elegy on plant metamorphosis ("...so that / The pair may join, may find the higher world"). In fact, the essay on the spiral tendency and the elegy on metamorphosis both posit "masculine" and "feminine" elements from beginning to end. In the 1790 essay on plant metamorphosis, Goethe foregrounds the development of sexual organs in the reproductive phase against the asexual phenomenon of growth. The newer model of vegetation preserves the androgynous frame while reshuffling the elements of masculinity and femininity. Though one or the other might dominate at any given moment, both masculine and feminine elements are constantly present—just as the poem joins male and female presences through the act of intuition.

Goethe's insistence on a "conclusion" [*Abschluß*] when describing the spiral tendency is striking. The conclusion in question could be empirical (for example, the "death" of the plant) or simply the imagined end of a growth cycle and Goethe's usage preserves this ambiguity. He defines the spiral tendency as the "conclusion of the blossoming stage"[133] and comments elsewhere that it reveals itself "most remarkably during endings and conclusions."[134] Moreover, as has already been mentioned in the context of Anaxagoras' homoiomeries, the spiral tendency is the movement "whereby the plant completes the course of its life and finally arrives at the conclusion and completion."[135] Nevertheless, the corresponding passages in the *Metamorphosis of Plants* (1790) which emphasize the formation of blossoms and fruit, and the subsequent transition to the formation of the seed and new plant, contain no mention of a "conclusion." Nor is there any question that Goethe modified his concept of metamorphosis between 1790 and 1831 in such a way as to question the notion of a continuum between generations of plants. Instead, with the notion of a "conclusion," Goethe reformulates the connection Herder made between the death of the individual and the growth of the species as a problem of contingency, without changing his understanding of the metamorphosis concept. After 1831, when Goethe speaks of the spiral tendency at the plant's "end" or "conclusion," the end of the life-cycle (as opposed to growth-cycle) is not excluded. For example, a note from the paralipomena to the spiral-tendency essay mentions "examples of the pathological manifestations of the spiral-tendency. Old age, dying, completion of its organic course."[136] The potential of the spiral tendency to manifest itself as a pathology recalls Goethe's description of the "third" or "chance metamorphosis," in the essay from 1790, where he introduced the possibility of contingency. The "pathological" potential of the spiral tendency, as an empirical manifestation, stands in contradistinction to an intuition of the spiral tendency as "producing," "continuing," or "passing through" (*vorübergehen*). The intuition of the spiral tendency as a transition necessarily confronts and coexists with the reality of the spiral tendency as an endpoint.

In this chapter I have argued for the mutual engagement of literature and science in Goethe's writings on metamorphosis. Goethe's poem, "The Metamorphosis of Plants," both contributes to the problems raised in the essay from 1790 and informs his later work on the spiral tendency. These problems include the role of contingency and, above all, the difficulty of finding a way to represent plant metamorphosis which corresponds to our intuition of the changing phenomenon. Not only does the poem take up the themes of language and the representation of metamorphosis, it incorporates new developments in Goethe's thinking, such as his work on experimentation as discussed in the context of "The Experiment as Mediator." The elegy contributes to Goethe's scientific work about metamorphosis by productively conjoining multiple trends in his thinking: the discomfort he feels with regard to the act of intuitive thinking (something which can lead to "a kind of insanity"); the role of contingency in otherwise predictable metamorphosis (and its intuition); the problem of representing intuition within the confines of our discursive language. Within this schema, gender plays a significant—if highly ambivalent—role. Goethe's poem grants the feminine a dual status: it has the ability to confirm "masculine" knowledge through the repetition of experimental process, but can also be associated with the element of contingency.

The next chapter will take a broader look at procreation in the context of literature's engagement with the life sciences. In the context of Hardenberg's aphorisms and novel fragment, *The Apprentices of Sais*, it advances in new directions central questions raised in the first chapter: the relation between theories of procreation and experimental thinking, the potential difficulties encountered when narrating organic processes, and the role played by genre (aphorism, elegy) and generation (as *Bildung*) at the interface between literature and science.

3 Friedrich von Hardenberg and the Discourse of Procreation

Der *Blick*—(die Rede)—die *Händeberührung—der Kuß—die Busenberührung—der Grif an die Geschlechtstheile*—der Act der Umarmung—dies sind die Staffeln der Leiter—auf der die Seele heruntersteigt—dieser entgegengesezt ist eine Leiter—auf der der Körper heraufsteigt—bis zur Umarmung.

(Friedrich von Hardenberg, 3:264, n. 126)[1]

The *gaze*—(the speech)—the *touch of hands—the kiss—the touch of the breast—the reach for the genitalia*—the act of embrace—these are the steps of the ladder—upon which the soul climbs down—opposed to it is a ladder—upon which the body climbs up—until the embrace.

In 1805, at the request of Friedrich Schlichtgeroll, editor of the *Necrology of Germans for the Nineteenth Century*, Carl Just put pen to paper to eulogize Friedrich von Hardenberg.[2] The resulting document, written four years after Hardenberg's death, portrays a man shaped by philosophy and literature: the author of a critique of Fichte, of the novels *Heinrich von Ofterdingen* and the unfinished *Apprentices of Sais*, and of the beautiful and elusive *Hymns to the Night*. These achievements are nonetheless secondary for Just, whose intention is to make sure that Hardenberg as scientist receives equal billing with the man of letters. His text can be read as an early draft of a scholarly program which would require almost two hundred years to take hold: a serious analysis of Hardenberg's scientific pursuits in addition to his literary output. Hardenberg as scientist: Just returns to this point time and again, as if speaking against the force of a convention starting to solidify during this time. For Just, Hardenberg does not *have* genius, he *is* genius. The abstract notion of a figure whose 'capacities of...spirit, to appear as independent inventor and virtuoso in every art and science that he will pursue' finds its embodiment in him. Nor does Hardenberg, according to his eulogist, eschew practical application for theoretical dilettantism: '*consequence* in thinking and acting, *aesthetic beauty*, and *science*' were the troika (of principles) defining his existence.[3] Of the three, science constitutes the main force of Hardenberg's life progress according to Just, who cites the study of halurgy and chemistry, physics, mathematics, geology, metallurgy, and mining.[4] The infamous "Sophie experience," the death of Hardenberg's young fiancée Sophie von Kühn in 1797 which would preoccupy generations of scholars, receives only a cursory glance: "His first letters to us after Tennstedt [after her death] testified to his unspeakable mourning, but also to the powerful spirit, which even in its hard fate found a call to new higher thoughts and perspectives."[5] Just clearly interprets this "call," rather than the mourning itself, as a prelude to Hardenberg's extensive scientific studies in Freiberg during the following year—a more pragmatic reading than those who would seek in Hardenberg's subsequent work the apotheosis of the dead bride.

Just's decision to write a necrology for Friedrich von Hardenberg, rather than Novalis, is not accidental. "Novalis" is the name Hardenberg chose for himself in one area of his intellectual output: his literary pursuits. One could paraphrase Just by saying that Novalis "has" genius, Hardenberg "is" genius. With oblique reference to Friedrich Schlegel and Ludwig Tieck, chief architects of the "Novalis" myth who published his works under that name a year after his death, Just claims that writing was only a "school" for Hardenberg:

> Die Schriftstellerey—so schrieb er mir darüber—ist eine Nebensache. Sie beurtheilen mich mehr billig nach der Hauptsache,—dem praktischen Leben. Wenn ich gut, nützlich, thätig, liebevoll und treu bin: so lassen Sie mir einen unnützen, unguten, harten Satz passiren. Schriften unberühmter Menschen sind unschädlich, denn sie werden wenig gelesen und bald vergessen. Ich behandle meine Schriftstellerey nur als Bildungsmittel...Nach meiner Meynung muß man zur vollendeten Bildung manche Stufen übersteigen; Hofmeister, Professor, Handwerker, sollte man eine Zeitlang werden, wie Schriftsteller. (Just, "Nekrolog," 237)

> Writing—thus he wrote to me—is a secondary thing. You will more appropriately judge me according to the main thing,—practical life. If I am good, useful, active, caring, and faithful: then allow me to utter a useless, unwelcome, and hard truth. Writings of unknown men are harmless, for they are little read and soon forgotten. I treat my writing only as a means of education ... In my opinion one must ascend several levels to complete an education; instructor, professor, craftsman one should become for a time, just as writer.

Somewhat surprisingly, though still faithful to Hardenberg's notion of the "practical life," the concise educational program he formulates in his letter to Just champions the "craftsman" above both instructor and professor. A central premise for both this chapter and the following one is that Hardenberg's ranking of literary creation alongside craftsmanship is by no means an anomaly, but an organizing motif which argues against an artificial division of his scientific and aesthetic production (between Just's "Hardenberg" and Schlegel and Tieck's "Novalis"). As a later aphorism from *The General Draft* will hint: "*Art*—science—handwork—play—nature—genius."[6]

This first chapter on Hardenberg charts the extent of his thinking about procreation in the early philosophical and scientific studies. It raises basic questions, such as the role of gender in the "Fichte Studies," a text usually associated with self-generation rather than gendered couplings. It also illustrates how the procreative roles Hardenberg assigns to the "masculine" and the "feminine" do not always match the traditional assumptions concerning both male and female agency in Romanticism. Just as important is Hardenberg's ambiguous relation to the larger debate on procreation at the end of the eighteenth century: his writing on this topic cannot be neatly capsulated within the framework of the two most hotly argued biological theories of the time, preformation and epigenesis. Whereas this chapter is designed to reveal the startling reach of Hardenberg's thinking about procreation, the next chapter works closely with the concept of the instrument (*Werkzeug*). It follows Hardenberg's cue about the importance of the craftsman to study the artisan discourses surrounding the instrument as they relate to procreation. This approach to reading Hardenberg takes up the duality of the instrument as conceived by the eighteenth century—its mechanical and organic properties—and requires that the familiar "organicism" of Romantic literature be reconsidered in connection with Hardenberg's interest in artisan craftsmanship and materiality. The second chapter on Hardenberg culminates in a new reading of his unfinished novel, *The Apprentices of Sais*, a text which deploys the instrument productively between science and poesy, between art and the artisan.

FIRST NOTES ON PROCREATION: THE "FICHTE STUDIES"

The "Fichte Studies"—written between 1795 and 1796 and extending well beyond an engagement with Fichte[7]—testify to the range of Hardenberg's early philosophical inquiry and form the foundation of his aesthetics.[8] This trove of "excerpts, reading notes and independent continuing thoughts"[9] which, as Herbert Uerlings points out, should not be confused with Romantic fragments, has usually been mined for its wealth of insights into Hardenberg's critique of Fichte, and to study his contributions to contemporary philosophical questions. Of particular interest is Hardenberg's discussion of the genesis of reflection and what Manfred Frank refers to as "the distinction between 'basis' (*Grund*) and 'result' in the self-consciousness" as it relates to the category of time. According to Frank, Hardenberg's "main discovery" in the "Fichte Studies" was the realization that "we have the result" of consciousness "*earlier* than that which produces it."[10] Frank's now canonical work on the figure of the "ordo inversus" illustrates Hardenberg's creative approach to a problem already formulated by Fichte: that the product of self-reflection is a falsification which impedes access to the original subject.[11] Fichte negotiates this problem through a law of reflection which posits the determination of knowledge through the simultaneous recognition of its opposite, while Hardenberg proposes a second negation of reflection. Through a double inversion which first acknowledges the falsity or *Schein* of reflection and then turns it on its head, Frank shows how Hardenberg believed the original, pre-reflexive state could be more closely approximated. Hardenberg calls for continuous philosophical activity, which, though it may never fully attain the pre-reflexive state, at least permits movement towards this goal.[12]

Hardenberg chooses various words to describe the undifferentiated and inaccessible pre-reflexive state which, on the one hand, precedes consciousness and, on the other hand, can only be approached belatedly and never in its totality. In addition to the frequent use of "ground" [*Grund*] and "feeling" [*Gefühl*] he also refers to the "mother sphere" [*Muttersfäre*, 2:105 n. 1] at the beginning of the "Fichte Studies." In *The Specular Moment*, David Wellbery reads this note within a narrative of loss and (prohibited) longing for recuperation. He writes that "a proscription seems to be operative here, and that proscription, that philosophical taboo, has a sexual character: reflection must not want to embrace the Mother; feeling must remain the sole path of access to Her."[13] For Wellbery, this note is of interest as it connects to his discussion of specularity in the work of Goethe. For my purposes, it suffices to integrate this note within a procreative context. Only mentioned a single time, the "mother sphere" is one of several biological metaphors to appear in the text. Though the "Fichte Studies" are better known for their discussion of a self-positing ego, they also refer to life processes in order to think through philosophical abstractions.[14] The biological language of the "Fichte Studies" figures into narratives of procreation as well. These fall within a general tendency Frank has identified as the "temporalization of the relationship ground-consequence" which ultimately takes part in a larger philosophical agenda, the "program of a genesis of space from time."[15] Hardenberg's references to procreation in the "Fichte Studies" assume a basic compatibility, or at least a productive tension, between two modes of generation: the positing of consciousness and the creation of life. Whereas Frank, in his brief comments on procreation, situates the topic within the Fichtean model of self-generation,[16] the purpose of the following discussion is twofold. It will explore the reciprocity between (philosophical) self-generation and the biological generation of life and analyze Hardenberg's first procreative narratives, especially their gender distinctions, as a template for understanding his later thinking of procreation in other domains.

Hardenberg's first mention of procreation in the "Fichte Studies" marks a subtle turning point. The context is a persistent rumination on the dialectical terms thesis, antithesis, and synthesis which he has already connected to a "biological" context (for example, the third note of the collection describes life as "synthesis, thesis and antithesis and yet none of all three."[17]) Hardenberg uses the dialectical structure as a heuristic tool throughout the "Fichte Studies."[18] He returns to it repeatedly, considering the three components from different angles, and using them (and their relations to each other) as a foil against which to distinguish the relationships between *Ich* and *Nicht-ich*, matter and form, feeling and reflection.[19] Hardenberg first introduces the concept of procreation into the dialectical structure in a note which considers the emergence of thesis, antithesis and synthesis as conceptual categories. The innovation of the note lies in the fact that Hardenberg does not just posit their relation as a static "original schema"[20] but describes an active development which is neither historical nor a linear narrative:

> Die These, Antithese und Synthese—jedes besteht aus 2 Theilen—darum kann jedes aus seinen 2 entgegensetzten construirt werden.
>
> These ist ein Satz, der auf die Antithese und Synthese bezogen wird—
>
> A[ntithese] und S[ynthese] haben ein gemeinschaftliches Merckmal, die Beziehung auf die These—zusammengezogen ist dis die These—Gattungsbegriff.
>
> Mit d[er] A[ntithese] und S[ynthese] ists eben so und wir sehn hieraus 3 Gattungsbegriffe entstehn. Jedes ist der Gattungsbegriff der beyden andern.
>
> /Zeugung. Mann und Weib./
>
> (2:161–2, n. 174)
>
> The thesis, antithesis and synthesis—each [one] is comprised of two parts—thus each one can be constructed[21] from the other two.
>
> Thesis is a proposition, which is related to the antithesis and synthesis—
>
> A[ntithesis] and s[ynthesis] have a common characteristic, the relation to the thesis—contracted into this the thesis—generic concept.
>
> With t[he] a[ntithesis] and s[ynthesis] it is also the case and we see three generic concepts emerge therefrom. Each is the generic concept of the other two.
>
> /Procreation. Male and Female./

The note connects to others in the "Fichte Studies" which also deny the primacy of any particular dialectical term at the expense of the remaining two: each can be constructed from the other two, and any given pair is defined in part by its relation to the third term. What distinguishes this note from others of its kind is a gentle shift of emphasis between the "being" and the "emergence" [*Entstehung*] of the three as "generic concepts" [*Gattungsbegriffe*]. Each of them both *is* and *forms* a generic concept which incorporates the other two, while *Gattung* conveys the meanings of category, class, or biological species.

The note's final phrase—"Procreation. Male and Female"—suggests an attempt to explain the relationship between the process of procreation and the dialectical model elaborated in the preceding sections. The dynamic nature of procreation aligns it with the verbs "comprise," "contract," and "relate" that respond to the emergence and interplay of thesis, antithesis and synthesis. Can, however, "procreation," "male," and "female" be considered three generic concepts in their own right, each composed of and defined by the other two? Even if Hardenberg seems to test procreation as a special case within a dialectical model, it is also possible to say that he contemplates more radical proposition: the "engendering" of philosophical activity. Hardenberg's note leaves open the degree to which procreation is either informed by dialectical thinking or reworks the dialectical triad within a procreative logic, yet it is striking that the very first mention of procreation is divorced from any immediate questions of birth and progeny. In general, the "Fichte Studies" contain few references to children, and none in connection with procreation. At the same time, there is a constant emphasis on philosophical activity and process in the broadest sense, which supports Frank's thesis of a temporalization of reflection. One consequence is that parents produce more parents, rather than offspring: "A concept is however, as anything produced, not composed of its parents, but rather it is an independent being, like one of its parents."[22]

In keeping with the broader discussion of processes in the "Fichte Studies," Hardenberg also takes up the concept of "force" to connect philosophical reflection and biological generation. A note from a manuscript group dating from the winter of 1795–1796 describes a "force of procreation" whereby "female = idea" and "male = intuition."[23] If Aristotelian conventions traditionally aligned the female with matter, and the male with the "imprint" of form, then Hardenberg's Fichte-inflected gender distinctions are analogous but detached from a material substratum.[24] Just as (at least for Aristotelian thinking) matter makes visible the stamp of form, intuition achieves consciousness through the reflection of the idea. Several notes in the "Fichte Studies" index the categories of "male" and "female" without greater differentiation than has been seen so far, offering glimpses into Hardenberg's early procreative thinking which can only lead to speculation. The following example, however, offers more detailed narratives of procreation which develop the distinctions between man and woman based upon their "tendencies" even further:

Erhaltung der Einzelheit—Erhaltung der Gattung—das sind ihre Naturzwecke bey der Zeugung. Der Erste, der weibliche, der andre d[er] Männliche.

Die Form der Befriedigung dieses Triebes ist seinerseits oder sein Genuß besteht in Sieg seines Triebes, seiner Kraft über das Entgegenstehende, Anziehende. Ihr Genuß besteht in Stillung ihrer Sehnsucht, ihres Bedürfnisses, durch Kraft*gefühl*—nicht Kraftempfindung.

Sie will—aber ihre Empfindung widerstrebt und läßt sich nur durch fremde Kraft einen Augenblick suspendiren.

Er empfindet—aber will nicht—und sein Wille läßt sich nur auf einige Augenblicke durch fremde Nachgiebigkeit suspendiren.

(2:260, n. 511)

Preservation of individuality—preservation of species—these are their [i.e., man's and woman's] natural purposes in procreation. The first, the feminine; the second, the masculine.

The form of the satisfaction of this drive is on his side, or his pleasure comprises the victory of his drive, of his force over what is opposing, attracting. Her pleasure comprises the quelling of her longing, her need, through the *feeling* of power, not sense of power.

She wants—but her sensibility resists and only allows itself to be suspended by foreign force for a moment.

He senses—but does not want—and his sensibility only allows itself to be suspended by foreign compliance for a few moments.

This note construes the "force of procreation" as a natural drive directed towards the preservation of the species (attributed to the masculine), as well as the preservation of the individual or *Einzelheit* (attributed to the feminine). Its rhetoric is one of reciprocity, balance, and the harmonizing of differences. Though not governed by dialectical thinking, it nonetheless maintains an essentially tripartite structure: each section contains a series of parallel statements describing the masculine and feminine roles in procreation. The first section of the aphorism distinguishes the preservation of group and individual by gender (i.e., the "natural purposes" of each in procreation), the second section theorizes the respective pleasure experienced by man and woman during procreation, and the final lines preserve the counterbalance of gender differences but alter the dynamic of the entire note by introducing a temporal dimension to an otherwise atemporal narrative. It is the mutual suspension of the sexes from their normal states which allows the temporality of procreation to occur, and which allows the new organism to be *made*.

The language of the aphorism is very close to that of Fichte's *Grundlage des Naturrechts nach Principien der Wissenschaftslehre* (*Foundation of the Natural Law according to the Principles of the Theory of Science*) from 1796. Fichte had lectured on this topic at the University in Jena during the winter semester of 1795–1796, and the first of two volumes was published in early summer.[25] The concept of procreation is absent from Fichte's 1794 *Wissenschaftslehre* (*Theory of Science*). In the *Foundations of the Natural Law*, however, he addresses masculine and feminine roles extensively in the "deduction of marriage." Fichte regards the propagation of the human race as nature's purpose. This purpose is ensured through a 'natural drive' in the two sexes.[26] It is helpful to read Hardenberg's note against the backdrop of Fichte's argument in *Foundations of the Natural Law* so as to emphasize those points which are essential to the development of Hardenberg's thinking about procreation.

With regard to the necessity of procreation and the role of the sexes, Fichte makes a few basic claims. The first concerns the desire to procreate as the "natural drive" which, he argues, only exists for itself and its own satisfaction: from the perspective of human nature it is a purpose [*Zweck*], and from the perspective of nature a means [*Mittel*] to ensure the continuation of the species. A species perpetuating itself can not be thought of as an "eternal becoming" of forms: were it always in transition, there would be no possible concept of being, no fixed points against which to discern change at all. In order to propagate itself, the species must have another organic existence, at which point Fichte introduces the idea of the (procreating) individual:

> Dies war nur dadurch möglich, dass die die Gattung bildende Kraft vertheilt, gleichsam in zwei absolut zusammengehörende, und nur in ihrer Vereinigung ein sich fortpflanzendes Ganzes ausmachende Hälften zerrissen würde. In dieser Theilung bildet jene Kraft nur das Individuum. Die Individuen, vereinigt, und inwiefern sie vereinigt werden können, sind erst, und bilden erst die Gattung. (Fichte, *Sämmtliche Werke*, 3: 306)

> This was only possible in that the force forming the species divides, as if it were split into two absolutely belonging halves which only compose a self-propagating whole through their union. In this division each force only forms the individual. The individuals, joined, and insofar as they can be joined, first are—and first form—the species.

There is a tension in this claim, between the creation of the category "species" and its function, which Hardenberg takes notice of as well. The pair of procreating individuals both "form" the species and "are" the species: they create it, and it defines them retroactively. Fichte then turns to the gendered roles of human procreation, beginning with the basic distinction that one sex must behave "actively" [*thätig*] and the other "passively" [*leidend*]. In woman, one finds united "the system of the entire conditions for the production of a body of the same kind" which is "set into motion" by the "first motive principle" provided by the man.[27] Most of Fichte's argument is concerned with the problematic role of the woman, who is at the nexus of conflicting imperatives. As a reasonable human being, she cannot have "passivity" as a purpose; neither can she make the fulfillment of the sexual drive (*Geschlechtstrieb*) her purpose without demeaning herself, as woman: "it is therefore necessary that in the woman this drive should appear in another form and, in order to exist alongside reason, itself appear as drive to activity."[28] Fichte suggests a resolution to this conflict through acknowledging that woman can grant herself to a nobler natural drive unique to her alone—love.[29] This solution would allow her to remain "active" while at the same time giving herself completely to the will of the man without (according to Fichte) devaluing herself.

Like the passages from Fichte's deduction of marriage, the narrative of procreation embedded in Hardenberg's note also begins with the bird's-eye view: the roles in procreation are assigned for the purpose of prolonging the existence of individual traits and of the species (as a whole).[30] For both male and female, whatever differences their roles may entail, their "natural purposes in procreation" are ultimately the satisfaction of a "drive." The aphorism's second paragraph narrows the focus to describe gender distinctions in the process of procreation. Just as the man, according to Fichte, is allowed to avow the drive to procreate openly, for Hardenberg "the form of the satisfaction of this drive" also occurs under the auspices of the male. His pleasure derives from the conquest of his drive over something which the note formulates in gender-neutral terms as simply "opposing" [*das Entgegenstehende*] and "attracting" [*das Anziehende*]. From this point of view, the feminine is pared down to a sexless "other," the object of his drive's conquest. The female's role in Hardenberg's narrative also shows affinities to Fichte's account—she is not permitted to avow procreation as a natural drive. Instead, Hardenberg states that her pleasure derives from "the quieting of her longing, of her need" (*Stillung ihrer Sehnsucht, ihres Bedürfnisses*). The choice of words is suggestive: *Stillung*, in addition to its meaning of "quieting" or "calming," can also refer to the nursing of a child at the mother's breast. When this latter inflection is taken into account, the moment of procreative "pleasure" doubles as the anticipation of birth and reinforces the idea that the activity of procreation, the process itself, is just as important as the question of progeny.

The female's longing [*Sehnsucht*], the state prior to her pleasure, is also an index of temporality in the narrative. This concept, which Hardenberg pursues with more rigor in his later aphoristic work, and which will be one of the key concepts in Ritter's thinking about procreation, scarcely is used in the "Fichte Studies."[31] That it appears in a procreative context, and as an attribute of the feminine, is all the more noteworthy when considered in tandem with the temporality of consciousness which Frank elaborates:

> Denjenigen Bewußtseinsmodus, kraft dessen sich das Ich seiner Abhängigkeit versichert, nennt Novalis—nicht ohne Tradition, wie man weiß, aber in Wahrheit doch erst Tradition schaffend—'Gefühl', später 'Erinnerung' oder 'Gedächtnis'. In dieser Substitution des Begriffs 'Gefühl' durch den des 'Gedächtnisses' kommt Bewußtsein der *Zeitlichkeit* jenes Selbstvermittlungsprozesses (Novalis spricht von 'Selbstberührung') zum Ausdruck. Das Ich erfaßt seine Dependenz als Vergangenheit . . . und

> sein Streben nach Komplettion [sic], welches Novalis 'Ergänzungstrieb' nennt, wird als Zukünftigkeit konstituiert. Die Trias 'Einbildungskraft-Gefühl-Reflexion' wird später ersetzt durch die 'Zeit-Gedächtnis-Ahndung.'" (Frank, *Das Problem 'Zeit,'* 140)[32]

> That model of consciousness, by virtue of which the I in its dependence secures itself, is what Novalis calls—not without precedent, as one realizes, but in truth establishing a precedent—"feeling," later "recollection" or "memory." In this substitution of the concept 'feeling' by that of "memory," awareness of the *temporality* in that process of self-mediation is expressed (Novalis speaks of "self-touching"). The I grasps its dependency as past . . . and its striving for completion, which Novalis calls "drive for completion," is constituted as futurity. The triad "imagination-feeling-reflection" is later replaced by "time-memory-intimation."

The narrative of procreation is a testing ground for the pivotal change Frank describes towards a model of consciousness whose key terms—feeling, imagination, reflection—are conceptualized as temporal relations in Hardenberg's later work. The locus of this change is the female: the temporality of longing and the positing of "feeling" [*Gefühl*] define her experience of the procreative process.[33]

The final two sentences of the note ("She wants—but her sensibility resists and only allows itself to be suspended by foreign force for a moment. / He senses—but does not want—and his sensibility only allows itself to be suspended by foreign compliance for a few moments") are defined by chiastic inversions which contract the temporality of procreation into the present moment. The activity of the woman's "will" is articulated as an (actively) passive compliance. Opposed to her will is a sensation [*Empfindung*] which allows itself to be suspended through a "foreign force," almost certainly the "conquering drive" of the man. The man, on the contrary, experiences a sensation to which his will is opposed: his will must be suspended through the woman's active passivity. The state of suspension, within which the act of procreation occurs, introduces the only precise temporal markers in a narrative whose sense of time is otherwise defined by the female's vague longing. The "moment" or "moments" of procreation, which intrude precisely when mutual resistance between the masculine and feminine is suspended, occur at the interface of feeling and temporality.

The "Fichte Studies" provide a rough template for Hardenberg's early thinking about procreation which will be refined during the course of his further poetic and scientific studies. The essential ingredients of procreation are present. Hardenberg takes the tendencies of "male" and "female" and positions them against the foil of a central problem, the genesis of reflection in relation to a basis ("feeling," "mothersphere"). Within the dialectical thinking of the "Fichte Studies," the categories of male and female undergo some degree of change, but they also show a certain resiliency. For Hardenberg, pairing of masculine intuition with female idea might fit well within the model of a productive imagination, but procreation also offers him an opportunity to expand the temporalization of the reflective process in a new metaphorical dimension which relies upon a preconceived model of heterosexual pairing. The following section will expand upon the structures and temporality of procreation in Hardenberg's thinking from the perspective of late-eighteenth century biological theories, which come with their own pre-packaged structural motifs and understanding of the timeframe within which procreation occurs.

THE PATTERNS OF PROCREATION

In the "Fichte Studies" Hardenberg adapts the language of biological generation to contexts abstracted from the physical act of procreation. This tendency in his early work gains momentum as he continues his studies of science and philosophy. The rest of the chapter explores the ways in which procreation bridges the different areas of his research and pursues the question already raised in the introduction, to what degree one can speak of a coherent strategy or approach—a "poetics" of procreation. Before turning to the wealth of procreative imagery and motifs found in Hardenberg's fragments and encyclopedia project, and in scientific notebooks, it is worth pausing for a moment to recall the cultural climate in which Hardenberg's thinking about procreation takes place. The introduction to this study outlined the two dominant theories competing during the last decades of the eighteenth century: preformation (including its permutations of "ovism" and "spermism") and epigenesis. Blumenbach was mentioned as a central figure in the shift of favor from the former to the latter. For both theories, the use of visual criteria—such as morphological similarities between the parents and progeny—was of extreme importance. If the preformationists profited from technological developments in the form of better microscopes, the epigenecists were able to counter with cases of physical deformities and monstrosities as well as interspecies hybridism, neither of which fit the preformationist model.[34]

A shift which took place in the use of morphological similarities as evidence has bearing on the discussion of Hardenberg. Blumenbach, who relied heavily on morphological similarities in his early work, modified his position in the years prior to 1800 through his reception of Kant's ideas on organic growth and natural history.[35] Fundamental to Blumenbach's developing point of view is a focus on the process of procreation itself: a "breeding criterion" gradually replaced the use of morphological characteristics to identify members of the same species. This idea is outlined in Kant's 1785 essay, "Determination of the Concept of a Human Race" (Bestimmung des Begriffs einer Menschenrace). Kant argues that if the task of natural history is to trace the genealogies of organisms, then it should employ such a standard whereby, if two animals are able to copulate and produce fertile offspring, then they belong to the same species.[36] The details of the dialogue between Blumenbach and Kant, which set the stage for a revolution in thinking about natural history, have been amply documented by Timothy Lenoir.[37] What is important in the context of Hardenberg's work are the implications of the gradual change towards a prioritization of functional characteristics over visual ones in the categorization of organisms. The retroactive nature of the argument for a "breeding criterion" effectively requires procreation to occur twice to say something about the parent generation. Only fertile offspring proves that the parents belong to the same species. Fichte advocates a similar argument in his discussion of how species are formed by individuals when he writes, "the individuals, united, and insofar as they can be united, first are, and first create, the species: for *being* and *creating* are One in organic nature. The individual is solely *comprised* of the tendency to create the species."[38] The potential for circularity in this thinking, whereby the individual "creates" a species to which it already belongs, was not lost on Hardenberg. He reframes the idea as the procreation of categories in general in the following excerpt from a note in *The General Draft* on "Encyclopedistics": "The basis of all sciences and arts must be a science and art—which one can compare with algebra—it will naturally, as do these, emerge later than most of the special arts and sciences—because the species or the common element emerges later than the singular—in that it is first produced through the contact of fully formed individuals—*hoc est* becomes flesh."[39] It is not coincidental that algebra comes closest to constituting the basis Hardenberg proposes. Like procreation, mathematics also functions as a bridge discourse that Hardenberg mobilizes to forge connections between different spheres of human thought, and the intersections between these two discourses will be discussed.

Unlike Goethe, Hardenberg does not state his position with regard to preformation and epigenesis directly, and it is helpful to contrast these two writers against each other in order to profile Hardenberg's contribution. Although in principle Goethe sided with Wolff and Blumenbach, throughout his career he remained skeptical with regard to the language of both theories. In his essay on the "Formative Drive" he writes that "evolution and epigenesis…seem to be words with which we only hinder ourselves."[40] Goethe finds preformation tautological—"a word that says nothing, how can something be formed before it is"[41]—and already in the "Observation on Morphology" he underscores the interchangeability of the theories with regard to simple organisms: "Phenomenon of the simplest [organic structures], which seem to be a mere aggregation of the parts, would however frequently be just as explainable through evolution or epigenesis."[42] The same criterion, more generally stated, holds for advanced organic structures as well, at least as far as Goethe's critique of the terms themselves is concerned:

Das Neue, Gleiche, ist anfangs immer ein Teil desselbigen und kommt in diesem Sinne aus ihm hervor. Dieses begünstigt die Idee von Evolution; das Neue kann sich aber nicht aus dem Alten entwickeln, ohne daß das Alte durch eine gewisse Aufnahme äußerer Nahrung zu einer Art von Vollkommenheit gelangt sei. Dieses begünstigt den Begriff der Epigenese. Beide Vorstellungsarten sind aber roh und grob gegen die Zartheit des unergründlichen Gegenstandes. (MA 4.2:197)

The new, same, is in the beginning always a part of the same [producing organism] and in this sense comes forth from it. This favors the idea of evolution; what is new can however not develop from the old, without the old having achieved a kind of completion through a certain intake of external nutrition. This favors the concept of epigenesis. Both ways of looking at things are crude and approximate however with regard to the delicacy of the unfathomable object.

Goethe's study on plant metamorphosis, the subject of the prior chapter, gains new emphasis in this context: his respect for the complexity of living phenomena, and skepticism with regard to the ability of language to describe it adequately, can also be read as a critique of those theories which would offer an overly simplistic picture. His contribution to the discourse of procreation is apparent both through his thinking about the limits of language in general as well as his willingness to experiment with scientific and poetic models.

Compared to Goethe, Hardenberg is a different case altogether. Given the fact that he was immersed within a climate of scientific debate on procreative theories, it is surprising that he makes no direct reference to epigenesis or preformation in his aphorisms and notes, and 'Evolution'—which was synonymous with preformation around 1800—appears only in a few passages which do not reference preformation. At the same time, readers of Hardenberg cannot help but marvel at the broad thematic presence of organic generation and the attention he devotes to modes of production and reproduction in the inorganic and organic realms. One can also detect an affinity between Hardenberg's writing and the figures and thought processes associated with epigenesis and preformation.

Different interpretations of epigenesis emphasize different aspects of the theory. It can be read as a triumph of self-development, but also as a reconceptualization of the (gendered) parental roles in the procreative process. Müller-Sievers discusses the former in depth. I choose to emphasize the latter just as strongly in my reading of Hardenberg because the discussion of autoproductivity in Early Romanticism has tended to divert attention away from procreative themes.[43] Epigenesis allows one to think of procreation as a synthesis between the two parents, rather than a trigger which initiates the growth of a pre-formed entity, and the synthetic view fits in well with Hardenberg's broader scientific interests. An example of an epigenetically-oriented note in his encyclopedic project is the following:

> Die org[anische] Masse wird durch die org[anische] Beschaffenheit der Mutter—und die org[anische] Besch[affenheit] des Vaters und die Verhältnisse dieser beyden Organisationen zu einander bestimmt. Ist dieses Verhältniß ein *vollk[ommen] Gesundes*, so werden auch die Kinder mit voll[kommen] ges[unden] Anlagen geboren werden. Zufälle in der Schwangerschaft und nachherige Behandl[ung] abgerechnet. (3:323, n. 437)

> The organic mass is determined by the organic composition of the mother—and the organic composition of the father and the relations of these two organisms to each other. If this relation is a *completely healthy* one, then the children will also be born with completely healthy developing organs [*Anlagen*]. Unpredicted events during the pregnancy and the following treatment excluded.

The word *Anlagen*, translated here only very approximately as "developing organs" to fit the context of Hardenberg's notes, has an important role to play in the discussion of epigenesis. In the *Critique of Judgment*, Kant puts forward epigenesis as a kind of "generic preformation" because "the productive faculty of the generator, and consequently the specific form, would be *virtually* preformed according to the inner purposive capacities which are part of its stock."[44] As John Zammito has observed, this model of a "preformed" species, which allows room for individual variation within certain limits, is the same one which Kant describes in the essay on the determination of the human race cited previously.[45] Hardenberg's aphorism is found under the heading of "Mathematical Physiology" in his encyclopedia project. In the same note, one encounters Hardenberg's speculations about diagramming the periodic "curves" of certain life processes which oscillate like the vibrations of a sting as well as a discussion of sickness and health infused with the language of Brownian medicine.

Hardenberg's encyclopedia project also mobilizes the concept of a "mathematical physiology" to connect mathematical models with procreative motifs associated with preformation theory. Although Hardenberg is certainly not a "preformationist" thinker in the tradition, for example, of Swammerdam—who, while dissecting silkworms, observed adult structures waiting to develop—his way of thinking and writing reveals some affinity with the characteristic structure of "embedding" (also referred to as *Einschachtelung* or *Emboîtement*) associated with preformationist theory. The idea of embedding required a leap of faith at the time it was proposed because it suggested a subdivision of space more minuscule than the eye could see. Bonnet referred to it as "one of the greatest victories that pure reason has ever achieved against the senses" because the infinite smallness assumed by this model "overwhelms Imagination without scaring Reason."[46] In her study of preformation theory, Clara Pinto-Correia makes the claim that "statistics and infinitesimal calculus both emerged in the age of preformation, and the coincidence was so fortunate that most likely it was not a coincidence at all. If you are going to posit the encasement of generations, the more scientific foundations for the concept of infinite smallness, the better."[47] In the following aphorism from *The General Draft* Hardenberg manipulates this embedded structure in order to develop connections between the procreative process and the activity of classification:

> Einfache Definitionen giebts nicht *zuerst*—je mehr man *zugleich definirt*—desto richtiger wird jede einzelne Definition. *Definiren en masse*—*Wissenschaft*. Die Definition ist die Constructionsformel d[er] Begr[iffe] etc. Aller Erzeugung—*Generation*—Erzeugung d[es] Geschlechts—geht eine Specification—der Specification eine Individuation voraus. Die Einheit ist Classe, Gattung, Art und Individuum zugleich—Mit der Mehrheit entsteht erst Classification, Generation, Specification und Individuation.[48] (3:433, n. 849)

> Simple definitions do not exist *first*—the more one *defines at the same time*—the more correct each single definition becomes. *Defining en masse*—*science*. The definition is the construction formula of concepts etc. All procreation—*generation*—procreation of a race [Geschlecht][49]—presupposes a specification—the specification in turn an individuation. Unity is class, species, kind and individual at the same time—Only with plurality do classification, generation, specification and individuation emerge.

The aphorism takes procreation out of its biological context and applies it more broadly as a metaphor for the production of categories one step removed from living organisms.[50] It begins with a statement that comes close to self-contradiction: what is the claim that "simple definitions are not given *first*" if not a preliminary definition about definitions strategically placed at the beginning of the aphorism? The would-be contradiction is annulled by the subsequent assertion that the more one defines, the more correct one's definitions become, thus relieving the first statement of its burden of being correct. The emphasis on a manifold of statements, as well as the oscillation between "definition" (as noun) and the act of "defining" (as verb) calls attention to a distinction between process and product which will carry over into the second half of the aphorism, which can also be read as an application of the opening propositions.

When it takes up the discourse of procreation, the aphorism creates a hyphenated chain that connects procreation of race to individuation. The

Friedrich von Hardenberg and the Discourse of Procreation 71

logic is "preformative" in that each link of the chain depends on the one which comes before. The fifth sentence moves in a contrary direction. Its beginning proposes a unity that is "class, species, kind and individual all at once;" the nexus of these contrary tendencies is the notion of an integrated individual which at the same time acts as a subset of broader categories. The aphorism then moves from the singular to the plural; plurality elicits a response on the part of the beholder, and the operations of classification, generation, specification and individuation occur, replacing the static terms of class and species.[51] When read together, the final two sentences of the aphorism form a structure of regression followed by one of progression. Between these two motions lies embedded the problem of the individual itself. If continued, the first sentence would lead inexorably to the question of what precedes individuation: the point at which preformationist theory relies upon a divine instance. The aphorism stops short of venturing into that territory. It recedes only as far the central unity, oversteps the metaphysical realm, and reverses momentum from regress to progress. Indirectly, the aphorism thus leaves the problem of accounting for procreation in the uncharted space between two contrary movements. The original creation of the individual remains a non-narrated gap between the contrary movements of the fragment, and procreation is also permitted to act metaphorically as a stop-gap for a non-narratable beginning.[52]

The examples cited previously illustrate Hardenberg's tendency to think about generation in abstract terms. The heading "Mathematical Physiology" found in the encyclopedia project is emblematic for this approach, but the procreative dimension of mathematical discourse needs further elaboration. Another note from the encyclopedia project, written under the title "Physics," provides a clue:

> Daß der Erzeugungspr[oceß] so früh und so vorzüglich die phil[osophischen] Physiker beschäftigt ist kein Wunder—Sie ahndeten wohl daß hier eine merckwürdige Grenzhöhe läge. Was ich begreife, das mus ich machen können—was ich begreifen will—machen lernen. Kommt die Physik hier an eine wirckliche Grenze, so muß sie die angrenzende Wissenschaft requiriren. (3:289, n. 275)

> That the process of generation preoccupies the philosophical physicist so early and so intensely is no wonder—they probably guessed that a peculiar upper limit [*Grenzhöhe*] lies here. What I comprehend, I must also be able to make—what I want to comprehend—learn to make. If physics arrives here at a real limit, it has to requisition the adjoining science.

This note foregrounds the relation between the observer and the world and between physical and intellectual modes of production. It asks how the process of generation relates to both knowing and making. The adjoining science is not specified, and subsequent examples will show that Hardenberg approaches the same question from various angles. At the same time, mathematics is the "science" which Hardenberg holds in higher esteem than the others for its ability to generate knowledge, or "products of intellectual autonomy [*Selbstthätigkeit*]."[53] Hardenberg underscores the relation between processes of mind and body—between intellectual making and physical generation—when he integrates mathematical notation with the language of procreation.

The general procreative patterns within Hardenberg's aphoristic work can be codified in relation to mathematical operations which relate to the structural features epigenesis and preformation. The synthesis of epigenetic pairs can be captured through arithmetical couplings and techniques of differentiation; and preformation, with its non-linear, sequential embedding, shares an affinity with the expansion or decline of a geometric series growing between the two poles of the infinitesimal and the infinite. Hardenberg was well-versed in mathematics, which he studied at the Freiburg Mining Academy in the academic year of 1798 through 1799.[54] From Johann Friedrich Lempe he learned arithmetic, geometry, and trigonometry while also attending Abraham Gottlob Werner's course on mining- and mineralogy-related fields and Wilhelm August Lampadius' lectures on chemistry and metallurgy.[55] Hardenberg's notes from 1798 connect mathematics to poetics, grammar, physics, philosophy, history, and even biological generation: "Geometric series—are living—progressive series. All *progressions are living.*"[56] Mathematics is a science with claims to universality ("all sciences should become *mathematics*") whose numerical system should be the model of our own language ("our letters should become numerals, our language arithmetic").[57] Like his friend Friedrich Schlegel, Hardenberg uses mathematical symbols as shorthand to capture oscillations between the infinitesimal and the infinite. In a manner comparable to Goethe's insistence on the relevance of algebraic functions for the understanding of plant growth and generation, Hardenberg also allows the intuitions of mathematical formulae to enter his writing as a supplement for discursive language.[58] The following aphorism not only takes procreation as its topic, it transposes the two procreative models into an abstract, speculative dimension and encodes their differences through mathematical operations.

PHYSIK. Sollte jede *Umarmung* zugleich die Umarmung des ganzen *Paars*—als Einer Natur, mit Einer Kunst (Einem Geiste) seyn und das Kind das vereinigte Produkt Der doppelten Umarmung.

Sollten die Pflanzen etwa die Produkte der weiblichen Natur und d[es] männlichen Geistes—und die Thiere die Produkte der *männlichen* Natur und des *weiblichen Geistes* seyn? Die Pflanzen etwa die Mädchen—die Thiere die *Jungen* der Natur?

Oder sind die Steine Produkte der Wurzelgeneration—Pflanzen der Generation^2—Thiere—der Generat[ion]^3—und Menschen—der Generation^n oder ∞? (3:255, n. 81)

PHYSICS. Should every *embrace* be at once the embrace of the entire *pair*—as one nature, with one art (one mind) and the child the united product of the doubled embrace.

Should plants perhaps be the products of feminine nature and masculine mind [*Geist*]—and animals the products of *masculine* nature and *feminine mind*? Plants then the *girls*—animals then the *boys* of nature?

Or are the stones products of the root generation—plants of generation^2—animals—of generation^3—and humans of generation^n or ∞?

Hardenberg begins with a procreative pairing which sees in every human embrace the coupling of nature and art—the children of such a union are physical and transcendental products. The following sentence remains within an anthropocentric model of generation which then expands to include other realms: Hardenberg detaches the word pair masculine/feminine from the human and integrates it within two distinct scenarios to account for the creation of plants and animals as well. He generates an entire organic economy through a set of arithmetical equations whose components are chiastically inverted such that "feminine nature + masculine spirit = plants [girls]" and "masculine nature + feminine spirit = animals [boys]." In each case nature, rather than mind (or "spirit"—Hardenberg uses the word *Geist*), determines the gender designation of the offspring. Up until this point the aphorism follows an arithmetical pattern, indexed by the synthesis of pairs and the structuring of the equations through additions and multiplications. The last sentence of the aphorism departs from the pairings to offer an alternate model of generation that integrates plants, animals and humans into an exponential series. Hardenberg's designation of stones as the "root generation" reflects both their proximity to the earth and their value within the exponential series—*Wurzel* also refers to the square root ($\sqrt{\ }$) or mathematical radical sign. The series then skips to plants, whose generation is raised to the power of two, followed by the generation of animals to the power of three. These first members of the series exist in approximate proportion to one another: the ratio of 3 to 2 is approximately the same as that of 2 to $\sqrt{2}$. Yet it is impossible to determine the latter ratio with precision. This is so because of a fact already discovered by mathematicians of antiquity, namely that $\sqrt{2}$ is an irrational number which cannot be precisely measured (hence "irrational" in the literal sense of without "ratio"). For that reason, the position of the stone generation in the series is subject to an infinite process of adjustment: its distance to the plant generation is immeasurable. The last term in the series, "humankind," forms a pendant to the stone generation: it too articulates an immeasurable gap through generation raised to a potentially infinite degree.

The speculative dimensions of the series can be situated within a scientific culture around 1800 which sought ways to connect inorganic and organic realms, a problem which the following section and the final chapters on Ritter will also take up with reference to electricity and magnetism. Irene Bark's monograph on mineral thinking in Hardenberg's work, *Steine in Potenz*, addresses precisely this problem and its ramifications:

> So implizierte der Versuch, die materiellen Ursachen des Lebendigen auf chemisch-physikalischem Wege zu ergründen, gleichzeitig den Anspruch einer wechselseitigen Annäherung mathematischer-mechanischer und organologischer Sichtweisen mit dem Ziel, über die Schließung der 'Kluft' zwischen den Reichen des Anorganischen und des Organischen hinaus auch einen Brückenschlag zwischen etablierten Erklärungsweisen rein materieller Phänomene ('Physik') und dem Versuch der wissenschaftlichen Ergründung von Vorgängen im Bereich des Bewußtseins ('Vernunftlehre') zu leisten. (Bark, *Steine in Potenzen*, 291)

> The attempt to ground the material causes of living things through chemical and physical processes thus also implied the claim of a reciprocal approximation of mathematical-mechanical and organological points of view with the goal—beyond closing the "gap" between the inorganic and organic realms—of building a bridge between established modes of explaining purely material phenomena ("physics") and the attempt of achieving the scientific establishment of processes in the realm of consciousness ("theory of reason").

Bark emphasizes the fact that comparisons between the organic and inorganic realms required a basic rethinking of how to understand and interpret the natural world. Mathematical or mechanical explanations would not suffice to explain 'organological points of view.' Relevant to this discussion is the proposal of an 'intuitive understanding' of organicisms put forth by Kant in the third critique that moves from an idea of the whole to the parts and encourages us to act as if nature were purposeful.[59] Against the backdrop of this discussion, one of the ambiguities of Hardenberg's 'living' geometric series stand out in sharper relief. Part of what makes the geometric logic an awkward fit is the imposition of mathematical notation upon living organisms. It creates a suggestive hierarchy of exponents, but also foregrounds the quantitatively (mechanically) unbridgeable differences between members of the series. The following section will continue examining the interaction between organic and inorganic realms in Hardenberg's procreative thinking, while paying greater attention to the use of scientific theory to affirm gender distinctions.

PROCREATION BETWEEN ORGANIC AND INORGANIC REALMS—CHEMISTRY AND GALVANISM

The interface between the organic and the inorganic realms is not necessarily defined by mathematical paradox, as Hardenberg's work on procreation in the context of chemical and galvanic phenomena will show. His notes and aphorisms dating from his studies at the Freiberg Mining Academy (1798–1799) and his subsequent appointment as saline assessor in Weißenfels are saturated with the chemical terminology of the day. In general, the research agenda of eighteenth-century chemistry was dominated by a handful of interrelated topics, including (but not limited to) investigation into the combustion process, the nature of heat, and attempts to break apart substances traditionally thought to be pure elements. With its emphasis on processes of synthesis (such as the formation of calxes) and separation (such as the decomposition of air and water), chemistry was a logical arena for Hardenberg's procreative thinking. His notes from this time, many of which comprise the foundation of a far-reaching encyclopedia project, index the language of both the empirical experimental regimes and the theories which drove them, and integrate the contemporary chemical discourse into narratives of procreation.

The widespread surge in scholarly interest devoted to the scientific thinking of German Romanticism has not bypassed chemistry. Among other contributions,[60] a monograph by Ralf Liedtke titled *The Romantic Paradigm of Chemistry: Friedrich von Hardenberg's Philosophy of Nature between Empiricism and Alchemical Speculation*,[61] deserves special mention for pushing this branch of research on Hardenberg in a new direction. Liedtke does not address procreation as a special topic, but his ideas on chemical productivity and Hardenberg's approach to it can serve as a foil against which to read the chemical and galvanic aspects of procreation in Hardenberg's work. Liedtke's primary thesis is that:

> The model of a processural collective activity, in which new aggregates, configurations or constellations are constantly forming with greater or lesser temporal stability, is paradigmatic for a "chemical" way of thinking which binds us today—in the form of a new thinking about nature—with the Romantic philosophy of nature. Already [it] found in chemistry its specific guiding and model science for the explanation of creative processes actively synthesizing spirit and nature and accentuating the context of discovery.[62]

In anticipation of the affinity between chemistry and procreation to be discussed, at least two items in this description require emphasis: the narrative potential of the chemical process, coupled with the formation of something "new"—"new aggregates, configurations or constellations"— whose substance and durability (i.e., the temporality of their formation and recombination) is called into question with regard to what came before. These same issues play a role in Hardenberg's chemical aphorisms on procreation and link them thematically to his notes for the encyclopedia project and the dialectical speculations of the "Fichte Studies" touched upon earlier in the chapter.

In the historical section of his study, Liedtke makes several observations about the development of chemistry which are programmatic for his subsequent interpretations of Hardenberg: that the history of chemistry goes hand in hand with the "art of experimentation"[63]; that it concerns itself with the "substantializing of chemical qualities" and the "identification of materials"; that there is a "mode of thought" associated with chemistry which is "productive-technical, instrumental, operational and functional;" and that occurrences of duality, polarity, and contradiction are germane to the science.[64] Of these points, the notion of "instrumentality" will eventually play a central role in my reading as well. Just as the history of chemistry and alchemy cannot be thought of without the concomitant development of their instrumentarium,[65] Hardenberg's expansive thinking about procreation as a mode of production incorporates a continued reflection upon its tools and instruments which will take center stage in the following chapter.

Hardenberg's most revealing notes on the chemistry of procreation can be found in two groups of manuscript pages written during his Freiberg student days at the mining academy, dated September and October of 1798. The first bears the title "Physical Fragments" (*Physikalische Fragmente*). In addition to Hardenberg's own notes, it comprises excerpts from Delamétherie's *On Chemistry* (1798) and Gren's *New Journal of Physics* (1796), Hardenberg's thoughts on Brownian medicine, a diagram from Johann Wilhelm Ritter's work on galvanism, and a response to a manuscript of aphorisms by Friedrich Schlegel titled "On Physics."[66] Apart from the processes of combustion and fermentation associated with chemistry, Hardenberg's manuscript also contains interwoven references to mineralogy, medical theory, and astronomy. The second group pertains to Hardenberg's encyclopedia project, *The General Draft*. Thematically there is considerable overlap between the two: in some cases Hardenberg transcribed a note from the "Physical Fragments" directly into *The General Draft*. Of particular interest is an extended narrative of procreation within each manuscript group that draws heavily upon the constellation of concepts and pertinent themes—a "narrative" in the sense that these notes integrate the language of chemistry and galvanism to construct procreative sequences from multiple perspectives, sometimes formulated with sentences and questions, and sometimes containing just a few suggestive words.

The procreative narrative Hardenberg formulates in the "Physical Fragments" recalls the "Fichte Studies" by positing an initial dialectical triad described through organic metaphors. In this case, the triad comprises three syntheses—designated as A, B, and C—each of which combines the

Friedrich von Hardenberg and the Discourse of Procreation

terms "life" and "organization." The first is an "absolute positive" synthesis of life and organization, the second an "absolute negative" one, and the third an "absolute absolute" synthesis.[67] A clue to decoding the three syntheses can be found in the passage immediately above, where Hardenberg distinguishes between life and death on the basis of conductivity. He notes that a body is dead when it functions merely as a conductor of a "solicitation"[68] without being awakened by it, or in the case where it is a total "non-conductor" of solicitation.[69] Between these two extremes, the "sensible life" of the living body functions within an intermediary state (*Halbzustand*) as an "incomplete conductor of solicitation."[70] This is what Hardenberg refers to as the "sphere" of C, which he also names "the incomplete conductor," and the "sphere of the *Philister*" (which could designate the proverbial Philistines or, more colloquially, any commoner).[71] It is within this "common" sphere—between life and death, or positive and negative life—that a speculative narrative of (emphatically epigenetic) procreation can unfold:

> *Gefühl* ist *gebildete* (organisirte) *Bewegung*. (Organisirter Stoff—organisirte Bewegung.) Zum Gefühle gehört hier jeder Affect der äußern Sinne. Empfindung ist d[urch] d[en] Verstand assimilirtes Gefühl.
>
> Empfindungen, Gefühle, und Gedanken sind wohl *Exkremente*? Eigentlich empfängt die Frau nicht, sondern das Ey empfängt. Das Ey ist Secretion des Weibes. Wenn das Ey empfangen hat, so wird es wieder durch Anwachsung—*Theil*—nicht Glied der Mutter.
>
> Der Mann befruchtet eigentlich nicht, sondern er ist nur das *Werckzeug der Befruchtung*—der Saame befruchtet—
>
> Ey und Saame sind polare Secretionen. Der Saame macht auch nur die Sollicitirende Potenz. Er *dringt nicht ein*—sondern er weckt blos die Erregbarkeit. Er hat eine größere Energie als das Ey, und *überwältigt die Erregbarkeit des Ey—Er entzündet das Ey*—Die Fortdauer der Entzündung liegt nun in der Natur der organischen Composition. (*Erzeugung thierischer Wärme.*)
>
> (Der Saame ist vielleicht ein flüßiger organischer (künstlicher) Stoff—das Ey—geronnener künstlicher Stoff. Der Saame wird die erste Nahrung des Ey—sobald die Entzündung geschehn ist—es saugt ihn ein—um seine Capacitaet zu vermehren—mit seiner größern Quantität abs[oluten] Wärmestoff.) (3:93)
>
> *Feeling* is *formed* (organized) *motion*. (Organized material—organized motion.) To feeling belongs here every affect of the external senses. Sensibility is feeling assimilated by understanding. Sensations, feelings, and thoughts are probably *excrements*? Actually the woman does not conceive, rather the egg conceives. The egg is secretion of the female.

If the egg has conceived, then it becomes again through accretion—*part*—not member of the mother.

The man does not actually fertilize, rather he is only the *instrument of fertilization*—the semen fertilizes—

Egg and semen are polar secretions. The semen also makes only the soliciting power [Potenz.] It *does not penetrate*—rather it merely awakens the excitability. It has a greater energy than the egg, and *overpowers the excitability of the egg—it inflames the egg*—The duration of the ignition now rests in the nature of the organic composition. (*Production of animal warmth.*)

(The semen is perhaps a fluid organic [synthetic] material—the egg—coagulated synthetic material. The semen becomes the first nutrition of the egg—as soon as the inflammation [*Entzündung*] has occurred—[the egg] absorbs it—to increase its own capacity—with its greater quantity of abs[olute] heat material.)

The tension in this note lies between excretion and assimilation. Its excretory logic encompasses both metaphorical "excretions" (sensations, feelings, and thoughts) and physical "secretions" (eggs and semen). Hardenberg takes a few liberties with the French word "excrement" as it was used at the end of the eighteenth century to designate anything which "leaves the body of the animal through a path of separation which is natural and ordinary,"[72] and he makes a few basic (if not completely rigorous) distinctions between excretions and secretions. Whereas excretions have the advantage of being "formed" (*gebildet*) and of potentially leaving the body as such, the secretions of egg and semen are yet undefined. Through the process of a fertilization conceived as a chemical combustion, they must first undergo a radical change before assimilation as aggregates or "accretions" (but not members) of the female body.[73]

The account of the actual conception is striking for the minimal roles of the male and the female. Just as the egg—not the female—conceives, it is the semen which fertilizes instead of the male, who remains the mere "instrument of fertilization." Even the semen is instrumentalized to the extent that its role is to "awaken" the egg, without penetrating it directly. The aphorism's insistence on an indirect mode of procreation connects it to a broad array of numerous other figures of reversal and deviation in Hardenberg's work, which have surfaced in the critical literature through names as various as "via negativa" (Molnar), "indirect technique" (Liedtke) and "indirect construction" (Gaier). In this regard, procreation opens a new domain for the further study of a familiar pattern.[74]

The concept of "excitability" (which, according to Hardenberg, is "overpowered" when the semen "inflames" the egg with its greater energy) draws from the medical theory of John Brown, the influential Scottish doctor whose *Elements of Medicine* Hardenberg and many of his contemporaries read. Brown defines life in terms of two principles: animal excitability and exciting powers, which can operate either internally or externally. In the *Elements of Medicine* he writes: "We know not what excitability is, or in what manner it is affected by the exciting powers. But whatever it be, whether a quality or a substance, a certain portion is assigned to every being upon the commencement of its living state."[75] Brown also believed that all illnesses were caused either by an excess or a deficit of stimulation (referred to as "sthenic" or "asthenic" diseases). Hardenberg's "sphere C"—as the sphere of excitability and exciting powers—falls within the parameters of Brownian medical theory. Beyond the field of medicine, Brown's ideas were also incorporated into new work on galvanism or "animal electricity" as well as the concept of an animal "life force" [*Lebenskraft*] conceptualized by Reinhold.[76] In Hardenberg's aphorism, the fertilization of the egg by the semen is also chemical: the semen inflames the egg to generate the warmth of the organism yet to be formed, and afterwards acts as nutriment for the egg, which in turn absorbs it. In addition to being one of Hardenberg's most detailed narratives of procreation, what this aphorism also brings to light is the degree to which the gender distinctions of the procreative process are dependent on scale (of the human body as opposed to the egg): the egg, though "feminine," does not play a completely passive role with regard to the semen. It is rather the case that they reciprocally act upon each other: the semen inflames the egg, but the egg then consumes the semen.

Hardenberg develops his scientific portrayals of procreation while retaining sensitivity to scale in the contemporaneous manuscript group belonging to *The General Draft*. As in the notes from the "Physical Fragments," the processes of combustion, digestion, and fermentation play a key role, with an important difference. Rather than casting procreation in terms of an indirect, abstract microprocess which occurs as a chemical and galvanic reaction between egg and semen, Hardenberg increases the scale of procreation by an order of magnitude so that "male" and "female" take the place of "semen" and "egg" in the electrical contact of procreation and subsequent combustions. One consequence is that the scientific processes of procreation need to be reformulated to adhere to a new gender-based logic. Whereas in the "Physical Fragments" the semen "inflames" the egg, to be subsequently consumed by it, in *The General Draft* Hardenberg reconsiders burning and digestion the following way:

NATURLEHRE. Je lebhafter das zu Fressende widersteht, desto lebhafter wird die Flamme des Genußmoments seyn. Anwendung aufs Oxigène. / Nothzucht ist der stärkste Genuß. / Das Weib ist unser Oxigène. (3:262, n. 117)

THEORY OF NATURE. The more animated the resistance of that which is to be consumed, the more animated the flame of the moment of pleasure will be. Application to oxygen. / Violation [*Nothzucht*] is the strongest pleasure. / The female is our oxygen.

The immediate scientific context of the note is the contemporary debate over phlogistic and antiphlogistic theories of chemistry sparked by the identification of the highly combustible oxygen gas. The "phlogiston" was originally conceived as an imponderable material released from the burning body during the process of combustion, a theory which was challenged when techniques of measurement became precise enough to determine that bodies gain weight during the burning process. The anti-phlogiston theory supported by Antoine Lavoisier and others reinterpreted the burning process in a new light. The French chemist's experiments gave new fuel to an old metaphor, allowing Hardenberg and his contemporaries to recast the "heat" and "flames" of procreative pleasure and grant the drive to procreate the necessity of a "productive" chemical process. At the same time, by coupling pleasure with combustion, Hardenberg's aphorism generates a certain ambivalence regarding the intersecting spheres of culture and scientific law. The ambivalence hinges on the reading of the word "violation" (*Nothzucht*). Although this word historically could refer to violence in the most general sense, by Hardenberg's day it was commonly understood as sexual violation, in keeping with its literal meaning of forced or necessary breeding. The ambivalence of the aphorism stems from the question of *whose* necessity. If the necessity is that of a scientific law, then—in the most generous interpretation—the aphorism grants human coupling the inevitability of a chemical combustion: oxygen, once ignited, tends to be consumed. Yet the deliberate use of the masculine narrative voice in this aphorism seems to suggest that "necessity" is not gender-neutral, and that the female is appropriated for masculine "consumption."[77] The fact that this aphorism was written in the same time period as the one from the "Physical Fragments" discussed previously suggests that Hardenberg actively employs a chemical vocabulary to create a more nuanced view of procreation which negotiates between interlocking micro- and macroscopic processes. Hardenberg's aphorisms use the logic of natural forces to posit with equal conviction that the egg "eats" the semen and that a flame "consumes" oxygen. He is equally assertive when using a scientific theory as a basis for a statement on gender relations—the necessity or *Nothzucht* of physical pleasure can describe a the law of chemical combustion just as chemistry can illuminate the process of procreation.[78]

"Physics"—the heading Hardenberg grants the lengthier procreative narrative in *The General Draft*—charts a relatively undifferentiated terrain between the inorganic and organic realms within which chemistry and galvanism operate. At the same time, the processes of combustion and consumption play pivotal roles in lending a certain dynamic to the aphorism, moving it from a focus on a general state of production into a clear narrative progression:

PHYSIK. Das Leben der Pflanzen ist gegen das Leben der Thiere gehalten—ein unaufhörliches Empfangen und Gebären—und lezteres gegen dieses—ein unaufhörliches Essen und Befruchten.

Wie das *Weib* das *höchste sichtbare* Nahrungsmittel ist, das den *Übergang vom Körper zur Seele* macht—So sind auch die Geschlechtstheile die höchsten, *äußern* Organe, die den Übergang von sichtbaren und unsichtbaren Organen machen.

Der *Blick*—(die Rede)—die *Händeberührung—der Kuß—die Busenberührung—der Grif an die Geschlechtstheile*—der Act der Umarmung—dies sind die Staffeln der Leiter—auf der die Seele heruntersteigt—dieser entgegengesezt ist eine Leiter—auf der der Körper heraufsteigt—bis zur Umarmung. *Witterung—Beschnüffelung—Act.* Vorbereitung der Seele und d[es] K[örpers] zur Erwachung des Geschlechtstriebes.

Seele und K[örper] *berühren sich* im Act—*chemisch*—oder galvanisch—oder electrisch—oder *feurig*—Die Seele ißt den Körper (und verdaut ihn?) *instantant*—der Körper empfängt die Seele—(und gebiert sie?) instantant. (3:264, n. 126)

PHYSICS. The life of plants is considered with regard to the life of animals—an incessant conceiving and giving birth—and the latter against this—an incessant eating and fecundation.

Just as *the female* is the *greatest visible* foodstuff that makes the *transition from body to soul*—so too are the genitalia the greatest *external* organs that make the transition from visible to invisible organs.

The *gaze*—(the speech)—the *touch of hands—the kiss—the touch of the breast—the reach for the genitalia*—the act of embrace—these are the steps of the ladder—upon which the soul climbs down—opposed to it is a ladder—upon which the body climbs up—until the embrace. *Scent—Sniffing—Act.* Preparation of the body and the soul for the awakening of the drive towards procreation.

Soul and body *touch each other* in the act.—*chemically*—or galvanically—or electrically—or as *fire*—the soul eats the body (and digests it?) *instantly*—the body conceives the soul—(and gives birth to it?) instantly.

In four succinct paragraphs which encompass the "physics" of eating, birthing, and bodily contact, the aphorism ascends from an emphatically material state of consumption and procreation rooted in the mutually dependent realms of animals and plants, to a coupling of body and soul which bears the hallmarks of its material origins: the transcendence of the aphorism still locates itself within the closed circuit of a galvanic chain. As in the aphorism which designated the female as oxygen to be consumed, here too the female is foodstuff; and like the mathematical aphorism discussed in the previous section (3: 255, n. 81), the human embrace is transcendent. The body becomes a galvanically excitable contact surface upon which the sparks to ignite the combustion process are generated. If on the one hand the female is reduced to her genitalia and other "contact points," on the other hand Hardenberg grants the female body the metaphoric function of the one who enables transformation (even transcendence) above and beyond her own limits.

A source for this aphorism can be found in Herder's essay "Liebe und Selbstheit" (Love and Selfhood) written in 1787 as a response to Hemsterhuis' "Lettre sur les désirs" (Letter on the Desires) and published together with the first German translation of Hemsterhuis. Hardenberg's aphorism responds to a section in Herder's essay on the "highest degree of love's rapture," the instant where the two lovers perceive their love's reciprocation, and speak aloud. Yet Herder immediately questions the apparent triviality of speaking, and brackets it in a discursive "parenthesis" just as Hardenberg does with "(the speech)." Herder then continues by ruminating on the kind of heavenly desire possible for creatures on earth now that, according to some mythologies, we have sunk from loving through glances, then kisses, contact and eventually "lower kinds of pleasure:"

> Der Augenblick jenes geistigen Erkennens, jenes Verrats der Seele durch Einen Blick setzt uns gleichsam in diese Zeit zurück, und mit ihr in die Freuden des Paradieses. In ihm geniessen wir *zurückempfindend*, was wir so lange suchten, und uns selbst nicht zu sagen wagten: in ihm geniessen wir *vorempfindend* alle Freuden der Zukunft. (Herder, *Werke*, DKV 4:414)
>
> The moment of that spiritual recognition, the betrayal of the soul through a glance, puts us as it were back into that time and into the joys of paradise. In [that moment] we enjoy retroactively, what we searched for so long and did not dare tell each other: in [that moment] we enjoy with anticipation all future joys.

Herder's description of earthly union merges two imagined trajectories. In terms of a mythological history, human coupling is a base, descended variation of what used to be a transcendental union of gazes; yet through mutual, unspoken recognition of human love, humans are able to lift themselves out of their history of decline. The moment of recognition is one of retroactive and anticipatory enjoyment: the collapse of a past paradise with a future one in the present moment. Christoph Holzhey interprets this passage as a narrative for the (psychoanalytic) constitution of the subject within a larger argument about the "indifference to sex(ual) difference" he reads in Herder's essay.[79] If for Holzhey, the passage in Herder's invokes the regression to a "pre-oedipal imaginary stage," the same material in Hardenberg's aphorism draws on the discourse of galvanism to take a different form altogether.

The sexual encounter of Hardenberg's aphorism also stages a transition through a series of steps, a ladder comprised of connecting words and dashes. After the first glance, the soul begins its descent, abandoning the relatively sophisticated faculties of vision and speech for a series of purely tactile gestures; these gestures intensify into an embrace, emphatically described as a procreative act. Between the glance and the first embrace there are no verbs. Instead, hyphens link the blocks of nouns to form the rungs of the ladder, creating a vertical structure out of syntactical units; the entire "act" is contained within an interlocking scheme.[80] On the opposing ladder, or "conductor,"[81] the body ascends towards the soul; their imagined crossing completes the act. After describing the two contrary motions of body towards soul, and soul towards body, each captured within the same embrace, the language of the fragment dilates from the microcosmic to the macrocosmic. The sequence of "scent,"[82] "sniffing," and "act" reinterprets sexual union as a process of crossing from the liminal sphere of sense impressions to the physicality of visible organs; it reverses the sequence found at the beginning of the fragment, which described the genitalia as the "greatest *external* organs that make the transition from visible to invisible organs."

The atemporality of the fragment vanishes precisely when the final sentence of the paragraph refers to a "preparation," a time before the awakening of the sex drive. The suggestion of a prior time opens up the possibility of repetition. In the following paragraph, the fragment continues by narrating a sexual union: "Soul and body *touch each other* in the act.—*chemically*—or galvanically—or electrically or as *fire* the soul eats the body (and digests it?) *instantly*—the body conceives the soul—(and gives birth to it?) instantly." Hardenberg links the four terms "*chemically*," "galvanically," "electrically," and "*fiery*" through his notion of touch, and creates a "potentialized" chain whose links comprise different types of electrical contact.[83] Body and soul become chemical conductors through which currents flow, and the "instantaneous" temporality of this union complements the (spatially complex) "atemporality" constituted in the first half of the note.[84] The constructions of unity and individuality emerge in this note through the dense, spatial "atemporality" on the one hand, and through the celebration of the "moment" on the other. The chapters on Ritter will show how his fragments also take up the discourse of galvanism to mark time through the changes of the female body more radically even than Hardenberg.

CONCLUSION

This chapter has discussed both the complexities and the constants of Hardenberg's procreative thinking in philosophical and scientific discourse. His aphorisms, whether fragmented notes or incipient narratives, tend to return to certain key themes. These include procreation as categorical thinking, a greater concern for process than progeny, the importance of scale for gender distinctions, and the temporality of procreative narratives. The next chapter focuses on the role of instrumentality in Hardenberg's aphorisms and novel projects, *The Apprentices of Sais* and *Heinrich von Ofterdingen*. It examines the same features of his procreative thinking from a different perspective and argues that Hardenberg's "tools" and "instruments" provide unexpected points of mediation between the scientific and philosophical writing on procreation and Hardenberg's literary poetics.

4 The Poet as Artisan and the Instruments of Procreation

> MENSCH[EN]L[EHRE]. Der Mensch soll ein *vollkommnes* und Totales *Selbstwerckzeug* seyn.
> (Friedrich von Hardenberg, 3:297, n. 321)

> THEORY OF MANKIND. Man should be a *complete* and total *instrument of the self.*

The previous chapter identified procreative tendencies in Hardenberg's philosophical and scientific aphorisms: where philosophical, chemical, or galvanic narratives of production were articulated as gendered couplings. Despite their diverse contexts, these narratives exhibited a few common tendencies. They draw freely from diverse theories of organic generation, they place as much emphasis on the process as on the product of procreation, and they are also interested in using organic procreation as a bridge discourse to downplay the differences between the intellectual and physiological spheres of human activity. Hardenberg's attention to these various aspects of the discourse on procreation also make it possible to distinguish between his approach and how Goethe unites organic and intellectual processes in his elegy on the metamorphosis of plants. As much as the process of an active intuition of the natural world informs the epistemological claim of the poem, it is equally concerned with the results: whether the genesis of a nascent "plant child," the coupling of the lovers, or the success of an experiment in joining discursive and intuitive thinking. Hardenberg's aphorisms which index the procreative process, either directly or through metaphors which transpose procreation into a different setting, are often bereft of progeny: what they produce is procreation itself. This chapter studies one aspect of Hardenberg's process-oriented thinking. It shows how the abstraction characteristic of his early writing on procreation (above all, in the "Fichte Studies") develops to include a marked interest in the materiality of the creative process which goes against the grain of a traditional notion of Romanticism. The aphorisms and narratives of craftsmanship and knowledge-building discussed in the following pages connect with physiological procreation in surprising ways.

The role of the instrument in Romanticism has long been underestimated. The manuscripts of Romantic literature may have been drafted with pen and paper, but Hardenberg makes use of a wider arsenal of instruments with which to hammer and file everything from poetic inscriptions to battleships. A persistent interest in "das Werkzeug"—a polysemous word which at the end of the eighteenth century could encompass everything from tool and instrument to organ and organon—runs throughout Hardenberg's fragment collections, aphoristic writing, and his two novels. In his father's workshop, the young Heinrich von Ofterdingen learns the skills and pleasures of manual craftsmanship before those of poetry. Even Hardenberg's literary *nom de plume*, Novalis, which was ostensibly chosen from a repertoire of ancestral names, deserves to be included within the discourse on tools circulating throughout his oeuvre: *Novale* refers to newly plowed land [*Neubruch*], a terrain of unknown fertility over which poets and plowmen must sow their seeds,[1] which is precisely what the epigraph to the best known fragment collection, *Pollen*, encourages the reader to do.

It is tempting to interchange the *Werkzeug* freely with other semantically related words, such as *Instrument*, *Organ*, and *Organon*. Although this has indeed been the general tendency of the critical scholarship,[2] one runs the risk of overlooking a clear hierarchy which prioritizes the *Werkzeug*. Its semantic elasticity allows for a free movement between the mechanical and the organic realms which the *Organ* is denied: in Hardenberg's day, bodily organs could be referred to as *Werkzeuge*, but it would not have been possible to refer to a chisel or hammer as an *Organ*. The *Werkzeug* rests at the top of a hierarchical tree which branches off into different metaphorical registers, and Hardenberg's fragments and novels exploit its potential for ambiguity and reveal affinities between its seemingly unconnected discourses.[3]

The instrument in Hardenberg's idiolect is an amalgam of tradition and philosophical innovation. It reflects the meanings in currency during the eighteenth century such as one might find in Zedler's *Universal-Lexicon* (1732 ff.),[4] and receives an additional impulse from Immanuel Kant's *Critique of Judgment* from 1790. The instrument in its capacity as organ is what Kant calls a "natural purpose" [*Naturzweck*], and he characterizes it as both organized and self-organizing. In other words, each part is there both *through* and *for* every other part and the whole; each part mutually produces every other part and is both *Zweck* and *Mittel*. Finally, a natural purpose appears to have a teleology, but this purpose cannot be discerned by human faculties.[5] Hardenberg's reception of the Kantian instrument amounts to a conceptual gain in complexity. The simple instrumentality of cause and effect relationships which characterizes the instrument prior to Kant transforms into a richer model of production built on reciprocal relationships. Hardenberg develops the new, organically influenced model of the instrument even further to include other types of productivity—such as the relation between artist, instrument, and artwork—as well as autoproduction, in keeping with his mandate that man should be a self-instrument [*Selbstwerkzeug*]. At the same time, he takes advantage of the instrument's fundamental ambivalence to explore new territory through the creative use of analogies. As a result, the scope of the instrument in the novels and aphoristic writing is vast. It ranges from the most mundane household tools and means of communication, such as the telegraph, to embrace literary forms, and abstractions: these include analogy itself, the faculty of judgment, and mathematics as the epitome of the scientific organon. Hardenberg's instrument is certainly not conceptualized as an idle tool, but just how it mediates between subject and object, man and world, remains to be addressed.

It is helpful to frame these questions within the broader context of Hardenberg's anthropology and the questions it addresses concerning both the study and conceptualization of the human. In an essay titled "'Macroanthropos'—Friedrich von Hardenberg's Literary Anthropology," Bianca Theisen describes the study of man around 1800 as a fundamentally paradoxical enterprise. The centuries prior had witnessed a growing focus on man's privileged position amongst other species, and a growing detachment from theological models of explanation. As a result, the established notion of man as microcosm gradually transformed into its opposite: the world became a "big man" or *Macroanthropos*. As she shifts her focus from the concept of the *Macroanthropos* to the developing discipline of anthropology, Theisen argues that there is a fundamental similarity between the two: both are indicative of an attempt "to formulate new forms of differentiation" in how human life is represented, and both "only do so on the basis of those forms the older order had already established."[6] The inclusion of older ordering structures in emerging ones implies a recursive relationship between part and whole and the recursive logic inherent in the *Macroanthropos* can be reformulated as a cognitive problem of self-observation, the fundamental activity of anthropology. Man's attempt to differentiate himself from something he is inextricably a part of, as Theisen argues, is increasingly thematized by the Romantics as an epistemological problem of self-reference. Simply put, the challenge is how can we—humans—find an adequate way of talking about our relationship to the world, given the inescapable problem of our self-implication in the object of inquiry? What Theisen concludes in her essay is that the theory of language Hardenberg develops provides him with a model which "could overcome the epistemological aporias of a differentiation between subject and object."[7] With reference to the posthumously published novel fragment, *The Apprentices of Sais*, she examines the language Hardenberg refers to as "true Sanscrit." In this model, the "code of human nature" is "laid out before our eyes like natural figurations."[8] This code—a kind of "pure language"—is not governed by a particular speaker. Rather, it is self-referential and suspends the separation between man and nature. Ultimately, Theisen argues, Hardenberg foregrounds the fictional action of poetic cognition. He conceives of a language that overcomes the difficulties of a differentiation between subject and object, man and world, "by means of a constructive process in which the constructing subject would figure its own operations of construction back into the object constructed. The object constructed, be it nature, the world, the subject as subject or man as man, would, in other words, rely on recursive observations or distinctions."[9]

Hardenberg's aphoristic writing on the instrument takes up precisely those problems central to Romantic anthropology. As a vehicle of mediation and production between man and world, the instrument must come to terms with the same paradox of self-implication (in other words: how do we distinguish the functioning of the tool from human agency?). If the instrument mediates between modes of production—even poiesis, understood as a characteristically human creative ability—then the question arises, to what degree can one connect the poietic function of the instrument with the fiction-building which, in Hardenberg's theory of language, overcomes the differentiation between subject and object. This chapter proposes to interpret Hardenberg's instrumental thinking—in its organic, mechanical, and epistemological inflections—as a joint theory of physiological and poetic production. Given how smoothly the instrument synchronizes with the key questions of Romantic anthropology, it has received surprisingly little critical attention.[10] The readings of individual aphorisms will focus on the problematic mediation of the instrument between subject and object, both in artisan contexts and those where the instrument is abstracted from its material origins. The following questions are of particular relevance: to what degree Hardenberg's emphasis on the instrument at the expense of agency posits an autonomous model of the instrument; what it means for the instrument to become a tool of language production; and finally, how to understand Hardenberg's interest in using the instrument to grant "immaterial" things—thoughts, judgments, etc.—a kind of plasticity. The second half of the chapter shifts from the aphorisms to Hardenberg's unfinished novel, *The Apprentices of Sais*, a text whose attempts to synthesize the various branches of Hardenberg's instrumental thinking grants it the status of a *Werkzeug* as well. Within the series of shifting epistemes indexed by the conceptual pairs man/microcosm and world/macroanthropos, Hardenberg's appeal for man to be an instrument of the self can be interpreted as the next logical step: it completes the transition from a definition of man based on representation to one based on function. What remains to be seen, however, is whether the instrument, which has always been defined through its purposefulness with regard to something else, retains its validity when it becomes—as Hardenberg would have it—a complete and total model of the human.

HARDENBERG'S 'WERKZEUG'

Generally speaking, most of Hardenberg's aphoristic writing on the instrument can be found in the manuscripts collected under the title *Preliminary Studies for Various Fragment Collections* and the notes for the encyclopedia project, *The General Draft*, which dates them approximately from the end of 1797 through 1799, a time period which also includes his work on *The Apprentices of Sais*.[11] Unlike the fragments belonging to *Pollen* or the *Athenäum*, which tend towards concisely pointed definitions and (particularly in Friedrich Schlegel's case) mathematical formulae, the aphorisms of the *Preliminary Works* and the encyclopedia project are, generally speaking, more expansive. In the case of the instrument, they elaborate multiple processes which need to be envisioned simultaneously. One of Hardenberg's longer, programmatic definitions of the instrument sets up a shifting balance between agent, instrument, and product:

> Alles Werckzeug ist Vehikel einer fremden Äußerung—Wircksamkeit. Es modificirt und wird modificirt. Die Ausführung ist ein Produkt der Individuellen Beschaffenheit des W[erck]Z[eugs] und der Gestion. Beyde können veränderlich seyn—so wird auch das Produkt veränderlich. Doch könnte der Fall eintreten, daß sie polarisch veränderlich sind— und dann ist das Produkt *beständig* und einerley. (2:552, n. 120)

> Every instrument is vehicle of a foreign utterance—efficacy. It modifies and is modified. The execution is a product of the individual composition of the instrument and of the *Gestion*. Both can be variable—thus too the product becomes variable. Yet the case could arise, that they are as poles variable—and then the product is *constant* and the same.

This definitive statement on the instrument, while focusing on its function, begins with a nod to the rhetorical tradition. As a vehicle of transferal, a medium between agent and product, the instrument performs the work of a metaphor. Moreover, by emphasizing that agent and tool modify each other, Hardenberg calls our attention to the fact that the instrument does not just act like a metaphor, it *is* one in the sense that it condenses mechanical and organic discourses. Much the same way in which the *Macroanthropos* collapses new and traditional epistemological orders, the instrument in this aphorism combines simple cause and effect relationships with a new way of thinking about the organism: the reciprocal relationship between agent and tool clearly invokes the relationship set up in Kant's definition of the instrument as organ or natural purpose.

The aphorism cited previously narrates the prolonged disenfranchisement of the agent in favor of the instrument. The stage for their potential alienation is set already in the first sentence. The insistence on the agent's "foreignness" is part of the handed-down definition of a *causa instrumentalis*: the instrument causes something else to happen, but because it is not automotive, needs to be manipulated by something foreign to it.[12] Hardenberg's aphorism recasts the standard definition in a new mold: instead of emphasizing the dependence of the instrument on foreign hands, he invokes alienation in subtle ways as a plea for the instrument's self-sufficiency.[13] The contours of the agent's individuality dissolve, and the choice of the

French word *Gestion* underscores both the agent's intangibility and its foreignness: *Gestion* is a more abstract word for gesture and is also a term which, in the French juridical system of the eighteenth century, referred to "management" in the most general sense.[14] In other words, it is as a intangible, "hands off" expression of agency as on can imagine.

The second paragraph of the aphorism draws the attention away from the agent altogether to configure a relation between instrument and product.

> Die *Gestalt* (Natur) des *Werckzeugs* ist gleichsam *das eine Element* des Produkts. / So ist der Punct ein *Element* der Linie, die Linie ein Element der Fläche—die Fläche ein Element des Körpers. Aus diesem Beyspiel erhellt sich, wie mir scheint, der Begriff des Elements sehr mercklich. (2:552, n.120)

> The gestalt (Nature) of the instrument is as it were *the one element* of the product. Thus the point is one *Element* of the line, the line is one element of the surface–the surface one element of the body. From this example, as it seems to me, the concept of the element is illuminated very noticeably.

The tool does more than scratch surfaces: it becomes an integral part of the product. When the aphorism allows the agent to reappear in the third paragraph, its role is once again limited:

> Ich kann mit einem Werckz[eug] auf keine andre Weise wircksam seyn—als auf die, die ihm seine natürlichen Verhältnisse bestimmen. So kann ich mit einem Meißel nur stoßen, schaben, schneiden oder sprengen, insofern er scharfes *Eisen* ist ihn electrisch, als Metall zum galv[anischen] Excitator gebrauchen. In beyden letzteren Fällen wirckt er nicht mehr, als Meißel. Ich fühle mich also durch jedes bestimmte W[erck]Z[eug] auf eine besonder Art von Wircksamkeit eingeschränkt—diese besondre Sfäre kann ich freylich unendlich variiren—ich kann so manches Stoßen, sprengen etc. so oft die Wirckung—modificiren—durch Aenderung des Stoffs—durch Variation der Elemente der Wirkung—die Resultate können unendlich verschieden seyn—das Resultat kann die Spaltung eines Steins—ein Pulverloch—eine Statüe etc. seyn. Jedes Werckzeug modificirt also Einerseits, die Kräfte und Gedanken des Künstlers, die es zum Stoffe leitet, und umgekehrt—die Widerstandswirckungen des Stoffs, die es zum Künstler leitet. (2:553, n. 120)

> I cannot be effective with an instrument in any other way except the one which determines its natural relations. Thus I can only push, scrape and cut or crush with a chisel, insofar as it is sharp *iron* use it electrically, as metal for a galvanic excitator. In the two latter cases it

no longer works as a chisel. I feel myself therefore through every specific tool limited to a certain kind of efficacy—this particular sphere I can of course vary endlessly—I can push various things, crush them etc.—modify—by changing the material—by varying the elements of the effect—the results can be endlessly diverse—the result can be the splitting of a stone—a powder-hole—a statue, etc.

The instrument as tool confines the agent's sphere of activity: although this leads us towards a model of production where the free will of the agent is conditioned by the tool, Hardenberg still claims that there is infinite variation within the constraints. The examples he gives seem to be transposed from the fragments with mathematical notation whose equations oscillate between zero and infinity: here, the differential swings between the hole and the statue, a completed work of art. When the aphorism concludes by restating the reciprocal relationship between agent, instrument, and product once more, it de-centers the agent and allows the instrument to take its place.

The same supplementary logic of part and whole which allows the instrument to stand in for the agent remains when the semantic emphasis shifts from "tool" to "sensory organs" or *Sinneswerkzeuge*. An aphorism from the *Preliminary Studies* which later appeared in the fragment collection *Pollen* suggests that both instruments and sensory organs make up the difference between potential and actual creativity. Man becomes a hybrid creature constructed through combinatory principles comparable to those which define the *Macroanthropos*:

> Werkzeuge armiren den Menschen. Man kann wohl sagen, der Mensch versteht eine Welt hervorzubringen, es mangelt ihm nur am gehörigen Apparat, an der verhältnißmäßigen Armatur seiner Sinneswerkzeuge. Der Anfang ist da. So liegt das Prinzip eines Kriegsschiffes in der Idee des Schiffbaumeisters, der durch Menschenhaufen und gehörige Werkzeuge und Materialien diesen Gedanken zu verkörpern vermag, indem er durch alles dieses sich gleichsam zu einer ungeheuren Maschine macht.
>
> So erforderte die Idee eines Augenblick oft ungeheure Organe, ungeheure Massen von Materien, und der Mensch ist also, wo nicht actu, doch potentia Schöpfer. (2:453, n. 88)

> Instruments [*Werkzeuge*] arm humans. One can certainly say, man understands how to bring forth a world, he only lacks the appropriate apparatus, the corresponding armature of his sensory organs [*Sinneswerkzeuge*]. The beginning is there. Thus the principle of a battleship lies in the idea of the master ship builder, who knows how to embody this thought through masses of men and the relevant instruments [*Werkzeuge*] and materials, in that through all of these at once he makes himself into an immense machine.

> Thus the idea of a moment may frequently require immense organs, immense masses of materials, and man is thus—if not actually, then potentially—creator.

The aphorism formulates a concept of agency which balances the intellectual faculty of understanding against sensory organs and tools. As in the previous aphorism, human agency gives precedence to the instrument from the very beginning: it is the instrument which, as grammatical subject, arms mankind. The transitive verb *armiren*, a Germanization of the French verb *armer* (or Latin *armare*), invokes the foreign dynamic which, as previously noted, inserted itself between agent and instrument in the case of the *Gestion*. The verb *armiren* also serves the purpose of indexing the instrument's dual citizenship: the organic and mechanical inflections already present within the word "arm."

Despite the prominent position granted to the instrument, the objection could be made that the tool is simply ancillary to its master, and that the aphorism ultimately celebrates absolute human creativity. Even without the accompanying instruments and materials, the principle of the battleship lies encapsulated within the idea of the master ship builder, merely waiting to unfold, and the instruments only cause to materialize what is already there in the first place. Such an objection neglects to take into account the requisite transformation the ship builder must undergo in order to begin the material construction work on his imagined ship. The transformation is of immense, even monstrous proportions: from a simple man with an idea he must become an immense—*ungeheur*—machine, because this is what his idea urgently demands: an immense man-machine with immense organs and equally immense masses of material at his disposal. It is precisely through the projected large-scale metamorphosis that the instrument reaffirms its importance. If we read the triply emphasized "immense" in the sense that Kant does in the *Critique of Judgment*, then it seems as if man must succumb to the machine and its instruments. According to Kant, an object may be called *ungeheuer* when, through its very enormity, it annihilates its own purpose and exceeds the ability of human imagination to intuitively grasp it as a whole.[15] If this were the case with Hardenberg's "immense machine" then the transition from potential to actualized human creativity requires a leap beyond the limits of human imagination into a conceptual realm where the machine and instruments are completely at home. And even though the eighteenth-century is crowded with post-Leibnizian man-machines, Hardenberg seems to integrate his into a model which more radically sacrifices an inherited fiction of the whole man. To put it in terms of part–whole relationships, one could say that the aphorism displaces poiesis, the definitive human ability, into the *Werkzeug* or armature which, while occupying a gray area between body and supplement, comes to stand in for the whole. In this regard the aphorism makes use of the same recursive logic to describe the relationship between man and instrument as elaborated in Theisen's *Macroanthropos* essay.

The Poet as Artisan and the Instruments of Procreation 93

Even if a master shipbuilder is not able to construct a water-tight ship through thoughts alone, Hardenberg does define a sphere where the instrument, through cognitive processes, can produce a language which has its own materiality. When manipulating language, the instrument performs multiple simultaneous functions, just as in the aphorisms cited previously which structured a reciprocal relationship between agent and product. On the one hand, it externalizes thoughts into near-tangible apparitions; on the other hand, it works in the opposite direction, moving from the acoustics of language to a supersensory poesy, which results in a hieroglyphic "total instrument" (*Gesamtwerkzeug*, 1:331), what Hardenberg will call "language to the power of two" (*Sprache in der 2ten Potenz*, 2:588, n. 264). The reciprocity between the sensory and the supersensory, internal and external, tangible and intangible can be thought of within the framework of late eighteenth-century physiology.

A theoretical model discussing the relations of organic forces to one another was familiar to Hardenberg, who had read Carl Friedrich Kielmeyer's 1793 essay, *On the Relations of the Organic Forces to one another in the Series of the Various Organizations, the Laws and Consequences of these Relations*. As was briefly mentioned in the prior chapter, Kielmeyer posited five forces in living organisms: sensibility (the capability of having impressions, such as on the nerves, produce ideas); irritability (the capability of the muscles or other organs to move when stimulated); reproduction (the capability to produce, either partially or wholly, beings which are self-similar); secretion (the capability of separating substances from the body); and propulsion (the capability of moving fluids through the body). He developed a theory of compensation, where a noticeable decrease in one force was balanced by the increase of another: in particular, the forces of reproduction, sensitivity and irritability exist in a perpetual delicate balance. Both sensibility and irritability together, however, decrease as the force of physical reproduction increases (for example, the relatively small number of offspring produced by the highly-organized element can be compared to the greater number spawned by less developed creatures such as the fly). This idea was taken up as a way of describing the balance between physical and intellectual faculties and to claim man's specificity as the creature with the greatest sensitivity: whose lessened physical reproduction, when compared to other species, was compensated by the production of ideas.[16]

When Hardenberg writes that the gestalt of the instrument is one element of the product, and when he describes the instrument as integral to all stages of the creative process, he suggests that a new understanding of the instrument is required. A question which arises is precisely what this new definition of the instrument implies—if one is to speak of the metaphorization of the instrument, then what model of production (or poiesis) does it serve? Those aphorisms where the instrument functions in the service of language production respond to this lacuna. Hardenberg keeps the instrument poised at the interface of organic and mechanical metaphors, but begins to think of language production in terms of a differentiation of form which will gradually move towards an aesthetics—towards the production of language or poesy for its own sake. With equal insistence on the organic and the mechanical, Hardenberg is able to say that any organ which serves another may be called its tongue or mouth, and the "language instrument" [*Sprachwerkzeug*] is precisely the "instrument which most willingly serves the spirit, [and] is the most readily capable of multiple modifications."[17] One example Hardenberg provides of an artificial language instrument is the human body conceived as an optical and electrical telegraph comprised of tongue and lips, telescopic eyes, and a hand whose multiple operations include being an "instrument of language," an "acoustic excitator and non-conductor," a "brush," and a "general instrument of direction."[18] This model of the human as an optical and electrical instrument closely resembles the aphorism discussed in the prior chapter which imagined the rising body and descending soul moving along the currents of a galvanic chain, facilitated by reciprocal contact points between man and woman through eyes, lips, and the touch of the genitalia (3:264, n. 126). Hardenberg's "artificial language instrument," which seems to function on its own, is nonetheless described with emphasis on the same erogenous body parts: eyes, tongue, and lips as well as a hand which can act as "excitator" and "brush" (*Pinsel*) whereby the latter term was commonly used in Hardenberg's day to refer to the penis, from which it also stems etymologically.

As Hardenberg's descriptions of the instrument become more abstract—retaining their organic and mechanical overtones, while departing from an easily visualizable context—he also shifts the emphasis on the instrument from a means to its own purpose:

> Eine Idee finden—i.e., in der Außenwelt unter mehreren Gefühlen herausfühlen—aus mehreren Ansichten heraussehn—aus mehreren Erfahrungen und Thatsachen herauserfahren—heraussuchen—aus mehreren Gedancken den rechten Gedancken—das Werckzeug der Idee herausdenken—unterscheiden. Hierzu gehört *physiognomischer* Sinn für die mannichfachen *Ausdrücke*, Werckzeuge der Idee. Ich muß die Kunst verstehn von der Idee auf ihre Erscheinung zu schließen. (2:588, n. 263)

> To find an idea—i.e., to feel around in the external world among several feelings—to look out among several perspectives—from several thoughts discern the right thoughtthe instrument of the idea. To this belongs *physiognomic* sense for the manifold *expressions*, instruments of the idea. I must understand the art of moving from the idea to its appearance.

This aphorism proposes a cognitive process whereby the thinking, feeling agent searches through a manifold of experience. The instrument develops both as a collective (the composite organon of the idea) and singly (as individual expressions couched in physiognomic terms, which are the "physical features" of the idea). It transforms the intangible and formless into something which can be differentiated through visual metaphors. What emerges, therefore, is an instrument which can be read and interpreted—an instrument which could be considered both a poetic product and a tool with its own creative potential.[19]

THE INSTRUMENT IN THE NOVEL

Hardenberg explores the instrument's potential for poetic creation in both his novels and his aphoristic writing. Between the two genres, however, it is the novel which more directly addresses the instrument as a problem for poetics and literary creativity, and each of Hardenberg's novels anchor their discussion of the instrument with references to artisan production. In *The Apprentices of Sais* (1802 posth.), which will be discussed in greater detail in the second half of the chapter, the pedagogical labor undertaken at Sais is posited against material craftsmanship and trade skills to which those students turn who leave the institution: a decision which, as the end of the fragment reveals, does not necessarily render them less competent in the eyes of their teacher. The same tension between the poetic and the artisan finds more provocative formulation in *Heinrich von Ofterdingen* in a conversation between Heinrich and Sylvester which takes place in the second part of the novel.[20] Sylvester finds in Heinrich a lost opportunity redeemed; years before, he had observed in Heinrich's father "signs of a great artist": "His eye was full of desire to become a true eye, a creating instrument."[21] Sylvester laments that the present world—including the dour skies of Thuringia—had already taken too deep a hold, causing Heinrich's father to ignore his true vocation and reduce poetic inspiration to the skills of an "adroit handworker."[22] Heinrich's counter-argument acknowledges his father's pragmatism without relinquishing his intuition. He claims that his father's "sober and entirely solid way of thinking, which allows him to look at all affairs like a piece of metal and a man-made product, still involuntarily and without even knowing it himself, to have a quiet reverence and fear of god before all incomprehensible and higher phenomena."[23] The argument for the compatibility of artisan skills with a sense for the holy, and even the sublime, comprises an important aspect of the instrumental thinking evident in *Heinrich von Ofterdingen* which will be discussed in *The Apprentices* as well. The hybrid status of the instrument also exhibits structural affinity to the genre where it finds its greatest elaboration in Hardenberg's writing: in general, the Early Romantic novel is also characterized by hybridity a well as the tendency to reflect on its own modes of production. Each of Hardenberg's novels connects the concept of the instrument directly to a particular literary genre. The second half of the chapter will show how *The Apprentices of Sais* grants the fairy tale the function of an epistemological instrument which filters natural history and human origins through poetic language, and it tests this theoretical premise by inserting a fairy tale in the center of its philosophical discussions. *Heinrich von Ofterdingen* experiments with different literary forms, poetry and the fairy tale, but identifies the fable as the "total instrument" which organizes Heinrich's world.

References to the fable appear in two discrete contexts immediately before and after the break between the two sections the novel: personified as an allegorical figure in a fairy tale told by the poet Klingsohr, and as a literary genre mentioned in a larger poetological discussion. These two aspects of the fable have more in common than meets the eye. In the poetological context, Heinrich introduces the fable at an unexpected moment. He and Sylvester have been pursuing a general discussion about travel, education, and man's relation to nature, and Sylvester suggests that the force of conscience [*Gewissen*] could effect a return to man's initial unity with nature. He gives conscience both an epistemological and a moral emphasis and suggests it has a creative function: either to build new worlds or expand our view of the world we already inhabit. Heinrich counters that the difference between building "new" worlds and expanding the present one is irrelevant: "I only know that for me the fable is the total-instrument of my present world. Even conscience, this sense- and world-generating power, this seed of all personality, appears to me, like the spirit of the world poem, like the chance of the eternal romantic gathering, of the infinitely changeable total life."[24] Heinrich invokes the genre of the fable as instrument in the sense of an organon, a construct which permits him to expand his knowledge and awareness beyond the present world: "thus in the theories of the fable the life of a higher world is replicated in the most marvelously arisen compositions in various ways."[25]

Heinrich's certainty that the fable, as poetic organon, completely informs his world laconically iterates a point of view articulated in great length in the fairy tale told by the poet Klingsohr. At the risk of vastly oversimplifying what many scholars have found to be a narrative of puzzling complexity, one can say that the fairy tale, among its other functions, allegorizes a metamorphosis from the individual to the total instrument—from tool to poesy. The fairy tale begins with a series of strange events at the king's court, including a morning card game between the king and the princess in which they try to predict a harmonious future by constructing relations between symbols and figures printed on the cards.[26] This game is observed by all members of the court, who, through strange pantomimes, behave as if they were each carrying an invisible instrument. These invisible objects might be musical instruments—though the description of the ambient music detaches it from any source[27]—or they might be scientific devices, given that the fairy tale also invokes electrical and galvanic phenomena. After the card game, the character "Fable" is introduced as a tiny child with uncanny abilities who plays a central role in Klingsohr's narrative.

Although a quest to save the kingdom is undertaken by other characters (Eros and Ginnistan), it is eventually Fable who performs this task and reestablishes harmony. In doing so, she performs her poetological function as well: eighteenth-century poetics defined the difference between the fairy tale and the fable in terms of the fable's ethical content.[28] Klingsohr's fairy tale enacts this moment of genre differentiation in as far as he invests his Fable with both creative potential and moral integrity: at the end of the fairy tale, Fable is given a spindle which she uses to spin "a golden unbreakable thread" from her own chest and the fairy tale closes with a song she sings which founds the "eternal realm."[29]

Hardenberg's poetological definition of the fable in the fragments refers to it as the "expression of an *entire* thought" and relegates it to "hieroglyphics squared" (i.e., to the power of two).[30] The fable has the ability to organize individual thoughts and the manifold of expressions (what Hardenberg called the "instrument of the idea") into just one. As the paragon of "language squared," it performs:

> poëtische Verdienste und ist nicht *rhetorisch*—subaltern—wenn sie ein vollkommener Ausdruck—wenn sie *euphonisch*²—richtig und praecis ist—wenn sie gleichsam ein *Ausdruck, mit* um des Ausdrucks willen ist—wenn sie wenigstens nicht, als Mittel erscheint—sondern an sich selbst eine vollkommne Produktion des *höhern Sprachvermögens* ist. (2:588, n. 264)
>
> poetic services and is not *rhetorical*—subaltern—if it is a complete expression—if it is *euphonic*²—correct and precise—if it is virtually an *expression, along with* and for the sake of the expression—if it at least does not appear as means—but rather is in itself a complete production of the *higher faculty of language*.

The aphorism emphasizes the totality of the fable which is a self-contained linguistic expression, a "complete production." The fable is not a means to something else—not an organon in the traditional philosophical sense. It therefore has something in common with the "pure language" sought by the travelers in *The Apprentices of Sais*: the fable expresses for the sake of expression. In its totality, the fable's claim of completeness would both fulfill Hardenberg's injunction for man to be a *"complete* and total *self-instrument"* and grant it an ethical dimension. Yet we have seen through several examples that there is a tendency in Hardenberg's fragments for the instrument to work against man's self-directed goal of totality and displace a centrally-positioned human agency. The same problem arises in *Heinrich von Ofterdingen*, in a dialog between Heinrich and Klingsohr which sets human faculties in counterpoint to a total poesy. When Heinrich asks whether a subject can be too effusive for poesy, Klingsohr replies in the affirmative, with the caveat that it is not poesy which has limits but rather humans: our "earthly means and instruments" (irdischen Mittel und Werkzeuge).[31] Just as the limits of the artisan lie within the technical skills of the handworker, the limits of the poetic are de facto the extent of human faculties. The negative side of poetic aspiration—that mankind, for all it can achieve, still wrestles with its own inadequacy—echoes the whisper of failure which threatened to undermine the act of intuition in Goethe's poem on metamorphosis. In an aphorism dating from 1799—an interim year joining his work on *The Apprentices* to the first drafts of *Heinrich von Ofterdingen*—Hardenberg comments that "naturally, on every higher level of formation [*Bildung*], poetics becomes a more significant instrument and a poem a greater product."[32] The remainder of the chapter explores the terrain Hardenberg charts for the limits of the human faculties through a reading of *The Apprentices of Sais* which considers both the role of the instrument and the instrumentalization of poetics.

THE APPRENTICES OF SAIS

Although Hardenberg never completed the draft of *The Apprentices of Sais*, it offers the most compelling testimony to the range of his instrumental thinking. In this text, the organic, mechanical, and epistemological dimensions of the *Werkzeug* which appear scattered throughout the fragments and aphorisms converge in the topos of procreation. Hardenberg's early writing on the novel dates from 1798, the same year in which he completed the fragments of *Pollen* and began early work on various fragment collections, the Freiberg Studies, and *The General Draft*.[33] In its subject-matter—various human philosophical perspectives of nature—*The Apprentices* does not depart from the scientific and philosophical studies of the previous years but rather shifts them into a more pronounced literary poetics, or an "aesthetic realm" (Mahoney).[34] The novel contains an abundance of references but does not attempt to reconcile philosophical differences, and thus becomes a veritable encyclopedic experiment: it takes part in an attempt to poeticize the sciences, as Hardenberg alludes in an oft-quoted letter to August Wilhelm Schlegel dating from February 24th, 1798.[35] William Arctander O'Brien has argued that the novel differs from the aphorisms of *The General Draft* in that it "does not seek to reconstitute the 'lost' unity of nature": instead, he argues, "nature and science are both irreversibly plural, and *Sais* elaborates a kind of prolegomenon to the future Romantic science."[36] Whereas O'Brien sees the novel as the preface of a science yet to come, the following reading prefers to speak of *The Apprentices* as the instrument or organon of a science in the process of discovery.

The temple of Sais traditionally belongs to Isis, the Egyptian goddess of wisdom, and it appears in Hardenberg's novel as a living collection of natural phenomena, a locus of intersecting questions and theories.[37] It is an educational institution guided by a single, unnamed teacher whose students comprise all those (the reader included) who visit the temple. The first, much shorter, chapter of the text introduces the reader to "the apprentice," an unnamed student who serves as a guide and living record of the disembodied voices whose clamor rises and falls throughout the course of the novel. In addition to the manifold of voices competing for legitimacy—to the confusion of student and reader alike—frequent interruptions undermine the continuity of the narrative of any linear progression. The consecutive mediations on human and natural history oscillate between hypothetical beginning points, the current fractured state of affairs where mankind has lost its innate understanding of the natural world, and the possibility of future reconciliation. These abstract meditations remain ungrounded in any tangible reference point. "Sais" does not index a precise historical or temporal coordinate and is perhaps best conceived as a disposition, a state of ongoing intellectual inquiry. The following pages explore the metaphorical potential of the instrument as a hermeneutic tool made available to the reader to mediate the otherwise irreconcilable perspectives of the text. With reference to the earlier analyses from *Heinrich von Ofterdingen* and the aphorisms discussed in the first half of the chapter, my readings examine its role in the novel to argue that the instrument offers a clue to the reader for negotiating the scientific, philosophical and poetological discourses of the novel without sacrificing their distinctions.

As most of the conceptual work on the instrument occurs in the longer second chapter, just a few pertinent details from the brief first chapter, "The Apprentice," will be mentioned here. The first words of the novel—"manifold ways"—are programmatic for its multiperspectival approach to human and natural relations. Yet the novel's opening also allows for the hint of a countertendency, the ability to recognize patterns which connect the most diverse figures of nature. Humans do not yet possess the key to these patterns of nature: they have intimations of their existence and sense a language beyond their immediate perception, yet the limits of the human faculties are the alkahest which separates them from the knowledge they are seeking. The first chapter sets up an epistemological scenario within which the philosophical dialogues of the second chapter are staged and also relativized. Through the point of view of a single apprentice we are introduced to the teacher of the institute and its pedagogical framework. Each apprentice searches for the patterns of nature on his own path. Two are allotted a messianic destiny— they are sent from the institute with the anticipation that, upon their return, all lessons will come to an end. Others, however, choose a seemingly more mundane future. They depart from the institute, return to their parents, and learn a trade. This need not be seen as a lesser choice, as the teacher's monologue at the end of the fragment reveals, and in *Heinrich von Ofterdingen*, Sylvester also comments that even mundane tools can be pleasing to the hidden sense.[38] The destiny of the narrating apprentice is still uncertain. Though less skilled than some, he has a sense of being on the right path, a journey which directs him inward rather than out into the field in search of stones and plants for the temple's collections. His path is also the reader's, who is permitted to accompany the apprentice for a while on his journey.

INSTRUMENT AND KNOWLEDGE

The second chapter of *The Apprentices* is a dense mixture of philosophical dialogues which generate a sensory confusion in their auditors and readers much like the alkahest which cloaks the human senses. The chapter begins with a series of philosophical meditations overheard by the solitary apprentice from the first chapter which are interrupted by a fairy tale told to him by one of his companions. The fairy tale then receives a commentary by the unhappy "nature voices" (*Naturstimmen*) belonging to the living objects collected in the temple; a discussion among four travelers and a monologue by the sole teacher of the institute concludes the manuscript as Hardenberg left it.

The theme which joins the multitude of perspectives is human relations to nature. The reciprocity of these perspectives, their non-linearity and interlocking dialogic structure cause them to function much like the instrument which swings between the artist and the material—modifying and modified by both—described by Hardenberg in *The General Draft*. The following reading of the nature chapter in *The Apprentices* is based on the premise that poetic and pedagogical function of the instrument cannot be overestimated. The strange topology of the narrative allows for Hardenberg's statement that poetics becomes an instrument in every higher level of formation to be conversely true as well. With its artisan and physiological inflections, the instrument not only figures into many of the discussions of nature, it offers itself as a metaphor elastic enough to expand from the individual parts to the work as a whole: in *The Apprentices*, a poeticized instrument and instrumentalized poetics go hand-in-hand.

The chapter begins by describing a distant era when mankind was just learning to differentiate and combine the objects of sensory experience in tandem with the development of its intellect. Thoughts about things or objects in the world stood in direct correlation with nature and were a "necessary result" of nature's condition (I:83). For early man, such unmediated thoughts become the best tools available "for observing the universe":

> Wir können daher die Gedanken unsrer Altväter von den Dingen in der Welt als ein notwendiges Erzeugnis, als eine Selbstabbildung des damaligen Zustandes der irdischen Natur betrachten, und besonders an ihnen, als den schicklichsten Werkzeugen der Beobachtung des Weltalls, das Hauptverhältniss desselben, das damalige Verhältniss zu seinen *Bewohnern*, und seiner Bewohner zu ihm, bestimmt abnehmen. (1:83)

Thus we can consider the thoughts of our ancestors about the things in the world to be a necessary result, to be a perfect image of the condition of worldly nature at that time, and in particular we can derive precisely from these thoughts, as the most appropriate instruments for the observation of the universe, its primary relationship, the universe's relationship at that time to its *inhabitants*, and they to it.[39]

It is precisely the function of thought as instrument—as a product derived from the sensory perception of nature, and something that can be deployed in the service of intellectual observation—that reveals a reciprocal relation of man to universe *and* universe to man like the relationship between artist and tool. The beginning of the chapter captures this doubled relationship through a metaphorization of the instrument inscribed within two points of view, one embedded within the other: the former condition of man's relation to nature is framed by the later "we" of the narrative present which, as the narrative voice, positions itself consciously in relation to its "ancestors." Though separated by time, these two perspectives are joined by a single intellectual and organic genealogy. The implicit transition from a time where thoughts occur "naturally" to a later perspective when naturally occurring thoughts can be framed and re-evaluated as instrument informs a creation history of human intellectual development and depicts the foundations of human reflection.

In its continued metaphorization of the instrument, the lengthy first paragraph moves beyond the epistemological claim of thoughts as scientific tools to include an instrumental understanding of the poetic arts as well. It relates how, at an even earlier stage of human history, man used "fairy tales and poems full of strange figural traits" populated by "humans, gods and animals as common craftsmen" and heard "the creation of the world described in the most natural way."[40] Not only do these fairy tales and poems imagine the "craftsmen" of the world and its "contingent, organic" origin,[41] the poetic arts themselves become "the favorite instrument of the true nature-friend, and the spirit of nature shines most brightly in poetic works."[42] By stating that the primary purpose of the instrument is to generate knowledge through the construction of literary and scientific narratives, the first paragraph of the chapter "Nature" sets an agenda followed consequently through the remainder of the text. The explorers and poets of nature are one people united by a single language; their cognitive activities—to dissect and tame the immensity of nature, to study its inner workings and follow its mutability—are extensions of the forces of attraction and repulsion which govern all natural activity.[43] What follows is a performance of these two functions: first, a series of philosophical perspectives which pursue to varying degrees the scientific dissection of nature at the hands of an increasingly powerful human agent; then, a fairy tale which carries out the poetic function of the instrument, to synthesize and transmit knowledge of nature through poetic narrative.

HYACINTH AND ROSENBLÜTCHEN

The tale of Hyacinth and Rosenblütchen transposes the discussion of nature from a historical-philosophical realm to an immediate problem of literary form and function. If the fairy tale does in fact operate as an epistemological instrument, as the opening paragraph of the chapter suggests, then the question of its application arises. Does the fairy tale attempt to reveal the "spirit of nature" to its listener and readers and thereby grant them a knowledge of nature they would not otherwise possess? And given that Hardenberg's instruments operate through reciprocity, to what extent are the speaker of the fairy tale and the narrative itself altered by the experience of being told, if at all? John Neubauer has proposed that the embedded tale provides a "blueprint" for the novel which indirectly reduces the opacity of the abstractions found in the philosophical dialogues and monologues surrounding it.[44] One consequence of reading the fairy tale as an instrument would be to acknowledge that, in a narrative whose multiple parts explain each other, the unique vantage point of a blueprint is eliminated. Just as Heinrich discovers a book in the hermit's cave which both charts and is charted by the course of his own life, the fairy tale of Hyacinth and Rosenblütchen both elucidates its framing elements and is defined by them at the same time. The line between instrument and product (or, poetologically speaking, between the frame and embedded narratives) blurs in *The Apprentices*, but in Hardenberg's aphorisms the distinction was never maintained to begin with.

With reference to the orality of *The Apprentices*, Ingrid Kreuzer has commented that the novel is "produced by speaking" (*sprechend erzeugt*).[45] Her observation has particular bearing on the second chapter, an extended auditory experience where the various meditations on man's relation to nature are articulated speech, whether as monologue or conversation. The fairy tale is also spoken aloud—it is the first time when the speaking voice can connected to a present persona—told by an apprentice to the one already introduced in the first chapter, who prefers to sit removed from the others in contemplation. His companion chastises the solitary apprentice for keeping to himself and surmises that this penchant for solitude is because he has not yet fallen in love: "with the first kiss, a new world is opened up within you."[46] The pedagogic function of the fairy tale is therefore also as procreative as Goethe's elegy on the metamorphosis of plants: to generate the experience of a new world through an imagined coupling, and to provide a short-cut to knowledge of love which the solitary apprentice has not yet gained through experience.

The events of the fairy tale are deceptively simple. Hyacinth, restless after encountering a traveler with tales of distant places, decides to leave his family and his beloved Rosenblütchen.[47] At the advice of an old woman in the woods he begins his journey in seemingly paradoxical directions, as a departure from his (biological) parents which is also a return to the "mother of all things." The fairy tale does not explain the cause of Hyacinth's restlessness, but it does describe the symptoms: a state of discord with nature, marked by a lack of understanding. The tension generated by an inability to read and interpret the signs of nature relates to Hardenberg's historical-philosophical definition of the fairy tale, in which "everything must be wonderful—secretive and disconnected—everything animated"; the fairy tale depicts a time of ". . .the *natural condition* of *nature*—the time before the *world* (state). This time before the world provides simultaneously the scattered traces of the time *after the world*."[48] The "scattered traces" surrounding Hyacinth are hidden within the voices of nature. The animals attempt to point him on the right path by communicating with him in human poetic genres such as songs, ballads, and fairy tales: in those genres, where the "spirit of nature" should reveal itself to mankind.[49] Yet even the lizard's highly suggestive song, which incorporates elements of the entire fairy tale, fails to elicit more than laughter in Hyacinth. In the song, Rosenblütchen "blindly" confuses Hyacinth with her mother, and it remains ambiguous which figure is real, and which is perceived.[50] Although the lizard's mocking tone trivializes the constellation of woman, man, and mother; these three elements are central to the fairy tale as a whole. Hyacinth is neither able to interpret his own fate in the lizard's song, and thus use it as a means of acquiring knowledge, nor is he able to interpret a second text—an illegible book left behind by the mysterious traveler.[51] At the advice of an old woman in the woods, Hyacinth burns the book, thereby returning it to nature, and begins his journey.

During Hyacinth's travels, time passes with increasing rapidity: as he approaches his terrestrial goal, he also nears the time "after the world" which, as predicted in the fragment on the fairy tale, bears remarkable resemblance to the "time before the world" as well. In the end, the distinctions between past and future, home and away, are annulled. The end of the journey releases Hyacinth from the constraints of time and place when he enters the temple of Isis and dreams the completion of his quest, and Rosenblütchen sinks into his arms. The union of Hyacinth and Rosenblütchen recalls the aphorism from the *General Draft* where the contrary motions of the rising body and falling soul incite a galvanized contact.[52] Just as in that aphorism the body ascends the electrically conducting "ladder" while the soul descends, here too the corporeal Hyacinth and the transcendental Rosenblütchen converge in an electric spark as Hyacinth touches her shining veil.[53] Like the aphorism, the end of the fairy tale equates sexual and intellectual productivity: in Neumann's words, "the love-act, simultaneously understood as an act of cognition . . . leads to the 'regeneration' of paradise."[54] The procreative emphasis of the fairy tale also guarantees its continuity. Countless children bless the union of Hyacinth and Rosenblütchen. Like the series geometric series which ended with mankind as generation "infinity," the apprentice's narrative (also an "account" or *Erzählung*) can never be told to its very end, and has only symbolic completeness.[55]

Critical readings of the fairy tale's conclusion have voiced strong arguments against the "reality" of Hyacinth's reunion with Rosenblütchen. Alice Kuzniar claims that because the end of the fairy tale occurs while Hyacinth is still dreaming, it is not certain whether the final events actually happen: "Their irreality casts an ironic light on any reading resounding of closure. Hyacinth's final self awareness is not assured."[56] Yet Neumann recalls that the concept of "dream" is inseparable from thought: "'Dream' rests for Novalis on the threshold between the organic and the inorganic . . . it is, as a condition of the 'relaxed' system, the very highest form of thinking which defies logic."[57] If, as Neumann suggests, the fairy tale posits sexual union and the acquisition of knowledge within a liminal state between the organic and inorganic, then the body, as locus of procreation and intellectual production, performs the same metaphorical function as an instrument.[58] The fairy tale, which has a textual materiality in the center of the novel, doubles as an intellectual and procreative source for the text as a whole.[59] It is the position of the fairy tale at the nexus of the creation of "thought" or "science" as opposed to a new "world" that leads Neumann to see already a new "mythology of thought" at stake" in the narrative.[60] Yet it is not simply a "key" for deciphering a novel which as Neubauer would have it, is otherwise "without unifying themes."[61] As much as the fairy tale interprets the novel, the novel reciprocates by interpreting the fairy tale: both beforehand, through its suggestion that poetry might function as "instrument," and afterwards, through an unusual act of interpretation which follows.[62]

At the end of the fairy tale, the two apprentices embrace and depart from the scene. Perhaps, as Ingrid Kreuzer argues, the tale does function as "substitute" knowledge for the solitary apprentice; she writes that his "novel" effectively comes to an end—"the fairy tale is the apprentice's 'Sais,' where he finds *his* truth..."[63]—yet several details suggest a more complicated scenario than Kreuzer's. For one, the apprentice has already described doubled experiences of the familiar and the foreign in the first chapter: these are intrinsic to his experiences at Sais, where the strangest pattern can suddenly have the familiarity of a household tool (1:82). What is more, the teacher is in accord with the solitary apprentice's wish to find his way alone: each individual figure that an apprentice inscribes has its own justification. An even more compelling reason for believing that the apprentice's private journey has not yet reached its conclusion can be found in the clamor of the nature voices [*Naturstimmen*] which resound throughout the temple halls once the apprentices have departed.

NATURE VOICES

They belong to the objects of the temple: voices of the precious stones and other artifacts which have been gathered and arranged into patterns by the

The Poet as Artisan and the Instruments of Procreation   105

teacher and the students. Collectively, these voices express a dissatisfaction which threatens to undermine the pedagogical project of the temple. Despite all the care taken by the students and the teacher to create harmonious orders—a process idealized in the first chapter by the unskilled apprentice who finds a stone which is the key to a complex pattern—all of the objects long for their freedom. Few stand in their "proper place" and the rest complain of "horrible agony and pain and lament their former glorious life in the lap of nature where a common freedom united them and each fulfilled its own needs."[64] In *Heinrich von Ofterdingen*, Sylvester explains to Heinrich that his personal sense of conscience is rooted in his love and respect for nature: he treats the flowers of his garden in accordance with their own wishes. Sylvester's willingness to allow natural objects their freedom stands in stark contrast to the teacher of Sais, who cannot be said to have a conscience in the sense which Sylvester describes.

The nature voices of the temple have their own diagnosis for the human behavior which has separated them so violently from their proper places. Their explanation takes up the same themes as the fairy tale: the current schism between humankind and nature, and the longing for a future union which would amount to a return to (or of) the Golden Age. Simply stated, the cause of mankind's disjuncture with nature is that it does not know how to feel:

> Lernt [der Mensch] nur einmal fühlen? Diesen himmlischen, diesen natürlichsten aller Sinne kennt er noch wenig: durch das Gefühl würde die alte, ersehnte Zeit zurückkommen; das Element des Gefühls ist ein inneres Licht, was in schönern, kräftigern Farben bricht. Dann gingen die Gestirne in ihm auf, er lernte die ganze Welt fühlen, klärer und mannigfaltiger, als ihm das Auge jetzt Grenzen und Flächen zeigt. (1:96)

> Will [man] ever learn to feel? He knows this heavenly, this most natural of all senses still too little: through feeling the old, longed-for time would return; the element of feeling is an inner light that breaks into beautiful, powerful colors. Then the stars would begin to burn in him, he would learn to feel the entire world more clearly and complexly, than the eye can now show him limits and surfaces.

This endorsement of "feeling" by the nature voices, the "most natural of all senses" can be read as an indirect caution against equating the fairy tale with an easy path to knowledge. Can its pedagogical function really succeed if there is no guarantee of a "feeling" to accompany the apprentice's "knowing"? Its success as a communicative act remains unsubstantiated in the version of the novel as Hardenberg left it.

The nature voices also take up a topic from the beginning of the second chapter in *The Apprentices* where the first instances of human philosophical reflection are described as the refraction of a light ray. The summons to feel is also a call to return to a moment of great creative potential, affirmed through cosmological metaphors as the birth of the stars. The earlier discussion of the "Fichte Studies" has already described the importance of feeling and reflection in Hardenberg's lexicon. As Manfred Frank has shown, "feeling" cannot be understood as pre-extant to reflection: the two are always already entwined with each other: "For without the apparently belated form of reflection, there would not be feeling as "material" for this reflection in the first place. Reflection is bound with [feeling] from the very beginning though [reflection] appears to be the effect of feeling in a "foreign shape."[65] One can interpret the nature voices to say that the purported philosophical and scientific activity of the temple is meaningless if there is no underlying "feeling" to accompany it. Drawing upon another metaphor Hardenberg introduced in the "Fichte Studies" one could say that, according to the nature voices, man has lost contact with the "mothersphere" (*Muttersfäre*). If "feeling" and the "mothersphere" are descriptors for the same conceptual realm, then the fairy tale of Hyacinth and Rosenblütchen and the lament of the nature voices appear as two versions of the same story, but with different endings. As many readers have noted, the fairy tale and the nature voices' response to it comprise a structural and organic center to the novel's second chapter. Less acknowledged, however, is that the chapter's center is marked by profound fissure which threatens the validity of the project as a whole and, at the very least, suggests an ironic ambiguity to the novel which has largely been overlooked. What remains to be seen is how the subsequent dialogues among four travelers visiting the temple, as well as the concluding monologue by the teacher, respond to the problem raised in the lament of the nature voices. The answer lies in a poetic counterpoint to Hardenberg's appeal for man to be a "total *instrument of the self*."

THE INSTRUMENT OF THE SELF

With varying degrees of optimism, both the fairy tale and the nature voices describe the possible unification of man and nature as well as man's ability to overcome his current state of discord through the retrieval of a lost sense: "feeling." Together, they comprise two lyrical interludes—two variations on the same theme—nestled between the philosophical monologues and the subsequent conversation among the four travelers. Their function is not just aesthetic, but also pedagogical. The solitary apprentice has been instructed to listen to the fairy tale in order to learn about a sense which he is lacking. The nature voices speak only to the empty halls and to the reader, who learns from them to approach the pedagogical project of the institution as a whole with greater skepticism. The polyvocality of the novel lies not just in the various perspectives on man and nature, but also the various paths through which to acquire knowledge.

From the beginning of the chapter, the "instrument" has served an epistemological function. As materialized thoughts and as poetic products, it has been conceptualized in such a way as to reveal the spirit of nature to mankind. The knowledge gained by the instrument allows man to "feel" nature once again, to appropriate the desires of nature as his own. Within the logic of instrumentality, the novel both establishes the instrument as the vehicle of thought and poetry, and posits the embedded fairy tale of Hyacinth and Rosenblütchen as precisely such an instrument. The function of the instrument shifts into new terrain with the advent of the travelers. Although they are newly arrived at the temple, their conversation seamlessly picks up where the nature voices left off. Each of the four travelers takes turn speaking, and their conversation moves through two cycles before the teacher interrupts. They are distinguished by nothing other than their intellectual points of view: the narrative provides no physical descriptions except to say that the fourth of the travelers—not coincidentally the one with the most passionate oratory—is a youth. As the various strains of their conversation begin to entwine, the travelers gradually develop the notion of the self as a procreative instrument. This is particularly the case in the second round of conversation, where the first, second, and fourth speakers propose three different perspectives which, read together, reframe the discourse of the instrument within a procreative language of self-generation.

The first speaker, who has already advocated the need for undivided attention at the beginning of any human endeavor, returns to this theme:

> Um die Natur zu begreifen, muß man die Natur innerlich in ihrer ganzen Folge entstehen lassen. Bei dieser Unternehmnung muß man sich bloß von der göttlichen Sehnsucht nach Wesen, die uns gleich sind, und den nothwendigen Bedingungen dieselben zu vernehmen, bestimmen lassen, denn wahrhaftig die ganze Natur ist nur als Werkzeug und Medium des Einverständnisses vernünftiger Wesen begreiflich. Der denkende Mensch kehrt zur ursprünglichen Funktion seines Daseins, zur schaffenden Betrachtung, zu jenem Punkte zurück, wo Hervorbringen und Wissen in der wundervollsten Wechselverbindung standen, zu jenem schöpferischen Moment des eigentlichen Genusses, des innern Selbstempfängnisses. (1:101)

> In order to comprehend nature, one has to let nature emerge in its entire sequence. Through this enterprise one need only let oneself be determined by the divine longing for creatures which are like us, and the conditions necessary to discover them, because the entire nature is truly comprehensible only as an instrument [*Werkzeug*] and medium of agreement for rational beings. The thinking man returns to the original function of his being, to creative observation, to that point where producing and knowing stood in the most marvelous reciprocal relation, to that creative moment of actual pleasure, of inner self-conception.

Just as Goethe's observer of nature rises above the real time of observation and recreates temporal unfolding in the mind's eye, the passage from *The Apprentices* suggests an atemporal overview of nature, from its origin to an imagined state of completion. Rather than striving for impartiality during this endeavor, as Goethe recommends, the passage in *The Apprentices* calls for an anthropocentric determination, a search for a human analog. It justifies the plea for a biased perspective with the claim that nature can only be comprehended as a human instrument, thereby inverting the traditional part/whole relationship so that the "microcosm" of nature takes part in the 'macrocosm' of man as rational being. The first traveler describes this intellectual exercise as an observation or intuition [*Beschauung*] of the original phenomenon [*Urerscheinung*] whose description leads to the "true theory of nature."[66] The person who performs this intellectual activity returns to his most primary function: "to that point, where generation and knowledge stand in the most fantastic relation of alternation, to that creative moment of actual pleasure, of inner self-conception."[67] From this moment of self-conception arise new temporal and spatial dimensions and with them, the possibility of a "you" to accompany the "I." Unlike the aphorisms of the "Fichte Studies," this theory proposes an active observation of nature akin to Goethe's intuition in which the eyes of the body and the mind work in coordination. The call for nature to be the instrument and medium of agreement between rational beings goes one step beyond Goethe and, by relegating nature to man's instrument, one step closer to Hardenberg's call for man to be a complete and total instrument of the self.

Whereas the second traveler does little more than express his wonder at the extent of nature's activity—"the great at-the-same-time in nature"[68]—the third traveler takes the relation of the instrument to the self a notch further when he replaces the "thinker" described by the first traveler with an "artist":

> Billig stellt der Künstler die Tätigkeit obenan, denn sein Wesen ist Tun und Hervorbringen mit Wissen und Willen, und seine Kunst ist, sein Werkzeug zu allem gebrauchen, die Welt auf seine Art nachbilden zu können, und darum wird das Princip seiner Welt Tätigkeit, und seine Welt seine Kunst. (1:102)

> Rightfully, the artist grants activity the foremost position, because his being is action and production with knowledge and volition, and his art is to be able to use his instrument [*Werkzeug*] for everything, to be able to represent the world in his own fashion, and thus the principle of his world becomes activity, and his world becomes his art.

The artist is praised for his activity and his ability to represent the world in his own manner; together, the thinker and the artist display the grandeur of human intellect through a capacity for personalizing and reinventing new

The Poet as Artisan and the Instruments of Procreation 109

worlds. Beneath the majesty of these extreme anthropocentric views, however, the view of nature as medium and instrument—as well as nature's pliability through human instruments (sensory or otherwise)—is what guarantees the success of the entire project. Applicable in the most diverse contexts, the instrument's resiliency overcomes any possible tautology in the statement that it *is* nature, *produces* nature and is also required for *understanding* nature. The conversation among the travelers can be read as an elaboration of the same ideas articulated in nuce within the aphorisms on the instrument discussed at the beginning of the chapter. Just like the instrument which swung between the artist and the artwork, or which armed humans to accomplish creations of immense proportions, the concept of the instrument in *The Apprentices* redefines the threshold of man and nature in such a way as to complete the transition ongoing since the Renaissance from man/microcosm to world/macroanthropos and beyond: from a definition of man based on representation to one based on function.

The plea of the nature voices for mankind to learn to feel returns when the youngest and most passionate of the four travelers concludes the conversation:

> So wird auch keiner die Natur begreifen, der kein Naturorgan, kein innres naturerzeugendes und absonderndes Werkzeug hat, der nicht, wie von selbst, überall die Natur an allem erkennt und unterscheidet und mit angeborner Zeugungslust, und inniger mannigfaltiger Verwandtschaft mit allen Körpern, durch das Medium der Empfindung, sich mit allen Naturwesen vermischt, sich gleichsam in sie hineinfühlt. (1:105)

> No one will understand nature who has no nature-organ, no inner nature-producing and dividing instrument, who does not, as if automatically, recognize nature and distinguish nature everywhere and with inborn procreative desire, and inner multiple relation with all bodies, through the medium of feeling, mix himself with all natural beings, and "feel" himself at once into them.

Neither thought nor reason suffices for an understanding of nature. Through the human "nature organ" as "instrument" man can "feel" relations with all kinds of natural beings. Procreative desire, enacted through the medium of feeling, allows him to forge relations with the natural world so that he may copulate with any aspect of nature: procreation and intellectual understanding are indistinguishable from one another. The concept of "feeling" is not identical the inaccessible, pre-reflexive feeling of the "Fichte Studies" but a conjuring of that original state which can be used as an instrument of mediation to join with nature and contribute to its creation. It is an approximation which will allow man to overcome the division lamented by the nature voices. Within the topos of procreation, the youth unites those ideas which have been circulating through Hardenberg's aphoristic work since the "Fichte Studies" and which he will continue to develop after setting aside *The Apprentices* to begin work on *Heinrich von Ofterdingen*.

CRAFTSMEN OF NATURE

As if to caution his students against the blind acceptance of the positions articulated by the travelers which, in varying degrees, assume nature to be the instrument of man's procreative faculties, the teacher's monologue concludes the novel fragment with a reminder that human knowledge has limits, and nature remains a mystery. As an apostle of nature, his profession requires him to reveal the "true evangelia" of nature to those students who are her instrument: "whoever follows an innate longing for nature, who seeks everything in her, and is at the same time a sensitive instrument of her secret actions, will only recognize as his teacher and as the confidante of nature he who speaks of her with reverence and faith."[69] The final speech of the novel, far from contradicting the more radical views of a nature manipulated by mankind, complements the opinions which have come before by returning to the reciprocity of the instrument. Not only does man possess the adequate instruments for understanding nature (or instruments *of* nature), as the youth and the other travelers suggest, human production also takes part in nature's greater plan. And though he refers to his own teaching as evangelia, the teacher's final comments reflect a pragmatism conspicuously lacking in the winged conversation of the travelers. One need not be an artist to understand nature. Her chosen are many:

> In allen Ständen, unter jedem Alter und Geschlecht, in allen Zeitaltern und unter jedem Himmelsstriche hat es Menschen gegeben, die von der Natur zu ihren Lieblingen ausersehn und durch inneres Empfängnis beglückt waren. Oft schienen diese Menschen einfältiger und ungeschickter zu sein als Andere, und blieben ihr ganzes Leben hindurch in der Dunkelheit des großen Haufens. Es ist sogar als eine rechte Seltenheit zu achten, wenn man das wahre Naturverständnis bei großer Beredsamkeit, Klugheit, und einem prächtigen Betragen findet, da es gemeiniglich die einfachen Worte, den gerade Sinn, und ein schlichtes Wesen hervorbringt oder begleitet. In den Werkstätten der Handwerker und Künstler, und da, wo die Menschen in vielfältigem Umgang und Streit mit der Natur sind, als da ist beim Ackerbau, bei der Schifffahrt, bei der Viehzucht, bei den Erzgruben, und so bei vielen anderen Gewerben, scheint die Entwickelung dieses Sinns am leichtesten und öftersten statt zu finden. (1:108)

> In all classes, in every age group and race, in all epochs and under every portion of the sky there have been people who were chosen as nature's favorites and gifted with inner conception. Frequently these

people seemed to be simpler and less skilled than others and remained their entire life in the darkness of the great mass. It is even considered to be very seldom that one finds true understanding of nature in great eloquence, intelligence and a splendid conduct, since [such understanding] usually produces or accompanies simple words, straight thinking, and a homely being. In the workshops of craftsmen and artists, and there where people are in manifold congress and conflict with nature, such as there is in agriculture, seafaring, the raising of livestock, mining and so many other occupations, the development of this sense [for nature] seems to occur most easily and frequently.

These final sentences are not meant to be the "last word" on human relations to nature, given that Hardenberg's plans to complete the novel never came to fruition. Their defense of a sense for nature rooted in the practical life of the craftsman is nevertheless a striking complement to the travelers' claim that the poet has the greatest sense for nature. The teacher's words also return the reader full circle to the beginning of the novel by invoking the image of the unskilled apprentice who moves blindly along his life's path. The same apprentice also explained that some students leave the temple to pursue trades: with hindsight, it is possible to see that this choice need not be read as a turn away from nature.

CONCLUSION

This chapter on the role of Hardenberg's instrumental thinking in the topos of procreation was written under the banner of his call for man to be a "complete and total instrument of the self." This call pushes the functional definition of the individual as far as it can go, but also raises the question whether such a goal is either attainable or desirable. As several of the readings have shown, were man to become a total instrument, he would risk losing both his agency and his specificity—the concept of the human would no longer retain its meaning. Yet the instrument has also proven to be a valuable poetological tool for Hardenberg's reader. Particularly in *The Apprentices of Sais*, it provides a key for understanding how the different discourses which participate in the topos of procreation can be reconciled, and how man's active relation to nature is a fundamentally poetic process.

As the past two chapters have shown, the topos of procreation in Hardenberg's writing covers a vast terrain: from scientific descriptions of chemical and galvanic processes, to the problem of categorizing living organisms and even the genesis of philosophical reflection. Within these diverse contexts, narratives of procreation exist in reciprocal relation to the particulars of the field. They provide a progressive model for thinking about the "before" and "after" of physical and philosophical changes, but they are also shaped by their discursive environments. Hardenberg's narratives of procreation, and in particular their gender distinctions, are sensitive to scale and to the scientific or philosophical logic which they invoke. Yet there is also a constancy to Hardenberg's writing on procreation which allows the topos such free rein. A poetics of procreation which would codify the common elements of Hardenberg's procreative narratives needs to be mindful of the new, functional definition of the human individual which characterized Romantic anthropological thinking. For Hardenberg, procreation is inseparable from categorization of the individual in its dynamic relation to a greater whole. His aphorisms avoid placing the individual within a static hierarchy: we find it circumscribed within geometrical series, or postulated through acts of progressive categorization. One consequence of this thinking is the problematic status of progeny: the procreative narratives we have focused on tend to outline the process of leading up to conception in greater or lesser detail, while omitting the subsequent stage of birth. Often it is the case that the "act" of procreation is coupled by the incursion of temporality into descriptions otherwise lacking in temporal markers. One speculation is that the interruption of time in procreative narratives indirectly indexes the advent of life. This is an idea which will be addressed much more concretely in the fragments of Johann Wilhelm Ritter.

5 Johann Wilhelm Ritter and the Writing of Life

> Der Mensch ist eine Vorrede zu der Natur. Der Autor hat darin einen hübschen Begriff von letzterer gegeben; er ersucht daher den gütigen Leser, sie ja zuerst zu lesen, es werde eine kleine Erläuterung geben.[1]
> (Johann Wilhelm Ritter, *Fragmente*, n. 684)

> Man is a prologue to nature. The author has given therein a nice concept of the latter; thus he petitions the good reader, to read it first, it will provide a small explanation.

> Die Vorrede könnte Blitzableiter betitult werden.
> (Lichtenberg, *Sudelbücher*, in *Schriften und Briefe* 1:604)

> The prologue could be called a lightning rod.

INTRODUCTION

If a procreative thinker around 1800 is someone whose writing incorporates the language of organic generation, and who uses it to reflect upon creative processes, such as poetic production or a scientific program, then Johann Wilhelm Ritter can take his place alongside Goethe and Novalis. He was an apothecary by training, and by vocation a physicist. Like the other two authors discussed in this study, Ritter instrumentalizes the language of procreation to make connections between diverse branches of scientific inquiry, through investigations of magnetic and electrical phenomena and chemical processes. Ritter was also a brilliant experimentalist with a penchant for excess recorded with fascination by friends and detractors alike. Between his arrival in Jena as a student in 1796 and his induction into the Bavarian Academy of Sciences in December of 1804, he earned a reputation for scientific research which reached far beyond the borders of the university town. He developed close ties to the early Romantics, gained the admiration of Goethe, and was intimate enough with Herder to read the *Oldest Document of the Human Race* under the tutelage of the author.[2] In scientific circles Ritter established himself through early experiments in the developing fields of electricity, galvanism, and chemistry. He not only "discovered" the ultraviolet end of the spectrum, he also constructed the first dry cell battery and proved the connection between galvanism and chemical reactivity. Ritter also made acute observations on the effect of electricity on muscles, sensory organs, plants. He ruthlessly subjected even his own body to numerous experiments at high voltage—what Stuart Strickland characterizes as "Ritter's use of his own body as an instrument, a source of knowledge, and an emblem of his individuality."[3] Ritter's best-known scientific work is the 1798 treatise on galvanism, the *Proof that a Living Galvanism Accompanies the Animal Realm*.[4] The *Proof* attempts to mediate between Galvani's theory of an innate animal electricity and Volta's theory that electricity in organic matter emerges from the contact of different elements as it would in inorganic contexts.[5] It solidified his status as one of the foremost experimenters of the decade and, though his work was later overshadowed by the discoveries of Maxwell, Ohm and Faraday, it helped garner him a niche in the reference books of scientific history.[6]

Ritter's contemporaries lauded his experimental ingenuity even as they identified a certain tendency at odds with his empirical studies, a tendency which, for example, allows aesthetics and theology to enter into his discussions of scientific ideas. In his autobiography, the philosopher and scientist Henrich Steffens describes Ritter's arrival in Jena and the publication of the *Proof*. He recalls that the writing was a mixture of "shrewdness" and a "rough" style due to Ritter's lack of a formal scientific education, and adds the following caveat: "although the experiments were chosen shrewdly and supported each other reciprocally, there hovered over the apparent precision of the account a darkness which could by no means to be ignored."[7] Steffens diagnoses the murkiness in Ritter's prose as the result of a methodological "internal rupture" between the pursuit of empirically-based science and speculative thinking.[8] He details the repercussions for Ritter's social and academic status in Munich as a gradual descent whereby "[Ritter] lost himself in dreams which made his experiments uncertain, from which point he was never able to work himself out of the darkness."[9] Already Ritter's 1806 address to the Bavarian Academy of Sciences, which dared give physics "the name of an art, and a higher art than all the rest,"[10] raised eyebrows over its content as well as its style (by consensus: "confused").[11] With the advantage of hindsight, one can see that the tarnish upon Ritter's scientific work—whether described in terms of a darkness, a rupture or even a "second soul," in biographer Klaus Richter's more charitable phrasing[12]—may have unfairly alienated Ritter from the larger scientific community. The opacity of his language, or the perception thereof, obscured his tangible contributions to science. In this chapter and the next, I will show how Ritter's contributions to the discourse of procreation are to be found precisely within those aspects of his work labeled dark, speculative, or guilty of excess. The language and images of procreation both inform the so-called darkness in his work and act as a bridge to those areas of his research legitimated by the scientific community. Strickland and others have commented that the body is the emblem of Ritter's individuality in the sphere of experimentation. By extending this argument to include Ritter's poetic work, I show how the portrayal of his life connects to his scientific thinking. The prior chapter argued that one of Novalis' contributions to the discourse of procreation was through a poetics of instrumentality that defined the self and its interface with the world by drawing on the language of organic generation. Ritter constructs a 'new' life by encrypting biographical details and joining them with various aspects of production (i.e. of scientific ideas, texts, and children). He instrumentalizes the self in the creation of a text which, with reference to other concepts in Ritter's lexicon, has qualities of both a 'hieroglyph' and a 'monument.' To advance this argument, I focus in the following pages on Ritter's fragment project. The next chapter will then elaborate how procreation functions as a bridge to connect different areas of Ritter's scientific research.

THE FRAGMENT PROJECT

Despite the title's suggestion of a posthumous publication, the *Fragments from the Estate of a Young Physicist* appeared shortly prior to Ritter's death in 1810. The work contains a prologue that is an autobiography in the third-person (an "editor" narrates the life of a recently deceased "physicist"), followed by seven hundred fragments in two volumes. The fragments, extracted from Ritter's scientific papers and personal diaries,[13] range from excerpts of scientific protocols and suggestions for future experiments, to literary witticisms and broad historical speculations.[14] As described by the author, they possess "honesty, naiveté, and often a boldness which will grant them their own charm;" compared to the writing of Ritter's contemporaries, the aphorisms "occupy the median between those of Novalis and Lichtenberg."[15] In short, the project is a child of Ritter's "two souls," not just because the fragments run the gamut of his scientific and speculative thinking, but also due to the prologue, the peculiar autobiography of the scientist which precedes them. The fragment project fuses two seemingly distinct bodies of knowledge: a corpus of scientific research into natural phenomena, and a poetic construction of the self as scientist.

In a letter to his friend Hans Christian Ørsted from 1806, Ritter reveals his intentions behind the writing of the prologue. The life portrayed should not necessarily be an example for humankind in general, but for scientists: "It shall not merely become a *collection* of my scribblings; it will be a kind of literary self-biography, perhaps interesting to everyone who wants to and must create of himself a physicist and experimentalist."[16] Dorinda Outram has observed that eighteenth- and nineteenth-century biographies and autobiographies of scientists' lives tend to describe different moments in the individual history. Whereas eighteenth-century autobiographies focus on vocational choices within a cultural context, she argues that later ones highlight the actual discoveries.[17] Even a superficial glance at Ritter's autobiography reveals that neither of these two categories is a good fit. On the one hand, Ritter is not overly concerned with factual accuracy. The editor who narrates the prologue gives out strategic misinformation such that biographical data (birthdays and deathdays) are falsified and deliberately exchanged with other events, such as key moments in the act of writing. On the other hand, the publication of the autobiography in tandem with the fragments, along with the prologue's interest in describing the methods of the scientist (though *not* his theory of physical phenomena, or experiments in the usual sense), need to be taken into consideration as well. Over the course of the prologue, the two 'bodies' of knowledge are thematized as two competing structures emerge. The first is 'ontological' in the sense that it relates to a narrative account of the physicist's existence. The second is 'epistemological' insofar as it has to do with the particular ways the prologue deals with the acquisition of knowledge. Both are connected to the activities of writing and scientific research, and both invoke the topos of procreation. To understand the enigma of Ritter's life as portrayed in the prologue is to understand the procreative dimensions of his text.

One could certainly argue that the "decoding" process is consistent with the autobiographical genre. The prologue plays with differences in identity between autobiographer and scientist, internalizing the same porous boundary between the "life" and "work" of the scientist that exists between the prologue and the fragments. It conforms to what is called "third person autobiography" or "autodiegetic narration in the third person," to speak with Lejeune and Genette.[18] Even if this kind of autobiography is a minority category in the genre, it serves an important function, reminding us that every act of narrative imposes a difference between the editor and narrated subject. According to Lejeune: "The figures of the third person furnish a range of solutions where it is the distanciation which is foregrounded, but always to express an articulation (a tension) between identity and difference."[19] We are in the realm of what Lejeune calls "fictive fictions:" "[t]he general system remains that of autobiography; it is only at the level of one of the instances of *récit*, the personage of the editor, that is grafted a kind of game: the autobiography tries to imagine to itself what would happen if it were *an other* who told its story or traced its portrait."[20] In addition to the game of writing oneself, i.e., the exercise of imagining oneself as other, there is a second one played by the reader. This is the game of decoding. According to Starobinski, in both first- and third-person autobiography, any infidelities to historical truth on the part of the editor, whether intentional or not, offer "a system of revealing indices, of symptomatic traits. . .No matter how doubtful the facts related, the text will *at least present an 'authentic' image of the man who 'held the pen.'*"[21] The same questions apply to the prologue: *who* exactly is the man holding the pen, upon what premises does he construct the identity of the physicist, and how do these personae connect to the life of Johann Wilhelm Ritter?

The usefulness of Ritter's prologue does not only lie in the fact that it offers the life of the scientist to an interested public as a model of imitation. It also suggests that the activity of reading, and the implied decoding of calculated distortions in his life-story, can contribute to the self-formation of the scientist ("those who want to *create of themselves* physicists and experimentalists"). In this context, the epigraph Ritter chooses for the fragment collection is programmatic. It acts as an umbrella to encompass the themes of life-writing, interpretation, and the acquisition of knowledge. It also alerts the reader to the fact that the following text imposes a hermeneutic challenge. To convey this message, Ritter chose a passage from the first Corinthian letter of Paul (the translation has been tailored to capture the idiom of Luther's German):

> Als ich ein Kind war, da redete ich wie ein Kind, und war klug wie ein Kind, und hatte kindische Anschläge: als ich aber ein Mann wurde, tat ich ab, was kindlich war. Wir sehen jetzt durch einen Spiegel ein dunkles Bild; dann aber von Angesicht zu Angesicht. Jetzt erkenne ich stückweise; dann aber werde ich erkennen, wie ich erkannt bin. Nun aber bleiben Glaube, Hoffnung, Liebe, diese drei; aber die Liebe ist die größte unter ihnen. (1 Corinthians 13, v. 11–13)

> When I was a child, I spoke as a child, and was clever like a child and had childish ideas: however when I became a man I put away what was childish. We see now a dark image through a mirror, but then [we will see] face to face. Now I recognize in part, but then I will recognize just as I am known. Still however remain faith, hope, and love—these three. But love is the greatest among them.

This passage was of particular significance in the eighteenth century, in part as a statement on the limits of human knowledge, as Andreas Herz has shown with regard to Herder.[22] When one considers that there is no Biblical tradition for reading Paul's first letter to the Corinthians within an autobiographical framework, however, the choice of epigraphs appears unorthodox.[23] Ritter's decision to place it at the beginning of a project nominally devoted both to autobiographical exposition and the accumulation of knowledge is nevertheless strangely fitting. The passage he cites from the epistle offers a capsulized autobiographical statement, and it also resonates with the epistemological concerns of a scientist who is deeply pious. Paul distinguishes between three stages of life differentiated by what one knows: the childish knowledge of the early years, the ignorance and partial understanding of the adult, and a futuristic condition of the total knowing which he anticipates upon coming face to face with God. Unlike the *Confessions* of Augustine, where the 'past self' is sinful and the 'present self' is saved, Paul refers to the stages of his life as epistemic states whose content, be it secular or esoteric knowledge, remains unspecified. Ritter's project occupies Paul's middle ground; the narrated time of the prologue begins and ends in adulthood and the scientist's pursuit of knowledge. This is the time of "seeing a dark image through a mirror," which may also be translated as a "riddle," a "dark saying" or "a truth clothed in the language of imagery."[24] The epigraph therefore articulates an enigma that functions both as a reflection on the title and on the following text.[25] In connection with the title, it allows us to read Ritter's fragments as the embodiment of the partial knowledge Paul describes, the dark sayings through which, indirectly, one may be permitted to approach the truth. In connection with the prologue and beyond, the epigraph also reminds us that the time of "partial knowledge" depicted in the prologue and embodied by the fragments is one of self-study, or gazing into a mirror at a distorted reflection. In the latter case, coming face to face with God so that one may know fully "just as one is known" has a secular counterpart in the fictional encounter staged between the doubled self (i.e., the "editor" and the "physicist") of the prologue. The epigraph therefore refers both to the premises of the autobiographical project (that it is a distorted and enigmatic representation of the self) and the challenge of deciphering (that Ritter is not in the business of "direct" truths but more concerned with the process of acquiring knowledge).

READING AND DECODING

From Ritter's prologue, readers can gain insight into the methods of the scientist and acquire a greater understanding of the organic relationship that exists between the story of his life and the evidence of his work. The distinction between the autobiography and the fragments is tenuous. One fragment in particular (also quoted as the first epigraph to this chapter) serves as a monition that the problem of representing life is also part of the scientific project. Towards the end of Ritter's fragment collection, the reader encounters the following: "Man is a prologue [*Vorrede*] to nature. The author has given therein a nice concept of the latter; thus he petitions the good reader to read it first, that it provide a small explanation" (684). The fragment alludes to the familiar topos of the 'book of nature' and suggests that 'man' (or Ritter's self-portrayal) is that book.[26] Hans Blumenberg finds in this claim a distinction between Novalis, for whom "reflection takes the path through nature," and Ritter, who takes the opposite path by finding "the reflection of the world totality [*Weltgesamtheit*] accessible through self experience."[27] Although, as Blumenberg suggests, the fragment reflects Ritter's general understanding of the self in relation to nature, its joint invocation of prologue, author and reader is unique. The fragment raises the question whether the reader of nature is also the reader of Ritter's book, an ambiguity derived in part from the non-specified "therein," which may either refer to the first sentence of the fragment, or to the prologue.

The question arises, how far Ritter is willing to take his metaphor of 'man as prologue,' and whether as a programmatic statement it can really do justice to the project as a whole. By flirting with a circular logic—do the fragments contain the key to the prologue or is it the other way around?—the aphorism also challenges us to reconsider its opening proposition. The strange claim that man somehow precedes nature, in which he also participates, holds true as long as we remain within the textual sphere of the fragment project and remember that Ritter writes himself as the prologue to his own account of the natural world.

Just as the ideal reader of the prologue is (like Ritter) largely an autodidact who instructs himself through the act of reading, the identity of the physicist is shaped by what he reads. The editor's claim that *"completely on his own*, our friend had formed himself to that which he to some degree was and became" only holds true in the sense that there is no institutional presence in the prologue—the physicist seems to exist in a sphere detached from the structure of a university system, tutored in part by friends but to a large degree by texts in the "school of the head" and "school of the heart."[28] Part of his education is based upon an enthusiastic reading of *Wilhelm Meister's Apprenticeship Years* and *Don Quixote* (where the author also notoriously stages his own intervention in the fictional life of his character), but what draws him to these books is beyond his capacity for reflection. He claims that unerring instinct rather than intention permits him to "live" the book he is reading:

> Was ihm überbleibe, wenn er so gelesen und fertig sey, würde ihm abermals schwer zu bestimmen seyn; es wäre etwas ins Gemüth und Leben selbst Eingegangenes und mit ihm bereits Verwobenes; seine Gegenwart und Wirkung spüre er wohl, aber er habe sich gewöhnlich wieder um den besten Theil davon gebracht, wenn er es hinterher zu einer strengern Analyse mit Gewalt hervorgerissen habe. (Prologue, xxvii)

> What remains for him, when he has read it and is finished, would however be difficult for him to determine; it would be something which has penetrated his mind and life and already woven itself into him; he would certainly be able to sense its presence and effect on him, but he would have robbed himself of the best part if afterwards he had with violence subjected it to a strict analysis.

The act of reading described here—akin to what Aleida Assman calls "wild reading"[29]—would remain instinctual, devoid of reflection, and decidedly un-Romantic were it not for the fact that the prologue splits the two activities of reading and reflection chronologically between the physicist and the editor (and reader). The belated moment of reflection imparts a logic onto the first to show that the physicist's intuition has a purpose, and also incorporates the reading into the life (while at the same time reflecting on the activity of this belated reflection). It falls upon the editor to create a "theory of life" and impart a logic to the physicist's activities even when, as the editor has occasion to admit, he is infected by the behavior of the physicist (who is, in turn, infected by reading): "how far I digress: almost as far as our friend when he learned so quickly how to read *Don Quixote*."[30]

Romanticism understands reading as an active "operation" and the reader as an "expanded author" (Novalis).[31] Even though Ritter thought his fragment project might be useful for the education of scientists, however, his readers will search in vain for the names of Volta, Galvani or any scientist (barring Goethe and Novalis) in the prologue. Instead, the physicist finds inspiration in unexpected places, such as "the *Prometheus* of *Aeschylus*, his *Eumenides*, *Shak[e]speare's Midsummer Night's Dream*."[32] In these he learns "an uncommon amount" directly applicable to his pursuit of science, even though "common physicists" might find such an idea humorous.[33] Whereas the actual selection process of reading material remains opaque (if well in keeping with mainstream Romantic literary taste), the process of reading iself is "polarized" and appears to follow the laws of magnetism. The self is the embodiment of a natural law: The physicist is pulled now towards one text, now towards the other, caught in oscillation between two poles with alternating values which, under certain circumstances, also change their 'charge.' This is the case with *Don Quixote* and *Wilhelm Meister*:

> Dann hören beynahe *beyde* jene Bücher auf, das vorige Interesse zu haben, oder, und eher, sie *wechselten* ordentlich die Rollen, und *Meister's Lehrjahre* würden es, die einem höchst komisch und drollig vorkommen könnten, während einem dagegen aus dem *Don Quixote* überall der dumpfste, finsterste, schneidenste Ernst entgegenkäme. (Prologue, xxvi)

> Then *both* those books would almost cease to have the previous interest, or, more likely, they would fairly *exchange* their roles, and *Meister's Apprenticeship Years* would become the one which could appear highly comical and droll, while from *Don Quixote* one would encounter everywhere the most dull, dark, biting seriousness.

There are clear parallels between the act of reading and the methods of both the physicist and the editor. The editor imposes order on the intuitive, unconscious method of the physicist and uses the opportunity to comment upon his own strategies of writing and organization of the physicist's fragments. At the same time, he will acknowledge a genetic connection between his work and the physicist's. If the editor is to be believed, the "method" of the physicist is one of unreflected spontaneity, and the fragments emerge as if they were natural and contingent products of nature: "In most cases they came to the paper through mere thinking" and, once drafted, were not subject to any revision.[34] The editor claims that the fragments were written in "the most varied sequence" as the physicist was inspired to "contemplate the entirety of creation."[35] The fragments capture the experience of perception, "just as things occurred to him, or as the objects of nature, lying amongst themselves, became noticeable to him in a human fashion."[36] In short, the fragments accumulate according to their own organic law, according to the "self-development" of the physicist's acquired experience [*Erfahrungsbesitz*].[37] The editor calls our attention to similarities between the writing and editing of the fragment collection, a convergence that should come as no surprise. He also acknowledges his indebtedness to the physicist: "I was familiar with his entire way of thinking, am myself to a certain degree only an offshoot of him and believe myself here and there in the position of continuing his work in a worthy fashion."[38] As much as the editor allows the physicist's spontaneity and tolerance for unclarity to permeate his own style, he also claims the advantage of being able to reflect upon the distinction between order and confusion at will. He retains those fragments "too difficult to understand" (because he cannot raise himself to the intellectual level of the author and they contain an obscure vocabulary[39]) and discards those which are too simple.[40] Working through a staggering volume of material—he claims that the published fragments are a fifteenth or twentieth of the original number—the editor disavows having followed any rigorous methodology. His selection process is "not very strict" and, in some cases, just as random as the writing process, given that he admits to including some fragments "without knowing why."[41] The division of the fragments into fifteen sections is equally arbitrary. Even if the editor claims that his motivation is based on principles of similarity and relation, he admits candidly that the distinguishing criterion is "by no means clear."[42] Appropriating a strategy reminiscent of Julius' "right to a charming confusion" in Friedrich Schlegel's novel *Lucinde* (1799),[43] the editor integrates a lack of clarity as a structural component of the collection. Although the reader may find some "relations of contiguity completely incomprehensible" he "does not lose too much thereby."[44] The editor chooses to disregard the categorical distinctions which a reader can find between the different sections—with their individual emphases on magnetism, chemical combustion, galvanic reactions, historical claims, etc.[45] Rather than separating fragments on the basis of scientific disciplines, he suggests a taxonomy which, if scrutinized closely, approaches a Borgesian absurdity: "Several fragments for example can certainly only be understood when one is smitten, others when one loves, others through the greatest, simplest contemplation of nature, and still others when one philosophizes even as one is speaking etc."[46]

It should be apparent by now that the editor is less concerned with scientific data than with the process of organization itself. The same can be said of the physicist's modus operandi. He does not subject his fragments to the exercise of judgment, preferring to leave them imperfect. They are "Sunday children" who are limited but "human" products in their own right.⁴⁷ Numbering among their "uncommonly human" qualities are contradiction, cloudy ideas which become clearer in the course of reading them, false assumptions which self-destruct within the individual fragment, and even "badness."⁴⁸ The exercise of thinking, the accidental "method of preservation" regarding these thoughts is what matters most, because in their progress one can observe the workings of a natural law. It is "the most human of all" to have a false assumption which reverses itself through contemplation such that "the entire *contrary part* from the beginning is the result of the end."⁴⁹ This is not because of the uniqueness of our psychological make-up but because there is a "general law of nature" behind this process which governs everything: "even in the case of electrical and magnetic excitation the process ends with the exact opposite of that with which it began; perhaps, however, one allows it to occur *precisely* for that reason—because a *general* law of nature must therefore be behind it."⁵⁰ Within this "law of nature" lies one of the keys to decoding the project. We have already seen evidence of it in the oscillations of the physicist between *Wilhelm Meister* and *Don Quixote*. In the context of scientific method, the editor now suggests that the same law governs both the thought process of the scientist and the material which he studies. Applied here, the law teaches us two things: that after deception the truth is revealed, and that the process of revelation is just as important as what is exposed at the end. A reader who connects these elements of Ritter's text (the epigraph, the activity of the physicist and editor) which point to the same message (obfuscation and error is a necessary precondition on the way to knowledge) will understand that he or she is implicit in this process as well.

THE ENIGMA OF LIFE

To comprehend that the general trend of the prologue is first to distort and then to begin revealing the truth still does not suffice to decode the greater enigma of the text, namely, how and why information about the life of the physicist and his personal relations is falsified. The prologue begins in the first-person voice of the editor, who takes pains to distinguish himself from the author of the fragments:⁵¹

> Indem ich dem Publikum die gegenwärtige Sammlung von "*Fragmenten aus dem Nachlaß eines jungen Physikers*" übergebe, übe ich eine Pflicht, die bestimmt war, meine erste dieser Art zu seyn. Der Verfasser derselben war, nahe seit 1796 schon, enger und vertrautester Freund meines Wissens, wie meines Lebens*); ich verdanke dem fast ununterbrochenen Umgange mit ihm unendlich viel—und sollte man die in diesen Fragmenten vorkommenden Gedanken und Ideen mit meinen eigenen Arbeiten vergleichen wollen, so wird man finden, daß viele ganz allein durch Ihn begründet wurden, und zu den meisten der

erste Gedanke von Ihm mir zugekommen seyn mußte. Aber ich hatte die vollkommenste Erlaubniß zu einem solchen Gebrauche seiner Mittheilungen an mich. (Prologue, i–ii)

By extending to the public the present collection of *"Fragments from the Estate of a Young Physicist"* I perform a duty which was destined to be the first of its kind for me. Their author was, almost since 1796 already, the close and most intimate friend of my knowledge, as of my life*); I owe the nearly uninterrupted accompaniment with him infinitely much—and should one wish to compare the thoughts and ideas which appear in these fragments with my own work, one will find that many were established by Him alone, and for most of them, the first thought must have come to me from Him. But I had complete permission for such a use of his communications with me.

The editor's hints may leave little to the imagination that he and the author of the fragments are one and the same person, but as he provides misinformation about the physicist's life and their relationship, he creates a radically new genealogy of biological and textual events. We learn, for example, that the two men have been intimates with each other's personal and professional life from 1796 (the year of Ritter's arrival in Jena) until the untimely "death" of the author that occasions the writing of the prologue and the publication of the fragments. To give further proof of the editor's place in the author's family circle, the asterisk—"*)"—directs the reader to a footnote at the bottom of the page:

*) Der Tag, wo ich ihn eigentlich erst *völlig* kennen lernte, war der 26ste October 1797. Wir feyerten an ihm den Geburtstag seiner *Mutter*—und die ältesten Fragmente dieser Sammlung sind von *jenem* Tage. (Prologue, i [note])[52]

*) The day where I actually first came to know him *completely* was the 26th of October, 1797. We celebrated on that day the birthday of his *mother*—and the oldest fragments of this collection are from *that* day.

The strange juxtaposition of fact and fiction in the prologue coalesces around two key dates. October 26th, 1797, is the birthday of Johann Wilhelm Ritter's mother. As Ritter describes it in a letter to Gotthilf Schubert, it is his own "day of resurrection" (*Auferstehungstag*).[53] The latter remark is less cryptic in light of the footnote in the prologue explaining that the first fragments were also drafted on that day. The "resurrection" of the physicist, the conceit of life after death, aligns squarely with the writing of the fragments. It also marks an important day in the relationship of the editor and the physicist, a day when they came to "know each other *completely*." Although their roles remain artificially divided through the contrivance of the narrative, they are "face-to-face," so to speak, which anticipates the temporal and epistemic senses Paul describes in the future state of complete knowing and being known. The editor identifies himself as both friend and protector of the physicist: shielding him from bad publicity, encouraging his writing, and above all respecting his wish for anonymity: "Perhaps I especially understood him in this regard; he would rather have had no name at all; and thus I appropriately will not name him, even there where he can no longer scold me."[54]

The friendship between the editor and the physicist continues through the physicist's death, at which point the editor assumes control over the latter's estate: "Already earlier our friend. . .had made me the erstwhile heir of all his journals and other papers, until finally the seventh of May, 1809, earlier than we ever would have believed, transformed the lighthearted joke into dark, bitter seriousness."[55] The prologue suggests that May 7th is the death date of the physicist (and, by implication, Ritter himself, permitting the illusion of a posthumous publication). Just as the first fragments are written on the birthday of his mother, marking the birth of the project, however, it is again the mother who symbolically brings the project to a close. In fact, the purported death of the author of the fragments coincides with the death of Ritter's own mother, who died on May 7th, 1809, at the age of fifty-six. A letter to Gotthilf Schubert written just a month later memorializes the day as auspicious:

> Viel Wunderbares begegnete mir am Tage ihres Todes, ohne daß ich an ihm, ihren Tod bestimmt geahnet hätte [. . .] Es geht mir viel Segen aus ihrem Tode hervor. Gerade mit einer Revision meines ganzen eigentlichen Lebens für neue Resultate beschäftigt, führte er mich tiefer und gründlicher in dasselbe zurück. (Rehm, *Briefe eines romantischen Physikers*, 55–56)

> Many strange things happened to me on the day of her death, without my having a precise intimation of it, her death [. . .] Many blessings are coming to me from her death. Currently occupied with a revision of my entire actual life for new results, [her death] led me more deeply and thoroughly back into it.

Ritter's remark that the death of his mother led to a deeper contemplation of life holds true within the prologue as well—the editor of the fragment collection takes the event of his friend's death as incitement to begin writing the biographical prologue. Herein lies one of the prologue's most important contributions to the discourse of procreation: the splicing of historical and poetic dates, and the biological lives of mother and son, defines the text as a procreative project. Under the pen of Ritter, the life of the physicist emerges as a hybrid of nature and writing. The choice of biological dates makes it a natural product; the fiction of third person makes it a poetic product.

ENCODED FRIENDSHIP

If the editor's biographical description of the physicist is puzzling, the portrayal of his friendships is hardly less so—they too are implicated in the construction of the self. We know from Ritter's correspondence and other documentation that he was intimate with, among others, the Danish scientist Hans Christian Ørsted, Adolf Ferdinand Gehlen (to whom Ritter left his estate) and Gotthilf Schubert, who took care of Ritter's wife and children after he died. That the only two friends to be mentioned by name in the prologue are Novalis and Herder reinforces the impression that Ritter's goal is not to characterize an epoch of his life in faithful detail, but rather to refer to those events with particular value for an understanding of his self and the project of writing. When the editor interprets the significance of the two friendships for the physicist, he understands them to be so integral to a formation as scientist and human being as to suggest a genealogical relation. Novalis becomes an extension of the self projected into the enigmatic future. Herder, who is for the physicist "like a father," also has a conspicuous part to play in a text indebted to the life and death of the mother, where the father is conspicuously absent.[56]

In the case of Novalis, the attraction is based upon the perception of similarity. During their first encounter—when Novalis pays an unexpected visit to the physicist's apartment—the editor records that they "understood each other at first sight: for [Novalis] there was not the slightest strangeness in their meeting; for the [physicist] it was virtually as if he could for once speak *aloud with himself.*"[57] This moment of near-perfect understanding, of speaking to oneself, invokes the motif of specularity in the epigraph of the fragment project and also suggests that the pursuit of self-knowledge is one aspect of the friendship. There is even stronger evidence for connecting the friendship to the themes of the epigraph, however: the editor goes so far as to graft Novalis' identity onto the physicist, who has until that point not been named at all. After describing Novalis' death and the physicist's mourning, the editor identifies him with the letter 'N': "In order to remain completely his own person, our N. fled from the place which had in many ways become dear to him through that time, and I accompanied him."[58]

From that point onward, through the remainder of the prologue, the editor refers to the physicist with the initial "N" as if to superimpose something of the deceased Novalis onto his continuing existence. As mentioned in Chapter 3, the name "Novalis" has its own intricate history. Chosen by Friedrich von Hardenberg from an ancestral registry, but used only in the publication of his poetic works, "Novalis" already doubles as a genealogical name and a literary nom de plume (and as discussed in the prior chapter, the name also connects to the discourse on tools and instruments). These connotations have further repercussions for the identity of the physicist: in the place of a proper name, he now bears an ambivalent symbol. The 'N' transcends the divide between life and art, as it did for Novalis, and it bridges the realms of the living and the dead. With reference to the epigraph, it functions between the present moment of imperfection and the future time of total knowledge. Read alongside the falsified birthdates and deathdates that comprise the life of the physicist, the 'N' adds one more piece to the puzzle that Ritter is creating of his life.

Whereas the physicist's friendship with Novalis begins within the private domestic sphere, his relationship with Herder thrives outdoors. On nature walks the physicist learns from him "what nature, man within it, and the actual physics are, and how the latter is immediately the ultimate religion."[59] These nature walks are informed by a reading of Herder's *Oldest Document of the Human Race* (1774–1776). According to the editor, the physicist "enjoyed the distinctive advantage of having the author himself as commentator for those passages which were more difficult for him to understand."[60] The form the commentary takes, however, is far from conventional:

> Gelesen hatte er in dieser Zeit wenig, aber viel: das Hauptwerk in derselben war ihm die *älteste Urkunde des Menschengeschlechts*,—wobey er den ausnehmenden Vortheil genoß, den Verfasser selbst zum Commen-tator derjenigen Stellen zu haben, die ihm schwerer zu verstehen waren. Dieser Selbst wurde hierdurch wieder ganz in jene Zeit, wo [die Stellen] Ihm entstanden, und die Er immer als eine vorzüglich seelige in Seinem Leben prieß, zurückversetzt, und jede Mühe wäre vergebens, die Feuerhimmel der Vorwelt, die dann sich ihm, und wer ihn sah und hörte, aufthaten, zu schildern. Er selbst beschrieb und schilderte nicht; Er *führte* blos zur Stätte *hin*, und *zeigte*; es *auszusprechen*, vermochte er nicht und unternahm es auch nicht. Aber *Er Selbst* in diesem Augenblicke, Sein ganzes Wesen, Sein Auge, Angesicht und Seyn, wurde zur lebendigen Hieroglyphe des Worts, für welches die Zunge das zureichende Organ nicht mehr war.
>
> So mußte man *Herder* sprechen sehen, um Ihn überhaupt zu hören und zu verstehen; *so* mußte man Ihn *gehört*—und *schweigen gesehen*—habe, um sagen zu können, man *lese* ihn. (Prologue, xxxvi–xxxvii)

[Herder] was once again completely transported back into that time where [the passages (*Stellen*)] were written, and which he always prized as an exquisitely blessed one in his life, and every effort to portray the empyrical heaven of the primitive world which revealed itself to him and to whomever witnessed and listened to him would be in vain. He himself did not describe and portray; he merely *led* to the place [*Stätte*] and *pointed*; he was not able, nor did he try, to *pronounce* it. But in this moment he himself—his entire being, his eye, his countenance and existence—became the living hieroglyph of the word for which the tongue was no longer the sufficient organ.

Thus one had to see *Herder* speak in order to even listen and understand him; *thus* one had to have *heard* him—and *seen him be silent*—in order to say, one were reading him.

Johann Wilhelm Ritter and the Writing of Life   127

In the description of Herder, the prologue stages another "face-to-face" encounter which, compared, to the physicist's relationship to Novalis, defines an epistemological difference between the two friendships. Between Ritter and Novalis, the act of encountering the other person "face-to-face" reveals a fundamental similarity between the two described as a moment of self-discovery. Expressed in Herder's countenance and his entire existence, the physicist observes a different kind of knowledge inscribed as a hieroglyph. As living hieroglyph, Herder is a text to be read—a medium for the acquisition of knowledge. The knowledge in question comprises both the natural world (nature, man, and physics) and human history, a knowledge of the "empyrical heaven of the primitive world" that informs Herder's *Oldest Document*.

The concept of the 'hieroglyph' has a special place in Ritter's lexicon, as it does in the writing of Novalis and Herder. It is an essential component of the prologue's textual poetics, but needs to be understood in its historical context. The history of the hieroglyph is not an easy one to map out, because its original function in the language of the ancient Egyptians was long obscured by a series of misinterpretations leading through Jean-François Champollion's deciperhing of hieroglyphs in 1822 (and even beyond[61]). Eighteenth-century language theories linked the hieroglyph to the idea of a universal language. In this view, hieroglyphs could transcend linguistic and cultural divides. They were also connected to "systems of communication with metaphoric or allegorical images."[62] In his reading of the *Oldest Document*, Ritter encounters what Herder calls a "really authentic old hieroglyph" contained in first seven days of creation in *Genesis*.[63] According to Herder, the hieroglyph in *Genesis* is not an arbitrary metaphorical image (he insists it has nothing to do with the "dreams" and "hypotheses" of Kircher and Warburton), but can provide an actual foundation for all branches of human thought.[64] It is nothing less than a "primal image [. . .] according to which gradually the entire script and symbolism of humans thus crafted so many inventions, arts and sciences."[65] Herder bases his discussion of the hieroglyph on an interpretation of the Egyptian God Theut as founder of the arts and sciences. Herder "reads" Theut in the hieroglyph through the first letter of his name (which Herder connects to the Greek letter 'theta' or a symbol comprised of a circle with a line or cross in the middle) and makes a case for understanding Theut as monument, writing, and hieroglyph all at once.[66] Herder also claims that the discovery of the hieroglyph will be "a new gateway of antiquity, of the most distant sanctums."[67] Ritter's description of Herder in the prologue draws upon this understanding of the hieroglyph and elevates Herder to a status whereby he is the embodiment of his text. Herder—as hieroglyph—is that gateway between the present and the past: both the historical past, when the text was written, and the more distant past of the "empyrical heaven" and the "primitive world."[68] It is the task of the physicist to read Herder, understand the *Oldest Document*, and gain knowledge of this theologically-inflected human history. The 'N' of

Novalis coorresponds to the hieroglyph to Herder—an association which the prologue encourages us to make[69]—and together they act as indices of the past and the future.

Ritter's understanding of the hieroglyph reaches well beyond his reading of the *Oldest Document*, however, with consequences that are relevant both for his self-portrayal in the prologue as well as his scientific study of acoustical and electrical phenomena. In this regard, Bernhard Siegert has drawn attention to the fact that the hieroglyph in Ritter's work spans two different epistemes. The first relates to the hieroglyphs participation in a universal language. In this tradition, the hieroglyph acts as metaphor "for the analytical symbols of a conceptual writing" and for a word understood as "an analytical forumla of the concept which it characterizes, so that every word of a universal language would at once define itself in the moment of being spoken."[70] This interpretation of the hieroglyph relies upon a concept of the sign whose signifier produces a distinct signified.[71] Siegert observes that Ritter stands with one foot in this tradition, to which Herder also belongs, but that his reception of Chladni's sound figures and Lichtenberg's electrical figures leads him in a very new direction. The "sound figures," for example, are patterns of acoustic vibrations captured in sand or some other substance. Both Ritter and Novalis understood these figures to be letters in a 'natural' language, and they incorporate the 'writing' of these figures into their concepts of the hieroglyph. As natural product, the hieroglyph still relates to universal language, but according to Siegert it manifests a different relationship between writing and word:

> Bei Ritter steht der mit explizitem Hinweis auf Herder verwendete Begriff der Hieroglyphe noch immer im Kontext einer Universalsprache (einer 'allgemeinen Sprache') und bezeichnet noch immer—als Klangfigur—eine Schrift, die vom Wort selbst unmittelbar geschrieben wird. Nur daß diese Schrift keine Selbstanalyse des Wortes im porphyrianischen System von Gattung, Differenz und Spezies leistet, sondern auf sich selbst als analoges Signal rekurriert.[72]

> Ritter's use of the concept of the hieroglyph still remains, with explicit reference to Herder, in the context of a universal language (a 'general langauge') and still indicates—as tone figure—a writing which is immediately written by the word itself. Only that this writing does not perform any self-analysis of the word in the porphyrian system of genus, difference and species, but refers back to itself as analog signal.

In terms of a new understanding of the sign, the distance between signifier and signified has collapsed. The signifier no longer 'produces' a separate meaning. Instead, meaning is recursively 'written in' to the act of writing. Ritter claims that "word and writing are just one in their origin, and neither is posible without the other."[73] He makes this point both in the fragments and the appendix. In the prologue, one finds traces of this new understanding of the hieroglyph in Ritter's portrayal of Herder, whose connection to the natural world is so strong as to leave an imprint on his countenance and being and who therefore has to be seen (or heard) in order for his texts to be read. The more radical consequences, however, are to be drawn from Ritter's portrayal of himself.[74] Bettine Menke has also described the peculiar phenomenality to the 'hieroglyphs' Ritter observes in the acoustic and electrical figures. In her reading, the acoustical (or graphic) trace, what Ritter calls 'writing,' has the structure of an "echo": a "repetition" "that first produces what it returns" (die erst erzeugt, was sie wiedergibt).[75] The history of the phenomenon's emergence is collapsed within the moment of its production. Like the hieroglyph of the acoustical figures, the portrayal of the physicist in the prologue also emerges as a radically singular and self-contained entity whose meaning is produced through, and confined to, the act of writing. The affinities between the prologue and the hieroglyphic 'nature writing' do not reduce the prologue to a poetic 'example,' as much as they affirm the genetic connection between Ritter's scientific and poetic endeavors. The remainder of the chapter will explore this affinity further by comparing the methods of scientist, editor, and reader under the rubric of another kind of construction and inscription: the edification of the 'monument.'

RITTER'S SPATIAL TURN: CONSTRUCTING THE MONUMENT

The physicist's method joins procreative and autobiographical elements through metaphors of space, direct thematic references, and a reflection on the generation of order. He takes care to emphasize to the reader that none of the fragments were written for publication, and that the reader is being granted a special glimpse into an intimate space: "[w]ith these fragments the reader therefore finds himself for all intents and purposes drawn into the *very secret workshop of the physicist*,—and can see things which have taken place there that are uncommonly human."[76] The "secret workshop" has a long tradition in hermetic literature; it also functions as a 'procreative' space of mystery and hidden labor.[77] The editor's comparison between reading the fragments and being inducted into the secret practices of the physicist both emphasizes the procreative dimension and signals a broader shift in his strategy of narration. His focus on method—the theory informing scientific practice—interrupts the chronological narrative of events in the physicist's life, which effectively suspends the sequential ordering of past, present, and future. The virtual expansion of space through the removal of temporal sequencing corresponds to Ritter's discussion of procreation in the fragments, where the moment of copulation is understood as a moment of indifferentiation between male and female, an exclusion of time.[78]

The secret workshop corelates to the construction of an analogous space in the editor's own project. Part of the task bequeathed to him by the physicist is to "collect the *Disjecti membra Poëtae*,"[79] "order them according to that basic organic law which no book teaches yet" and "build them into *a Temple with the God inside*."[80] The editor leaves no doubt that this ediface is the book itself: "that day demands its own monument (*Denkmal*) and it is enough for me to know that I have laid it in place for him with this book, whatever the opinion of others about it might be."[81] The task of the editor—at once procreative and palingenetic—is to resurrect the physicist, to collect his *disiecti membra* or the scattered fragments of his writing, and to order them into a "body" of work for publication.[82] Because of the passage's insistence on moving from the transitory to the permanent—from the "body" to the "monument"—we can also think of the editor's work in terms of the difference between "documents" and "monuments." Aleida Assman (with reference to Foucault[83]) describes the difference as follows: "Document we call a sign that is constituted as such from an observer standing on the outside, monument on the other hand a sign, which is related directly to an addressee."[84]

As "documents" within the "monument" of the book, the fragment project connects to a broader theme of architecture in Ritter's writing. In *Physics as Art* he distinguishes architecture from other arts because (like music but unlike painting) it "internalizes" the artist as hieroglyph:

> So sieht man in der *Baukunst* höchster Periode nur des Menschen eiliges Bemühen, die *Kraftgewalt* seines ersten Geschlechts durch Häufung ungeheurer Massen des Dauerhaftesten auf Erden, für alle folgende Zeit der Vergessenheit zu entreißen, und noch erscheint ihr Ordner selbst an ihnen, nur im als Hieroglyphe veräußerten Ebenmaaße seiner eigenen Gestaltung. (Ritter, *Physik als Kunst*, 57–58)

> Thus one sees in the *architecture* of the greatest period only man's hasty effort to rescue from oblivion for all following times the *force* of his first race by piling immense masses of what is most durable on earth, and still the arranger of these masses appears upon them, just in the harmony of his own formation expressed as hieroglyph.

In the fragment project, Ritter's references to architecture can be traced back to two sources: Winckelmann and Vitruvius. The prologue states that one of Herder's most valuable services to the physicist was to introduce him to Winckelmann's *History of Art* (1764) which left him as if "newly born" and revealed to him already on the first page that a remarkable similarity exists between human art and the more general art of the world, that they both erect monuments.[85] The fragments also refer to Winckelmann's *Comments on the Architecture of the Ancients* (1762).[86] Reading Winckelmann taught Ritter about the large-scale monuments associated with Egyptian and Greek culture built to preserve the memory of the dead for all eternity. From Vitruvius Ritter receives a different impression altogether of what can be included under the heading of "architecture." The ten volumes of *De Architectura* written during the 1st century BCE provide more than a history of human architectural projects. They also contain Vitruvius' observations on mechanics, advice about harvesting, and general thoughts about the human procreation in relation to natural cycles.[87] Together, Winckelmann and Vitruvius contribute to Ritter's understanding of the monument which is at once permanent and connected to the periods of the natural world (offering an unusual synthesis of the two temporalities which both Aleida and Jan Assman's discussion of the monument understands as distinct[88]). Ritter synthesizes the two viewpoints in a fragment that explains what it means to recollect the departed through a monument:

> Wenn etwa nun der *Tod* in nichts bestände, als im Wegfallen des *willkührlichen* Bewußtseyns, so könnte dem Verstorbenen noch immer wieder Bewußt—und Daseyn,—Leben—hervorgerufen werden, und ein Leben, was alles Vergangene enthielte, und auch die Zukunft auschließbar vor sich hätte,—durch das bloße Andenken der zurückgebliebenen Lebenden. Hier enthüllte sich die Bedeutung so vieler Anstalten, dieses Andenken zu feyern und es zu unterhalten: der *Sinn des Monuments*,—der vielleicht das Einzige war, was nie von Menschen wich. Denn das Monument enthält geradezu im Leben und giebt Leben dem, dem es gesetzt ist. (*Fragmente*, n. 478)

> If for example *death* was not comprised of anything other than in the disappearance of the *arbitrary* consciousness, then consciousness, being, life, could be summoned again for the dead person, and a life which contained everything past, and which also could have the future revealed before itself—merely through the recollections of the living left behind. Here the meaning of so many institutions would reveal itself, to celebrate this memory and sustain it: the *sense of the monument*, which was perhaps the only thing which never left men. For the monument precisely maintains life and gives life to whom it is dedicated.

Ritter makes an important distinction in this description of the monument's function. Rather than simply invoking the memory of departed, the "sense of the monument" is also to return the departed to life. We summon the consciousness, being, and even life of the dead on their behalf and permit their continued existence. Ritter's claim that the monument both "preserves" (enthält) life and "gives" (giebt) life recalls the peculiar phenomenality of the hieroglyph. Here too, we have a preservation of life that functions as repetition or return to life. Ritter's monument, which relies in part upon the experience of the *Lebenswelt*, does not fit well into traditional schemes which understand the temporality of the monument as "eternal" (instead of implicated in transitory life) and its function removed from uses of daily life as Jan Assman has discussed in the context of ancient Egypt. It comes closer to Deleuze and Guattari's discussion of the monument in *What is Philosophy?* where they write the monument does not celebrate something *as* past. Instead, "it is a bloc of present sensations that owe their preservation only to themselves and that provide the event with the compound that celebrates it. The monument's action is not memory but fabulation. We write not with childhood memories but through blocs of childhood that are the becoming-child of the present."[89] Deleuze and Guattari's emphasis on fabulation over memory helps elucidate Ritter's insistence on a generative and perpetual monument. It also explains why Ritter's monument, implicated as it is in an ongoing activity of construction, cannot be viewed as "eternal" in the sense of existing in a separate mode of time and has more in common with Ritter's concept of the hieroglyph.

CONCLUSION: MARRIAGE AND PROCREATIVE SPACE

The "spatial turn" in the prologue, from the chronology of the physicist's life to a discussion of method, serves as a screen for another event: his marriage and the birth of his children.[90] For someone who sees in both friendships and works of literature intimations of a higher science, it is not surprising that marriage is an occasion of the greatest significance in the physicist's life. With marriage and the new kind of (carnal, "Biblical") knowledge it brings, a veil drops so that the physicist's mind is no longer transparent to the editor. There is a space more secret, more intimate than even the workshop. With regard to the turn from narrative chronology to methodology—a procreative removal of time which occurs as the collapse of story through an expansion of discourse—the coupling between knowledge and procreation is now cast in even sharper relief.

In compliance with the "scientific law" whereby things become their opposite, the prologue ends with a series of turn-arounds. The dead physicist and the living editor are one.[91] What began with the artificial coupling of two deaths, a mother's (Ritter's mother) and a son's ("the physicist"), concludes in the presence of a mother on the birthday of the child. In the act of writing the prologue ("through the method of preservation") the original premise has been discarded and its opposite is embraced as truth. While these theatrics are taking place, the reader is by no means a passive observer. Quite the contrary: through a series of direct addresses using the second person, the reader is drawn ever closer to the scene of the events. Up until the end of the prologue, the pronoun "you" has been mediated through the letters of the physicist. The addressee was not presumed to be present in the moment of narration, and the act of writing did not correspond to the writing of the prologue. When the narrator addresses the reader directly, he does so with reference to the fragment project: its "interesting, often unusual paths" are there for him to follow, "and more often than not these paths will themselves be more instructive, than that which was put upon them as a place holder [*Markstein*] or memorial stone [*Denkstein*]."[92] By the same token, the editor/physicist can not say with any degree of certainty either "What it *actually* is...which I offer you here" nor "What it will *become* for you" except to hope that the prologue may be included in this process of transformation.[93]

By the time the reader has been fully implicated in the continuation of the physicist's life work, the narrative shifts to address the mother of his children. The most private space now transparent to the reader, who becomes a voyeur to the domestic life of the physicist and his wife on the occasion of the youngest child's first birthday.[94] The physicist addresses the final paragraph of the prologue directly to his wife as witness (*Zeugin*) and the one who knows him best. When he marvels "*you* created from *nature*, and no one has yet to fathom *its* treasures,"[95] he shifts his focus from the animosity of the outside world to the "now" of the domestic moment. His suggestion that they "take advantage" of the fact that the children are sleeping is accompanied by a discrete break in the text. The prologue ends with a celebration of procreation and birth, but also the renewed absence of the father, couched in eschatological overtones: "tell [the child]: *the father has been there and will soon come again.*"[96] His book, that "single monument" commemorating the death of Ritter's mother, becomes the birthday gift of the child, for whom it should remain a token of the father in his absence. The enigma of the text is only half-resolved with the reader's induction into the "secret workshop" and the even more private sanctum of the family's living space. The solution to the puzzle leads to the further development of the monument. Once he departs from the procreative space of the husband and wife, the reader should follow the "paths" of the fragments, carrying the book with him, as Ritter suggests, and continuing the work of the physicist.

6 Procreative Thinking—Scientific Projects

Das Weib wird immer Indifferenz seyn, der Mann dagegen Differenz, Pol. (*Fragmente*, n. 485)

The female will always be indifference, the male on the contrary difference, pole.

INTRODUCTION

This chapter discusses how Ritter relates procreation directly to his broad interest in forging connections between the organic and inorganic realms. It also examines the special role that Volta's construction of the pile in 1799 plays in Ritter's writing on procreation. Before the pile, there are few traces of procreative motifs in Ritter's scientific work. The treatise that established his scientific reputation, the *Beweis, daß ein beständiger Galvanismus den Lebensproceß in dem Thierreich begleite* (1798, Proof That a Constant Galvanism Accompanies the Life-process in the Animal Realm), is entirely lacking procreative language. The "hints" (*Winke*) Ritter allows himself at the end of that text, when he departs from his prior discussions of empirical work in paragraphs twenty-five and twenty-six, fantasize about a gender-neutral universal-animal of nature (an *All-Thier*).[1] Just a few years later, the three-volumes of the *Beyträge zur nähern Kenntniss des Galvanismus* (Contributions to the Better Understanding of Galvanism, 1800–1805) tell a different story: of procreation and death, of beds for brides and corpses.[2] Ritter's writing after 1800 betrays a 'Romantic' interest in generation that runs the gamut of scientific and non-scientific contexts. In his aphorisms one will find the credo of Romantic procreation, "The female gives birth to humans, the man to the work of art."[3] He also imports procreative language into his work on magnetism, electricity, and chemistry and infuses his physiologically based discussions of procreation with a technical vocabulary—for example, when he provides his readers with scientific diagrams to analyze the charges and polarizations of the female body during conception and gestation.[4] As Ritter's lexicon expands to include a growing instrumentarium of scientific apparatuses and techniques, he takes advantage of the new vocabulary by fashioning it into metaphors to explain procreative processes. The breadth of his procreative thinking grows too, away from the context of the body towards the historical development of mankind.

We can think of Ritter's goal as a scientist—to unify the scientific study of chemical, magnetic, and electrical phenomena by conceiving them as a single principle in the organic and inorganic realms[5]—as something he wanted to prove experimentally and perform through language. In a scientific article from 1800, he writes that reducing all processes on earth to a single one effectively dissolves "all prior divisions of physics. . .into word games [*Wortspiele*]."[6] According to contemporary lexicons such as Adelung's, "word games" take place when individual words are connected for pure amusement, without concern for meaning.[7] In this regard, we can read Ritter's remark as a criticism against those who would impose arbitrary disciplinary divides onto different areas of scientific research. We can also interpret this remark in another sense, discussed by Novalis. In the "Monologue," Novalis uses the expression "word game" to make an important linguistic claim: that language, like mathematical formulae, is a "world for itself" and speaks only "for itself."[8] As a consequence, Novalis writes, "real conversation is a mere word game."[9] When Ritter criticizes arbitrary disciplinary divides in favor of a single science, he counters the word games of others with one that plays by different rules, one that bears close resemblance to Novalis'—with an important caveat. Novalis' "Monologue" describes the operations of language. Ritter's generalization about physical processes and empirical phenomena has to do with knowledge. Yet when he insists that everything can be reduced to a universal principle or, conversely, that all phenomena are manifestations of this principle—Ritter proposes an approach to science that resembles Novalis' "word game." Just as Novalis' "Monologue" suggests that there is nothing external to langauge, Ritter finds in the electrical spark a template of all forms in the organic and inorganic realms, natural phenomena that he also describes as a kind of language. The question this chapter explores is how the discourse of procreation fits in to the Romantic 'word game.' Is procreation simply a rhetorical bridge between different areas of scientific discourse? Or does procreative thinking become part of the scientific project?

In light of the diversity of his scientific work—which ranged from the fields of optics and electricity to chemistry, animal magnetism, and the infamous pendulum experiments—it would be a disservice to categorize Ritter too rigidly. At the risk of imposing too narrow a girdle on someone who shared Friedrich Schlegel's ambivalence toward systems,[10] a focus on three closely connected topics will show just how ingrained procreation is in his scientific program. The first is "indifference." In the fragments, Ritter aligns this concept with the female body, the process of procreation more generally, and a range of scientific phenomena. The second, related topic is the apparatus of the pile, whose working can also be understood in terms of difference and indifference. Shortly after the pile was constructed by Volta, it was used to refine the process of water electrolysis and the decomposition of other substances, an area of research Ritter also pursued. With reference to the fragments and the *Contributions*, I discuss how the pile provides Ritter with a model which facilitates his thinking about procreation across scales. The third topic marks a return to the point of departure in Chapter 1 to show how Goethe's theory of metamorphosis proves instrumental to Ritter in his search for a unifying principle in the sciences.

INDIFFERENCE

Indifference is a mobile concept for Ritter, which he transfers between the processes of the human body and the passage of historical epochs. In the context of the human body, indifference provides both a natural (biological) and a cultural basis of differentiation from the male. For Ritter, the female is intrinsically 'indifferent,' the male intrinsically 'different.' Such a distinction is clearly an anomaly within a Western cultural tradition which has tended to assign the categories of identity and difference to the masculine and the feminine, respectively.[11] Reversing the categories does not, however, make Ritter an unusually progressive thinker. Structurally, gender differences and hierarchies are still in place. The masculine subject position remains central with regard to the objectivity of the female. They have simply exchanged what they signify—a reminder that these values are arbitrary to begin with. After a quick sketch of indifference's historical background I will start with a narrow focus to consider what it means for a woman's body to be indifferent from a physiological point of view before following Ritter through scenarios of increasing complexity: first by bringing the male into the picture, and then by considering gender differences in the procreative process. As was the case with Novalis, an awareness of the time in which procreation occurs, its narrative structure, and the uniquely feminine perception of temporality is key to understanding Ritter's endeavor. Procreation is a process of indifference and polarization, and "all polarities [are] only to be understood as temporal."[12]

The concept of indifference has a long history before it enters the scientific discussions around 1800. The Stoic philosophers espoused a kind of indifference through freedom from passions (*apatheia*) for the better use of reason.[13] After the Stoics, one finds indifference as a principle for relating the individual to the universal in the work of Medieval philosopher Ockham,[14] in Descartes' musings on the principle of freedom,[15] in the moral philosophy of Hume,[16] and as a topic for the developing field of experimental psychology, where indifference was understood as a lack of desire.[17] Around 1800, indifference took root in the sciences. It is commonly associated with Schelling's discussion of magnetism in the *Ideen zu einer Philosophie der Natur* (1797, Ideas for a Philosophy of Nature), and *Von der Weltseele* (1798, On the World Soul).[18] Schelling's use of indifference can be traced back to the work of Dutch scientist Anton Brugmans, who describes a plane of indifference between the two poles of the magnet.[19] With varying degrees of rigorousness, Ritter and his contemporaries refer to indifference in their discussions of chemistry ("only what is indifferent forms solutions"[20]), physiology (where female reproductive organs were considered indifferent prior to puberty[21]) and even electricity.[22] Ritter's project to unify the sciences actively draws from "indifference" as it is found in each of these contexts around 1800; the fragments, as records of Ritter's scientific work throughout his career, reflect these nuances as well.

As far as procreation is a biological phenomenon entrenched in cultural practices, Ritter's writing on it can also be understood as an attempt to think more broadly about nature and human culture within a single historical framework. David Wellbery has suggested that we can read Ritter's writing as an effort "to invent a unified language of description for the realms of nature *and* culture," arguing that "the key words of Ritter's lexicon are to be read as doubled: on the one hand in relation to their original area, on the other hand as generalized concepts which encompass the natural as well as the cultural."[23] Wellbery's insight into the scope of Ritter's thinking can be formulated with even more precision in the case of the gendered language of procreation. Due to the fact that Ritter returns multiple times to narrate processes of procreation in different contexts, enacting precisely the *Aufhebung* that Wellbery describes, the merger between the natural and the cultural is perhaps not as firmly in place as has previously been assumed. There exists a tension between them—more precisely, between the specific context and a more generalized narrative of procreation—which is precisely what Ritter's procreative discourse tests out heuristically.[24] There is also an innate circularity to this process. When procreative language is exported beyond its home discourse of physiology to the degree that it is in Ritter's work, to serve figuratively for other processes of different contexts and scales, the coherence of the procreative narrative can no longer be taken for granted. The way Ritter brings together different aspects of nature and culture around one term lends new meaning to it and also allows him to unify nature and culture conceptually. The logic of physiological procreation informs scientific discourse, and these discourses imprint themselves upon procreative models.

The textbook example for physiological indifference around 1800 is Johann Christian Reil, an acquaintance of Ritter's who tried unsuccessfully to bring him to the university in Halle for an academic appointment in 1804. His essay, "On the Polar Deviations of the original Forces of Nature in the Uterus at the Time of Pregnancy, and their Exchange at the Time of Birth, as Contribution to the Physiology of Pregnancy and Birth, from Professor *Reil*" (1807), gives an anatomical description of a female's original "indifference." Although the title places the reader in the middle of things, the essay begins by describing the female prior to pregnancy and the "polarities" it generates. Before conceiving, the female body exists in a state of indifference, a balance of latent forces which are yet to be activated. Reil explains this condition as follows: "The female genitalia have remained on the lowest levels of formation as indifferent and indistinguishable mass, in which the higher powers of its actual life, nubility, pregnancy and birth are certainly potentially contained but are still at rest."[25] The female is technically in a neutral state until the indifference "in the substratum of the basic forces of the uterus" is removed (*aufgehoben*) upon conception.[26] Ritter, without differing from Reil in any significant way, calls the state of potentiality before conception a state of "longing" ("the female in longing = indifference"[27]). Both Reil and Ritter envision the female before conception as purely forward-looking, a strange creature with no past and scarcely a present in contrast to a boundless future that unfurls under the banner of "not yet."[28] The state of longing as the future-oriented condition of the feminine can also be connected back to Hardenberg's "Fichte Studies," in particular the aphorism discussed in Chapter 2 in which Hardenberg describes the "longing" of the female prior to the moment of procreative pleasure.[29]

By functioning as a gender distinction, "indifference" illustrates the doubling of concepts to encompass the natural and the cultural which Wellbery claims to be characteristic for Ritter's lexicon. The following fragment couches indifference in a social context and complements the examples of 'physical' indifference in the female body:

> Die Stelle in Goethe's Tasso: 'Willst du genau erfahren, was sich ziemt, so frage nur bey edlen Frauen nach;.... Und wirst du die Geschlechter beyde fragen: Nach Freyheit strebt, der Mann, das Weib nach Sitte;'[30]—giebt ganz vortreflich den Ort des Webes in der natürlichen Welt an. Die Erde in ihrer höchsten freyesten Erscheinung ist die Sitte selbst; das extraplanetarische auf Erden ist im Manne verklärt. Das Weib wird immer Indifferenz seyn, der Mann dagegen Differenz, Pol. (*Fragmente*, n. 485)

> The passage in Goethe's Tasso: "If you want to learn exactly what is proper, then inquire with noble women [*Frauen*];....And should you wish to ask both sexes: towards freedom strives the man, the female [*das Weib*] towards custom;"—indicates most excellently the place of the female in the natural world. The earth in its greatest, most free appearance is custom itself; the extra-planetary on the earth is transfigured in the man. The female will always be indifference, the man on the other hand difference, pole.

The fragment shifts easily between cultural values (freedom, propriety) and their correlating physical co-ordinates (the earth-bound female, the extra-planetary male). It also engenders a distinction within woman herself, separating the learned and noble women (*Frauen*) from the striving female (*Weib*);[31] for Ritter, the female as *Weib* embodies the autochthonic, the "continuation of the earth" upon which she is "native" and man is "foreign."[32] The pairing of female-indifference and male-difference within a relationship of polarity raises the question, to what degree either male or female can exist or act autonomously of the other. Though the word "indifference" suggests that the female is integral to herself, she cannot be said to function apart from the male who occupies her future horizon. What about the "difference" of the male? To what extent are his extraterrestrial vagaries truly free if they only exist in a relation of difference to her? Winfried Menninghaus reads Ritter's "basic formula" of difference–indifference as departing little from the Romantic canon. It is "the traditional opposition of feminine natural unity and masculine dividedness (*Gespaltenheit*) stamped by will and intellect."[33] Ritter would likely not have objected to being placed squarely in the Romantic tradition, but there is more to the "formula" than meets the eye. A gendered, masculine will has a specialized role to play in the discourse on procreation for Ritter, in the context of animal magnetism where the will of the *Magnetiseur* overcome is the pliant *Somnambulistin*.[34] In his distribution of gender roles, Ritter places more emphasis on the activity of the male as the one who generates difference rather than being differentiated. The fragment which begins with the transition of the female from indifference to difference puts this question into sharp relief:

> Das Weib in Sehnsucht = Indifferenz.
> Das Weib auf dem Wege zur Erfüllung = beginnender Differenz.
> Das Weib in vollendeter Erfüllung = totaler Differenz.
> (*Fragmente*, n. 501)

> The female in longing = indifference.
> The female on the way to fulfillment = beginning difference.
> The female in complete fulfillment = total difference.

Conception requires contact, whether it is the abstract "cohesion" of two heterogeneous things into a new "egoity" (*Ichheit*),[35] an electrically charged touch,[36] or low-tech copulation. The moment of conception not only symbolically sparks the life of the embryo, it begins what Ritter calls a magnetic transition whereby the previously neutral female becomes polarized. With the advent of this polarity—of differentiation—comes awareness and temporal perspective. Ritter writes that "the female must be able to say with certainty when she conceived" and the man must be able to say with equal certainty at which point he has "caused difference" even before there is visible "proof."[37] Conception therefore also initiates a time horizon of past and present co-ordinates. Prior to it, in the undifferentiated future horizon of the female, every union was simply a hope. Suddenly she gains a past, a history of which her body is the index, and which every subsequent copulation will recall.

The temporalization of the female body during the sex act recalls Novalis' claim that the virgin *only* lives for the future, with neither remembrance nor experience:

Das schöne Geheimniß der Jungfrau, was sie eben so unaussprechlich anziehend macht, ist das Vorgefühl der Mutterschaft—die Ahndung einer künftigen Welt, die in ihr schlummert, und sich aus ihr entwickeln soll. Sie ist das treffendste Ebenbild der Zukunft. (Novalis, *Schriften*, 2:407)

The beautiful secret of the virgin, which makes her so inexpressibly beautiful is the premonition of motherhood—the intimation of a future world which slumbers within her and should unravel itself from her. She is the most accurate replica of the future.[38]

Novalis emphasizes the mystical singularity of procreation by invoking an immaculate conception that "unravels" from a mere intimation. Ritter shares his reverence,[39] but articulates a different point of view when he writes that the female can, relatively speaking, cycle back to the state of indifference and recapture her forward-looking perspective in anticipation of the next act of conception. He differs from Novalis not only in this regard. That conception opens up a past horizon is, for Ritter, what separates animals and humans—men included: the male undergoes a parallel change. Whereas for the female the past is a history of the body, for the male the past is shaped by the knowledge of what he has done. As if in anticipation of Menninghaus's comment, Ritter approaches the question of male "dividedness" directly:

Der Mann wird indifferent im Eingang in die Differenz der Frau. Das Weib giebt ihre Individualität *auf*; die Einheit geht zur Zweiheit über, und Sehnsucht nach Aufgabe derselben ist überhaupt die Sehnsucht des Weibes. Welche Trennung aber wird im Manne in der Liebe aufgehoben?–ist es der so oft genannte Kampf zwischen Wissenschaft und Liebe?–besser: zwischen Wissenschaft und Sehnsucht?–Der Mann *sucht* Individualität. Erst wenn er als *Mann* in die Familie eingeht und in derselben steht, hat er Individualität gefunden, und ist Eins geworden. (*Fragmente*, n. 501)

The man becomes indifferent when he enters into the difference of the woman. The female gives her individuality *up*; unity goes into division, and longing for release is in general the longing of the female. Which separation, however, is released in the male, during love? Is it the struggle named so often between science and love? Better: between science and longing? The man *seeks* individuality. Only when he enters into the family as *man* and stands within it, has he found individuality and has become One.

The shifting polarities during copulation emphasize the fact that gender categories are dynamic, rather than fixed. In Ritter's version of the procreative act, they can switch entirely, approximating the law of nature cited in the prior chapter, where one thing becomes the opposite. Man and woman are "different" relative to each other as they unite, but in the moment when the woman's body differentiates, the man, in the act of differentiating, becomes indifferent. The woman's longing has driven her to give up her individuality (in the literal sense that Ritter equates with indifference) and become double. As for man, if he could be said to embody a "dividedness" to begin with, between "science and love" or "science in longing," it disappears in the moment of conception and in the constellation of the family (Ritter writes in the prologue to the fragments: the family is where the physicist feels "*completely integrated* for nature and science"[40]). Ritter's understanding of male individuality cannot be limited to the male artist, scientist, or "intellect" in isolation. It exists as an integrated part of the whole. The cultural claim also functions as a scientific analogy whereby the "typus of the family" demonstrates the "triplicity in every (here organic) chemical process."[41] In general, the acts of coupling, conception, and birth described in Ritter's writing on procreation define procreation as a complex of spatial and temporal figures kept in flux through the displacement and reinstatement of gender roles. Procreative narratives are never simple for Ritter. They superimpose physiological generation, the language of other scientific discourses (such as magnetism and electricity), and reflections upon their own temporality. The time of procreation will play a greater role in the following discussion of the pile. Its importance reaches well beyond definitions of gender categories to include the study of life—in Ritter's words, "the history of the embryo is means to a theory of the organism."[42]

A WATERY BRIDGE

The Voltaic pile, and the chemical processes it facilitiates, are central to the Ritter's writing on procreation. Simply put, the pile's ability to decompose and re-compose substances operates as a bridge metaphor. On the one side these processes are rooted in the body, including the brain. On the other side, in the processes of analysis and synthesis facilitated by the pile, Ritter finds metaphors of remarkable elasticity which can be mapped across scales of time and space. These metaphors provide an important common reference point to connect Ritter's procreative language and his interest in joining the sciences through a single principle: not just as they currently are, but as they have developed historically. As has often been observed, science *is* history for scientists conducting research into natural phenomena in Ritter's time.[43] Understanding a phenomenon requires understanding how it came to be. Or, in Ritter's succinct statement: "Not history *of* physics, but rather history = physics = history."[44]

Water decomposition is the process of separating water into hydrogen and oxygen. In 1789, Adriaan Paets von Troostwijk and Jan Rudolf Deiman demonstrated that decomposition could be achieved through combustion using electric sparks—and even earlier scientists were aware that the combustion of water produced a gas[45]—but it took another decade after the "Amsterdam experiments" for the role of electricity in the process to be understood. One piece of the puzzle was provided by Alessandro Volta's construction of a device in 1799 that was able to generate a current through contact electricity.[46] The Voltaic battery or "pile" is literally a pillar of metal disks interspaced with rags or pieces of paperboard. The disks were of alternating metals such as copper or silver and zinc, the rags were initially dampened in salt water (NaCl) which is an electrolyte. It contains free-floating positively charged sodium ions and negatively charged chloride ions as a result of salt crystals having been dissolved in the water; these ions display a natural tendency to couple with copper and zinc to form more stable compounds. When this happens, electricity is released and electrical charge accumulates on the metals. The Voltaic pile—acting as a simple battery—converts the chemical energy of the ions into electrical energy, and Ritter observed that this phenomenon is the same as that which forms the basis of the galvanic chain.[47] The pile's early applications were based on the fact that its electric current generated a polarity of positive and negative charge. When two wires connected to the ends of the pile are inserted into water, the electric field produced near the tips of the wires overcomes the bond between hydrogen and oxygen in water. The positively charged wire (the anode) attracts the negatively charged oxygen, while the negatively charged wire (the cathode) will have the same effect on the positively charged hydrogen. The English scientists Nicholson and Carlisle, who learned about the pile even before Volta's announcement was published, were the first to use the pile for the process of water electrolysis (literally: separation through electricity). Ritter then improved upon their experiments and was the first to collect and measure the oxygen and hydrogen gases in separate containers. He was also intrigued by the fact that the activity within the individual components of the pile mirrored the process of electrolysis on a smaller scale, in the sense that he also interpreted the interaction of metals and salt water in terms of ongoing decomposition and re-composition.

As knowledge of water electrolysis spread, it made waves outside of the laboratory. For Ritter, it provides an important link between productive and reproductive processes in the body. In the fragments he observes how the analysis and synthesis of water, which can also be thought of in terms of "differentiation" and "indifferentiation," function both within a regime of self-generation (in terms of the working of the brain) and in procreation (in the watery element of the womb). The former can be explained with reference to Kant and Sömmering:

> Da *Kant* Wasserzersetzung als Vehikel der Seelenthätigkeit vorschlägt, und es fast bewiesen ist, daß im Wasser die beyden Grundkräfte, welche das Lebensprinzip constituiren, im gleichsam ruhenden Zustande liegen, so wäre es wohl möglich, und im Grunde mit dem Sinn

der Kantischen Hypothese ganz gleichstimmend, daß das Ich bey seiner Thätigkeit zunächst auf diese Kraft (die Wasserzersetzung), in und mit ihr, wirkte. (*Fragmente*, n. 400)

Since *Kant* proposes water decomposition as vehicle of the soul's activity, and it is almost proven that in water both basic forces which constitute the principle of life are found in equally stable condition, then it would certainly be possible, and basically in complete accordance with the Kantian hypothesis, that the ego (*Ich*) in its activity was first of all operative on this force (the decomposition of water), in and with it.

Ritter does not specify in which of Kant's texts the hypothesis can be found, but there is only one text where water decomposition and *Seelenthätigkeit* intersect: Kant's review of Samuel Thomas von Sömmering's *Über das Organ der Seele* (On the Organ of the Soul, 1796). Sömmering's text argues that the "seat" of the human soul is located within the fluid element of the brain cavity. Kant, faced with the dilemma whether to ground his comments in a perspective and discourse more sympathetic to "doctors as physiologists" or "philosopher as metaphysicians," opts to bypass the problem of the soul's locality altogether.[48] He is entitled to do this, Kant says, since the notion of a "seat" would demand a "spatial relation" for something which is only an object of the inner sense and thus leads to a contradiction. We should also not allow a "virtual presence" to yield a concept which would make it possible to treat the question of *sensorium commune* simply as a physiological task. For example, if headaches and other twinges might suggest we "feel" ourselves thinking, we run the risk of confusing the cause of the sensation in a certain place on our head with the sensation of the cause. According to Kant, we can keep the physiological question free of metaphysics by focusing on that matter "which makes possible the conjoining of all sensory perceptions in the mind."[49] Excavation of the brain cavity by skilled anatomists such as Sömmering has shown that the "matter" in question is nothing but "water."[50]

Kant suggests that we abandon the spatial/mechanical model of the brain cavity in favor of a dynamic organization based on chemical principles. Just as a space (the brain cavity and its water) can be divided into infinite subdivisions, so too can we think of the chemical division of water which also occurs *in indefinitum*. With oblique reference to recent developments in the field of chemistry, Kant reminds us that, unlike in earlier times, water is no longer conceived of as a single, pure element but should rather be thought of as a composite which itself can be further decomposed to facilitate organic processes. Just as the decomposition of common water can provide for an immeasurable variety of processes in the plant kingdom, so too can we imagine the manifold of organs on the nerve endings which react with the water in the brain.

144 *German Romanticism and Science*

On the basis of his claim that the physiological activity of the brain cavity is, at least in part, a process of chemical decomposition, Kant suggests the following:

> Wenn man nun als Hypothese annimmt: daß dem Gemüth im empirischen Denken, d.i. im Auflösen und Zusammensetzen gegebener Sinnenvorstellungen, ein Vermögen der Nerven unterlegt sei, nach ihrer Verschiedenheit das Wasser der Gehirnhöhle in jene Urstoffe zu zersetzen, und so, durch Entbindung des einen oder des andern derselben, verschiedene Empfindungen spielen zu lassen (z.B. die des Lichts, vermittelst des gereizten Sehenervens, oder des Schalls, durch den Hörnerven, u.s.w.), so doch, daß diese Stoffe, nach aufhörendem Reiz, so fort wiederum zusammenflössen; so könnte man sagen, dieses Wasser werde continuirlich organisirt, ohne doch jemals organisirt zu sein: wodurch dann doch eben dasselbe erreicht wird, was man mit der beharrlichen Organisation beabsichtigte, nämlich die collective Einheit aller Sinnenvorstellungen in einem gemeinsamen Organ (*sensorium commune*), aber nur nach seiner chemischen Zergliederung begreiflich zu machen. (Kant, *Werkausgabe*, 12:34)

> If one takes as hypothesis: that in empirical thinking, that is, in the dissolution and composition of given sensory impressions, a faculty of the nerves underlies the mind in order, in keeping with their differences, to decompose the water in the brain cavity, and thus, by unbinding one or the other [of the nerves], to allow various impressions to come into play (for example, the impression of light through the irritated nerve of sight, or of sound, through the nerve of hearing, etc.) so, however, that these materials, after the irritation has ended, at once flow back together; then one could say that this water becomes continuously organized, yet without being organized: whereby, however, exactly the same thing is achieved which one intended with constant organization, namely the collective unity of all sensory impressions in a common sensory organ (sensorium commune), but only to be comprehended according to its chemical analysis.

Kant's description of brain activity, in terms which anticipate the electrolysis of water, serves a special purpose.[51] It allows him to speak of a process of organization whereby the sum total of chemical activities accounts for the "collective unity of all sensory impressions." He can describe in nonmetaphysical terms a "common organ" which functions like the mind yet which does not require the metaphysical underpinnings. For Ritter too, water is the "medium" for all five of the senses, a thought which leads him to the conclusion that "water is the bridge of all possible things from the world to us. Even in the sex act it has the main role."[52] He will also state that "everything is modified water:"[53] it is both the origin and the state to which one returns. In his interpretation of the Kantian hypothesis, however, Ritter re-introduces a dimension into the model that Kant himself seems deliberately to have excluded. He envisions the ego (*Ich*) in its activity as both motivating cause and component of the water decomposition process: the ego has an effect "upon," "in," and "with" the process. For Caroline Welsh, the role of the ego is paramount. She argues that Ritter does not limit himself to a "resonance model" (where external stimuli act upon the nerves of the brain, which then responds directly), nor does he endorse an "arbitrary relation between objects and conscious ideas."[54] There is also an "immutable part of the personality," an "absolute subject" that belongs to the "conscious perception."[55] Welsh's argument helps account for Ritter's insistence upon an ego that is both agent (acting 'upon') and reagent (acting 'in' and 'with' the mind and body). It can also be extended to other contexts, such as the playful division of a life narrative into the first and third person in the autobiographical project, and a tension between the immediacy of the hieroglyph and the permanence of the monument.

Ritter's experiments with the Voltaic pile led to the conviction that what was originally understood as a problem for chemistry needed to be reframed for the study of electricity and galvanism. In a journal article from 1800 he marvels at the ability of the pile to allow the experimenter to perform processes of decomposition at will.[56] The pile demonstrates that "every production of oxygen and hydrogen under circumstances where one described it as the product of a decomposition of water, and thus actually everything which one earlier assigned this name is nothing other than the product of a purely galvanic process."[57] Ritter thereby claims that all chemical processes are galvanic. In the same article that raises the question of the "word game" in the first place, Ritter muses that he could push his results even further:

> Ich könnte weiter gehen. Ich könnte alle chemischen Processe, die es nur eigentlich sind, auf Oxy- und Desoxygenationsprocesse, und alle mit diesen wieder auf Wasserzersetzungs- und nach Umständen auch Wiederzusammensetzungsprocesse reduciren, und nur etwas Geduld würde alle Schwierigkeiten überwinden können, die sich mir entgegenstellen möchten, wenn ich es unternehmen wollte, das *Wasser zum Indifferenzpunkt aller chemischen Qualität*, und die angenommenen *Bestandtheile desselben* zu den *beyden Armen des gemeinschaftlichen Hebels aller Kraftäußerung jener*, zu erheben. (*Physisch-Chemische Abhandlungen*, 1:239–240)

> I could go further. I could reduce all chemical processes, which actually are [chemical], to oxy- and disoxygenation processes, and with these reduce everything again to water decomposition and, circumstances permitting, water recomposition processes, and only a bit of patience would overcome all difficulties which would confront me, if I wanted

> to try to raise *water to the point of indifference of all chemical quality*, and the assumed *components of the same* to the *two arms of the common lever of all its expression of force.*[58]

With these words Ritter embarks on an argument which will receive its most flagrant elaboration eight years later in an essay on the history of chemistry. Its orientation is both regressive and progressive. Ritter wishes to restore water to its original concept of a single, indivisible element, yet he does not deny the phenomenon of decomposition and instead interprets it in a different light. What if water was in fact "simple" and "ponderable"? What if, under certain conditions, water merely transformed itself into oxygen and hydrogen, giving the *"appearance"* of a water *decomposition"*?[59] Having proven through experiment that water is a compound, Ritter now tried to re-establish its simplicity.[60]

Ritter's argument that water is an element and oxygen a compound, as well as his emphasis on experimental regimes where it is a product, sets him in contrast not only to his contemporary scientists, but also to the Early Romantics Schlegel and Novalis, whose fragments predate the construction of the pile.[61] Novalis appears to have been aware of experiments in water electrolysis,[62] and perhaps also their metaphorical potential in Ritter's hands. He mentions "Ritter's perspective on the creation and disappearance of substances" in his aphorisms, in a context as broad as Ritter himself: with reference to death, life, and the thought of a "single kind of generation" applicable to all bodies.[63] Schlegel and Novalis nonetheless focus their attention on traditional processes of combustion. If the female is "our oxygen" for Novalis it is because she is consumed through combustion, not released by electrolysis. Even if, after Lavoisier, the burning process should also be viewed as a synthesis, Novalis' aphorisms emphasize the "consumption" of the oxygen rather than its union with a combustible substance. Ritter, for his part, articulates gender roles in other narratives of generation beyond combustion. In his essay *Physics as Art* (1806) he critiques the "French chemistry" of Lavoisier, to which Novalis' statements on chemistry are strongly indebted, by replacing it with a cyclically-driven "water science."[64] Like Novalis, he preserves the correlation between oxygen and the feminine, hydrogen and the masculine, but the fact that these gases have different roles to play in burning processes as opposed to water electrolysis leads him to different results. Whereas Novalis and Schlegel negotiate between metaphors of the transient (the burning of the "disposable," "consumable" female-oxygen) and the permanent (for example, the female in her organically continuous state), Ritter is able to incorporate the differentiation and indifferentiation of gender within an ongoing process of decomposition and re-composition. This amounts to the creation of a second conceptual framework to consider in tandem with the burning process, one where the feminine principle is not consumed but rather "produced" and then "re-integrated" with the masculine.

Ritter's post-pile meditations on the procreative process are most pronounced in the *Contributions*, in a postscript to the first volume published in 1802. The context is a lengthy homage to the universal importance of the galvanic chain, from which I will highlight just the main points. First of all, Ritter understands the galvanic chain as symbol of self-renewing organic life, a process of constant rebirth. Secondly, the medium in which that rebirth takes place is water. With this claim, Ritter makes both a technical comment and a speculative one. From an empirical point of view, water is decomposed in the chain: "The *oxygen* on the one side *combines* with the metal itself to oxide; the *hydrogen* appears on the metal of the other."[65] Using this fact as the basis for further reflection, Ritter describes water as "the last union of the terrestrial with the sun, the last bodily indifference" (die letzte Vereinigung des Irdischen mit der Sonne, die letzte Körperindifferenz).[66] It is both "the true corpse of nature on earth into which everything loving dies" (der wahre Leichnam der Natur auf Erden, in den jedes Liebende entstirbt) as well as a scene of regeneration.[67] The strangeness of this line of thought does not lie in its scale. In a letter to Gilbert from 1801, Volta also wondered whether there exists "a continuous galvanic process between the earth and the moon which is modified by the influence of the sun."[68] Instead, it lies in the coupling of scientific process with the discourse of procreation. The same scene in Ritter's imagination reads as follows:

> Aus ihm [Wasser], in welches sich alle Individualitäten verlieren, können eben darum alle wiedergeboren werden, ja sie müssen es, so wahr das Wasser das umfassendste gemeinschaftliche *Seyn* ausdrücken soll, zu dem Erde und Sonne endlich gekommen sind [. . .] Das Wasser wird, Statt zu einem Todtenbette, zum schönsten Gegentheil das Brautbett der Natur, in dem Sonne und Erde jeden Augenblick ihrer Unendlichkeiten letzte Vermählung feyern, deren Frucht dieselbe Vermählung derselben Sonne und Erde, neu erstanden, selbst wieder ist [. . .] So wüssten wir also, dass das Wasser die Instanz ist, an die sich jedes Zeugen und Umschaffen auf Erden zu wenden hat. (Ritter, *Beyträge*, 1.3:177)

> From [water], into which all individualities lose themselves, can yet therein all be born again, certainly they must, as truly as water should express the most inclusive common *being* to which the earth and the sun have finally come [. . .] Instead of becoming a death bed, water becomes in the most beautiful opposition the bridal bed of nature in which the sun and earth celebrate in every moment the final marriage of their infinitudes, whose fruit is the same marriage of the same sun and earth, risen anew [. . .] Thus we would also know that water is the instance towards which every procreation and re-creation [*Umschaffen*] on earth must turn.

A review of the *Contributions* published in 1805 praises the scientific experiments but condemns the fantasies of the postscript as mocking the seriousness of science.[69] The reviewer gives his approval to the over two hundred pages of experimental analysis, most of which connects in some way to the decomposition or recomposition of water through the use of the Voltaic pile, but rejects the author's metaphysical speculations, even when they are bracketed within a postscript. He objects to Ritter's language in the moment when it switches from the transparence of empiricism to the opacity of metaphors. After being tested in countless scientific experiments, water cannot bear the metaphors of corpses and bridal beds without Ritter being accused of flying in the face of the seriousness of science.

Undeterred by negative reviews, Ritter's empirical work and his speculative departures from it emphasize the continuous, repetitive, aspects of water decomposition and re-composition as a palingenesis in action. Within this process Ritter finds nothing less than the death and rebirth of the organic world in miniature *and* enjoyment of the godlike power of controlling it. Ritter encapsulates the process as a temporal and spatial unity which can be extrapolated through space and time without losing its essential structure. The example of Fragments 447 and 448, dating from approximately the same time period,[70] will show how the result is a speculative historical thinking indebted to its laboratory origins.

The two fragments consider the epochs of organic and inorganic nature, respectively. The first corresponds closely to the flow of electricity within the galvanic chain:

> Die zwey Mittel-Epochen des Organischen scheinen überall das Herrschen zweyer Differenzen zu bezeichnen, die dritte—wieder die erste—ist die Zeit, wo die Indifferenz herrscht. Eben darum, weil die Indifferenz sie macht, ist sie die Hauptepoche. Symbole sind: Zink, Silber und Wasser. Im Wasseralter blüht alles und empfängt sich neu. Die Galvanische Kette wird Bild des Lebens. Ihre Glieder sind die Indifferenzen, bey denen das Leben einkehrt, die Grenzactionen, die Uebergänge aus dem einen Alter in das andere. (*Fragmente*, n. 447)

In lieu of a translation, the fragment can be diagrammed as follows:

1. Indifference	2. Difference	Difference	3. Indifference
water	zinc	silver	water
(main epoch)	(transitional epochs)		(main epoch)

Ritter reads the galvanic chain as a composite image [*Bild*] whose members can be translated from a spatial schema to a temporal one. He imagines a historical progression that functions according to the logic of the pile, where periods of relative stability (the main epochs of indifference) are followed by periods of relative transition of differentiation. The tension in the fragment lies in the fact that it abounds with the activity of individual organic life (blossoming, conception, etc). Its indefinite units of epochs and ages could, however, just as well refer to the life of man as to the ages of mankind. In this case, Ritter uses the "bridge" of procreation to cross scales of temporal measure.

In Fragment 448, the same units of currency are mapped onto "inorganic nature" whose unity with the organic is reaffirmed by naming epochal differences after stages in human development:

> Die anorgische Natur als Ganzes hat auch ihre drey Alter: das magnetische, das electrische, und das chemische,—oder: das des Embryo, das des Kindes, und das des Jünglings....oder der Sehnsucht. Hierauf-Zusammenstürzen, wo von neuem Magnetismus empfangen wird. *Fragmente*, n. 448.

To heighten the comparison with Fragment 447, it can be diagrammed as follows:

1. Magnetic	2. Electric	3. Chemical
embryo	child	youth/longing
(from indifference to difference)	(difference)	(return to indifference)

The two fragments form a chiastic crossing. The first one posits that organic life—and, by extension, its history—can be reduced to the working of the galvanic chain. The second suggests that the inorganic realm has a cyclical history whose three ages can be defined in stages of human development. Read together, they illustrate the extent to which the language, temporality and structural motifs of procreation are inextricably bound to the working of the pile of the galvanic chain.

BACK TO GOETHE

This study began with a discussion of Goethe's theory of metamorphosis and will end, in the spirit of both procreation and metamorphosis, by revisiting Goethe's theory in a new interpretive framework. We have already seen how Ritter uses the pile as the chief instrument in his arsenal so that, with recourse to the language of procreation, he can pursue his agenda of joining diverse aspects of scientific research through a common principle. Ritter's essay on the history of chemistry from 1808 introduces Goethe's theory of metamorphosis into his discussion of the pile and is one of the last steps in the argument. His reading of Goethe has tangible consequences both for his scientific arguments and for the coupling of "nature" and "culture" because it reclaims a law that governs both.[71]

The "Versuch einer Geschichte der Schicksale der chemischen Theorie in den letzten Jahrhunderten" (Attempt at a History of the Fates of Chemical Theory in the Past Centuries)[72] was published in Gehlen's *Journal for Chemistry, Physics and Mineralogy*. Ritter drafted it at approximately the same time as he was working on a second historical project: the autobiographical prologue to the fragment collection. Like the prologue, the chemistry essay can be read as an act of self-revision. After writing the main text, Ritter appended lengthy footnotes, several of which span multiple pages. In contrast to the prologue, however, the chemistry essay navigates more openly between political, scientific, and cultural narratives, and the two stages of constructing the essay devote attention to different spheres of human activity. The motivation to write is also the result of a politically charged request. Ritter admits to his readers that it was a "task" assigned to him by one of the "first statesmen in Bavaria, whom the new flourishing of the sciences in this land has to thank for the greatest possible personal engagement, apart from the greatest ministerial interest."[73] The unnamed minister to whom Ritter refers is likely Maximilian von Montgelas (1759–1838), who codified his plans for the modernization of Bavaria—its administration, economy, and university system—in the "Ansbacher Memoir" of 1796. Montgelas also drafted the latest version of constitution for the Royal Academy of Sciences in Munich, to which Ritter belonged.

The political interests behind the assignment to write the history of a chemistry are unmistakable given the competition between French and German theories during the past century. Just as the names Johann Joachim Becher and Georg Ernst Stahl are associated with the phlogiston theory, so too, as discussed in the chapters on Novalis, is Antoine Lavoisier's with the rival "anti-phlogiston" theory. Ritter's essay acknowledges the work of other scientists—Priestley in England, Paets van Troostwyck in the Netherlands—without relinquishing its foothold in the French–German rivalry, and he clearly relishes taking an occasional snipe at the French scientists. He concentrates his politically-charged account of the history of chemistry in the main body of the text, which was written first. He later added the footnotes, where he pursues a separate if tangential line of thought and makes fundamental changes both to the structure and the content of his essay—changes in which the discourse on procreation will have a central role to play. The end effect is one of disequilibrium: approximately twenty-five out of the sixty-five pages of printed text are notes, some of which extend to fill three or four pages at a time. Ritter's supplementary writing blurs the relation between center and the periphery, creating a narrative topology whose "outside" and "inside" are not firmly defined.

Ritter introduces the theme of procreation in his essay at a point of bifurcation. He has begun by framing his essay with "epistemic objects" (in Hans-Jörg Rheinberger's sense of this term[74]) rather than historical dates. Against an undifferentiated backdrop of mankind's long interest in the processes of life and burning,[75] the history of chemistry begins for Ritter with the epoch-making phlogiston theory. At this point in his narrative, as if to accentuate this historical differentiation with a textual one, we find the first of a series of lengthy footnotes. In the main body of text, Ritter will continue with a description of the principle of the phlogiston, with reference to the work of Becher and Stahl. The footnote takes a different direction in the name of Goethe. In the note, Ritter ponders what it means for an epoch to begin in the history of science, and whether the history of the theory of chemical process can be equated to organic growth in the sense that they follow the same path, have the same periods, and obey the same laws. The notion that human history—as the history of scientific research and the establishment of scientific theory—should be compatible with the laws of organic nature is an idea with strong resonances of Herder. Ritter chooses instead to focus his attention on Goethe's theory of metamorphosis. The precedent he cites for a proposed organic relation between man and nature does not, however, only come from Goethe's scientific essays:

> Sonst—wird es dem Verfasser nicht allein aufgefallen seyn, wie, daß ein natürliches Factum, besonders von so allgemeinem Range, als eben das des chemischen (dynamischen) Prozeßes, z.B., zum klaren menschlichen Verständniß gelange, es, auf seinem Wege dahin, d.i. in der Geschichte seiner Theorie, den nemlichen Gang nehme, und dieselben Perioden nach denselben Gesetzen durchlaufe, als irgend ein andres äußerliches organisches Gewächs. (Man vergleiche hierzu *Goethe's* Metamorphose der Pflanzen, die völlig ähnliche Um—und Ausbildungsgeschichte der Thiere, und, wer es billigt, vor allem *Goethe's* Elegie im ersten Bande der Cotta'schen Ausgabe seiner Werke, p. 341—343.) (Ritter, *Versuch einer Geschichte*, 8–9 [note])[76]

> Otherwise—it will have occurred not only to the author how a natural fact, in particular [one] of such general stature as that of the chemical [dynamic] process, for example, could be comprehended clearly by the human mind, how [the process], on its way there, that is, in the history of its theory, could take the same path and run through the same periods according to the same laws, as any other outwardly organic growth. Compare here *Goethe*'s metamorphosis of plants, the entirely similar history of animal transformation and development, and, whoever approves of it, above all *Goethe*'s elegy in the first volume of Cotta's edition of his works, 341–343.

Goethe's wish that poets might be "beneficial" to scientists finds a receptive audience in Ritter, who is of one mind with Goethe when it comes to a broad understanding of the theory of metamorphosis and, as the quote suggests, the contribution that literature can make. He endorses a very broad interpretation of metamorphosis when he writes to Ørsted, in a letter dated July 25th, 1802, "I understand the metamorphosis of plants, of animals, of humans, of the earth, of humanity etc. like *Goethe* and no one else. In short: the *metamorphosis of everything finite*." [77] His placement of the 1798 elegy alongside (and perhaps even above) the 1790 essay on plant metamorphosis imports a familiar question into a new context: the question of what Goethe's poem might contribute to an understanding of scientific principles that the scientific essay does not. Walter Wetzels, one of the few to have published commentaries on this passage, takes as his point of departure the phrase, "the history of its theory could take the same path and run through the same periods according to the same laws, as any other outwardly organic growth."[78] He interprets a comparison between "three phases in the metamorphosis of a scientific theory" and the blossoming of a plant: between the idea, its analysis, and then a reconfirmation of the idea "on a higher level" (when the details of the analysis are joined into a composite image) and the organic model of the seed, the leaves, and the blossom.[79] For Wetzels, the poem is irrelevant. He claims we can still understand the comparison between organic growth and theoretical progress "even without Ritter's reference to Goethe's elegy."[80]

In my reading, the elegy's mention in the chemistry essay is not at all incidental. At the beginning of the poem, the narrator's beloved confronts a 'Linnean' bombardment of names and details, an empirical confusion to be transcended. The opening of Ritter's essay gives voice to the same lament when he writes how difficult he finds it "to raise himself for the moment to a general and uniform overview from the midst of the detail which preoccupies him so unavoidably in its most elaborate particularity."[81] Both the poem and the chemistry essay are concerned with what Ritter refers to as the "errancy of our mind"—that is, the historical traces of the mind's vagaries when faced with the challenge of organizing empirical data. The cognitive dimension, not thematized in Goethe's essay but emphasized in the elegy on metamorphosis, is important for Ritter: "from this point of view the errancy of our mind achieves an even more serious interest than that which is usually so gladly granted to it, in that it becomes a necessary link wherever truth wants to renew itself on a higher level."[82] Goethe believed that an intuition of the living phenomenon—above all, in the context of the metamorphosis of plants—could be gained by running through the individual images of development in the mind's eye, and grasping the whole and the parts at the same time.[83] Ritter's language reveals another remarkable affinity to Goethe when he writes:

> Erst dann aber ihre [i.e. der Idee] Wiedererscheinung völlig klar verbleiben, und jeder Zukunft fortleuchten, läßt, wenn alle Seiten oder Weisen, nach welchen die Betrachtung sich in das von der Idee umfaßte Detail verlieren kann, nach der Reihe, und so, daß zwischen je zweyen derselben allemal ein solcher Durchbruchsmoment letzterer (der Idee) selbst vorkam, durchlaufen sind. (Ritter, "Versuch einer Geschichte," 10 [note])

Only then will [the idea] come forth completely clear in its re-appearance and illuminate every future, if all aspects or ways are run through on the basis of which observation can lose itself in the detail gathered from the idea, down the row, and so that in general between any two of them such a break-through moment of the latter (the idea) itself appeared.

From Ritter's description it is a small step to Goethe's method, which encourages us to take a series of empirical observations and organize them such that we create (or recreate) the living phenomenon in our mind's eye. The "row" and "break-through" moments Ritter envisions are, however, not attached to the plant, but rather to the Voltaic pile. In other words, whereas for Goethe the "break-through" moment is the one we intuit between stages of plant growth observed in real time, for Ritter it is the electrical charge which bridges the two contact metals of the pile. Ritter therefore invokes Goethe in order to stage his own delicate transitional moment, bridging between the organic and inorganic realms, as well as between the idea and its empirical manifestation. Just as Goethe's elegy paired cognitive processes of the observer with patterns of growth in organic nature, Ritter finds the metamorphoses of the organism and the development of ideas compatible. He emphasizes the ways in which both, in the process of transformation, "go beyond" themselves: "Everything advancing organically, (and nothing is of another kind, just more or less), advances through the reconstruction of itself going beyond its prior being, and, as the average organism, in its metamorphoses [. . .] so too the intellectual component of the idea."[84] The comparison has a broad resonance in Ritter's work. In the fragments he writes that just as "ideas consume violently," so too does the mother die away from the embryo, the embryo from the child, the child from the man, etc.[85] It is also the premise of the autobiography to the extent that the "death" of the physicist was the precondition for the writing of his life through the prologue.

Ritter mobilizes these arguments in order to make the case for reading the "mechanical" production of the pile as organic generation. If in mechanical production, Ritter says, a body reconstructs itself "in place," then organic procreation can be loosely described as the disappearance of a body in one place and its return in another place. Ritter realizes that the idea of inorganic material obeying the laws of organic procreation (i.e., that mechanical propagation, or locomotion, where spaces are exchanged, should follow organic laws) will be met with skepticism. He assures his readers that he does not want to rehash alchemical theories, just consider the possibility that, in its earlier state, inorganic matter might have practiced the same kind of production as organic matter, and that remnants of this earlier state can be observed still today in a few chemical processes. He cites several cases where he believes this to be the case before turning again to the "more striking example" of the Voltaic pile. As an example, he mentions experiments by Hisinger, Berzelius, and subsequently Davy, where acids and bases were thought to decompose on one pole of the pile and then recompose on another, crossing over in diluted form in between.[86] Ritter lauds the experiments for demonstrating a "true organic propagation."[87]

Ritter could have ended his essay with the analogy between Goethe's theory of plant metamorphosis and Volta's work on the pile, but he has created a suggestive constellation without yet coming to his main point. The discourse of procreation, and the themes raised with reference to Goethe's elegy, have still not exhausted their usefulness.

As discussed in Chapter 2, at the heart of Goethe's theory of metamorphosis is the notion of a "transcendental organ" enabling all empirical manifestations of plant organs. With reference to experiments conducted with the pile and other electrical machines, Ritter posits an analogous concept. It is an electrical spark which would serve as a template for every organic and inorganic form:

> Nehmen wir jetzt alles zusammen,—und wie Vieles ist hier in der Kürze übergangen! so bietet sich uns im *bloßen electrischen Funken*, seinen Hauptmomenten nach, genau das Nemliche dar, was uns auch jedes Organische, sey es Pflanze oder Thier, bloß äußerlich, durch bloße Formreduction, gewährt: ein *System von ramificirtem Hohlem*, ein *gegliedertes Gefäß*. (Ritter, "Versuch einer Geschichte," 58)

> If we now take everything together, and how much is passed by here for the sake of brevity! Then in the *mere electrical spark* is offered to us, according to its main moments, precisely the same thing which every organic thing, be it plant or animal, affords us merely externally, through mere reduction of form: a *system of ramified space*, a *divided vessel*.

Ritter sees in the spark and its electrical figures a template for the natural world—an 'Urfunke' comparable to Goethe's 'Urpflanze.' Persistence with the electrical machine would leave "no single leaf- and twig-form appearing in the plant kingdom unrepeated."[88] Not only does the electrical machine capture the forms of the organic and inorganic realms, however, it captures their history:

> Überdies würde, da alle Form und Figur *Schrift* (Natur-Schrift) ist, alle solche aber nur Bahn der *That* bezeichnet, diese aber wieder in der *Zeit* geschieht, oder, und eigentlicher, die *Zeit selbst—ist*, alle jene Schrift in Form und Figur zugleich *Zeit-Schrift, Zeit-Geschichte*, seyn. (Ritter, "Versuch einer Geschichte," 59)

> What is more, since all form and figure is *writing* (nature writing), all such writing however only traces the path of the *deed*, but this in turn

happens in *time*, or, and more accurately, *is time itself*—all that writing in form and figure would be also *time-writing, time-history.*

It follows, continues Ritter, that the electrical figure is both a "spatial organizational scheme" as well as the "first type of *temporal*-organization."[89] This natural "law" inscribes a history which contains the key to all forms of the organic and inorganic realms. The imprint of the electrical spark, whether generated by a table-top electrophor (Volta) or a gigantic "electrical machine" (Teyler) is a script. As described in the prior chapter, this writing generated by nature itself is "hieroglyphic." The reading of Ritter's fictional biography showed how it joined the concepts of writing (and monumentalizing) the self to the phenomenon of 'nature writing.' In broader context of Ritter's scientific program, the hieroglyph as 'nature writing' or a 'natural language' is a powerful instrument in his project to unify all phenomena under a single principle. As a natural letter in a natural language, the hieroglyph of the electrical spark plays a word game akin to that of Novalis' "Monologue." It writes itself, is concerned only with itself, speaks for itself, and still—according to Ritter—functions as a general language.[90] It appears as if Ritter could not possibly push his argument any further. He has made his case for a universal principle that will not only unite empirical phenomena, but also disciplinary divides and the unfolding of history as well. Yet there is one problem remaining to be solved, which Ritter attempts with a return to the language of procreation.

CONCLUSION

Ritter is troubled by a discrepancy between what he sees and what he knows. Experiments with electrical machines have shown conclusively that "individual electricities are subjugated to the law of continuous division into three,"[91] but only two kinds of electricity had been identified—positive and negative. Following his dream of a universal law whereby every "original thing" is organized in patterns of three (his examples include the poles and the center of the light spectrum, the three components of the galvanic chain, and the Holy Trinity), Ritter doubts that the polarity of electricity is an exception. Could there be an invisible third kind of electricity, one which we cannot see with the eyes of our body? To answer this question affirmatively, Ritter turns once more to the discourse of procreation. He uses the example of sexuality to ask whether "in the realm of the *organic* the true number of different sexes is not exhausted with two."[92] The "best commentary," he claims, is "an attempt at a law of the sexes for humans, of a first [law] in general, what everywhere would command attention and consideration for a third [sex] external or superior to the two others. (*Goguet*, etc.) Law is however always only pronounced necessity of nature, and a human [law] pronounced the necessity pertaining to an entire animated creation.[93] Without explaining exactly what the characteristics of this "third sex" might be, Ritter claims that it is visible both to the "*inner* eye, if it only looks closely,"[94] and available for empirical observation. Ritter does not specify what kind of creatures he has in mind. He could have in mind the hermaphrodites of the plant kingdom, those flowers which have both stamens and pistils, which Goethe describes in both the essay and the elegy on plant metamorphosis. It is also possible that he refers to the mystical or cabbalistic traditions, such as Jakob Böhme's third principle, a synthesis of male and female.[95] In each case, the third sex is "external" to the other two, but also needs to be defined in terms of them.[96] The fact that Ritter needs the example of sexual difference to justify his scientific theory suggests that the language of procreation does not just function as a rhetorical bridge, but also has a constitutive role to play in the scientific project.

Conclusion

This book explores Romantic responses to the mystery of procreation: a quintessentially 'female' mystery, localizable in woman's body and therefore intrinsic to the field of physiology, but also one exported beyond the domains of anthropology and medicine into other areas of literary and scientific practice. The discourse of procreation cuts a broad swath through those fields appropriated by the Romantics in their efforts to gather the sciences and the arts within a single project of encyclopedic scope. From philosophy, mathematics and history to the study of magnetic, chemical and electric phenomena, procreation bridges the organic and inorganic realms to include all facets of human physical and intellectual activity. In response to this phenomenon, my study has sought to identify common tendencies in the work of different writers and their ways of narrating processes of procreation. It argues that, as varied as Goethe, Novalis and Ritter are in terms of their literary and scientific backgrounds and interests, they are united by the contributions that they make to the discourse of procreation—contributions that reach well beyond a simple thematic interest in procreative motifs. For these three writers, the problem of organic generation is never far removed from other modes of production: processes of observation, the acquisition of knowledge, and the production of 'literature' broadly defined. At the same time, they are aware that descriptions of procreative processes, as well as comparisons of growth, generation, and other modes of production pose very real challenges. In the case of Goethe, the question arises as to whether human language may well be insufficient to capture the vicissitudes of a natural phenomenon in a constant state of flux. Writing on procreation therefore also means coming to terms with writing itself and the constraints of language.

The twin questions that motivate this book from beginning to end—namely, what Goethe, Novalis, and Ritter have to say about procreation and what they are able to 'do' with it—are associated with a number of ancillary topics. These topics, which play greater or lesser roles in each chapter, include sex and gender hierarchies in procreation, the temporality of procreative processes, and the question of genre, i.e., what literature can contribute to the mystery of the day (Blumenbach) for the scientific community. I chose to focus on Goethe's theory of metamorphosis in the opening chapter because it offers a broad introduction to the problem of procreation and affords us the opportunity to connect the manifold of procreative themes and questions through the reading of a single literary text—the elegy on plant metamorphosis. For Goethe, metamorphosis is a joint activity of growth and reproduction. Because he defines these two words in terms of one another, calling growth "asexual reproduction," we are entitled to read his work on metamorphosis as a theory of (plant) procreation that eventually extends into domains beyond the botanical kingdom. The chapter identified certain problems Goethe encountered while developing his theory and expanding the reach of his scientific investigations. One of these is the use of figurative language, including metaphor. Goethe's views on metaphor in scientific investigations undergo a significant change in the 1780s and the 1790s. An organic metaphor should not just foreground a structural similarity, but be flexible enough to have a predictive value as well. As a result of this shift in thinking, Goethe adapts his use of metaphor to include dynamic, functional comparisons of how things change and develop over time. The second problem area discussed had to do with the observer, whose role also undergoes changes in the course of Goethe's scientific studies. His notes from the late 1780s demonstrate a willingness to define certain stages of organic development based on observations from the outside: from this anthropocentric perspective, for example, a birth occurs when we become aware of a separation between parent and progeny. Subsequent years witness a prolonged engagement with the basic question, what happens when we engage in the active beholding or 'intuition' of a living phenomenon. The fruit of this labor is Goethe's conclusion that we must be as dynamic as nature herself and recreate the phenomenon in our mind's eye. This idea is Goethe's most tangible contribution to the discourse on procreation, and it connects directly to the third main problem area: the process of experimentation, and the necessity of repeating experiments (and experiences) at will. My reading of Goethe's poem on plant metamorphosis situated it at the junction of these three areas of inquiry to show how the poem takes the theory of intuition as the basis for an experiment through a staged repetition. At the same time, it allows for the interruption of contingency in the otherwise predictable process of metamorphosis. These distinctions are coded in Goethe's poem through gender roles. The challenge of communicating the intuition of the phenomenon, as well as the burden of repeating (and therefore validating) the experiment, is concentrated on the figure of the silent female addressee. If all organic signs point to success, the poem still leaves open the possibility of failure because the silent addressee is also a figure of contingency. Drawing on examples from the botanical essay of 1790, the elegy of 1798 and Goethe's late work on the spiral tendency, the chapter also exposes a countertendency running throughout Goethe's work on metamorphosis that manifests itself as a doubt of the possibility to accomplish the kind of intuition he has in mind. The "missing word" of the 1790 essay and the "word which unlocks" the elegy point to the fact that the discursive structure of language does not allow us to run through the parts and experience the whole all at once with ease (as Goethe claims is necessary to understand metamorphosis), and that such an endeavor can lead to "a kind of madness." For my reading, this aspect of Goethe's theory is less of an admission of failure (after all, his theory of metamorphosis still holds) than an example of how the study of procreation around 1800 is closely paired with a careful attention to the capacities and limits of language in scientific and poetic contexts.

The two chapters on Novalis transfer the questions raised during the readings of Goethe into the arena of early Romantic poetics and develop them further. The relation between intellectual productivity and organic generation, the question of how best to narrate procreative processes, and the gender roles defined by these narratives are all problems that Novalis addresses in his aphorisms and two unfinished novels. In examining how procreation acts as a bridge discourse between different realms of nature and human activity, a tension emerges between the coherence of procreative models and the transformative power of the individual areas of scientific study. Procreation articulates a common denominator between the diverse spheres of research and poetic writing, but Novalis' narratives of procreation also adapt in significant ways to the individual contexts. This distinction is not always an easy one to make: the synthesis of pairs typical for procreative narratives abounds in the dialectical thinking of the "Fichte Studies" and in processes of chemical combinations, and is part of what grants these contexts an affinity to procreation in the first place (or vice versa).

Novalis' thinking about procreation is tied to the most basic questions he grapples with in his early philosophical work. His reading of Fichte encouraged him to ask about the structure of philosophical reflection and the relation between the categories of space and time. The aphorisms he writes during this epoch probe the process and temporality of the procreative act, an emerging timescale Novalis associates with the female perspective. Even though Novalis' early philosophical studies draw directly from Fichte's *Natural Law*, which contains a "deduction of marriage," the language and tone of the aphorisms are far removed from the material situation of women in the world. In general, Novalis is more concerned with abstractions and tendencies than with the materiality of bodies. In his scientific and philosophical writings they appear in terms of galvanic and chemical reactions, or as mathematical quantities. This holds for his literary work a well, where "bodies" are rarely described in detail (who could paint a picture of Mathilde?). Novalis' willingness to consider procreation abstractly testifies to the pervasiveness of the discourse in his work. This abstraction is the reason why procreation, for example, fits well with Novalis' understanding of mathematics (another universal discourse) as a science of abstract production. What Novalis does not acknowledge is that the seemingly unlimited ability of procreative narratives to function within other discourses of production has a reciprocal effect on gender roles. Chemistry is a case in point. Thanks in part to the work of Antoine Lavoisier and other scientists who re-interpreted the process of combustion during the latter part of the eighteenth century, 'burning' was no longer considered a purely destructive activity since a burning substance gains in weight when it combines with oxygen during the process of combustion. This and other developments in chemical theory allow us to read certain episodes in Novalis' oeuvre (for example, the burning of the book in the fairy tale of Hyacinth and Rosenblütchen) with the nuances they merit. Yet, as I discuss in Chapter 3, Novalis' willingness to invoke the discourse of procreation in the context of chemical combustion has its consequences. It may well follow a chemical logic that woman, as 'oxygen,' is 'consumed' by the burning process against her will (as a 'Nothzucht') in the production of something new. In this case, however, the chemical comparison is easily vulnerable to accusations of misogyny regarding the role of women in procreation. As troubling as they are, these aphorisms are one aspect of Novalis' far-reaching contribution to the discourse on procreation, and need to be considered within a broad spectrum of other ideas. To that end, the chapter also described a larger tendency in Novalis' work, showing how early references to procreation's temporality are later complemented by models of increasing spatial complexity. We can observe this tendency in procreative narratives that function on different scales (for example, between male and female, sperm and egg), in Novalis' willingness to integrate mathematical figures, and in spatially-driven metaphors such as the rungs of the "ladder" in the galvanic chain.

The second chapter on Novalis raised the question of agency, i.e., of the productive and procreative subject. I based my arguments on Novalis' clearly formulated premise that artisan production and the figure of the craftsman need to be considered in tandem with the creation of art as well as organic generation. The readings of the aphorisms and novels identified the ways in which these modes of production interact with one another. Part of the inquiry was linguistically motivated, due to the fact that the German language allows the word *Werkzeug* to refer to an instrument, a tool, a bodily organ, or a philosophical organon. Novalis' aphorisms exploit this ambivalence, which leads to a language of production that cannot be clearly defined in terms of mechanical or organic régimes (a distinction which in many regards was also deemed problematic by late-eighteenth century discussions of the human). The problem of the *Werkzeug* is also one of part–whole relationships, their interdependence, and by extension, the place of the creative subject to the world. In this regard, Novalis' discussion of instrumentality raises questions similar to those addressed in the Goethe chapter, though from a different perspective. Like Goethe, Novalis is interested in learning how the acquisition of knowledge (as a mode of "intellectual procreation") relates to organic processes. These questions are treated discretely in the aphorisms, but come together in the two novel projects. In *Heinrich von Ofterdingen*, Novalis posits the craftsmanship of the father against the poetic talent of the son. The encyclopedic *Apprentices of Sais* is, as I argued, both instrumental and organic in its structure. It offers Novalis' most comprehensive contribution to the discourse of procreation by synthesizing its philosophical, scientific and aesthetic dimensions and makes the strongest claim about thinking as an organic activity. In general, a poetics of procreation which would codify the common elements of Novalis' procreative narratives needs to be mindful of the new, functional definition of the human individual characteristic of Romantic anthropological thinking. It needs to be sensitive to context, to scale, and—as is the case with Goethe as well—to the mutability of the participant in the procreative act.

The final chapters, devoted to Johann Wilhelm Ritter, demonstrated how the themes and questions introduced earlier in the study can be pushed to extreme conclusions. Although the amount of attention paid to Ritter's work has increased dramatically in Germany during the past decade, his texts are still awaiting the full attention they deserve from an Anglophone audience—from scholars of literature as well as historians of science. The two chapters were therefore designed to emphasize Ritter's importance as a Romantic writer and approach his works with the interest of literary studies in mind. With a focus on his fragment project, they discussed both the idiosyncrasies of his work and the tangible contribution he makes to the discourse on procreation. I began the first chapter on Ritter with a reading of the prologue to the fragment project in order to show how the joint interests of narrating life on the one hand and the acquisition of knowledge on the other are as inseparable for Ritter as they are for Goethe and Novalis. Ritter's prologue is like a puzzle where the easiest answer is perhaps not the most correct. As a case of hidden identity it is not difficult to solve: the unnamed, supposedly deceased physicist is Ritter himself, as is the 'editor' who undertakes the task of narrating his life. Yet the obviousness of the answer serves as a screen for a mystery of another kind. The physicist portrayed in the biography differs in significant ways from the historical figure of the author. He is instead a composite of forged dates (from the mother) and borrowed names (from Novalis): someone who exists in a highly intricate network of relationships which, if decoded correctly, point directly to the epistemological questions governing the narrative: questions about life and human knowledge.

The chapter argued that the prologue—through the voice of the editor—makes the claim that both life processes and the pursuit of knowledge follow the logic of natural phenomena. This logic invokes three figures central to the prologue's textual poetics: pairs of polar opposites, hieroglyphs, and the monument. Just as in nature the poles of a magnet can exchange their charges, in life one state can become its opposite. This figure cuts across narrative frames to account for the thought processes of the physicist, the activities of the editor, and the reader's own change of state from confusion to clarity. The hieroglyph is the second key figure of the prologue, also connected with natural phenomena, and it serves several functions. As far as the hieroglyph is a sign to be read, it links the physicist to his friends. At the same time, the hieroglyph functionalizes the friendships for the gain of the physicist: for knowledge of himself (in the case of the 'N' of Novalis) and the natural world (in the case of Herder as hieroglyph). In anticipation of the final chapter on Ritter, I also introduced the special role of the hieroglyph in Ritter's scientific work, as developed in the context of electrical and sound figures. It expands prior scholarship on Ritter by reconsidering Ritter's scientific hieroglyph in the context of a literary poetics. The novelty of Ritter's work on the hieroglyph is due to his reading of this sign-system as a natural language with a particular phenomenal structure and a particular relation to the subject. It is a sign generated recursively, whereby meaning emerges in the moment of inscription (Siegert), as an "echo" which first creates that which it reproduces (Menke), but whose meaning for an 'ego' (*Ich*) is non-arbitrary (Welsh). Without reducing the prologue to a poetic "example" of this natural phenomenon, my reading underscores affinities between the two in order to emphasize the degree to which Ritter's poetic and scientific writing cannot be easily distinguished. The genre of the fictional biography (or third-person autobiography) is, thus, already fertile ground for patterns of recursion: all signs point back to the author, who cannot write anything (be it historical facts or deviations from them) without implicating himself. At the same time, the life portrayed by the prologue emerges under very special circumstances. As much as it is beholden to a historical context, it emerges as a radically singular and self-contained entity. The beginning and endpoints of the life cannot be mapped onto any referential sphere outside the conditions of its writing and its meaning is produced through the act of writing. The genesis of such a text, which writes its own history, can be compared to a particular 'hieroglyphic' understanding of the phenomenon in Ritter's scientific work, but the prologue also draws upon the additional concept of the 'monument' to make its claim to permanence. The chapter concluded by discussing the claim that the fragment project as a whole shall serve as a monument (*Denkmal*) to the physicist by collecting his 'scattered limbs'—the fragments of his work—into a temple.

The final chapter argued that Ritter makes the most radical contributions to the Romantic discourse of procreation. Each aspect of procreation discussed by the prior chapters returns in his work in amplified form: a theory of gender differences based on scientific phenomena, the direct implementation of scientific instruments into narratives of procreation, and a willingness to think about the temporality of procreation in terms of historical epochs rather than mere months or years. And that is just the beginning: the chapter showed the extent to which Ritter relies upon procreation to make his case for the unification of all phenomena to a single principle. His reception of Volta's pile is one cornerstone of the project, and the language of procreation in Ritter's scientific writing can be shown to be a response to the pile. The other cornerstone to Ritter's project is, surprisingly, Goethe. My study comes full circle by returning to Goethe's theory of metamorphosis—and in particular, the elegy—because this is the model Ritter draws upon to conceptualize a primal phenomenon in nature. With reference to Goethe's 'transcendental leaf,' Ritter argues for an electrical spark to serve as a template of all organic and inorganic forms and their histories. The spark is a template for time and space, but this template, as I argued at the conclusion of the chapter, is still indebted to Ritter's work on procreation.

There is no final word on procreation—such is the nature of the discourse—and this study does not claim otherwise. The cross-section of Romantic writing on procreation presented in these chapters is one possible constellation of writers among many. In the spirit of inconclusive conclusions, I will end with Ritter:

> Alles zeigt, daß das Wesen der Zeugung durchaus tiefer zu suchen ist, als in den bloßen Gesetzen der Materie. (Fragmente, n. 504)

> Everything shows that the essence of procreation is to be sought entirely more deeply than in the mere laws of matter.

Notes

NOTES TO CHAPTER 1

1. "Kehren wir in das Feld der Philosophie zurück und betrachten Evolution und Epigenese nochmals, so scheinen dies Worte zu sein, mit denen wir uns nur hinhalten." Goethe, "Bildungstrieb," MA 12:101.
2. "Alles zeigt, daß das Wesen der Zeugung durchaus tiefer zu suchen ist, als in den bloßen Gesetzen der Materie" Ritter, *Fragmente*, n. 504.
3. "die Entdeckung des wahren Verhältnisses der Erzeugung der Säugethiere, den Menschen mit einbegriffen." Ibid., 317.
4. "der allgemeinste Gegenstand für Untersuchung der nachdenkenden Köpfe." Blumenbach, *Bildungstrieb*, 11.
5. "Was geht im Innern eines Geschöpfes vor, wenn es sich der süßesten aller Regungen überlassen hat, und nun von einem zweyten befruchtet einem dritten das Leben geben soll?" Ibid., 9.
6. Blumenbach's treatise was first published in 1781, and then revised for the second edition in 1789. A third edition appeared in 1791. All quotes are from the 1791 edition.
7. Ibid., 10.
8. Humboldt, who insists upon the ability of humans to call into life something which previously existed only in matter, positions himself in direct opposition to those who would see in human reproduction the unfolding of preformed life: "Bei allem Erzeugen entsteht etwas vorher nicht Vorhandenes. Gleich der Schöpfung, ruft die Zeugung neues Daseyn hervor, und unterscheidet sich nur dadurch von derselben, dass dem neu Entstehenden ein schon vorhandener Stoff vorhergehen muss. Dieser Nothwendigkeit ungeachtet, hat indess das Erzeugte dennoch eine von dem Erzeugenden unabhängige Kraft des Lebens, und weit entfernt, dass diese aus demselben erklärbar wäre, bleibt es vielmehr ein unergründliches Geheimniss, wie nur sein Daseyn daraus hervorgeht." W. von Humboldt, "Über den Geschlechtsunterschied," *Gesammelte Schriften*, 1:315–316.
9. See also Peter Hanns Reil, "Science and the Construction of the Cultural Sciences in Late Enlightenment Germany: The Case of Wilhelm von Humboldt" *History and Theory* 33.3 (Oct., 1994), 345–366.
10. Blumenbach, *Bildungstrieb*, 11.
11. The sentence, which begins "Der Mann ist leicht zu erforschen, die Frau verräth ihr Geheimniß nicht," ends with a comment about how otherwise the loquacity (*Redseligkeit*) of women makes it impossible for them to keep things to themselves. Kant, *Werkausgabe*, 7:303–4.
12. Alles zeigt, daß das Wesen der Zeugung durchaus tiefer zu suchen ist, als in den bloßen Gesetzen der Materie." Ritter, *Fragmente*, n. 504.

13. "Bey der Zeugung *braucht* die Seele den Körper und vice versa vielleicht—Mystizism dieser Operation." Novalis, *Schriften*, 3:458, n. 1008.
14. The expression "poetics of procreation" has also been used by Stefan Willer, in an essay that focuses on Clemens Brentano's novel *Godwi* (1801). See Willer, "'Eine sonderbare Generation'. Zur Poetik der Zeugung um 1800.'" In *Generation: zur Genealogie des Konzepts, Konzepte der Genealogie*, edited by Sigrid Weigel. Munich: Wilhelm Fink Verlag, 2005.
15. "Die geistige Zeugungskraft ist das Genie." W. von Humboldt, "Über den Geschlechtsunterschied." *Gesammelte Schriften*, 1:316.
16. "(1800.) Ist thierischer Magnetismus blos ein Spiel der Zeugungskräfte, so müssen sie, durch Batterien gesammelt, Wunder thun, z.B. wirklich befruchten, durch bloße Berührung. Giebts nicht schon in der Natur Befruchtung durch bloße Berührung? Was ist überhaupt menschliche Berührung verschiedener Geschlechter zum Theil schon anders?" Ritter, *Fragmente*, n. 466.
17. For an introduction to the history of these disciplines around 1800 see Wolf Lepenies, *Das Ende der Naturgeschichte: Wandel kultureller Selbstverstandlichkeiten in den Wissenschaften des 18. und 19. Jahrhunderts* (Munich: C. Hanser, 1976) and more recently, John V. Pickstone, *Ways of Knowing: A New History of Science, Technology and Medicine* (Manchester: Manchester University Press, 2000).
18. "Wer sich mit der Naturforschung der Romantik beschäftigt, wird zugleich stets über die historische Analyse hinaus zu allgemeinen Reflexionen angeregt: über Wesen und Wirkung der Naturwissenschaften, über die Verantwortung des Naturforschers für Natur und Gesellschaft, über die Beziehungen der Naturwissenschaften zu Kunst, Theologie und Philosophie." Engelhardt, "Naturforschung im Zeitalter der Romantik," 19.
19. "Die *Reproduktionskraft* ist bei weitem die allgemeinste und in größtem Maaße an die Organisationen verschwendete Kraft." Kielmeyer, *Ueber die Verhältnisse der organischen Kräfte*, 24.
20. "Hier legte sie sich in einer ungeheuren Moles des Körpers zu Tage, dort in Pünktchen, die unser Aug mit Licht kaum mehr zu betasten und zu begränzen vermag, hier erscheint sie ewig einförmig, dort unter der Gestalt einer wandelbaren Fee." Ibid., 25.
21. "Schon *Boerhaave*'s Lehrer, *Drellincourt*, hat allein 262 grundlose Hypothesen über das Zeugungsgeschäfte aus den Schriften seiner Vorgänger zusammengestellt, und nichts ist gewisser, als dass sein eignes System die 263te ausmacht." Ibid., 13.
22. "Procreation and development are essentially seen as growth within the seed of a miniature organism already structured in its entirety" (Zeugung und Entwicklung werden im wesentlichen als Wachstum des im Keim bereits fertig angelegten verkleinerten Organismus angesehen). Joachim Ritter, *Historisches Wörterbuch der Philosophie*, s.v. "Zeugung." For a thorough and entertaining recent study of the achievements and failures of preformation theory, see Clara Pinto-Correia's *The Ovary of Eve: Egg and Sperm and Preformation* (Chicago: Chicago University Press, 1997).
23. See Timothy Lenoir's essay "Kant, Blumenbach, and Vital Materialism in German Biology" for an explanation of how Kant, reformulating Blumenbach's own ideas, came up with a solution for Blumenbach to "insist on the functional and teleological aspects of his views without espousing vitalism," as well as advocating the "mechanical features" of his description of the organism "without adopting a reductionist philosophy of organic form" (Lenoir, "Vital Materialism, 88). Kant describes Blumenbach's "formative force" or "formative drive" (*nisus formativus*) as something intrinsic to the self-organization of organic life yet still obedient to the laws of mechanics.

Cf. Immanuel Kant's *Critique of Judgment*, in particular paragraphs 81 and 81.
24. Gould, *Ever Since Darwin*, 203.
25. See Book 1, Chapters 17 and 18. Although early epigenetic theory is linked to Aristotle's name, the word "epigenesis" does not appear in *On the Generation of Animals*.
26. See Aristotle, *On the Generation of Animals*, Book 2, Chapter 1.
27. Wolf Lepenies describes Haller's view of natural history as one which accepts "no temporalized concept of development" (keinen temporalisierten Begriff der Entwicklung) and "no becoming" (kein Werden); in short, "the 'nil noviter generari' of Haller does not permit a concept like procreation at all" (das 'nil noviter generari' Hallers läßt einen Begriff wie den der Zeugung gar nicht zu), Lepenies, *Das Ende der Naturgeschichte*, 45–46.
28. Roe, *The Natural Philosophy of Albrecht von Haller*, vi-vii. For Roe's full argument, see "The Development of Albrecht von Haller's Views on Embryology," *Journal of the History of Biology*, 8:167–90.
29. In his *Natural History*, Buffon writes that "every hypothesis which admits an infinite progression ought to be rejected not only as false but as destitute of every vestige of probability. As both the vermicular and ovular systems suppose such a progression, they should be excluded for ever from philosophy," quoted in Needham, *A History of Embryology*, 215.
30. Ibid.
31. Pinto-Correia, *The Ovary of Eve*, 69–70.
32. See "Theories in Early Embryology. Close Connections between Epigenesis, Preformationism, and Self-Organization" by Linda Van Speybroeck, Dani de Waele, and Gertrudis van de Vijver in *Annals of N.Y. Academy of Sciences* 981 (2002) 7–49. The authors illustrate points of contact between the theories and discuss recent scientific attempts to bridge them, citing Waddington's concept of "epigenetics" as well as Jacob's and Monod's genetic program.
33. Gould, *Ever Since Darwin*, 205–206.
34. Von Baer, *Selbstbiographie*, 317.
35. Ibid., 319.
36. *Self-generation: Biology, Philosophy, and Literature around 1800* (Stanford: Stanford University Press, 1997) is a translated and significantly expanded version of Müller-Siever's earlier book, *Epigenese*, which discussed the language theory of Wilhelm von Humboldt.
37. In *Self-generation*, Müller-Sievers does not extend his discussion of epigenesis to engage with early Romantic literature, nor does he discuss the work of Novalis and Johann Wilhelm Ritter.
38. Müller-Sievers, *Self-generation*, 4.
39. Ibid., 5. To give just one example, Needham discusses how Christian Wolff, in *De Formatione Intestinorum* from 1768, offered "incontrovertible proof" against preformation which, however, had "little impact on the debate": "he demonstrated that the intestine is formed in the chick by the folding back of a sheet of tissue which is detached from the ventral surface of the embryo, and that the folds produce a gutter which in course of time transforms itself into a closed tube. The intestine, therefore, could not possibly be said to be preformed" Needham, *A History of Embryology*, 221.
40. Michel Foucault, *History of Sexuality* (New York: Vintage, 1988), 1:35.
41. Ibid., 32–33.
42. Ibid., 54.
43. Ibid.
44. Ibid., 54–55.

45. See Clara Pinto-Correia's discussion of the homunculus in *The Ovary of Eve*, 211–241.
46. Foucault, *History of Sexuality*, 54–55.
47. "eine anständige und doch wie Naturkenner wissen, sehr bedeutungsvolle Vorstellung des Genusses, der dann den Bildungstrieb zur Folge hat." Blumenbach, *Bildungstrieb*, 7. Both images were added for the 1791 edition.
48. See Barbara Duden, *The Woman Beneath the Skin: A Doctor's Patients in Eighteenth-Century Germany*, trans. Thomas Dunlap (Cambridge: Harvard University Press, 1998) and Ludmilla Jordanova, *Sexual Visions: Images of Gender in Science and Medicine Between the Eighteenth and Twentieth Centuries* (Madison: University of Wisconsin Press, 1989).
49. See also David Wellbery's introduction to the English translation of Friedrich Kittler's *Aufschreibesysteme*: "Romanticism is the discursive production of the Mother as the source of discursive production. Before the phantasm of the Mother and before the attachment of desire to this phantasm, in other words, there is a discursive network, and both phantasm and desire are functions of and within this network. The Romantic (and psychoanalytic) origin derives from a beginning, from a network of technologies themselves empirical, historical and other." Wellbery, *Discourse Networks*, xxiii.
50. Menninghaus argues for the fixity of Romantic oppositional pairs, even in cases of apparent experimentation. Schlegel, *Theorie der Weiblichkeit*, 214.
51. Johann Heinrich Zedler, *Grosses Vollständiges Universal-Lexicon aller Wissenschaften und Künste*, 1731f.
52. Frevert, *Mann und Weib*, 26.
53. Ibid., 22.
54. "Schon 1747 gibt das Weib offensichtlich mehr Rätsel auf als der Mann; es ist, zumindest in der Imagination der Lexikonautoren, präsenter, verlangt nach Definitionen, Abgrenzungen, diskursiven Erörterungen." Ibid., 49.
55. "Die Generalisierung des Mannes zum Menschen der Humanwissenschaften und die Besonderung der Frau zum Studienobjekt einer mit philosophischen, psychologischen und soziologischen Ansprüchen auftretenden medizinischen Teildisziplin." Honegger, *Die Ordnung der Geschlechter*, 6.
56. Jordanova, *Sexual Visions*, 21–22.
57. Ibid., 23.
58. Tantillo, "Goethe's Botany and His Philosophy of Gender," 123.
59. Kuzniar, "Hearing Women's Voices," 1197.
60. Ibid., 1196.
61. Helfer, "Male Muses," 305.
62. Ibid.
63. Müller-Sievers, *Self-generation*, 9–10.
64. Astrida Orle Tantillo, *The Will to Create: Goethe's Philosophy of Nature* (Pittsburgh: University of Pittsburgh Press, 2002).
65. Robert J. Richards, *The Romantic Conception of Life Science and Philosophy in the Age of Goethe* (Chicago: University of Chicago Press, 2002).
66. See, for example, Frederick Amrine's "Metamorphosis of the Scientist" in *Goethe's Way of Science: Towards a Phenomenology of Nature*, eds D. Seamon and A. Zajonc (Albany: SUNY Press, 1998), 33–54.
67. WA IV 13:271–272.
68. Lenoir, "Teleology Without Regrets", 297.
69. English translation: Gregor and Sullivan, 62. In German: "die Verbindung zweier Personen verschiedenen Geschlecht zum lebenswierigen, wechselseitigen Besitz ihrer Geschlechtseigenschaften" Kant, *Werkausgabe*, 6:277.

70. Gregor and Sullivan, 62. "In diesem Act macht sich ein Mensch selbst zur Sache, welches dem Rechte der Menschheit an seiner eigenen Person widerstreitet." Kant, *Werkausgabe*, 6:278.
71. Gregor and Sullivan, 62. "Indem die eine Person von der anderen gleich als Sache erworben wird, diese gegenseitig wiederum jene erwerbe; denn so gewinnt sie wiederum sich selbst und stellt ihre Persönlichkeit wieder her." Kant, *Werkausgabe*, 6:278.
72. Ibid., 6:280.
73. "Man kennt, was der Zeugung vorhergeht, und sieht das Daseyn, das darauf erfolgt; wie beides verknüpft ist? umhüllt ein undurchdringlicher Schleier." W. von Humboldt, "Über den Geschlechtsunterschied," *Gesammelte Werke*, 1:316.
74. "Fluxion of time" is a term from Newton's differential calculus (published in 1736 as *Method of Fluxions*).
75. "Die Historisierung der Natur wird mit der Historisierung des Wissens von der Natur in einen inneren Zusammenhang gebracht. Identität und Differenz, Extraktion und Kontraktion, Verwandlung und Steigerung haben ihre Gültigkeit in der Natur wie im individuellen Leben und der gesellschaftlichen Welt." Lepenies, *Das Ende der Naturgeschichte*, 43.

NOTES TO CHAPTER 2

1. Goethe to Karl Christian Adolf Neuenhahn, July 14th, 1798.
2. The original letter, which Goethe later reprinted in the *Italienische Reise*, is addressed to Herder and dated May 17th, but the commentary in the Leopoldina edition suggests that the correct date of composition is the 8th or 9th of June, 1787. LA II 9A:365.
3. See Eckart Förster, "Die Bedeutung von § § 76, 77 der Kritik der Urteilskraft für die Entwicklung der nachkantischen Philosophie." *Zeitschrift für Philosophische Forschung* 56.2 (April–June 2002), 169–190.
4. Schiller, *Nationalausgabe*, 34.1:32.
5. Goethe drafted these two essays in 1817, and they were published in a new edition of his morphological writings in 1820. In "Effect of Recent Philosophy," he describes his pleasure at reading that poetry (*Dichtkunst*) and comparative studies of nature (*vergleichende Naturkunst*) are closely connected through being submitted to the same kind of judgment (MA 12:96). In the essay "Intuiting Judgment" Goethe describes how "through the intuition of an ever creating nature we make ourselves worthy to intellectual [*geistig*] participation in nature's production" (daß wir uns, durch das Anschauen einer immer schaffenden Natur, zur geistigen Teilnahme an ihren Produktionen würdig machten), and that nothing could hinder him for participating in Kant's "*adventure of reason*" (*Abenteuer der Vernunft*). MA 12:99.
6. The full entry reads "18. Metamorphosis of Plants. Poems in order. Afternoon at Prof. Fichte's. Evening at Schiller's, on the possibility of a portrayal of the theory of nature by a poet" (18. Metamorphose der Pflanzen. Gedichte in Ordnung. Nachmittags bey Prof. Fichte. Abends zu Schiller, über die Möglichkeit einer Darstellung der Naturlehre durch einen Poeten). WA III 2:212.
7. Wilhelm Lötschert's article, "Goethe und die Pflanze," analyzes poems and dramatic excerpts that foreground Goethe's unified vision of nature and plant (i.e., the "Wald und Höhle" scene from *Faust*, "Gingko Biloba" from the *West-Östlicher Divan*, and the poem "Parabase"). See Wilhelm Lötschert, "Goethe und die Pflanze" in *Jahrbuch des freien deutschen Hochstifts* (1982), 216–230.

8. The botanical essay, *Versuch die Metamorphose der Pflanzen zu Erklären* (*Attempt to Explain the Metamorphosis of Plants*), was first published as a single volume in 1790.
9. "This poem was most welcome to the actual beloved, who had the right to relate the dear images to herself" (Höchst willkommen war dieses Gedicht, der eigentlich Geliebten, welche das Recht hatte die lieblichen Bilder auf sich zu beziehen). MA 12:77.
10. "Da versuchte ich diese wohlwollenden Gemüter zur Teilnahme durch eine Elegie zu locken, der ein Platz hier gegönnt sein möge, wo sie, im Zusammenhang wissenschaftlicher Darstellung, verständlicher werden dürfte, als eingeschaltet in eine Folge zärtlicher und leidenschaftlicher Poesien." MA 12:74.
11. Much of Goethe's early botanical research fed into his later studies on morphology. In the 1780s, however, the field of morphology had yet to be conceptualized; Goethe is credited with coining the word *Morphologie*, which appears in journal notes dating from 1796. For biographical information on Goethe's early fascination for botany, see Günter Peters' *Die Kunst der Natur*. Beginning with the refuge grandfather Textor's garden offered the young Goethe, Peters then traces the development of Goethe's natural scientific interests. Peters provides a biographical framework for Goethe's natural-scientific studies (with emphasis on the significant move to Weimar), but his emphasis on the contextualization of Goethe's metamorphosis poem alongside the work of Brockes and Gautier is less relevant for my analysis.
12. Hence at best, the frequent descriptions of the poem as "pure representation" [*reine Darstellung*] of Goethe's theory of metamorphosis, as Gertrud Overbeck writes ("Goethes Lehre," 41), and at worst, a total skepticism towards both Goethe's botany *and* the poem. Compare Lisbeth Koerner, "Goethe's Botany: Lessons of a Feminine Science" *Isis* 84.3 (September 1993) 470–495. Koerner describes Goethe as a "dilettante" ("Goethe's Botany," 478), his botany as a "private hobby" (ibid., 487), and the poem as an attempt to "naturalize" Goethe's and Vulpius' imperfectly socialized union" (ibid., 491). For a recent discussion which situates the poem in the broader scope of Goethe's work on morphology, see Dorothea von Mücke, "Goethe's Metamorphosis: Changing Forms in Nature, the Life Sciences, and Authorship." Von Mücke investigates the effect which Goethe's concept of metamorphosis might have had on his conception of authorship (with particular reference to the botanical research he conducted during the 1790s and his publication of *Zur Morphologie* in 1817).
13. Nehemiah Grew, *The Anatomy of Plants*, 1682. Charles Linné, whose binomial system of classification is still in use today, became famous in the 1730s for basing his categories on morphological differences in the plant's reproductive organs (the "male" stamen and the "female" pistil). Linné's binomial system developed over time. His first attempts at nomenclature, which could be called "polynomial" and used lengthy descriptions to identify and describe individual species of plants, were not as streamlined. See Jerry Stannard, "Linnaeus, Nomenclator Historicusque Neoclassicus," in *Contemporary Perspectives on Linnaeus*, ed. J. Weinstock (Lanham, Md.: University Press of America) 17–35. In addition to invoking Linné in the name of poetry and science, Goethe cited him as one of three thinkers who profoundly affected his development (the other two were Shakespeare and Spinoza). Yet in the same letter where he grants Linné this accolade, Goethe adds that what he learned from Linné was not botany per se, but rather an approach to observing nature (see the letter from Goethe to Zelter dated Nov. 7th, 1816, in WA IV 27:219). This topic is also discussed in Walter Wetzels' essay "Goethe and Linné," *Contemporary Perspectives on Linnaeus*, 135. Goethe's relationship

to Linné and his terminology was an ambiguous one. His gradually developing critique of Linné says much about his own changing perspectives on botanical language and theory. In particular, one can observe a trend away from morphologically-based comparisons (where structures of a plant are observed and compared to other organisms) to comparisons which attempt to capture the dynamic processes of growth and procreation.
14. Londa Schiebinger gives a good example of the fascination for detail that accompanied contemporary descriptions of plant reproductive organs: "... in the male the filaments of the stamens are the vas deferens, the anthers are the testes and the pollen that falls from them is the seminal fluid; in the female the stigma is the vulva, the style becomes the vagina, the tube running the length of the pistil is the fallopian tube, the pericarp is the impregnated ovary and the seeds are the eggs. The French physician Julien Offray de La Mettrie, along with other naturalists of the time, even claimed the honey reservoir found in a plant's nectary gland to be equivalent to mother's milk in humans." Schiebinger "The Loves of the Plants," 112. Schiebinger quotes from de La Mettrie's "L'homme plante," in *Oeuvres Philosophiques*, 1:255.
15. Linné's criteria were not entirely accurate; for example, different plants of the same species can produce flowers with varying numbers of stamens. Schiebinger, "The Loves of the Plants," 113.
16. "The debate surrounding Linnaeus's notions of plant sexuality did not focus on this fundamental (mis)reading of the laws of nature. No one at the time or since then, for that matter, objected to this flaw in his system. Rather debate centered on scientific and moral questions surrounding the nature of plant sexuality and the language Linnaeus and his disciples used to describe the loves of the plants." Schiebinger, "Nature's Body," 126. From a twentieth-century vantage point, Linda Schiebinger interprets "two levels in the sexual politics of early modern botany—the *implicit* use of gender to structure botanical taxonomy and the *explicit* use of human sexual metaphors to introduce notions of plant reproduction into botanical literature." Ibid., 123.
17. MA 12:74.
18. Unless otherwise specified, all English citations of the poem are from "The Metamorphosis of Plants" in *Selected Poems*, trans. Michael Hamburger et al. (Princeton: Princeton University Press, 1994).
19. "Nun weiß ich noch recht gut, daß mir bei der Bildung der Geschlechter die Lehre zu weitläuftig wurde, als daß ich den Mut hatte, sie zu fassen. Das trieb mich an, der Sache auf eigenem Wege nachzuspüren und dasjenige zu finden, was allen Pflanzen ohne Unterschied gemein wäre, und so entdeckte ich das Gesetz der Metamorphose." MA 19:214.
20. Goethe contrasts his methods against Linné's on several occasions in his botanical works. In "The History of My Botanical Studies," Goethe recalls his study of Linné and comments that his attempt to master Linné's system left him as divided as the natural world in the wake of the Swedish botanist: "For as I tried to incorporate his precise and ingenious dividing, his fitting, purposeful, but often arbitrary laws, I was divided within myself" (Denn indem ich sein scharfes, geistreiches Absondern, seine treffenden, zweckmäßigen, oft aber willkürlichen Gesetze in mich aufzunehmen versuchte, ging in meinem Innern ein Zwiespalt vor). MA 12:22.
21. "What he sought to hold apart by force, had to strive for union according to the innermost need of my being" (das was er mit Gewalt auseinander zu halten suchte, mußte, nach dem innersten Bedürfnis meines Wesens, zur Vereinigung anstreben). Ibid.
22. Herder's earlier work (i.e., the *Viertes Wäldchen*, 1769, and *Vom Erkennen und Empfinden der menschlichen Seele*, 1778) already explores comparisons

between human and vegetative life cycles. For a discussion of early "biological" metaphors in Herder's thinking, see Edgar B. Schick's "Art and Science: Herder's Imagery and Eighteenth-Century Biology," *The German Quarterly*, 41.3 (1968), 356–368.
23. "Die Pflanze hat eine Art Leben und Lebensalter, sie hat Geschlechter und Befruchtung, Geburt und Tod." Herder, *Werke*, DKV 6:59.
24. "Wie sie, wird Mensch und Tier aus einem Samen geboren, der auch als Keim eines künftigen Baums eine Mutterhülle fodert. Sein erstes Gebilde entwickelt sich Pflanzenartig im Mutterleibe...Unsere Lebensalter sind die Lebensalter der Pflanze; wir gehen auf, wachsen, blühen, blühen ab und sterben." Herder, *Werke*, DKV 6:59. In the *Viertes Wäldchen*, Herder also uses the concept of "plant feeling" (*Pflanzengefühl*) to describe both primitive man and the human child. Ibid., DKV 2:274, 276.
25. "die Blüte, wissen wir, ist bei den Pflanzen die Zeit der Liebe. Der Kelch ist das Bett, die Krone sein Vorhang, die andern Teile der Blume sind Werkzeuge der Fortpflanzung, die die Natur bei diesen unschuldigen Geschöpfen offen darlegt und mit aller Pracht geschmückt hat." Herder, *Werke*, DKV 6:61.
26. "Ihr großer Zweck sollte erreicht werden...dieser Zweck ist *Fortpflanzung, Erhaltung der Geschlechter*." Ibid.
27. The phrase that became the motto of Goethe's botanical work was first jotted down during field work in Italy; see LA II 9A:58.
28. The precise date of the manuscript is not known. The editors of the Leopoldina edition estimate that it was around the time of other botanical studies conducted in 1785 and 1786. See LA II 9A:515.
29. OED, s.v. "placenta."
30. "aufgebläht, unförmlich, unausgebildet und mit einer einfachen Massen ausgefüllt... ohne daß Gefäße sonderlich mercklich würden." LA II 9A:97.
31. "Bey Lineen selbst nur Deckmantel des unentdeckten." LA II 9A:97.
32. "Es sind daher die Vergleichungen der Kotyledonen mit dem Mutterkuchen der verschiedenen Schalen des Samens mit den Häutchen der thierischen Geburten, nur scheinbar, und um desto gefährlicher als man dadurch abgehalten wird genauer die Natur und Eigenschaft solcher Teile kennen zu lernen." LA I 10:65.
33. "Da alle Geschöpfe welche wir lebendig nennen darin überein kommen, daß sie die Kraft haben ihres gleichen hervorzubringen, so suchen wir mit Recht die Organe der Zeugung *wie* durch alle Geschlechter der Thiere *so auch* im Pflanzenreich auf." LA I 10:64.
34. John Neubauer notes that Goethe had "harshly criticized" *Naturphilosophie* for "careless use of language, overuse of analogies, unreflected adoption of terminology from other fields, and reification of signs," Neubauer, "Organic Form in Romantic Theory," 220.
35. LA I 10:45.
36. *Elements of Geometry*, Part One, first definition.
37. Harvey describes his observations of the *punctum saliens* in the fourth chapter of *De motu cordis* and connects the term to Aristotle: "'The punctum saliens,' says Aristotle, 'is already possessed of spontaneous motion, like an animal.' Because an animal is distinguished from that which is none, by the possession of sense and motion. When this point begins to move for the first time, consequently, we say well that it has assumed an animal nature." *On the Motion of the Heart*, 238–239. In *Die Mechanisierung des Herzens*, Thomas Fuchs compares the first clot of blood in the embryo to the Aristotelian *arché*, "the first self-developing and auto-motive organ" (das erste sich entwickelnde und bewegende Organ) that later divides to form the heart and the circulatory system. *Die Mechanisierung des Herzens*, 92–93.

38. Goethe also uses the "point" in conjunction with the "organ" to compare the development of plants with varying degrees of complexity. Whereas in simpler organisms (for example, the so-called "Infusions-Thiere," which Goethe refers to as little point-animals or "Punkttierchen," see LA I 10:25–40) one assumes a living "point" which constantly reproduces itself, development of greater complexity is monitored through the transformation of a basic organ into multiple, more complete ones.
39. LA II 9A:34.
40. Ibid.
41. "Da in allem diesem eine Art von Zeugung, und nicht blos eine Art von Entwickelung und Absonderung vorzugehn scheint so fragt sichs, in wie fern eine solche Zeuchung [sic], wenn man sie annehmen könte und dürfte mit iener welche durch den Blumenstaub geschieht eine Ähnlichkeit hätte. Wäre aufs genauste zu untersuchen, und die Spuren davon eifrig zu verfolgen, das Resultat mag ausfallen wie es will." LA II 9A:34.
42. Goethe's intuitions were very much in line with a new trend in the scientific study of living organisms. Blumenbach describes the "Bildungstrieb" (formative drive) as "the first most important force for all procreation, nourishment, and reproduction (die erste wichtigste Kraft zu aller Zeugung, Ernährung, und Reproduction). *Über den Bildungstrieb*, 32.
43. This is the historical argument proposed by Franz Mautner, who describes the aphorisms migration from a "scientific mode of expression" into the fields of moral philosophy and anthropology until finally, as if through the force of tradition, it has become "a *creative* [gestaltenden], and in narrower sense "literary" form with its own claims and laws, a poetic *genre*" (daß er so zu einer *gestaltenden*, im engeren Sinne "literarischen" Form mit eigenen Ansprüchen und Gesetzen, zu einer poetischen *Gattung* geworden ist). Mautner, "Der Aphorismus als literarische Gattung," 36.
44. Gerhard Neumann, *Der Aphorismus* (introduction), 9.
45. Ibid.
46. Neumann, *Ideenparadiese*, 14.
47. Gerhard Neumann, *Ideenparadiese*, 14. Herder discusses the historical basis of the affinity between aphorism and the organic in his work *Zerstreute Blätter*; Goethe received the first volume in March 1785.
48. This is the term used by editor Harald Fricke in the Frankfurt edition of Goethe's aphorisms.
49. One product of the discussions with Moritz is the essay, "Einfache Nachahmung der Natur, Manier, Styl" (Simple Imitation of Nature, Manner, Style) published in the February 1789 volume of the journal *Teutsche Merkur*. In the essay, Goethe promotes an ideal of artist as scientist, with specific reference to botany. "It is apparent that such an artist must become all the greater and more authoritative, if in addition to his talent he is also an educated botanist" (Es ist offenbar daß ein solcher Künstler, nur desto größer und entschiedener werden muß, wenn er zu seinem Talente noch ein unterrichteter Botaniker ist). MA 3.2:189.
50. Goethe will return to the idea of a single individual with two sexes as the best way of conceptualizing plant reproduction at various stages of his studies.
51. This word should be read with the double emphasis of activity and perfection. See Adelung, *Grammatisch-Kritisches Wörterbuch* (1811), s.v. "Ausübung."
52. Just as there are two moments, there are two *Augenblicke*: *Augenblick* stems from the regard of the observer, but there is also the continuum of nature defined as, *in jedem Augenblick*.
53. Julius von Sachs' *History of Botany* is indicative of a certain point of view which aligned Goethe's position "exactly" with the "position of the so-called

nature-philosophy" and criticized him for a "confusion of notion and thing, idea and reality, subjective conception and objective existence" that in the later writings on the spiral tendency became "still more obscure." Sachs, *History of Botany*, 158–159.

54. "Die *regelmäßige* Metamorphose können wir auch die *fortschreitende* nennen: denn sie ist es, welche sich von den ersten Samenblättern bis zur letzten Ausbildung der Frucht immer stufenweise wirksam bemerken läßt, und durch Umwandlung einer Gestalt in die andere, gleichsam auf einer geistigen Leiter, zu jenem Gipfel der Natur, der Fortpflanzung durch zwei Geschlechter, hinauf steigt." MA 12:30.

55. Adolf Portmann remarks that the thought behind Goethe's laconic central statement concerning the *Urphänomen*, "everything is leaf," had already been discussed by the English naturalist Nehemiah Grew as early as 1672. In other words, Grew connected various organs of the plant to the single notion of leaf without making a leap from empirical evidence to a purely intellectual envisioning or *Anschauung*. He also argues that Goethe's interest in the "inner forces" of the plant marks a stage in the history of science that the field of botany was about to outgrow, partly due to the cell theories that originated during the first decades of the nineteenth century. See Portmann, "Goethe and the Concept of Metamorphosis," 135–142. In Günter Altner's reading, Goethe's theory of metamorphosis illustrates what "went lost" in modern biology, where the research of forms [*Gestaltforschung*] "concentrates on the molecular preconditions of form, but not on the particularity of forms themselves" Altner, "Gestaltwandel der Welt," 79.

56. "Es versteht sich hier von selbst, daß wir ein allgemeines Wort haben müßten woedurch wir dieses in so verschiedene Gestalten metamorphosierte Organ bezeichnen, und alle Erscheinungen seiner Gestalt damit vergleichen könnten." §120, MA 12:67.

57. The notion of "leaf" as an *Urphänomen* which manifests itself in different forms throughout plant growth is the central thought of Goethe's *Attempt to Explain the Metamorphosis of Plants*. Goethe summarizes his conclusions in §119: "Just as we have tried to explain the various organs of the growing and blooming plant from a single one, namely *the leaf*" (So wie wir nun die verschiedenscheinenden Organe der sprossenden und blühenden Pflanze alle aus einem einzigen, nämlich *dem Blatte*...zu erklären gesucht haben). MA 12:67.

58. The Goethe scholarship has pointed out that the use of the word "leaf" to signify the *Urphänomen* was to be only temporary, until a better solution suggested itself. Dorothea Kuhn comments on the use of "Blatt" as a placeholder until a more adequate expression can be found: "Goethe tries to identify individuation as 'leaf.' Here, he grapples with the word. He wants to say 'leaf' only tentatively, wants to introduce a new concept, [he] does not do it however; later he speaks of the 'transcendental leaf.' Therefore temporarily he calls that which the plant produces as organs 'leaf' and in the course of the plant's development ascertains a regular series of differently shaped 'leaves.'" Kuhn, *Typus*, 135.

59. "Denn wir können eben so gut sagen: ein Staubwerkzeug sei ein zusammengezogenes Blumenblatt, als wir von dem Blumenblatte sagen können: es sei ein Staubgefäße im Zustande der Ausdehnung." §120, MA 12:67.

60. The chapter on Novalis' fragments and novel examines the late eighteenth century's understanding of "organ" more closely; see also Manfred Frank's *Der kommende Gott*, Part One, Lecture Six.

61. Goethe iterates the significance of these two central concepts on several occasions in his correspondence. In a letter to Johann Schweigger dated April 25th, 1814, he writes "Since our excellent Kant says with sparse words:

no matter can be thought of without attraction and repulsion, (that really means, not without polarity), I am greatly comforted to be able to continue my world-view [Weltanschauung] under this authority in accord with my earliest convictions, in which I have never gone astray" (Seit unser vortrefflicher Kant mit dürren Worten sagt: es lasse sich keine Materie ohne Anziehen und Abstoßen denken, (das heißt doch wohl, nicht ohne Polarität,) bin ich sehr beruhigt, unter dieser Autorität meine Weltanschauung fortsetzen zu können, nach meinen frühsten Überzeugungen, an denen ich niemals irre geworden bin.) WA IV 24:227.

62. Goethe's description of plant development conforms to the notions of "polarity" [Polarität] and "intensification" [Steigerung]. These concepts are present throughout his oeuvre through the movements of expansion and contraction, polar pairs, the diastolic and the systolic, and optical phenomena (one could refer to, for example, "The Effect of Recent Philosophy," the preface to the Farbenlehre, or to prose works such as the Wilhelm Meister novels). Goethe also describes polarity and intensification as the "two great gears [Triebräder] of all nature:" polarity is the gear "of matter, to the extent we think of it materially," and intensification belongs to matter "to the extent that we think of it spiritually" (jene der Materie, insofern wir sie materiell, diese ihr dagegen, insofern wir sie geistig denken, angehörig). MA 18.2:359. For Goethe, polarity is just as active a concept as intensification and implies a constant oscillation between two extremes.

63. The two concepts are central to Goethe's understanding of plant development, and they play a role in his later work on the spiral tendency where are associated with gendered metaphors of masculinity and femininity.

64. Goethe construes "idea" as independent from space and time; for this reason, "the simultaneous and the successive" [Simultanes und Sukzessives] are interlocked within an idea, but separate from the point of view of experience. See "Bedenken und Ergebung." MA 12:99–100.

65. "An denen Körpern, welche wir Pflanzen nennen, bemerken wir die doppelte Kraft ihres gleichen hervorzubringen: einmal ohne sichtbare Wirkung der Geschlechter, einmal durch ihre sichtbare Wirkung." LA I 10:56. Here too, Goethe underscores a distinction between growth and reproduction on the basis of visibility ("seeing" the birth, etc.)

66. Arber, Goethe's Botany, 103.

67. Goethe questions Wolff's claim to see a constant "contracting" and "shrinking" during plant metamorphosis. This one-sided motion, argues Goethe, finds itself in constant alternation with a force of expansion that Wolff failed to notice: "He saw that it reduced in volume and did not notice that it simultaneously refined itself, and thus counter-intuitively attributed it to completion, or to a weakening." (Er sah daß es sich an Volum verringere und bemerkte nicht daß es sich zugleich veredle, und schrieb daher den Weg zur Vollendung, widersinnig, einer Verkümmerung zu.) MA 12:85. Goethe praises Wolff's observations and methods for their precision: they guided Wolff towards the correct answers, but as a result of misinterpretation, he remained in constant contradiction with himself.

68. "Anastomosis" indicates the union of an organism's parts so as to "intercommunicate" or create a network. It derives from the Greek ana + stoma (the latter means 'mouth'). In the section of the essay on metamorphosis titled "Repetition," Goethe returns to the notion of anastomosis and groups it with, in his view, the most important concepts of the essay. He also elaborates that this particular process is not limited to plant reproduction, but may also be observed as early as the first stage of growth, in the appearance of the cotyledons (see §117 and §118).

69. "und wenn die genaue Verwandtschaft desselben mit dem männlichen uns durch diese Betrachtung recht anschaulich wird, so finden wir jenen Gedanken, die Begattung eine Anastomose zu nennen, passender und einleuchtender." MA 12:49–50. With the emphasis on illumination or making visible, Goethe also emphasizes one aspect of metaphors as defined by Quintilian: to "place things vividly before the eye." Quintilian, *Institutio Oratorio*, 311.
70. In addition, Goethe's reference to procreation as a *"geistige"* anastomosis both covers and reveals the "secret" of procreation. *Geistig*, translated here as "immaterial," is opposed to the corporeal, but can be read as finely particulate (as is pollen), and carries the meanings both of the "intellectual" and the "spiritual." In this reading, the moment of plant procreation hovers between the physical and the metaphysical.
71. "Bei der fortschreitenden Veränderung der Pflanzentheile wirkt eine Kraft, die ich nur uneigentlich Ausdehnung und Zusammenziehung nennen darf. Besser wäre es ihr ein x oder y nach algebraischer Weise zu geben, denn die Worte Ausdehnung und Zusammenziehung drücken diese Wirkung nicht in ihrem ganzen Umfange aus. Sie zieht zusammen, dehnt aus, bildet aus, bildet um, verbindet, sondert, färbt, entfärbt, verbreitet, verlängt, erweicht, verhärtet, theilt mit, entzieht." LA I 10:58.
72. Seeing in this context is always emphatically active, not passive. Jost Schieren comments that activity is necessary to perceive differences between phenomena, and that both Goethe and Schiller emphasize how important it is "to remain active" within the experiment. Schieren, *Anschauende Urteilskraft*, 103–104. With reference to Hegel's reception of the *Urphänomen* in Goethe's work, he also locates the *Urphänomen* at an transitional position between the "idea" and the "empirical." Ibid., 175.
73. Förster, "Goethe and the 'Auge des Geistes,'" 93.
74. Ibid., 94.
75. Ibid., 93.
76. Goethe's travel journal from the first Italian voyage also comments on the continued metamorphosis of engendered organisms: "Das Gezeugte und Gebohrne schreitet unaufhaltsam fort wieder zu zeugen und zu gebähren, und verändert sich in jedem Augenblick." This observation collapses the two moments of *Zeugung* and *Gebären* into a single organic instance. LA II 9A:52.
77. "Der Mensch kann ohne diese nur das was gesondert ist erkennen, eben darum weil es gesondert ist. Er muß um zu erkennen, dasjenige sondern, was nicht gesondert werden sollte; und hier ist kein ander Mittel als das, was die Natur gesondert unserer Erkenntniß vorgelegt hat, wieder zu verbinden, wieder zu Einem zu machen." LA 10:58.
78. With reference to Husserl, Schieren notes that "every perception is...first of all limited. Our perception traces an object from its proper continuum." (Jede Wahrnehmung ist...zunächst beschränkt. Unser Wahrnehmen grenzt einen Gegenstand aus dem ihm eigenen Kontinuum aus). Schieren, *Anschauende Urteilskraft*, 91. Goethe's metaphors actively connect biological and intellectual processes. In a text on morphology, he suggests that physiological observations amount to a "palingenesizing" from isolated phenomenon so that one can construct the organism again as living and healthy. MA 4.2:198.
79. Goethe drafted the essay in 1792. "Der Versuch als Vermittler zwischen Subjekt und Objekt" was first published in an edition of Goethe's scientific studies (vol. 2, no. 2, 1822).
80. MA 12:687.
81. See MA 4.2:329. Goethe also makes specific reference to his optical experiments in the following passage, and there is documentary evidence that he

developed his ideas about the experiment while working on the treatise on color theory (see MA 4.2:1075–1077).
82. "Sie stellt die Formel vor, unter welcher unzählige einzelne Rechnungsexempel ausgedruckt werden" (MA 4.2:330). Goethe's notion of a composite series of experiments has been compared to the traditional model of the *scala naturae* still popular during the eighteenth century: the idea (supported by numerous scientists, including Linné, Haller and Bonnet, as well as Buffon) that a "chain of being" connects all things of the world, from the simplest matter through the inorganic and organic realms through man and the realm of angels. Dorothea Kuhn, who observes that the *scala naturae* transcended theories of epigenesis and preformation, argues that *Kette, Stufenfolge,* and *Konsequenz* designate continuity as well as unity; according to Kuhn, this logic inspired Goethe's experimental methodology, which orders observations into series. See Kuhn, "Typus und Metamorphose," 103. The comparison between Goethe's concept of the experiment and the *scala naturae* captures a certain linearity present in both, but can lead to an overly biased view of Goethe's methodology. Though the idea of perfection does enter Goethe's essay on plant metamorphosis, and in the metaphors of the poem, it is misleading to view his experiments as rows of observations leading towards perfection. If the composite experiment provides us with a formula of mathematical knowledge, as Goethe claims, it is based upon a discursivity where each element of the "proof" participates equally in the whole. The notion of interconnectedness in Goethe's essay on the experiment relates it to a broader philosophy of nature, but equally important is the scientist's ability to construct a new series: to detach, arrange, and reiterate certain phenomena. Margrit Wyder argues that Goethe's morphology contributes to a breaking down in the hierarchy of the linear nature model in the 18th century and provides a more critical reading of Goethe and the *scala naturae*. See Margrit Wyder, *Goethes Naturmodell: Die Scala Naturae und ihre Transformationen.* Cologne: Böhlau, 1998.
83. MA 4.2:330.
84. This is true also when the empirical seems to contradict intuition. In reference to such an apparent contradiction, Goethe iterates these necessary elements in a letter to Wackenroder dated January 21st, 1832: "thus we must always have imagination, judgment, comparison, all intellectual forces together, in order as it were to corner the incomprehensible" (so müssen wir doch immer Einbildungskraft, Urtheil, Vergleichung, alle Geisteskräfte beysammen haben, um das Unbegreifliche gewissermaßen in die Enge zu bringen) WA IV 49:210–211.
85. "When we are able to survey an object in every detail...grasp it correctly and produce it again in our mind...we can say that we intuit it in a real and higher sense" (LA II, 11:165). This passage is cited and discussed by Eckart Förster in "Auge des Geistes," 93.
86. MA 4.2:1077.
87. Tantillo, *Will to Create*, 182.
88. There is not much to be gained in a biographical reading of the *Geliebte* as Christiane Vulpius when the language of the poem insists on the same movement "to the general" that defines Goethe's botanical studies. In my reading, the *Geliebte* is more an articulation of a female tendency.
89. For Robert Richards it is important that Goethe conceptualized the poem days after his reading of Schelling's *Weltseele*. See Richards, *Romantic Philosophy of Life*, 466. Lisbet Koerner relates her reading of Goethe's poem to Erasmus Darwin's 1789 *Loves of the Plants*, a work which Goethe praised as a "teaching poem" but also critiques in a letter to Schiller from January, 26th, 1798. See LA II 9B:130.

90. Peters, *Die Kunst der Natur*, 170–171.
91. "Man vergaß daß Wissenschaft sich aus Poesie entwickelt habe, man bedachte nicht daß, nach einem Umschwung von Zeiten, beide sich wieder freundlich, zu beiderseitigem Vorteil, auf höherer Stelle, gar wohl wieder begegnen könnten." MA 12:74. Both Astrida Tantillo and Karl Richter take this text as a point of departure.
92. Matthew Bell has observed that this dualism also echoes Goethe's aphorism, "from procreation to procreation from birth to birth is a ceaseless progress" (von Zeugen zu Zeugen von Gebähren zu Gebähren ist ein unaufhaltsamer Fortschritt). WA II 6:274, also quoted in Bell, *Goethe's Naturalistic Anthropology*, 226. In particular, he emphasizes the importance of a cycle of reproduction for the anthropological dimension of the poem: "The botanical lesson is structured so as to begin and end with the process of reproduction, highlighting the stage of reproduction within the whole metamorphic cycle. If it were understood simply as a didactic poem on the metamorphosis of plants, this emphasis would not be significant. However, the poem demands consideration as an anthropological venture as well, since the life cycle of the plant is expressed at each stage in metaphors describing the metamorphosis of the human being." Ibid., 225.
93. The English translation substitutes "Growing" for *Werdend*, which actually encompasses the more general meaning of "becoming."
94. The task of the *Geliebte*—to find the law which governs plant metamorphosis, and decipher that which is in front of her very eyes—has been read in connection to the familiar topos of "the apparent secret" (das offenbare Geheimnis) in Goethe's work. See Marlis Helene Mehra, *Die Bedeutung der Formel 'Offenbares Geheimnis' in Goethe's Spätwerk*. Stuttgart: H.-D. Heinz, 1982.
95. "Eine jede Erfahrung die wir machen, ein jeder Versuch, durch den wir sie wiederholen ist eigentlich ein isolierter Teil unserer Erkenntnis, durch öftere Wiederholung bringen wir diese isolierte Kenntnis zur Gewißheit." MA 4.2:326–327.
96. For another reading of the "word" in Goethe's poem, compare Günter Peters, *Die Kunst der Natur*, 167–203. Peters understands the word as a puzzle which must be solved "so that it can unite the manifold to one"; to accomplish this, however, "an entirely different *word* must be found, a word of an entirely different kind, a word which acts differently than names. Can there be such a word?" (Ein ganz anderes Wort müßte gefunden werden, ein Wort von ganz anderer Art, ein Wort, das anders verfährt als die Namen. Kann es ein solches Wort geben?). Peters, *Die Kunst der Natur*, 182 and 203.
97. For a detailed discussion of this passage in Goethe's poem, see Jean Lacoste's *Goethe. Science et Philosophie*. Lacoste not only reads the "erotic and pagan vision" as the center of the "mystery" of metamorphosis, he also describes the unseen union as a kind of turning point, a "fugitive" moment of intense contraction followed by "the greatest extension" of fructification before the final production of the fruit (Cette vision érotique et païenne constitue le coeur de ce poème à la fois élégiaque et didactique qui explique à la bien-aimée, la jardinière Christiane Vulpius, le mystère de la métamorphose des plantes. Mais elle est assez fuigitive). Lacoste, *Goethe*, 20.
98. Luhmann, "Liebe als Passion," 153–154. For a detailed discussion of "incommunicability" see Edgar Landgraf, "Romantic Love and the Enlightenment: From Galantry and Seduction to Authenticity and Self-Validation" in *The German Quarterly*, 77.1 (Winter 2004), 29–46.
99. It occurs not only in the realm of plants and animals, but also exists as an intrinsic part of the human condition. Cf. Lötschert, "Goethe und die Pflanze," 219 and Kirchhoff, "Die Idee der Pflanzen-Metamorphose," 20.

100. The English is my translation. The standard English translation misses several key elements of these crucial final verses in the poem, including the indirect reference to the pair; the intellectual activity which is formulated as an "intuition" (and not a marriage); and the subjunctive mood of the final verse. With regard to the unprecedented use of the third person in "the pair," Günter Peters comments that the muteness of the narrator's companion, whom the narrator addresses without bringing to speech, contributes to the strangeness of the third person: "One does not see how the pair here too could be bound in word, in speech" (Man sieht nicht, wie das Paar hier auch im Wort, in der Rede, verbunden sein könnte). Peters, *Die Kunst der Natur*, 184.
101. Tantillo, *Will to Create*, 185–186.
102. Bell, *Goethe's Naturalistic Anthropology*, 227.
103. Portmann, "Goethe and the Concept of Metamorphosis," 142.
104. At that point in the essay, Goethe issues a command to his readers that we "turn our attention away" from this kind of metamorphosis, "because it could lead us astray from the simple path we have to follow and displace our goal" (Dagegen werden wir von der dritten Metamorphose. . .unsere Aufmerksamkeit wegwenden, weil sie uns von dem einfachen Wege, welchem wir zu folgen haben, ableiten und unsern Zweck verrücken könnte). MA 12:30–31.
105. Schiller characterizes the naïve poet as one who "follows simple nature and feeling [Empfindung] and limits himself to the imitation of reality" (der einfachen Natur und Empfindung folgt und sich bloß auf Nachahmung der Wirklichkeit beschränkt) *Nationalausgabe* 20:440. The "sentimental" poet "*reflects* on the impression which objects make on him" (Dieser *reflektirt* über den Eindruck, den die Gegenstände auf ihn machen) Ibid., 441; the object therefore relates to an idea. The sentimental poet glides between "reality as limit" and the infinity of the idea. A tendency towards the first results in satire, according to Schiller, while the second case results in the elegy. Contemporary readings of Schiller such as Peter Szondi's essay, "Das Naive ist das Sentimentalische," have questioned the integrity of these two categories, but they serve the purpose of a foil against which to consider Goethe's notion of the elegy.
106. Ibid.
107. "Der elegische Dichter sucht die Natur, aber als eine Idee und in einer Vollkommenheit, in der sie nie existiert hat, wenn er sie gleich als etwas Dagewesenes und nun Verlorenes beweint" Ibid., 450–1.
108. Günter Peters' reading of the elegiac distance structured by the poem as a distance between the observer and the "closed world" of the plant or nature, with its unique law, goes against the grain of Goethe's scientific thinking. Peters, *Die Kunst der Natur*, 179.
109. Peters reads "das lösende Wort" as that which is pronounced by the "language of nature" and with which "der Betrachter der Natur Grundform und Bildungsprinzip des Planzenlebens entdeckt, darüber hinaus aber den Aufstieg in die "höhere Welt" des Menschenlebens findet. Wer im Buch der Natur zu lesen versteht, sieht sich gedrängt, das lösende Wort ihrer Rede ins poetische Gespräch zwischen Menschen zu steigern" Peters, *Die Kunst der Natur*, 169. Peters does not explain why the "lösende Wort" cannot be transmitted immediately. Overbeck reads "das lösende Wort" as "die volle anschauliche Erscheinung." Overbeck, "Goethe's Lehre," 57.
110. In Peters' interpretation, it is "the language of nature" in Goethe's poem which "pronounces 'das lösende Wort'", that poetic language is the most suitable for speaking the natural law (Die Sprache der Natur. . .spricht . . .'das lösende Wort' aus, mit dem der Betrachter der Natur Grundform und Bildungsprinzip des Pflanzenlebens entdeckt, darüber hinaus aber den Aufstieg in die 'höhere Welt' des Menschenlebens findet. Wer im Buch der Natur zu

lesen versteht, sieht sich gedrängt, das lösende Wort ihrer Rede ins poetische Gespräch zwi-schen Menschen zu steigern). Peters, *Die Kunst der Natur*, 169.
111. "Daß ich nahe am End meiner Laufbahn noch von dem Strudel der Spiraltendenz ergriffen werden sollte, war auch ein wunderlich Geschick." LA I 4:251.
112. The existing literature on Goethe and the spiral tendency is limited to a handful of essays (primarily on the spiral tendency as a literary motif in Goethe's work), histories of botany such as Sachs', and the commentary of the various Goethe editions. See Hans Froebe, "Ulmbaum und Rebe"; Robert Stockhammer, "Spiraltendenzen der Sprache, Goethes *Amyntas* und seine Theorie des Symbols"; and chapter five of Aeka Ishihara's, *Makarie und das Weltall: Astronomie in Goethes 'Wanderjahren.'* titled "Die Vertikal- und Spiraltendenz: Makarie und die Naturwissenschaftler."
113. "Above all...I notice, that the basic view which I have the honor of presenting here, is not just the result of my research, but rather that it at least in part has already been accepted and is really the result of the morphological perspective of the blossom for which we can thank our great poet Goethe" (Vor Allem...bemerke ich, daß die Grundansicht, welche ich hier vorzulegen mir die Ehre gebe, nicht etwa bloß das Resultat meiner Forschungen ist, sondern daß sie theilweise wenigstens von vielen bereits angenommen worden und überhaupt das Resultat jener morphologischen Ansicht von der Blume ist, die wir unserem großen Dichter Goethe danken) Martius, "Über die Architectonik der Blüten," column 334.
114. "Die Konstruktion einer Blüte beruht...auf einer, für jede Gattung eigentümlichen Stellung und Anordnung einer gewissen Anzahl metamorphosierter Blätter." LA I 10:339.
115. "eine symbolische Bezeichnung für die Einzelnheiten zu unternehmen und ein neues System darauf zu erbauen." LA I 10:339–340.
116. See Goethe's journal from November 6th, 1830, on vertical and spiral tendencies in the mineral realm, WA III 12:327.
117. "Versuche einer Witterungslehre 1825 / Wiederaufnahme: "...wir versinnlichen sie [die Bewegung der Welt] als lebendige Spirale, als belebte Schraube ohne Ende" (FA 25:294–295). See also Helmut Müller-Sievers' essay, "'Belebte Schraube Ohne Ende,' Zur Vorgeschichte der Doppelhelix" in *Trajekte* 16 (2008), 25–28. Müller-Sievers discusses the figures of the spiral, the helix and the screw as they relate to the work of Kant, Goethe, and subsequent theories of mechanics. With regard to Goethe, Müller-Sievers reads a direct connection between the spiral tendency of the earth and the spiral tendency of vegetation (27).
118. "[Makarie] wandelt seit ihrer Kindheit um die Sonne, und zwar, wie nun entdeckt ist, in einer Spirale, sich immer mehr vom Mittelpunct entfernend und nach den äußeren Regionen hinkreisend." MA 17:677.
119. He writes "daß die Wesen, insofern sie körperlich sind, nach dem Zentrum, insofern sie geistig sind, nach der Peripherie streben." Ibid.
120. "Will man [der Menschheit] auch eine Spiralbewegung zuschreiben, so kehrt sie doch immer in jene Gegend, wo sie schon einmal durchgegangen." MA 10:475.
121. "Wir betrachten sie als die kleinsten Teile, welche dem Ganzen dem sie angehören vollkommen gleich sind...ihm ihre Eigenheiten mitteilen und von demselben wieder Eigenschaft und Bestimmung erhalten." LA I 10:340.
122. Jonathan Barnes explains Anaxagoras' cosmology in terms of three basic principles: "In the beginning, everything was mixed together"; "There is no smallest portion of anything"; "Now, everything is mixed together" (Barnes, *The Presocratic Philosophers*, 249. There follows a more detailed description of what is meant by "thing" on pages 250–252.

123. "Lassen wir bei Seite, daß eben diese Homoiomerien sich bei urelementaren einfachen Erscheinungen eher anwenden lassen; allein hier haben wir auf einer hohen Stufe wirklich entdeckt, daß spirale Organe durch die ganze Pflanze im kleinsten durchgehen, und wir sind zugleich von einer spiralen Tendenz gewiß, wodurch die Pflanze ihren Lebensgang vollführt und zuletzt zum Abschluß und Vollkommenheit gelangt." LA I 10:344.
124. In a draft of an unposted letter to Karl August Varnhagen von Ense dated January 5th, 1832, Goethe reflects on how, at the end of his life, he finds himself surrounded by things from his past and makes reference to the spiral tendency of plants. See WA IV 49:398.
125. "neither one can be thought of as separated from the other, because one only appears living through the other...But it is necessary, for a more precise understanding...to separate and investigate them in observation: how then one or the other prevails, first its opposite overpowers, then is overpowered, or contrives to establish itself as equal" (keins kann von dem andern abgesondert gedacht werden, weil nur eins durch das andere lebendig wirkt...Aber nötig ist, zur bestimmteren Einsicht...sie in der Betrachtung zu trennen und zu untersuchen: wie denn eins oder das andere waltet, bald seinen Gegensatz überwältigt, bald von ihm überwältigt wird, oder sich mit ihm ins Gleiche zu stellen weiß). LA I 10:340. What Tantillo describes a "struggle for power between the masculine and the feminine" in Goethe's botanical thinking is particularly applicable here. Tantillo, *Will to Create*, 152.
126. "The great difficulty of keeping vividly within the intuition verticality and spirality, bound and absorbed into one, the impossibility of doing this forces me presently to a parable, if I may be allowed to insert it here" (Die große Schwierigkeit jenes Zusammenwerkens der in Eins verbundenen und verschlungenen Vertikalität und Spiralität dem Anschauen lebendig zu erhalten, die Unmöglichkeit dieses zu leisten drängt mich neulich zu einem Gleichniß, sey es erlaubt solches hier einzuschalten). WA II 7:54.
127. "Freylich paßt dieses Gleichniß auch nicht ganz." WA IV 49:446–447.
128. On January 5th, 1832, Goethe wrote to Varnhagen: "Mit den neu hervortretenden Betrachtungen über die Spiralität übergeben wir den Nachkommen mehr einen gordischen Knoten als einen liebevollen Knaul." LA II 10B:745.
129. LA I 10:341.
130. "das männlich stützende Prinzip." LA I 10:345.
131. "das eigentlich Produzierende Lebensprinzip." LA I 10:341; "auf die Peripherie angewiesen." LA I 10:345.
132. "das Fortbildende, Vermehrende, als solches Vorübergehende, sich von jenem gleichsam isolierend" and "abschließend, den Abschluß befördernd." LA I 10:357.
133. "Abschluß des Blütenstandes" LA I 10:355.
134. "erweist sie sich am auffallendsten bei Endigungen und Abschlüssen." LA I 10:342.
135. "wodurch die Pflanze ihren Lebensgang vollführt und zuletzt zum Abschluß und Vollkommenheit gelangt." LA I 10:344.
136. "Beyspiele der pathologischen Manifestationen der Spiral-Tendenz. Alter, Absterben, Vollendung seines organischen Laufes." WA II 13:94.

NOTES TO CHAPTER 3

1. All citations of Hardenberg are from the Historisch-Kritische Ausgabe and refer to the volume, page number, and (when relevant) the aphorism number.

2. "Nekrolog für Friedrich von Hardenberg" in *Nekrolog der deutschen für das neunzehnte Jahrhundert*, ed. Friedrich Schlichtegeroll (Gotha: Justus Perthes, 1805), 4:187–241.
3. Ibid., 199. This passage and subsequent ones from Just's text are also cited at length in Manfred Frank's book, *The Philosophical Foundations of Early German Romanticism*. Frank's chapter on Novalis focuses on his philosophical position with regard to Fichte, whereby the following sentences from Just receive particular emphasis: "Fichte gave the word 'science' (Wissenschaft) a new meaning; and this had much value for my friend. For his wish and aspiration was, not only to attribute everything, which up until then had been called art and science, to one principle and so to achieve a true science, but also to unify into one all sciences and arts" (Fichte hatte dem Worte 'Wissenschaft' eine neue Bedeutung gegeben; und diese hatte viel Werth für meinen Freund. Denn sein Wunsch und Bestreben war, nicht nur Alles, was man bisher Kunst und Wissenschaft nannte, auf ein Princip zurückzuführen, und so zur wahren Wissenschaft zu erheben, sondern auch alle Wissenschaften und Künste in ein Ganzes zu vereinigen). Just, "Nekrolog," 200–201; translation in Frank, *Philosophical Foundations*, 162.
4. In the recent publication of Hardenberg's "saline writings" [Salinenschriften] relating to his professional activities in Weißenfels and elsewhere, the editors of the critical edition raise the same question: "Hardenberg or Novalis?" (6.3:xv).
5. "Seine ersten Briefe an uns nach Tennstedt zeugten von seiner unsäglichen Trauer, aber auch von dem mächtigen Geist, der selbst in seinem harten Schicksal einen Aufruf zu neuen hohen Gedanken und Ansichten fand." Just, "Nekrolog," 205.
6. "*Kunst*—Wissenschaft—Handwerck—Spiel—Natur—Genie." 2:262, n. 521. Hardenberg granted his encyclopedia project the working title *Das allgemeine Brouillon* (The General Draft); it encompasses 1151 aphoristic notes written between September 1798 and March 1799. See 3:207.
7. Manfred Frank comments: "through their choice of the title *Fichte-Studien (Fichte Studies)*, [the editors of the critical edition] have presented an entirely inappropriate picture of the young Hardenberg with respect to his appropriation of Fichte's early idealism, and have thus distorted. . .the history of the public reception of Novalis' work." Frank, *Philosophical Foundations*, 41.
8. Although the importance of Fichte's philosophy for Hardenberg is universally acknowledged, Hardenberg's actual philosophical position with regard to Fichte continues to be disputed. Bernward Loheide argues for a reading of Hardenberg as a Fichtean, against the current of recent Hardenberg scholarship. See Loheide, *Fichte und Novalis*, 14–16; also Uerlings, *Friedrich von Hardenberg*, 136.
9. "Es handelt sich bei den philosophischen Aufzeichnungen aus den 'Fichte-Studien,' den Hemsterhuis- und Kant-Studien, den 'Vorarbeiten zu verschiedenen Fragment-Sammlungen' und dem 'Allgemeinen' Brouillon' auch keineswegs um 'romantische Fragmente,' sondern um Exzerpte, Lektürenotizen und eigenständige weiterführende Überlegungen, um Texte also, die ohne ihren ganz spezifischen Kontext nicht verständlich sind." Uerlings, *Friedrich von Hardenberg*, 105.
10. Ibid., 137.
11. As Frank points out, Novalis was already dead by the time Fichte returned to address this topic: "Es ist die Unterscheidung von 'Grund' und 'Resultat' im Selbstbewußtsein, in deren prozessualer Vermittlung Novalis in seinen

letzten Lebensjahren das Werk der 'allein tätigen' Zeit erkannte." Frank, *Das Problem 'Zeit,'* 130.
12. Cf. Manfred Frank and Gerhard Kurz, "Ordo Inversus. Zu einer Reflexionsfigur bei Novalis, Hölderlin, Kleist und Kafka" (*Geist und Zeichen*, Herbert Anton et al., Heidelberg: Carl Winter, 1977, 75–97) and Frank, *Das Problem 'Zeit,'* 148. For a contemporary analysis of Frank's work, see also Mario Zanucchi, *Novalis—Poesie und Geschichtlichkeit* (Paderborn: Schöningh, 2006), Chapter 1.
13. Wellbery, *The Specular Moment*, 67–68.
14. In Hardenberg's appropriation of "feeling" (*Gefühl*), Friedrich Strack finds not just "another word for the 'intellectual intuition'" but also, and with a glance towards Hardenberg's Pietist heritage, a word which invokes "our *emotional* stake in 'the whole.'" Strack, "Novalis und Fichte," 195.
15. "die Temporalisierung des Verhältnisses Grund-Folge," "das Programm einer Genese des Raums aus der Zeit." Frank, *Das Problem 'Zeit,'* 170, 163.
16. Ibid., 185.
17. "Leben ist ein aus Synthese, These und Antithese Zusammengesetztes und doch keins von allen dreyen" 2:107, n. 3.
18. Manfred Frank has commented that the "dialectical structure present in things to be explained" is for Hardenberg only the "empirical symbol of the absolute unity of all oppositions in the absolute basis [Grunde]," which is then used as a "heuristic principle of philosophy." See also Mario Zanucchi, *Novalis*, 37–45, on dialectical language in the "Fichte-Studies."
19. As Manfred Frank and others have shown, Hardenberg's template for thinking about the relationship between thesis, antithesis and synthesis is a reading of Fichte whereby the conscious, knowing *I* and the and *not-I* are not statically opposed to one another but rather originally joined in the absolute ego itself. The figure for "internal differentiation within the *Identical*" is that of *Wechselbestimmung* or "reciprocal determination," one of the central motifs in Hardenberg's thinking. Zanucchi, *Novalis*, 41; see also Manfred Frank, *Das Problem 'Zeit,'* 141.
20. "Jedes dieser drey ist alles Dreyes und dis ist Beweis ihres Zusammengehörens. Die Synthese ist These und Antithese oder kann es seyn. So die These; so die Antithese. Ursprüngliches Schema. / Eins in allem / Alles in Einem." 2:109, n. 3; also quoted in Frank, *Das Prblem 'Zeit,'* 141.
21. The German *construiren* comes from the French *construire* which, around 1800, could refer either to constructing a building ("Bâtir, faire un édifice") or, in a grammatical context, arranging the parts of a sentence ("Arranger des mots suivant les règles et l'usage de la Langue"). *Dictionnaire de L'Académie française* (1798), s.v. "construire." The ambiguity fits well with the heuristic, exploratory nature of the "Fichte Studies" as a document of Hardenberg's early philosophical "grammar."
22. "Ein Begriff ist aber wie alles Erzeugte nicht aus seinen Eltern zusammengesetzt, sondern er ist ein selbstständiges Wesen, wie Eins von seinen Eltern." 2:260–1, n. 512.
23. "*Zeugungskraft*. Weib = Vorstellung—Mann = Anschauung. Unmittelbare, mittelbare Producte." 2:189 n. 255.
24. "The female always provides the material, the male that which fashions it, for this is the power that we say they each possess, and this is what is meant by calling them male and female. . .While the body is from the female, it is the soul that is from the male." Aristotle, *On the Generation of Animals*, 738b.
25. Hardenberg was no longer a student in Jena at this time, but he read the first volume during the summer when it was published.

26. For a feminist reading of the *Foundations of Natural Law*, see Marion Heinz and Friederike Kuster, "'Vollkommene Vereinigung.' Fichtes Eherecht in der Perspektive feministischer Philosophie" DZ Phil, Berlin 46 (1998) 5:823–839, esp. 830ff.
27. "Auch von dieser näheren Bestimmung lässt sich der Grund angeben. Das System der gesammten Bedingungen zur Erzeugung eines Körpers der gleichen Art musste irgendwo vollständig vereinigt seyn, und einmal in Bewegung gesetzt, seinen eigenen Gesetzen nach sich entwickeln. Das Geschlecht, in welchem es liegt, heisst durch die ganze Natur hindurch das *weibliche*. Nur das erste bewegende Princip konnte abgesondert werden; und musste abgesondert werden, wenn bestehende Gestalt seyn sollte. Das Geschlecht, in welchem es, von dem zu bildenden Stoffe abgesondert, sich erzeugt, heisst durch die ganze Natur hindurch das *männliche*." Ibid.
28. "Es ist daher nothwendig, dass dieser Trieb beim Weibe unter einer anderen Gestalt und, um neben der Vernünftigkeit bestehen zu können, selbst als Trieb zur Thätigkeit erscheine." Ibid., 307.
29. There is a long tradition of feminist scholars who have read these passages with a critical acumen tinged with disgust and disbelief. Gertrud Bäumer laments Fichte's "relapse" into a "pre-Kantian metaphysical experiment" and describes Fichte's thoughts on sexual relations as a "strange construct of emotional incompetence, metaphysical arrogance and Philistinism" (Dieses merkwürdige Gebäude aus seelischer Inkompetenz, metaphysischer Überheblichkeit und Philisterei). Bäumer, *Fichte und Sein Werk*, 58–60. See also a slightly more forgiving reading by Marianne Weber, *Ehefrau und Mutter in der Rechtsentwicklung* (Tübingen: J. C. B. Mohr, 1907), especially 307–311, as well as Heidemarie Bennent's *Galanterie und Verachtung* (Frankfurt/New York: Campus Verlag, 1985). Bennent describes the regressive elements of Fichte's discussion of marriage and sexuality in more detail both in contradistinction to Kant and with regard to the material situation of women around 1800.
30. See Frank's comment on Hardenberg's variable terminology, which includes "species" [*Gattung*] and "individual" among the possible substitute pairs for *Grund* and *Folge*: "Im Verlauf der Fichte-Studien wählt Novalis als Termini für die bekannte Entgegensetzung die in der Sekundär-Literatur überschätzte Unterscheidung von 'Zustand und Gegenstand,' die er selbst mit der negativ beantworteten Frage: 'Qualificiren sich die Begriffe—Zustand und Gegenstand—zu Grundlagen' aufgibt und einer andern Differenzierung, der von 'Wesen und Eigenschaft,' 'Grund und Folge'...'Gattung und Individuum' hintanstellt." Frank, *Das Problem 'Zeit,'* 170.
31. Nor does Fichte deal with "longing" in *Foundations of the Natural Law* (either as noun, *Sehnsucht*, or verb, *sehnen*), but it does play a significant role in the *Foundations of the Entire Theory of Science* (1795). Manfred Frank discusses how for Fichte, the concept of "longing" describes the "unconscious striving" of the I as something that we "feel" passively. Frank, *Philosophical Foundations*, 168.
32. See also Zanucchi on the Romantic notion of "the lost" in relation to feeling; Zanucchi, *Novalis*, 33. Loheide comments that time for Hardenberg is both "expression of a fundamental lack"—the separation of the I from its "inaccessible ground"—and the mitigation thereof. Loheide, *Fichte und Novalis*, 222.
33. Mario Zanucchi shows how Hardenberg's distinction between *Gefühl* and *Empfindung* derives in part from his reception of Jacobi, who distinguishes between *Empfindung* as sensation of one's own body and the *Gefühl* as feeling (or the French *sentiment*) of existence more generally. See Zanucchi, *Novalis*, 30. According to Zanucchi, Hardenberg "mobilizes...Jacobi's argument,

that being does not amount to self-consciousness" ibid., 32. *Gefühl* and *Empfindung* can also be related to the preceding aphorism (i.e., 2:260, n. 510). "Empfindung," usually defined as physical sensitivity, governs the nature of woman but is the servant [Untertan] of the man. "Kraftgefühl"—as opposed to "Kraftempfindung"—can be read as woman's fleeting experience of her own will, and as a momentary leap from the particular to the general in the moment of procreation.

34. A difference of opinion about the use of morphological criteria to differentiate species is one aspect of the debate over Buffon's *Histoire Naturelle*. See Timothy Lenoir, "Vital Materialism," 79.
35. Timothy Lenoir has discussed this in detail in the "Vital Materialism" essay.
36. Kant makes a provisory distinction, for the sake of argument, between a "Nominalgattung" where species kinship is supposed on the basis of similarity, and a "Realgattung" where species kinship is proven through generations of fertile offspring. Whereas the first category lies under the purview of "describers of nature" (Naturbeschreiber), the second is the business of natural history. Kant, *Werkausgabe*, 8:102.
37. Kant's essay also critiques Blumenbach's early preformationist position which was later revised. Timothy Lenoir explains how Blumenbach's reading of Kant led him to rework key passages in the *Bildungstrieb* between the first and second editions. While Blumenbach was a student of Haller, he advocated preformation. Although he later abandoned this view in favor of epigenesis, Blumenbach initially tried to retain certain characteristics, such as the morphological criteria of distinguishing species. Lenoir, "Vital Materialism," 91–92.
38. "Die Individuen, vereinigt, und inwiefern sie vereinigt werden können, sind erst, und bilden erst die Gattung; denn *seyn* und *bilden* ist in der organischen Natur Eins. Das Individuum *besteht* lediglich als Tendenz, die Gattung zu bilden." Fichte, *Sämmtliche Werke*, 3:306.
39. "Die Basis aller Wissenschaften und Künste muß eine W[issenschaft] und Kunst seyn—die man der Algéber vergleichen kann—Sie wird freylich, wie diese, später, als die meisten speciellen Künste und W[issenschaften] entstehn—weil die Gattung oder das Gemeinsame später, als das Einzelne entsteht—indem es erst durch den Contact der gebildeten Individuen erzeugt wird—h[oc] est ins Fleisch kommt." 3:257, n. 90.
40. The passage continues with Goethe voicing his dissatisfaction with both theories: preformation is "distasteful" to any "educated person" but epigenesis still cannot relinquish the need of something—however it might be called—which comes before. "Kehren wir in das Feld der Philosophie zurück und betrachten Evolution und Epigenese nochmals, so scheinen dies Worte zu sein, mit denen wir uns nur hinhalten. Die Einschachtelungslehre wird freilich einem Höhergebildeten gar bald widerlich, aber bei der Lehre eines Auf- und Annehmens wird doch immer ein Aufnehmendes und Aufzunehmendes vorausgesetzt, und wenn wir keine Präformation denken mögen, so kommen wir auf eine Prädelineation, Prädetermination, auf ein Prästabilieren, und wie das alles heißen mag, was vorausgehen müßte, bis wir etwas gewahr werden könnten." MA 12:101.
41. "Praeformation ein Wort das nichts sagt, wie kan etwas geformt seyn eh es ist." FA 1, 13:312. The note dates from 1788 and is grouped by the editors under the heading, "Studien zur Entwicklungslehre Patrins." The 1788 work, *Zweifel gegen die Entwicklungstheorie. Ein Brief an Herr Senebier von L(ouis) P(atrin). Aus der französishcen Handschrift übersetzt von Georg Forster.*

42. "Phänomen der einfachsten, die eine bloße Aggregation der Teile zu sein scheint, oft aber ebenso gut durch Evolution oder Epigenese zu erklären wäre." MA 4.2:197. The precise date of this text is uncertain; the editors of the Leopoldina edition place it at approximately 1795–1798. LA II 9B:421.
43. Hardenberg also integrates the two dimensions, as the following note from the encyclopedia project can attest: "Imagination *came* to the *world*, or *became*, the most easily and first—reason *perhaps at the end*. On this *outward formation*—and spiritual *secretion*. Seed and irritation secretion—first feminine—last masculine. *Development of our nature*. First procreation—2nd—third etc. cumulative." (Die Einbild[ungs]Kr[aft] ist am leichtesten und ersten zur *Welt gekommen*, oder *geworden*—die *Vernunft vielleicht zulezt* [sic]. Über diese *Herausbildung*—und geistige *Secretion*. / Keim und Reitz Secretion—erstere weibliche—letztere männlich. / *Entwicklung unsrer Natur*. Erste Zeugung—2te—dritte etc. cumulative). 3:252, n. 70. The editors of the critical edition connect the note to Hardenberg's reading of Alexander von Humboldt's *Aphorismen aus der chemischen Physiologie der Pflanzen* (Leipzig 1794) and provide further commentary on his reading of Spinoza. 3:903–904.
44. "Dieses letztere [= das System der *Epigenesis*] kann auch System *der generischen Präformation* genannt werden: weil das productive Vermögen der Zeugenden doch nach den innern zweckmäßigen Anlagen, die ihrem Stamme zu Theil wurden, also die specifische Form *virtualiter* präformirt war" Kant, *Werke*, 5:423. English translation in J. H. Bernard, 272. For a discussion of this passage see also Zammito, *The Genesis of Kant's 'Critique of Judgment,'* 217–218.
45. Ibid., 218.
46. Pinto-Correia, *Ovary of Eve*, 57.
47. Ibid., 282. Both Pinto-Correia and Gould have observed that before the advent of cell theory, there was no lower limit for the size of organisms. The idea of miniature creatures with miniscule organs was therefore not implausible to the eighteenth-century imagination. See Gould, *Ever Since Darwin*, 204.
48. *Erzeugung* can refer either to organic generation or, more broadly, to any kind of production (Adelung's dictionary lists the organic definition first). *Constructionsformel* also has a special place in Hardenberg's lexicon: he refers to this term both in his mathematical studies ("Definitionen...sind *Constructionsformeln*," 3:125) and also in political sense whereby the constitution is the construction formula of a nation (3:257, n. 91).
49. As was discussed in the introduction to this study, the word *Geschlecht* was not narrowly defined around 1800. Adelung's dictionary notes that it is frequently interchanged with *Art* ("kind") and *Gattung* ("species" or "genus") although it is usually broader in scope than either of the other two (Art, Gattung und Geschlecht werden oft mit einander verwechselt; doch wird das letztere am beständigsten von der Ähnlichkeit der Gattungen, Gattung von der Ähnlichkeit der Arten, Art aber von der Ähnlichkeit einzelner Dinge gebraucht). *Grammatisch-Kritisches Wörterbuch* (1811), s.v. "Geschlecht."
50. The aphorism also recalls those passages from Fichte's *Foundation of the Natural Law* discussed in the context of Hardenberg's "Fichte Studies" where Fichte suggests that the concepts of genus and species are consequences of the procreative act ("The individuals, joined, and insofar as they can be joined, first are—and first create—the species." Fichte, *Sämmtliche Werke*, 306).
51. Adelung defines *Gattung* broadly as "things, which go together, which are like one another, things of one kind, as a collective" ("Dinge, welche sich zusammenschicken, welche einander ähnlich sind, Dinge einer Art, als ein Collectivum"). In a narrower, philosophical sense, "...animals are the group which

comprises the four-footed animals, birds, fish etc. as species, (". . .die Thiere die Gattung, welche die vierfüßigen Thiere, Vögel, Fische u.s.f. als Arten unter sich begreift). Adelung also lists a third usage, the *Gattung* or *Genus* of temporal expressions in language, such as the "the active *Gattung*" and "the passive *Gattung*," *Grammatisch-kritisches Wörterbuch* (1811), s.v. "Gattung."

52. For comparison with another note from the encyclopedia project which makes use of preformative structures, see the following, titled "Physics and Theory of the Future": "A *generation* is the seed of *endless generations*—which encapsulates the world drama. The true generation is our becoming human. The usual *generations* are only conditional processes of the true generation." (Eine *Generation* ist der Keim der *unendlichen Generationen*—die das Weltdrama beschließt. Die ächte Generation ist unsre Menschwerdung. Die gewöhnlichen *Generationen* sind nur BedingungsProcesse der ächten Generation). 3:254, n. 79.

53. "Die Mathematik ist ächte Wissenschaft—weil sie *gemachte Kenntnisse* enthält—Produkte geistiger Selbstthätigkeit." 3:473, n. 1126. The commentary to the critical edition has pointed out this connection (3:920).

54. Ibid., 4.

55. Ibid., 4–5.

56. "Geometrische Reihen—sind lebendig—progressive Reihen. Alle *Progressionen sind lebendig.*" Ibid., 92.

57. "Alle Wissenschaften sollen *Mathematik werden*. . .Das Zahlensystem ist *Muster* eines ächten Sprachzeichensystems—Unsre Buchstaben sollen Zahlen, unsre Sprache Arythmetik werden." Ibid., 50.

58. See Martin Dyck, *Novalis and Mathematics* (Chapel Hill: UNC Press, 1960) and Käte Hamburger's "Novalis und die Mathematik; eine Studie zur Erkenntnistheorie der Romantik," *Romantik Forschungen* 16 (Halle, 1929).

59. Cf. Förster, "Die Bedeutung von § § 76, 77 der Kritik der Urteilskraft," 177.

60. An early milestone in this field is Johannes Hegener's *Die Poetisierung der Wissenschaften bei Novalis* (Bonn: Bouvier, 1975), which contains several sections devoted to chemical theory; for a more recent contribution see Michel Chaouli's *The Laboratory of Poetry: Chemistry and Poetics in the Work of Friedrich Schlegel* (Baltimore: Johns Hopkins University Press, 2002).

61. *Das romantische Paradigma der Chemie: Friedrich von Hardenbergs Naturphilosophie zwischen Empirie und alchemistischer Spekulation* (Paderborn: Mentis, 2003).

62. "Das Modell eines prozessualen Gesamtgeschehens, in dem sich permanent neue Aggregate, Konfigurationen oder Konstellationen mit mehr oder weniger großer zeitlicher Stabilität bilden, steht paradigmatisch für eine 'chemische' Denkform, die uns heute—in Gestalt des neuen Naturdenkens—mit der romantischen Naturphilosophie verbindet. Bereits die romantische Naturphilosophie fand in der Chemie ihre spezifische Leitund Modellwissenschaft zur Erklärung schöpferischer, Geist und Natur aktiv synthetisierender und den *context of discovery* akzentuierender Prozesse." Ibid.,14.

63. There is a play on words here: *Probierkunst* technically refers to the (al)chemical process of "fire assaying", although in the context of Liedtke's sentence it can also be read as "experimental art."

64. ". . .das allgemeine heuristische Interesse der Chemie als klassischer experimenteller 'Probierkunst'. . .das Problem der Substantialisierung von chemischen Eigenschaften / Identifikation von Stoffen. . .die insgesamt produktiv-technische, instrumentelle, operationale und funktionale Denkform der Chemie. . .das Charakteristikum des Widerspruchs, der Dualität oder Polarität des Chemieparadigmas." Ibid., 19.

65. See the introduction to Bettina B. Meitzner, *Die Gerätschaften der chemischen Kunst: der Traktat* De sceuastica artis *des Andreas Libavius von 1606: Übersetzung, Kommentierung und Wiederabdruck* (Stuttgart: Franz Steiner Verlag, 1995).
66. "Zur Physik. Im Sommer 1798 zu Dreßden angefangen," HKA 18:144–151.
67. "A. abs[olute] Positive Synth[ese] von Leben und Organisation–
    B. abs[olute] Negative Synth[ese] v[on] Leben und Org[anisation]
    C. abs[olute] abs[olute] Synth[ese] von Leben und Organisation." 3:93.
68. Cf. Kant, *Metaphysische Anfangsgründe der Naturwissenschaft*: "The effect of a moving force on a body in a moment is the solicitation of [the body]" (Die Wirkung einer bewegenden Kraft auf einen Körper in einem Augenblicke ist die Sollicitation desselben). *Werkausgabe*, 4:551.
69. "Wir nennen den *Körper todt*—der bloßer Leiter der Sollicitation ist—den die Sollicitation nicht *weckt*. Der absolute Nichtleiter der Sollicitation ist wieder todt zu nennen." 3:92.
70. "So sehn wir, daß das *sensible Leben an sich* ein *Halbzustand* ist—worinn wir die Körper *unvollkommne Leiter der Sollicitation* nennen." 3:92.
71. The entry on "Philistines" in Adelung suggests that current usage in Germany and Austria does not refer to the ancient Philistines who lived on the border of Judean lands, but rather designates commoners or soldiers in employment of the state. This usage derives from a corruption of the Latin *Balistarii*, a name for low-ranking soldiers who shot with crossbows ("Balistis"), and later spread to a more general, and pejorative, designation of all commoners. *Grammatisch-kritisches Wörterbuch* (1811), s.v. "Philister."
72. "Ce qui sort du corps de l'animal, par la voie d'une séparation naturelle et ordinaire." *Dictionnaire de l'Académie française* (1798), s.v. "excrement."
73. Elsewhere in the same manuscript Hardenberg compares the products of combustion to progressively more complex excrements. See 3:84.
74. See Geza von Molnár, *Novalis' "Fichte Studies"* (The Hague: Mouton, 1970), esp. Chapter 1; Liedtke, *Das romantische Paradigma der Chemie*, 147; Ulrich Gaier, *Krumme Regel* (Tübingen: Niemeyer, 1970).
75. Brown, *The Elements of Medicine*, 1:7; see also John Neubauer, "Dr. John Brown and Early German Romanticism." Nebauer discusses how Hardenberg's reception of Brown's medical theory was mixed: on the one hand, Hardenberg did not agree with Brown's attempt to reduce the human body to a complex of mechanical principles largely sustained by outside influences (375); on the other hand, Brown's attempts to classify health and disease on a single continuous scale appealed to Hardenberg (377).
76. Johann Christoph Leopold Reinhold believed that the degree of "life force" of an organism was connected to the degree of its excitability when exposed to external irritants [*Reize*]. Reinhold's description follows in the wake of the arguments made by Alexander von Humboldt against Alessandro Volta who believed that there is an intrinsic electricity to living beings. Humboldt borrowed Brown's notion of excitability to express a general quality of living matter.
77. Menninghaus' comment that these and similar passages belong to the "most suppressed" of the scholarship on Hardenberg still holds true. See Menninghaus, "Theorie der Weiblichkeit," 169, as well as Hardenberg's equally provocative "Theorie der Wollust," which could be approximately translated as a "Theory of Lasciviousness" (3:425). Gerhard Schulz has noted that the word "Sexualität" (sexuality) was not yet in use in Hardenberg's day, and that "Wollust" and "Sinnlichkeit" were common although ambivalent in their relation to either sensuality or spirituality, ibid. His claim requires some qualification, given that "Sexualität" was a word already in currency,

used to describe the reproductive habits of plants. Gerhard Schulz, "Novalis' Erotik," 214. Cf. Mähl's defense of Hardenberg through a contextualization of this aphorism in *Novalis und die Wissenschaften*, 233.
78. Gerhard Schulz has observed that there is a broad range of eroticism in Hardenberg's writing and cites both familiar examples (the "Unio mystica" of two souls) as well as unfamiliar ones (including necrophilia). Ibid.
79. Holzhey, "On the Emergence of Sexual Difference," 14.
80. The containment of a transferral from one pole to the other depicted in this fragment is reminiscent of the blocks of opposing pairs in the previous one.
81. "*Leiter*" can refer to either a step-ladder or an electrical conduit; the field of galvanism provided Novalis with metaphors to describe "electrical transfers" between bodies; elsewhere in *The General Draft*, he writes that the tongue and lips are "parts of a telegraph." 2:690, n. 639.
82. *Witterung* had various connotations in Hardenberg's day. Adelung gives the definitions: 1) "atmospheric conditions" (more specific than "weather"), 2) in mining, the vapors which emerge from the drifts, and 3) in hunting, from the verb *wittern*, to scent or smell, *Witterung* refers to animal scents. *Grammatisch-kritisches Wörterbuch* (1811), s.v. "Witterung."
83. Elsewhere in *The General Draft* Hardenberg also links the chemical and mystical aspects of procreation in an aphorism where he writes "[i]n procreation the soul *uses* the body and vice versa perhaps—mysticism of this operation" (Bey der Zeugung *braucht* die Seele den Körper und vice versa vielleicht—Mystizism dieser Operation). 3:458, n. 1008.
84. Gerhard Neumann reads the mutual consumption or conception of body and soul as a "reciprocal metamorphosis" emblematic of the "act of love": "The soul becomes embodied, bound, the body approaches the soul, becomes free. Just as the first contact delivers love, the second delivers knowledge." (Die Seele wird verkörperlicht, gebunden, der Körper nähert sich der Seele, wird frei. Wie diese Berührung Liebe entbindet, so jene Erkenntnis.) Neumann, *Ideenparadiese*, 270.

NOTES TO CHAPTER 4

1. See Zedler, *Universal-Lexicon*, s.v. "Neubruch."
2. In *Die theuren Dinge*, Ulrich Stadler takes up the special case of the "indirect" *Werkzeug* in Hardenberg. Because he focuses his analysis on how the indirect *Werkzeug* and related figures of mediation ultimately dissolve subject–object distinctions, Stadler is less concerned with discussing their nuanced differences.
3. The ambiguity of the *Werkzeug* creates a problem for translators: insofar as "instrument" is the literal, and "organ" the metaphorical meaning (the organs as "instruments" dates to an earlier mechanistic view of the body), I translate *Werkzeug* as "instrument" and let the context grant the inflection of organ or organon.
4. Zedler categorizes the *Werkzeug* into *instrumenta artis* (such as hand-held instruments or tools), the *organum* (bodily organ), and *causa instrumentalis* (insofar an instrument is a cause, but operates through a foreign agency). See *Universal-Lexikon*, s.v. "Werkzeug."
5. Cf. Kant's *Critique of Judgement*, §65 and §80.
6. Theisen, "Macroanthropos," 245.
7. Ibid., 254.
8. Ibid., 248.
9. Ibid., 254.

10. Apart from Stadler's *Die theuren Dinge*, see Florian Roder, *Menschwerdung des Menschen*.
11. The title *Preliminary Studies for Various Fragment Collections* (*Vorarbeiten zu verschiedenen Fragmentsammlungen*) was chosen by Hardenberg's editors and includes manuscripts which date from 1797 to 1798). Hardenberg's correspondence dates his work on *The Apprentices of Sais* to 1798 and most likely the first months of 1799 (1:71–2). Hardenberg suspended work on the novel when he began *Heinrich von Ofterdingen*; plans to take up *The Apprentices* at a later point were never realized.
12. This corresponds to the definition of *Werkzeug* as *causa instrumentalis* in Zedler. Ulrich Stadler also makes reference to the "foreign" element of the *Werkzeug*. *Die theuren Dinge*, 153.
13. For example, by invoking the "composition of the instrument" ("Beschaffenheit des Werkzeugs") which is a general way to describe the instrument's self-sufficiency. The entry "Beschaffenheit" in Adelung's dictionary describes "The expanse of all inner determinations of a thing ("Der Umfang aller innern Bestimmungen einer Sache") and more generally, also the external and contingent determinations and circumstances of a thing (äußere und zufällige Bestimmungen, Nebenumstände eines Dinges). *Grammatisch-kritisches Wörterbuch* (1811), s.v. "Beschaffenheit."
14. The more customary translation of *Gestion* as "gesture" does not allow for a reading of agency in the more general sense permitted within the jurisprudential discourse. For example, Diderot and D'Alembert's *Encyclopédie* defines *Gestion* as the "*administration* of some buisness, like the *gestion* of a tutelage, the *gestion* of the good of someone absent or of some other person" (*administration* de quelque affaire, comme la *gestion* d'une tutelle, la *gestion* des biens d'un absent ou de quelque autre personne) *Encyclopédie*, 7:653.
15. "Denn in dieser Art der Vorstellung enthält die Natur nichts, was ungeheuer (noch was prächtig oder gräßlich) wäre; die Größe, die aufgefaßt wird, mag so weit angewachsen sein, als man will, wenn sie nur durch Einbildungskraft in ein Ganzes zusammengefaßt werden kann. Ungeheuer ist ein Gegenstand, wenn er durch seine Größe den Zweck, der den Begriff desselben ausmacht, vernichtet." Kant, *Werkausgabe*, 5:253.
16. Hardenberg had noted that Kielmeyer's idea of a "transition from one force into another"—and "their successive and simultaneous existence"—was a model which could be used for "the synthesis between antiquity and modernity," an idea which finds its correlate in Kielmeyer's text as well, in a lengthy passage on the durability of the force of reproduction. Not only does the "wealth of forms" which the force of reproduction can assume generate wonder, along with its ability to occur in the "points" of the tiniest organisms as well as the immense volumes of the largest creatures: reproduction's temporality is also cause for astonishment. If in some cases it can go "for hundreds of years unused" in others "it is a moment which contains [reproduction's] effects" (hier dauert sie Jahrhunterte lang unabgenuzt fort, dort ists eine Zeitfluxion die ihre Wirkungen enthält." Kielmeyer, *Ueber die Verhältnisse der organischen Kräfte*, 25.
17. "Das Werckzeug, was dem Geiste am willigsten dient, am leichtesten mannichfacher Modificationen fähig ist." 2:588, n. 264.
18. "Zunge und Lippen etc. sind Theile eines Telegrafs. Telegraf ist ein künstliches Sprachwerkzeug. Die Augen sind Fernröhre—die Fernröhre Augen—die Hand, als Sprachwerkzeug—acustischer Excitator und Nichtleiter—als Pinsel—als allg[emeines] Directionswerkzeug—*Hebe*, Griff—als Unterstützung, Unterlage." 3:400, n. 690.
19. This would distinguish the "poetic" instrument from the "scientific" instrument which, as in the case of mathematics, is excluded from being an aesthetic

concept: "Am Ende ist die ganze Mathemat[ik] gar keine besondre Wissenschaft—sondern nur ein allgem[ein] wissenschaftliches *Werckzeug*—ein schönes Werckzeug ist eine Contradictio in adjecto." 3:251, n. 69.
20. Parts One and Two of *Heinrich von Ofterdingen* were published posthumously under the editorship of Ludwig Tieck in 1802.
21. "Ich bemerkte in ihm die Anzeichen eines großen Bildkünstlers. Sein Auge regte sich voll Lust ein wahres Auge, ein schaffendes Werkzeug zu werden." 1:326.
22. Ibid.
23. "Mein Vater scheint mir, bei aller seiner kühlen und durchaus festen Denkungsart, die ihn alle Verhältnisse, wie ein Stück Metall und eine künstliche Arbeit ansehn läßt, doch unwillkürlich und ohne es daher selbst zu wissen, eine stille Ehrfurcht und Gottesfurcht vor allen unbegreiflichen und höhern Erscheinungen zu haben." Ibid., 326–327.
24. "Ich weiß nur so viel, daß für mich die Fabel Gesamtwerkzeug meiner gegenwärtigen Welt ist. Selbst das Gewissen, diese Sinn und Welten erzeugende Macht, dieser Keim aller Persönlichkeit, erscheint mir, wie der Geist des Weltgedichts, wie der Zufall der ewigen romantischen Zusammenkunft, des unendlich veränderlichen Gesamtlebens." 1:331.
25. "so bildet in den Fabellehren das Leben einer höhern Welt sich in wunderbarentstandnen Dichtungen auf mannigfache Weise ab." 1:333. The emphasis of this passage is on the impossibility of communicating the idea of a moral conscience. The difference in Heinrich's and Sylvester's perspectives is marked by the distinction between nature and literature: whereas Sylvester's sense of conscience emerges as an ethical responsibility to the flowers in his garden, Heinrich's ethics are construed as literature with reference to the fable and the Bible.
26. The scene parallels the opening chapter of the *Lehrlinge*, where the apprentices strive to align stones into appropriate constellations.
27. The concept of the "indirect *Werkzeug*," as elaborated by Ulrich Stadler in *Die theuren Dinge*, is relevant here.
28. In addition to its more general definition as a fictional narrative, Adelung's dictionary defines the fable as a fiction "with which the poet combines a moral intention, in distinction from a fairy tale, which has no moral intentions, and only serves for amusement" ("mit welcher der Dichter eine sittliche Absicht verbindet, zum Unterschiede von einem Mährchen, welches keine moralische Absicht hat, sondern bloß zur Belustigung dienet."). *Grammatisch-kritisches Wörterbuch* (1811), s.v. "Fabel."
29. 1:314.
30. "Language to the second power. For example fable is expression of an entire thought—and belongs in the hieroglphics to the second power—in the *language of sound and written images^2*" (Sprache in der 2ten Potenz. z. B. Fabel ist Ausdruck eines ganzen Gedanckens—und gehört in die Hieroglyphistik der 2ten Potenz—in die *Ton und Schriftbildersprache^2*). 2:588, n. 264.
31. 1:285–286.
32. "Freylich wird auf jeder höhern Stufe der Bildung die Poëtik ein bedeutenderes Werckzeug und ein Gedicht ein höheres Produkt." 3:688, n. 681.
33. Novalis put aside work on *The Apprentices* project in order to develop ideas for a second novel. Though he did return to *The Apprentices* after publishing the first book of *Heinrich von Ofterdingen*, he died before completing the project.
34. Mahoney, *The Critical Fortunes of a Romantic Novel*, 113.
35. In the same letter Hardenberg requests that Schlegel publish his future writings under the name *Novalis* and includes fragments as well as the promise of

a few reams of "logological fragments, poëticisms, and a beginning under the title, the apprentice of Saïs—also fragments—only all in relation to nature" (Ich habe noch einige Bogen logologische Fragmente, Poëticismen, und einen Anfang, unter dem Titel, der Lehrling zu Saïs—ebenfalls Fragmente—nur alle in Beziehung auf Natur). 4:251. A subsequent passage of the letter contains Hardenberg's well-known proclamation, "In the future I will pursue nothing other than poesy—the sciences must all be poeticized—this real, scientific poesy I hope to discuss with you intensely" (Künftig treib ich nichts, als Poësie—die Wissenschaften müssen alle poëtisirt werden—von dieser realen, wissenschaftlichen Poësie hoff ich recht viel mit Ihnen zu reden). Ibid., 252.

36. O'Brien, *Signs of Revolution*, 208.
37. An extensive treatment of the Isis motif in the eighteenth century can be found in Monica Birth Hoesch's *"I Am All That Is, That Was, and That Shall Be, and No Mortal Has Lifted My Veil": Kant, Novalis, Goethe, and the Veiled Goddess Isis* (dissertation Johns Hopkins University, 2006) and Pierre Hadot, *Le Voile d'Isis: Essai sur l'histoire de l'idée de Nature* (Paris: Éditions Gallimard, 2004).
38. "unser Hausgeräte ward durch wohlerdachte Arbeit auch den verborgenen Sinnen angenehm." 1:334.
39. "Wir können daher die Gedanken unsrer Altväter von den Dingen in der Welt als ein notwendiges Erzeugnis, als eine Selbstabbildung des damaligen Zustandes der irdischen Natur betrachten, und besonders an ihnen, als den schicklichsten Werkzeugen der Beobachtung des Weltalls, das Hauptverhältniss desselben, das damalige Verhältniss zu seinen *Bewohnern*, und seiner Bewohner zu ihm, bestimmt abnehmen." 1:83.
40. "Noch früher findet man statt wissenschaftlicher Erklärungen, Märchen und Gedichte voll merkwürdiger bildlicher Züge, Menschen, Götter und Tiere als gemeinschaftliche Werkmeister, und hört auf die natürlichste Art die Entstehung der Welt beschreiben." 1:83.
41. Hardenberg refers to a "zufälligen, *werkzeuglichen*" origin of the world depicted by the fairy tales. Cosmologies which advance a logic of contingency rather than determinism are compatible with the Kantian view of organic generation as well (cf. *Critique of Judgement*, §§ 72–73).
42. "Daher ist auch wohl die Dichtkunst das liebste Werkzeug der eigentlichen Naturfreunde gewesen, und am hellsten in Gedichten ist der Naturgeist erschienen." 1:84.
43. "Naturforscher und Dichter haben durch Eine Sprache sich immer wie Ein Volk gezeigt. Was jene im Ganzen sammelten und in großen, geordneten Massen aufstellten, haben diese für menschliche Herzen zur täglichen Nahrung und Notdurft verarbeitet, und jene unermeßliche Natur zu mannigfaltigen, kleinen, gefälligen Naturen zersplittert und gebildet. Wenn diese mehr das Flüssige und Flüchtige mit leichtem Sinn verfolgten, suchten jene mit scharfen Messerschnitten den innern Bau und die Verhältnisse der Glieder zu erforschen." 1:84.
44. Neubauer, *Bifocal Vision*, 117.
45. Kreuzer, "Die Lehrlinge zu Sais," 285.
46. "Du hast noch nicht geliebt, du Armer; beim ersten Kuß wird eine neue Welt dir aufgetan." 1:91.
47. The element of chance is central to Kristin Pfefferkorn's reading of the fairy tale as the interruption of contingency in an orderly state of affairs, and "the product of man's creative ability in which our relation to chance and our insight into its qualitative nature are presented in one imaginative tableau." See Pfefferkorn, *A Romantic's Theory of Language and Poetry*, 158. Although the notion of contingency is not central to my reading of *The*

Apprentices, it will play a crucial role in the chapter on Schlegel's *Lucinde* where a chance interruption is integrated into a chaotic poetics. Also Karl Grob considers the possibility of a "poetics" or contingency in Novalis' work, and in the fairy tale.

48. "In einem ächten Märchen muß alles wunderbar—gehimnißvoll und unzusammenhängend seyn—alles belebt...der *Naturstand der Natur*—die Zeit vor der *Welt* (Staat.) Diese Zeit vor der Welt liefert gleichsam die zerstreuten Züge der *Zeit nach der Welt*." 3:280, n. 234.
49. See 1:84.
50. See 1:92. Birrell identifies the song as a "veiled summary of the entire tale, with the roles of the two lovers reversed," and notes that "In both cases, the mother unexpectedly turns out to be none other than the beloved...the song thus makes a pedagogical and prophetic point." Birrell, *The Boundless Present*, 66.
51. Unlike the lizard's song, however, the book exemplifies a different kind of "pseudo-knowledge where acquaintance with the letter does not yield insight." Neubauer, *Bifocal Vision*, 119.
52. Gaier interprets a relation of mutual influence between Hyacinth and nature that conforms both to the model of activity and passivity and, as I argue, to the concept of the instrument: "nature influences Hyacinth (through his senses)," and "Hyacinth influences nature (through shape, Gestaltung)." Gaier, *Krumme Regel*, 20.
53. The paralipomena to the novel contain a alternative ending to the search for "the secret sleeping chamber" of Isis whose procreative elements are less chastely described: "He entered and saw—his bride, who received him smiling. As he looked around he found himself in his sleeping chamber and a sweet night music resounded under his windows" (Er trat ein und sah—seine Braut, die ihn mit Lächeln empfing. Wie er sich umsah, fand er sich in seiner Schlafkammer—und eine liebliche Nachtmusik tönte unter seinen Fenstern). 1:110.
54. Neumann, *Ideenparadiese*, 412. It has been frequently observed that in the paralipomena to *The Apprentices*, the "regeneration of paradise" occurred as a narcissistic rather than a procreative moment: the raised veil reveals an image of the self. (Einem gelang es—er hob den Schleyer der Göttin zu Saïs—Aber was sah er? Er sah—Wunder des Wunders—Sich selbst) 1:110. Cf. Helfer, "Male Muses," 300.
55. If inclined, one could push the comparison between the fairy tale and the geometrical series whose members are stones, plants, animals, and humans even further. Readers of *The Apprentices* have observed that the names "Hyacinth" and "Rosenblütchen" have their own minerological and organic significance: a "Hyacinth" is both a type of stone and a flower, and Rosenblütchen's organic name speaks for itself. In other words, all of the elements of the geometric series are assembled in the fairy tale, in approximately the proper order. For further information on the names of the fairy tale, see Birth, *Kant, Novalis, Goethe, and the Veiled Goddess Isis*, 180–181; and Gaier, *Krumme Regel*, 63–64.
56. Kuzniar, "Reassessing Romantic Reflexivity," 82–83.
57. "'Traum' steht für Novalis auf der Schwelle zwischen Organischem und Anorganischem...er ist, als ein Zustand des 'gelockerten' Systems, höchste Form des die formale Logik sprengenden Denkens überhaupt." Neumann, *Ideenparadiese*, 410.
58. "Körper ist das Werckzeug zur Bildung und Modification der Welt; Wir müssen also unsern Körper zum *allfähigen* Organ auszubilden suchen." 2:587.
59. Readings such O'Brien's, who describes the fairy tale as an "allegory of scientific epistemology," emphasize the intellectual aspect of the narrative. See O'Brien, *Signs of Revolution*, 211.

60. Neumann, *Ideenparadiese*, 406.
61. Neubauer, *Bifocal Vision*, 117.
62. This position has been argued by Haywood as well, for whom the "correct interpretation of one without the other. . .is impossible, yet the connections he draws between the novel and fairy tale, such as between the figure of the apprentice and Hyacinth, tend toward the literal." See Haywood, *The Veil of Imagery*, 30.
63. Kreuzer, "Novalis: Die Lehrlinge zu Sais," 299.
64. "Wenige standen auf ihrem eigentlichen Platze, und sahen in Ruhe dem mannigfaltigen Treiben um sich her zu. Die Übrigen klagten über entsetzliche Qualen und Schmerzen, und bejammerten das alte, herrliche Leben im Schoße der Natur, wo sie eine gemeinschaftliche Freiheit vereinigte, und jedes von selbst erhielt, was es bedurfte" 1:95.
65. "Denn ohne die scheinbar nachträgliche Form der Reflexion gäbe es erst gar nicht das Gefühl als "Stoff" dieser Reflexion. Sie ist von vornherein mit dem verflochten, dessen Wirkung in einer "fremden Gestalt" sie zu sein scheint," Menninghaus, *Unendliche Verdopplung*, 86. Peter Pfaff connects Novalis' speculative writing on "feeling" to the organ of the body and to woman and argues for an "erotic allegoresis of transcendental relations of nature" ("erotische Allegorese der transzendentalen Naturverhältnisse"). See Pfaff, "Natur-Poesie," 97.
66. "die wahre Theorie der Natur." Ibid.
67. "zu jenem Punkt. . .wo Hervorbringen und Wissen in der wundervollsten Wechselverbindung standen, zu jenem schöpferischen Moment des eigentlichen Genusses, des innern Selbstempfängnisses." Ibid.
68. "das großße zugleich der Natur." 1:102.
69. "Wer eine innige Sehnsucht nach der Natur spürt, wer in ihr alles sucht, und gleichsam ein empfindliches Werkzeug ihres geheimen Tuns ist, der wird nur den für seinen Lehrer und für den Vertrauten der Natur erkennen, der mit Andacht und Glauben von ihr spricht." 1:108.

NOTES TO CHAPTER 5

1. *Fragmente aus dem Nachlass eines jungen Physikers. Ein Taschenbuch für Freunde der Natur.* A facsimile of the first edition (Heidelberg: bey Mohr und Zimmer, 1810). Afterword by Heinrich Schipperges. Heidelberg: Lambert Schneider, 1969. All quotations of Ritter's fragments in German are cited from this edition by the fragment number. All translations of Ritter are my own.
2. *Die Aelteste Urkunde des Menschengeschlechts* (Riga: J. F. Hartknoch, 1774–76).
3. Strickland, "The Ideology of Self-Knowledge," 454. See also Simon Schaffer's article "Self Evidence" in *Critical Inquiry* 18, no. 2 (Winter 1992) 327–362.
4. Johann Wilhelm Ritter, *Beweis, daß ein beständiger Galvanismus den Lebensproceß in dem Thierreich begleite* (Weimar: Industrie-Comptoir, 1798).
5. For more information see Strickland, "Reopening the texts of Romantic science: The language of experience in J. W. Ritter's 'Beweis'" in *Trends in the historiography of science* (1994); and Eva-Maria Tschurenev, "Hegels Abwehr der Totalisierung des Galvanismus bei Ritter" in *Hegels Jenaer Naturphilosophie*, Klaus Vieweg, ed. (Munich: Wilhelm Fink, 1998): 319–345, esp. 323–327.

6. The most thorough depiction of Ritter's life, including an excellent bibliography of Ritter's work and references to him in the writing of his contemporaries, is Klaus Richter's *Das Leben des Physikers Johann Wilhelm Ritter* (Weimar: Hermann Böhlaus Nachfolger, 2003). Also valuable as an earlier re-evaluation of Ritter's legacy for the history of science: Dr. Wilhelm Ostwald, *Electrochemistry. History and Theory*. N. P. Date, trans. (Leipzig: von Veit & Comp., 1896; translation: New Delhi: Amerind Publishing, 1980).
7. "Diese Schrift war mit großem Scharfsinn ausgearbeitet. Der Mangel an früherer wissenschaftlicher Bildung zeigte sich besonders durch einen harten unbehilflichen Stil, aber die Schrift machte mit Recht Aufsehen, und dennoch, obgleich die Versuche scharfsinnig gewählt waren und sich wechselseitig unterstützten, schwebte über der scheinbaren Bestimmtheit der Abfassung eine Dunkelheit, die auf keine Weise zu verkennen war." Steffens, *Was ich erlebte*, 73–74.
8. Ibid., 77.
9. "Ritter lebte mit sich selbst in einem inneren Zwiespalt, in einer geistigen Verwirrung, die immer mehr überhand nahm und für seine bürgerliche wie für seine wissenschaftliche Stellung die unglücklichsten Folgen hatte. Diese verbitterte sein Dasein, isolierte ihn immer mehr; er verlor sich in Träume, die seine Untersuchungen unsicher machten, daher er sich selbst nie aus der Dunkelheit herauszuarbeiten vermochte." Ibid.
10. "so wage ich es ohne Anstand, Ihr [i.e., der Physik] Selbst den Namen einer *Kunst* zu geben, und einer Höheren, als Alle Uebrige." *Physik als Kunst*, 57.
11. Carl Ployer wrote to Karl Ehrenbert von Moll on November 10th, 1807: "This speech is completely like this distracted and confused [individual]. I understand not a single word of the entire speech" ("Diese Rede ist ganz dem zerstreuten und verwirrten ähnlich. Ich verstehe kein Wort von der ganzen Rede"). Moll, *Mitteilungen aus seinem Briefwechsel*, 2:596. In a letter to his friend Achim von Arnim, Clemens Brentano writes of having read the speech with pleasure "except for the style" ("bis auf seinen Stil"). *Clemens Brentano. Briefe*, 1:312.
12. Richter, *Das Leben des Physikers*, 40.
13. Ritter's entire estate has vanished with the exception of his correspondence and three volumes of his diary, held in the in the Bavarian State Library in Munich.
14. Ørsted, *Correspondance*, 2:228f.
15. On March 31st, 1809, Ritter wrote a letter to the Danish scientist Hans Christian Ørsted to report on the current state of his research projects. Ritter promised his friend two works for the following book fair. The first concerned his controversial experiments with pendulua and divining rods; the second was to be a collection of fragments in the Romantic style: "These fragments, 700 in number, are collectively taken from my diaries and other papers. Not a single one was written with the thought of future publication, whereby they have reached an honesty, naiveté, and often a boldness which will grant them their own charm. By and large they occupy the median between those of *Novalis* and *Lichtenberg*." (Diese Fragmente, 700 an der Zahl, sind sämmtlich aus meinen Diarien u. andern Papieren gezogen. Kein einziges war mit dem Gedanken an den einstigen Druck geschrieben, wodurch sie zu einer Ehrlichkeit, Naivität, u. oft Kühnheit, gekommen, die ihnen einen eignen Reiz lassen werden. Im ganzen halten sie ohngefähr die Mitte zwischen denen von *Novalis* und *Lichtenberg*). Ibid., 228.
16. "Es soll nicht bloss eine *Sammlung* meiner Schreibereyen werden; es wird eine Art von literarischer Selbstbiographie vielleicht jedem interessant, der sich aus sich selbst zum Physiker u. Experimentator bilden will u. muss."

Ritter to Ørsted, February 2nd, 1806, in Ørsted, *Correspondance*, 2:147. See also a letter dated March 31st, 1809, in which Ritter explains that "The prologue contains the biography of the departed, his inner one; it is my own, and I wrote it with much honesty and feeling. The entire thing is thereby a greatly serious jest, dedicated to the friends of the deceased" (Die Vorrede enthält die Biographie des Verstorbenen, seine innere; es ist meine eigene, und ich habe sie mit viel Ehrlichkeit und Rührung geschrieben. Das Ganze ist somit eine höchst ernsthafte Posse; den Freunden des Verstorbenen gewidmet). Ibid., 2:229.

17. "Whereas eighteenth-century autobiographies are powerful vehicles which talk about mobilising a *life*, the nineteenth-century autobiographies focus on a single 'Eureka' *moment* of disovery, and fail to engage with their surrounding culture as a whole." Outram, "Autobiography, Science and the French Revolution," 98.

18. See the chapter "L'autobiographie à la troisième personne" / "narration autodiégétique à la troisième personne" in Philippe Lejeune, *Je est un autre. L'autobiographie de la littérature aux médias* (Paris: Éditions du Seuil, 1980).

19. "Les figures de la troisième personne fournissent une gamme de solutions où c'est la distanciation qui est mise en avant, mais toujours pour exprimer une articulation (une tension) entre l'identité et la différence." Lejeune, *Je est une autre*, 39. Ritter was certainly not the first to take on a separate voice, or persona such as "editor," and describe his own life in the third person. Well-known examples include the commentaries of Julius Caesar and the *Life* of Leon Battista Alberti.

20. "Le système général reste celui de l'autobiographie; c'est seulement au niveau d'une des instances du récit (le personnage du narrateur) que se greffe une sorte de jeu: l'autobiographe essaie de s'imaginer ce qui se passerait si c'était *un autre* qui racontait son histoire ou traçait son portrait." Lejeune, *Je est une autre*, 52–53.

21. Starobinski also writes, "Not only [. . .] can the autobiographer lie, but the "autobiographical form" can cloak the freest fictive invention...In these cases, the *I* of the narrative [. . .] is assumed by a nonentity; it is an *I* without referent, an *I* that refers only to an arbitrary image. However, the *I* of such a text cannot be distinguished from the *I* of a "sincere" autobiographical narrative." Starobinski, "Style," 75.

22. Herz, *Dunkler Spiegel*, 16. Herz discusses the importance of this passage for Herder's sermons and historical essays against the backdrop of the eighteenth century. Ritter cites the passage from the Corinthians frequently in his work, for example, in the dedication of his book, *Das electrische System der Körper* (1805, The Electrical System of Bodies) to C. S. Weiss.

23. For examples of autobiographical writing in the epistles, scholars of Paul have traditionally reached for his letter to the Galatians or passages from the second letter to the Corinthinas. See B. R. Gaventa, "Galatians 1 and 2: Autobiography as Paradigm" in *Novum Testamentum*, vol. 28, Fasc. 4 (October 1986) 309–326 and Paul E. Koptak, "Rhetorical Identification In Paul's Autobiographical Narrative" in *Journal for the Study of the New Testament* 40 (1990), 97–113.

24. Gill, "Through a Glass Darkly," 427.

25. Genette, *Paratextes*, 145–147.

26. Neumann has compared Ritter's fascination with this topos to Lichtenberg's. See Neumann, *Ideenparadiese*, 198–199.

27. "Während bei Novalis die Reflexion den Weg über die Natur nimmt, an ihr die transzendentale Selbstdarstellung des Ich wahrnehmend, bevorzugt Ritter den

umgekehrten Weg, an der Selbsterfahrung die Abbildung der Weltgesamtheit zugänglich zu finden." Blumenberg, *Die Lesbarkeit der Welt*, 263.
28. "*Völlig aus sich selbst* hatte unser Freund sich zu dem gebildet, was er etwa war und wurde, und früh schon war er dazu genöthiget." Prologue, xvi.
29. A. Assman, "Die Domestikation des Lesens," 96–97.
30. Prologue, xxviii.
31. Schriften, 2:470, n. 125.
32. Prologue, xxvii. These titles remain ciphers; Ritter does not explain the sense in which they might have inspired his scientific research.
33. Ibid.
34. "in den meisten Fällen kamen sie auf ein bloßes Denken auf dem Papier zurück." Ibid., xci.
35. Ibid., lxxxvi.
36. "In den Papieren des Verfassers folgten sie sich gewöhnlich in der buntesten Reihe, und zuweilen schien es, als habe er an Einem Tage die ganze Schöpfung bedenken wollen, und keinesweges nach der Ordnung, sondern wie es ihm eben *ein-*, oder die Gegenstände in der Natur, selbst durcheinander liegend, ihm, menschlicher Weise, eben *anf-*fielen [sic]." Ibid., lxxxvii.
37. "Es komme dann nur auf die gute Gelegenheit an, und jeden Augenblick entwickele sich das ganze System unseres Erfahrungsbesitzes wieder von selbst." Ibid., xci.
38. "Ich war mit seiner ganzen Gesinnungsart vertraut, bin selbst gewißermaßen nur ein Sprosse von ihm, und glaube mich hie und da im Stande, ihn seiner würdig fortzusetzen." Ibid., ciii.
39. Ritter specifies: with words that are found neither in Gehler (Johann Samuel Traugott Gehler, *Physikalisches Wörterbuch*. Leipzig: Schwickert, 1791) nor Fischer (Johann Carl Fischer. *Physikalisches Wörterbuch*. Göttingen: Johann Christian Dieterich, 1799) Prologue, lxxxix.
40. Ibid.
41. "Es wird überhaupt blos der fünfzehnte oder auch der der zwangzigste Theil des gesammten vorgefundenen Vorraths seyn, den ich hier mittheile, und ich muß gestehen, daß ich bey der Auswahl eben nicht sehr strenge war, und manche Fragmente aufnahm, ich weiß selbst nicht, warum." Ibid., lxxxvii–lxxxviii.
42. "Nur um Aehnliches und Verwandtes etwas zusammen zu bringen, habe ich alle 700 Fragmente unter 15 Abtheilungen gebracht, aber auch diese Scheidung ist keinesweges scharf." Ibid., lxxxviii.
43. Julius claims "das Recht einer reizenden Verwirrung." F. Schlegel, KA 5:9.
44. "manchmal kann es wohl kommen, daß man dort manche Nachbarschaft ganz unverständlich findet; man verliert aber damit nicht viel." Ibid., lxxxviii.
45. A note on chronology: although the fragments are not organized according to the date of their composition, the editor leaves the dates on the fragments and encourages friends to take the "small trouble" of organizing the fragments chronologically for the sake of the "interesting results" about his intellectual development which could be gained. See Prologue, xi.
46. "Mehrere z. B. werden sicher nur, wenn man verliebt ist, andere, wenn man liebt, verstanden, andere bey der höchsten, einfachsten Naturandacht, wieder andere, wenn man eben, wie man spricht, philosophirt, u.s.w." Ibid., lxxxix.
47. Ibid., xcv.
48. Ibid., xciii–xcvii.
49. "einige Male fängt sogar eine *falsche* Annahme an, durchgeführt zu werden, zerstört sich aber nach und nach durch sich selbst, und das *ganz Entgegengesetzte* vom Anfang ist das Resultat des Endes. Letzteres ist dann das

Allermenschlichste, weil man im Leben allaugenblicklich dergleichen trifft." Ibid., xciv–xcv.

50. "noch bey Electricitäts—und Magnetismus-Erregung der Proceß mit dem Umgekehrten von dem anfängt, womit er endet; vielleicht aber läst man es *eben darum* hingehen,—weil, so, ein *allgemeines* Naturgesetz dahinter seyn muß." Ibid., xcv.

51. "J. W. Ritter" only appears on the title page as editor. It is no secret that the anonymous life detailed in the prologue is a version of Ritter's. The narrated life events, the constellation of named friends, including Herder and Novalis, reveal his identity while concealing only the name.

52. Note that, contrary to Richter's statement, the textual record suggests that the project began just over ten years prior to its eventual publication date.

53. "Ihr Geburtstag, der 26ste Oct[ober], war 1797 mein eigentlicher Auferstehungstag, und noch in den Fragmenten, die ich jetzt herausgebe, hatte ich ihn gefeiert." Ritter to Gotthilf Heinrich Schubert, June 9th, 1809. Rehm, *Unbekannte Briefe*, 55–56.

54. "Ich vielleicht besonders verstand ihn hierüber; er hätte am liebsten gar keinen gehabt; und so nenne ich ihn billig auch selbst da noch nicht, wo er mich nun nicht mehr schelten kann." Prologue, iv.

55. "Schon früher hatte mich unser Freund, doch immer noch erst mehr im Scherze—wenn ich ihn nemlich gar zu sehr darum bat—zum einstigen Erben aller seiner Tagebücher und anderer Papiere eingesetzt—bis endlich der 7te May 1809, früher, als wir irgend geglaubt, den heitern Scherz in finstern, herben Ernst verwandelte" (iv); the language recalls the "ernsthafte Posse" Ritter describes in his letter to Ørsted. See Ørsted, *Correspondance*, 2:228.

56. Prologue, xxxii.

57. "*Novalis* und unser Freund verstanden sich den Augenblick; fürs erste lag auch nicht die geringste Merkwürdigkeit in ihrem Zusammenkommen; letzterem war schlechterdings nur eben, als wenn er einmal *laut mit sich selber sprechen könnte*," Prologue, xviii. Novalis' correspondance also testifies to his affection for Ritter, who is "in spirit and heart the most glorious person in the world" (von Geist und Herz der herrlichste Mensch von der Welt.) Letter to Dietrich von Miltitz, January 31st, 1800. Novalis, *Schriften*, 4:319.

58. "Um völlig sich selbst sicher zu bleiben, entfloh unser N. auf einige Zeit dem Orte, der ihm in äußerst mannichfacher Hinsicht bisher theuer geworden, und ich begleitete ihn." Prologue, xxxi.

59. "*hier* habe er gelernt, was die Natur, der Mensch in ihr, und eigentliche Physik, seyn, und wie die letztere Religion unmittelbar." Prologue, xxxiv. For further information on Ritter's friendship with Herder's family, see also Klaus Richter, "Der Physiker Ritter und Johann Gottfried Herder," in *Impulse. Aufsätze, Quellen, Berichte zur deutschen Klassik und Romantik*. Folge 3. Berlin und Weimar: Aufbau-Verlag (1981), 109–119.

60. Prologue, xxxvi.

61. J. Assman, "Ancient Egypt," 17.

62. Ibid.," 31. Jan Assman discusses how a text by the Egyptian priest Horapollon (fifth or sixth century) containing false interpretations of hieroglyphs was influential for establishing "a hieroglyphic worldview that understood the world as a complex of meaningful signs." (Ibid.).

63. Herder, *Werke*, DKV 5:269.

64. Ibid.

65. "wie ihm etwa davon das *erste Urbild* worden, von dem man sich weiter *versucht*, an und nach welchem sich allmählich die *ganze Schrift* und *Symbolik* der Menschen also so viel *Erfindungen, Künste und Wissenschaften*

gebildet?" Herder, *Werke*, DKV 5:269. For Herder's use of the "hieroglyph" see also Dieckmann, *Hieroglyphics*, 151.
66. Herder, *Werke*, DKV 5:319.
67. "Eine neue Pforte des Altertums, des fernesten Heiligtums eröffnet." Angelika Rauch's comment that hieroglyphs of the past contain a truth which is "lost to the modern reader" and are "enigmatic signs that stimulate the fantasy and the desire to know what they *could* mean" is relevant here. See Rauch, *Hieroglyph of Tradition*, 127.
68. Herder mutely gestures to a "place" Ritter refers to as a *Stätte* rather than a *Stelle* (which one would expect for a textual passage). The first definition in Adelung's dictionary cites an example from the Bible (Moses 1:2, v. 21), suggesting that "Stätte" can also connote a more elevated "Stelle." *Grammatisch-kritisches Wörterbuch* (1811), s.v. "Stätte."
69. In his account of Novalis' death, the editor reports that a letter was delivered to the physicist from Novalis' estate which encouraged the physicist to continue his projects and which was treasured by the latter like a holy relic "[The letter] contained encouragements for him to remain true to his previous aspirations as well as several prospects which he would necessarily have to complete. Concerning both matters was expressed a saying of great meaning and our friend has preserved and cared for the word like a relic" (Er enthielt Ermunterungen an ihn, seinem bisherigen Streben treu zu bleiben, und mehrere Aussichten, die dann ihm ganz nothwendig in Erfüllung gehen müßten. Ueber beyde war hier ein Wort von außerordentlicher Bedeutung gesagt, und wie ein Heiligthum hat unser Freund dasselbe verwahrt und gepflegt). Prologue, xxxi. The letter—if it existed—presumably disappeared with the remainder of Ritter's estate.
70. "In der auf Bacon zurückgehenden Tradition war die Hieroglyphe (worunter man ja nicht nur die ägyptischen Piktogramme, sondern auch die chinesischen Schriftzeichen verstand) Metapher für die analytischen Zeichen einer Begriffsschrift, für die 'real characters' gewesen, bei Athanasius Kircher bei Wilkins, bei Leibniz e tutti quanti, die am großen Universalsprachenprojekt des 17. Jahrhunderts teilgenommen hatten. Die Hieroglyphe war Metapher für ein Wort, das zugleich eine analytische Formel des Begriffs ist, den es bezeichnet, so daß jedes Wort einer Universalsprache sich im Moment des Aussprache zugleich selbst definierte." Siegert, *Passage des Digitalen*, 259.
71. See Siegert, *Passage des Digitalen*, 256; also Bettine Menke, "Töne—Hören" in Joseph Vogl, ed. *Poetologien des Wissens*, 69–95.
72. Siegert, *Passage des Digitalen*, 259.
73. "Wort und Schrift sind gleich an ihrem Ursprung eins, und keines ohne das andere möglich." *Fragmente* (Appendix), 229.
74. Compare this formulation to the same sentiment, more weakly expressed, in a letter from Ritter to Oersted dating April 1st, 1806: "With the Document [Herder] will have written a word all the more immortal, since he could seldom *say* everything that he felt and saw" ("er wird nur um so mehr ein unsterbliches Wort an der Urkunde geschrieben haben, als er selten *sagen* konnte, was er alles fühlte u. sah.") Ørsted, *Correspondance*, 2:158–159.
75. Menke, "Töne–Hören," 264. Menke describes an example from Ritter's work where a tone is produced when breath meets resistance, and shows how this logic applies to a broader range of phenomena. See also Caroline Welsh's book *Hirnhöhlenpoetiken* (Rombach: Freiburg im Breisgau, 2003), for an in-depth discussion of Ritter's work on acoustical and electrical figures in the context of Englightenment and Romantic anthropology.

76. "Der Leser findet sich also mit diesen Fragmenten durchaus in die *geheimere Werkstätte des Physikers* geführt,—und kann da Dinge vorgegangen seyen, die ungemein menschlich sind." Prologue, xciii.
77. See Steven Shapin, "The House of Experiment in Seventeenth-Century England" in *Isis* 79.3 (September 1988), 373–404. In his essay, he refers both to the prevalence of this image in the visual arts of the seventeenth century (378), as well as an effort to dispel it (as in Robert Boyle's stated agenda to bring the "chymist's doctrine" from the "dark and smokey laboratories" to "the open light," *Works* 1:461, also quoted by Shapin on page 378). It is not certain how extensively Ritter had read in the hermetic tradition, but the symbolism of alchemy is prevalent in his fragments through references to alchemical transubstantiations, mystical unions, and texts.
78. "Absolute indifference would be exclusion of time" (*Fragmente* 597). For Ritter, the beginning "differentiation" of the female occurs after the "indifferentiation" between the two sexes. The heightened spatial descriptions during the time of procreation in Goethe's elegy on plant metamorphosis also come to mind here.
79. "scattered limbs of the poet" from Horace, *Satires* I 4:62.
80. "die *'Disjecti membra Poëtae'* zu *sammeln*, sie nach jenem organischen Urgesetz, was noch kein Buch gelehrt, sondern das überall nur *schaffend*, im *Werke selbst*, sich offenbaren mag, und in dessen Besitz er so bestimmt sich wüßte, zu *ordnen*, sie zum *Einen "Tempel mit dem Gott darin" aufzuerbauen*: *dazu* gebrach ihm die würdige Ruhe und Muße." Prologue, cxiii.
81. "Ein eignes Denkmal forderte jener Tag durchaus, und es sey genug für mich, zu wissen, mit diesem Buche es ihm gesetzt zu haben, was irgend auch die Meinung Anderer darüber seyn könnte." Prologue, v. The day in question doubles as the death day of the physicist and Ritter's mother, who has received her own monument: "We took it upon ourselves to have the children leave a monument (*Denkmal*) for the grandmother....I did not want, however, for it to be a monument of stone; it should remain *living green*, like the good mother now, and our own remembrance of her." (Wir haben uns vorgenommen, unsere Kinder der Großmutter ein Denkmal setzen zu lassen....Ich wollte aber nicht, daß es ein steinernes Denkmal würde; *lebendig grünen* soll es, wie die gute Mutter jetzt, und unser eigenes Andenken an sie). Rehm, *Unbekannte Briefe*, 56.
82. The passage refers both to Horace's "scattered limbs" and Corinthians: "What? Know you not that your body is the temple of the Holy Ghost which is in you, which you have of God, and you are not your own?" Bible, American King James Version, Corinthians 1:6, v. 19.
83. See Foucault, *Archaeology of Knowledge*, esp. 7–8.
84. See A. Assmann, "Kultur als Lebenswelt und Monument," 13–14.
85. Prologue, liii. Winckelmann, Johann Joachim. *Geschichte der Kunst des Alterthums*. Leipzig: Breitkopf, 1764.
86. Winckelmann, Johann Joachim. *Anmerkungen über die Baukunst der Alten*. Leipzig: Johann Gottfried Dyck, 1762. See *Fragmente*, n. 132.
87. Fragment 460 paraphrases the passage from *De Architectura* which connects the seasons to human reproduction. See Marcus Vitruvius Pollio, *The Ten Books on Architecture*. Morris Hicky Morgan, trans. (Cambridge: Harvard University Press, 1914): "in Spring all trees become pregnant, and they are all employing their natural vigour in the production of leaves and of the fruits that return every year. The requirements of that season render them empty and swollen, and so they are weak and feeble because of their looseness of

texture. This is also the case with women who have conceived. Their bodies are not considered perfectly healthy until the child is born" (Vitruvius 58). Ritter's citations of Vitruvius in the fragments also draw from the chapters on mechanics (*Fragmente*, n. 624) and the construction of temples for the most appropriate worship of God (*Fragmente*, n. 617).
88. For an attempt to synthesize Assman's two temporalities see Hartmut Winkler, "Discourses, Schemata, Technology, Monuments: Outline for a Theory of Cultural Continuity" trans. Geoffrey Winthrop-Young and Michael Wutz, in *Configurations* 10 (2002) 91–109.
89. Deleuze and Guattari, *What is Philosophy?*, 167–168.
90. Ritter married his housekeeper on June 17th, 1804. If the scale of the scandal was several orders of magnitude smaller than the one which ensued in the wake of Goethe's marriage to Christiane Vulpius, the commentaries of Ritter's peers were no less vitriolic. See Ritter's letter to Ørsted from May 20th, 1803 ("I love a maiden of glorious nature. She lives with me, is my housekeeper or whatever you want to call it") and Clemens Brentano's less flattering description ("one of the most common Jena street whores, horribly dirty") in Ørsted, *Correspondance* 2:33, and R. Steig, ed. *Achim von Arnim und die ihm nahe standen*. Achim von Arnim und Clemens Brentano. Stuttgart 1894), 1:116.
91. See also Richter, *Das Leben eines Physikers*, 148.
92. "öfters werden diese Wege selbst belehrender seyn, als was auf ihnen, als Mark- oder Denkstein gleichsam, niederliegen blieb." Prologue, cxv.
93. "Was es aber, daß ich eine *völlig* treffende Beschreibung gebe, *eigentlich* ist, was ich Euch hier biete, wüßte ich selbst nicht in der Kürze zu sagen ..... Was es Euch *werden* wird, wird es seyn,—und vielleicht darf diese Vorrede auch dazu genommen werden. So viel nun weiß ich, daß ich es Euch *schuldig* war." Prologue, cxv-cxvi.
94. Ritter closes his narrative on the date of September 14th, 1809, the first birthday of his youngest son August.
95. "denn Du schöpftest aus der *Natur*, und ihre Schätze hat noch *keiner* ergründet." Prologue, cxxiii.
96. "Erzähle ihm: *der Vater sey da gewesen, und komme bald wieder.*" Prologue, cxxv.

NOTES TO CHAPTER 6

1. *Beweis*, 170.
2. *Beyträge*, 1:177.
3. *Fragmente*, n. 495. "Das Weib gebiert Menschen, der Mann das Kunstwerk."
4. See *Fragmente*, n. 501.
5. For an introduction into this aspect of Ritter's work see: Walter D. Wetzels, *Johann Wilhelm Ritter: Physik im Wirkungsfeld der deutschen Romantik*. (Berlin: Walter de Gruyter, 1973) 75–87.
6. He proposes the unity of chemical, electrical, magnetic, and galvanic processes—"all processes on earth"—so that "all prior divisions of physics are ultimately dissolved into word games" (alle bisherigen Abtheilungen der Physik zuletzt in Wortspiele auflöst) "Bemerkungen über die Art, auf welche der Zutritt der Luft auf die Wirksamkeit der Galvanisch-chemischen Kette von Einfluss ist," *Physisch-Chemische Abhandlungen*, 1:227–244, 242. (Note: the article was written in 1800 for Gilbert's *Annalen der Physik* but unpublished until the *Physisch-Chemische Abhandlungen*).

7. See Adelung, *Grammatisch-kritisches Wörterbuch* (1811), s.v. "Wortspiel."
8. Novalis, *Schriften*, 2:672. The date of Hardenberg's text is uncertain. I am very grateful to Thomas Glaser for the reminder about the *Wortspiel* in Novalis' "Monologue."
9. "das rechte Gespräch ist ein bloßes Wortspiel." Ibid.
10. See Ritter, Prologue, xciii.
11. The bibliography which considers the problem of the female as the "second sex" (Beauvoir) the "object," "the other" within the context of the Western philosphical tradition is vast; it has also been increasingly observed in more recent criticism that a white feminist perspective has internalized this dualism without moving beyond it. Cf. Milner and Browitt, *Contemporary Cultural Theory* (New York: Routledge, 2002), esp. 132–139. For a critical perspective which focuses on the historical time period in question see, for example Martha Helfer's essay "Male Muses," which questions the "centrality of the feminine to Romantic poetic production" and the role scholarship has granted woman as the one who "grounds Romantic poesy." Helfer, "Male Muses," 300.
12. "Alle Polarität, alle Differenz, muß als zeitlich betrachtet werden." *Fragmente*, n. 597.
13. Sellars, *Stoicism*, 118. See also Gründer and Ritter eds, *Historisches Wörterbuch der Philosophie*, s.v. "Indifferenz." In the *Metzler Philosophie Lexikon*, the "negativity" of indifference receives particular emphasis, in the sense of a "lack of decision" or a "lack of difference" which only depends on the discursive context. Burkard and Prechtl, *Metzler Philosophie Lexikon*, s.v. "Indifferenz."
14. See Simon Francis Gaine OP, "Fruition, Freedom and Indifference: William of Ockham." In *Will There Be Free Will in Heaven?* London: Continuum, 2003.
15. "If I always saw clearly what was true and good, I should never have to deliberate about the right judgement or choice; in that case, although I should be wholly free, it would be impossible for me ever to be in a state of indifference" Descartes, *Meditations on First Philosophy*, 40.
16. *A Treatise of Human Nature: Being an Attempt to Introduce the Experimental Method of Reasoning into Moral Subjects*. London: John Noon, 1739–1740.
17. See *Historisches Wörterbuch der Philosophie*, s.v. "Indifference."
18. See F. W. J. Schelling, *Erster Entwurf eines Systems der Naturphilosophie*. Wilhelm G. Jacobs und Paul Ziche eds. (Stuttgart: Frommann-Holzboog, 2001). In this work from 1799, Schelling describes a state of indifference as one where natural phenomena exist with the forces acting upon them in balance. He does not use gender metaphors to discuss indifference, nor does he connect it to the topos of procreation. See also Bernhard Rang, *Identität und Indifferenz. Eine Untersuchung zu Schellings Identitätsphilosophie* (Frankfurt: Klostermann, 2000).
19. This is an antiquated concept of the magnet, which was replaced by magnetic fields after Ritter's death (and later by quantum theory). See Brugmans, *Philosophische Versuche über die magnetische Materie*, Leipzig 1784. See also Stein, *Naturphilosophie der Frühromantik*, 12–13.
20. Ritter, *Fragmente*, n. 271.
21. Reil, "Über das polarische Auseinanderweichen," 429.
22. It was not commonplace to think of electricity, which was either positive or negative, as having a state of indifference, but Ritter prosposes an electric indifference in his *Electrical System of Bodies* from 1805.

23. "eine einheitliche Beschreibungssprache für die Bereiche der Natur *und* der Kultur zu erfinden. So sind die Schlüsselwörter des Ritterschen Lexikons doppelt zu lesen: zum einen mit Bezug auf ihren Herkunftsbereich, zum andern als generalisierte Begriffe, die sowohl Natürliches als auch Kulturelles umfassen." Wellbery, "Kunst-Zeugung-Geburt," 18–19. For a discussion of the Ritter–Hegel connection see Eva-Maria Tschurenev, "Hegels Abwehr der Totalisierung des Galvanismus bei Ritter," and Henricus A. M. Snelders, "Hegel und der romantische Physiker J. W. Ritter" in *Hegels Jenaer Naturphilosophie*.
24. The same question is also to be considered from a slightly different angles (such as from the point of view of the history of medicine) in Ludmilla Jordanova's book, *Sexual Visions. Images of Gender in Science and Medicine Between the Eighteenth and the Twentieth Centuries* (Madison: University of Wisconsin Press, 1989). Jordanova also argues that polarities such as woman/nature and man/culture have been oversimplified and that, when considered alongside other dichotomies, sexual disctinctions become blurred. See Jordanova, *Sexual Visions*, 21–22.
25. "Die weiblichen Geschlechtstheile sind auf den untersten Bildungsstufen als indifferente und ununterscheidbare Masse zurückgeblieben, in welcher die höheren Potenzen ihres eigenthümlichen Lebens, Mannbarkeit, Schwangerschaft und Geburt zwar schon potentialiter enthalten sind, aber noch ruhen" Reil, "Polar Deviations," 429.
26. Ibid., 416.
27. "Das Weib in Sehnsucht = Indifferenz." *Fragmente*, n. 501.
28. Ritter's experiments with the pendulum also rely upon the concept of a polarized body. In a letter to Karl Hardenberg from February 1st, 1807, writing about the method of using the divining rod, Ritter describes the positive and negative polarities of various body parts (the head positive, the feet negative) as well as points of indifference in between. The feminine genitalia and eyes as well as the feminine mouth are also brought into the "positive" relation to masculine "negativity." Rehm, *Briefe eines Romantischen Physikers*, 30.
29. See Hardenberg, *Schriften*, 2:260, n. 511, as well as Dietrich Henrich's chapter on "Theories of Imagination and Longing and Their Impact on Schlegel, Novalis and Hölderlin" in *Between Kant and Hegel: Lectures on German Idealism*. Cambridge: Harvard University Press, 2003.
30. The reference to Goethe is from *Tasso* 2,1. See also *Fragmente*, n. 486.
31. The word *Weib*, usually as the diminutive *Weibchen*, distinguishes sex in living species, including humans (how pejorative it is, depends on the context). The word *Frau* is limited to human women. In this passage from *Tasso*, *Frau* also connotes social status and propriety.
32. *Fragmente*, n. 482.
33. The only new thing for Menninghaus is "the radicality and the concreteness does not seldom provoke one to laughter, with which Ritter brings all bodily properties, all phenomena of love, procreation, and birth to the common terms indifference and difference apparently borrowed from Schelling's philosophy of nature." (In dieser Grundformel der Ritterschen Reflexionen steckt schwerlich mehr als die herkömmliche Gegenüberstellung von weiblicher Natureinheit und männlicher, von Wille und Intellekt geprägter Gespaltenheit. Neu ist denn in der Tat auch nur die Radikalität und die krude, nicht selten Lachen provozierende Konkretheit, mit der Ritter alle körperlichen Eigentümlichkeiten, alle Phänomene von Liebe, Zeugung und Geburt auf die offenbar der Schellingschen Naturphilosophie

entlehnten Nenner Indifferenz und Differenz bringt). Menninghaus, "Theorie der Weiblichkeit," 218–219.
34. See *Fragmente*, n. 477.
35. Ibid., n. 43.
36. Ibid., n. 299.
37. Ibid., n. 501.
38. Unraveling—*entwickeln*—is Ritter's verb as well: "The woman *unravels*, and the man *ravels* himself" (Die Frau entwickelt sich, der Mann verwickelt sich). *Fragmente*, n. 504.
39. See, for example, *Fragmente*, n. 501, where the Madonna and child are the "most beautiful symbol of polarity."
40. "Als *Gatte* und *Vater*, in der *Familie* erst, behauptete er mehrmals, für die Natur und ihre Wissenschaft sich *vollkommen integrirt* zu fühlen." Prologue, cx.
41. "Offenbar zeigt der Typus der Familie die Triplicität in jedem (hier organisch-) chemischem Process." *Fragmente*, n. 501.
42. See *Fragmente*, n. 484.
43. See Engelhardt, "Naturforschung im Zeitalter der Romantik," 42–43.
44. "Nicht Geschichte *der* Physik, sondern Geschichte = Physik = Geschichte." *Fragmente*, n. 140.
45. In a letter to de la Metherie they explain the relevance of their observations for the ongoing debate between the "old" and "new" theories in French chemistry, the phlogiston and the anti-phlogiston theories: "Although we acknowledge that the new theory of French chemists regarding the nature of water has not so far been strictly established we are all the same far removed from the desire to defend the old theory. On the contrary, we believe we can contribute a good deal for confirmation of the new theory because we have been successful in discovering the means of converting water simultaneously into combustible air (hydrogen gas) and life-giving air (oxygen), and therefore decomposing it in a manner which appears to us to preclude the attribution of these products to any other source." Ostwald, *Electrochemistry*, 22.
46. The first published correspondence was in 1800 in a letter from Volta to Joseph Banks titled "On the Electricity excited by the mere Contact of conducting Substances of different kinds." In a comparison with the "*organe électrique naturel*" (natural electric organ) of the torpido fish, Volta decides to call his new instrument an "*organe électrique artificiel*" (artificial electrical organ). Volta, "On the Electricity," 405. Two pages later, Volta switches the terms of his comparison: it is no longer the pile which imitates nature, but "an extremely slow torpedo fish" which imitates the effects of a weak pile. Ibid., 406–407.
47. Through his invention of the pile, Volta developed the first wet-cell battery. Ritter himself later developed the first dry-cell one, which did not depend on moist cloths or paperboard to facilitate conductivity between the pairs of metals.
48. Kant, *Werkausgabe*, 12:31.
49. "welche die Vereinigung aller Sinnen-Vorstellung im Gemüth möglich macht." Ibid., 12:32.
50. Kant writes, "The only thing which is qualified for it (to be *sensorium commune*) is [. . .] contained in the brain cavity, and merely water" (Die einzige aber die sich dazu (als Sensorium commune) qualificirt, ist [. . .] in der Gehirnhöhle enthalten, und bloß Wasser). Ibid. In a letter to Goethe dated September 1st, 1795, Sömmering comments "these old Nile-sources

of the soul are certainly not common water, as Kant thinks" but rather as distinct as humans are from one another. LA 2:9A, 451.
51. For additional historical background on Ritter's reception of Kant and Sömmering, see Caroline Welsh, *Hirnhöhlenpoetiken*, 72–73.
52. "Das medium des *Hörens* ist das *Wasser*. Es ist in allen Gehörorganen vorhanden, und seine Erschütterung wird die des Nervens, der in ihm liegt. Das Medium des *Sehens* ist das Wasser gleichfalls, denn in sofern Pole hervor-gerufen werden, wird gesehen, indiferenzirt. Das Medium des *Schmeckens* ist es ebenfalls, auch das des *Geruchs*, und das des *Fühlens* abermals, nur hier mehr innerlich. Also ist das Wasser die Brücke alles Möglichen von der Welt zu uns. Sogar im Geschlechtsact hat es die Hauptrolle." *Fragmente*, n. 445.
53. Also quoted in Wetzels, *Johann Wilhelm Ritter*, 24.
54. Welsh, *Hirnhöhlenpoetik*, 78.
55. Ibid.
56. "Volta's Galvanische Batterie, nebst Versuchen mit derselben" in *Voigt's Magazin für den neuesten Zustand der Naturkunde* (1800), 2:356–400. Reprinted in *Physisch-Chemische Abhandlungen*, 1:195—226.
57. "Wie wichtig dies alles einst werden müsse, wenn sich ausweisen wird, dass jede Erzeugung von Oxygen und Hydrogen unter Umständen, wo man sie für das Product einer Zersetzung des Wassers ausgab, und somit überhaupt alles, was man bisher mit diesem Namen belegte, nichts als das Product eines rein Galvanischen Processes sey, ja dass alle chemischen Processe, als, um noch in der bisherigen Sprache zu reden, sich alle in Oxy- und Deseoxydationsprocesse auflösend, und so wieder einzig durch sogenannte Wasserzersetzung vermittelt werdend, nichts als bald so, bald anders, verkleidete Galvanische Processe seyen, bedarf keiner näheren Erläuterung." *Physisch-Chemische Abhandlungen*, 1:220.
58. "Ich könnte weiter gehen. Ich könnte alle chemischen Processe, die es nur eigentlich sind, auf Oxy- und Desoxygenationsprocesse, und alle mit diesen wieder auf Wasserzersetzungs—und nach Umständen auch Wiederzusammensetzungsprocesse reduciren, und nur etwas Geduld würde alle Schwierigkeiten überwinden können, die sich mir entgegenstellen möchten, wenn ich es unternehmen wollte, das *Wasser zum Indifferenzpunkt aller chemischen Qualität*, und die angenommenen *Bestandtheile desselben* zu den *beyden Armen des gemeinschaftlichen Hebels aller Kraftäußerung jener*, zu erheben." "Bemerkungen über die Art," 239–240.
59. Ibid., 240.
60. Drawing upon Ritter's own vocabulary, Lothar Müller discusses Ritter's attempt at a paradigm change in terms of an electrical "fire science" to replace the reigning "water science." Müller, "Die 'Feuerwissenschaft," 280.
61. According to Wetzels, "the two gases were, according to Ritter's explanation, the result of a compositional rather than a decompositional process in which water was, as it were, galvanized to combine with the two electricities generated by the two electrodes" Wetzels, "J. W. Ritter and Romantic Physics," 209.
62. In the aphorisms collected under the title "Physicalische Fragmente" is: "*Noteworthy Phenomenon*: Decomposition of Water through Iron and Zinc—Perhaps through More Metals" (*Merckwürdiges Phaenomén*: Zersetzung des Wassers durch Eisen und Zink—vielleicht durch mehrere Metalle.) Novalis, *Schriften*, 3:73, n. 1.
63. Ibid., 3:559, n. 27.

64. *Physics as Art*, 45.
65. *Beyträge*, 1, 3:175.
66. Ibid., 174.
67. Ibid.
68. Quoted in Ostwald, *Electrochemistry*, 207. Ritter also compares the earth to the positive wire of a pile, where the negative wire is on the moon (*Fragmente*, n. 543).
69. Anonymous review of the *Beyträge*, *Allgemeine Literatur Zeitung* 311 (Thursday, November 28th, 1805): col. 410–416. See also Wetzels, *Johann Wilhelm Ritter*, 168.
70. Ritter generally arranges his fragments chronologically by section; these two fragments likely date from 1802–1804.
71. The following pages are devoted to Ritter's reception of Goethe and its importance for his thinking about procreation. The exchange of ideas between the two writers was by no means one-sided: Joseph Vogl has shown the importance of Ritter's work on chemistry for Goethe's *Elective Affinities*. See Vogl, "Nomos der Ökonomie. Steuerungen in Goethes *Wahlverwandtschaften*." MLN 114.3 (1999): 503–527.
72. J. W. Ritter, "Versuch einer Geschichte der Schicksale der chemischen Theorie in den letzten Jahrhunderten," *Journal für die Chemie, Physik und Mineralogie* 7.1 (1808): 1–66.
73. "von einem der ersten Staatsmänner Baierns, dem der neue Flor der Wissenschaften in diesem Lande, außer dem höchsten ministeriellen Interesse, auch noch möglichste persönliche Theilnahme verdankt." Ritter, "Versuch einer Geschichte," 1. The new charter of the *Bavarian Academy of Sciences* is the *Konstitutions-Urkunde der königlichen Akademie der Wissenschaften*. (Munich: Zängl, 1807). See also Richter, *Das Leben eines Physikers*, 126.
74. "'Epistemic things' are material entities or processes—physical structures, chemical reactions, biological functions—that constitute the objects of inquiry. As epistemic objects, they present themselves in a characteristic, irreducible vagueness. This vagueness is inevitable because, paradoxically, epistemic things embody what one does not yet know." Rheinberger, *Towards a History of Epistemic Things*, 28.
75. "The first objects of chemistry were in every epoch *life* and *burning*." (Die ersten Gegenstände der Chemie waren zu jeder Zeit das *Leben* und das *Verbrennen*). Ritter, "Versuch einer Geschichte," 2.
76. See also Ritter's letter to Ørsted from July 19th, 1806, where he refers to the publication of Goethe's collected works by Cotta. Ørsted, *Correspondance*, 2:182.
77. "Ich verstehe die Metamorphose der Pflanzen, der Thiere, der Menschen, der Erde, der Menschheit etc. wie *Goethe* noch sonst jemand nimmermehr. Kurz: die *Metamorphose alles Endlichen*." Ørsted, *Correspondance*, 2:19.
78. Ritter, "Versuch einer Geschichte," 9 (note).
79. Wetzels, *Johann Wilhelm Ritter*, 78. See Fragment 490, which also links the notion of the first idea as the best idea to metaphors of botanical growth and human metamorphosis (cycles of life and death, as cycles of difference and indifference).
80. "Diese Dreiphasentheorie über die Entwicklung einer wissenschaftlichen Idee ist offensichtlich—auch ohne Ritters Hinweis auf Goethes Elegie—nach dem organischen Modell Keim—Blätter—Blüte konzipiert." Wetzels, *Johann Wilhelm Ritter*, 78.

81. Zwar immer im Geiste des Ganzen mit seinem Gegenstande umgehend, fiel es doch auch ihm schwer, sich in der Kürze mitten aus dem Detail, was ihn in ausgedehntester Einzelheit so unvermeidlich beschäftigt, zur allgemeinen und gleichförmigen Uebersicht zu erheben." "Versuch einer Geschichte," 1–2.
82. Ritter connects this idea to epochal thinking. One of the patterns we observe is governed by the number three ("what doubtlessly is based upon a great law governing *all* distinction in space and time, as in nature and mankind—to which one of the following comments will return once more"). "Versuch einer Geschichte," 10–11 (note).
83. Cf. Förster, "Auge des Geistes" 93–94.
84. "Alles organisch Vorschreitende, (und nichts ist andrer Art, blos mehr und weniger), schreitet durch außer sein voriges herausfallende Reconstruction seiner selbst vor [. . .] auch das Geistige der Idee." "Versuch einer Geschichte," 9 (note).
85. See *Fragmente*, n. 490.
86. See, for example, Hisinger's and Berzelius's results in Gehlen's *Neues Allgemeines Journal der Chemie* 1 (1803), under the title "Versuche, betreffend die Wirkung der electrischen Säule auf Salze und auf einige von ihren Basen."
87. "Versuch einer Geschichte," 18—19 (note).
88. Ibid., 56.
89. Ibid.
90. In his correspondence with Ørsted Ritter writes that Lichtenberg figures generated by positive and negative electricity form the first and final letters of the alphabet.
91. "Versuch einer Geschichte," 62–63.
92. "Ist doch auch im reiche des *Organischen* die wahre Anzahl der verschiedenen Geschlechter mit zwey nicht abgethan" Ritter, "Versuch einer Geschichte," 63.
93. "Bester Commentar: Versuch eines Geschlechtsgesetzes für Menschen, eines ersten überhaupt, was überall die Auf- und Rücksicht auf ein Drittes außer oder über beyden mit befahl. [*Goguet*, u.a.] Gesetz ist aber immer nur ausgesprochene Naturnothwendigkeit, und ein menschliches sprach die einer ganzen belebten Schöpfung zukommende aus." Ibid., 63.
94. This suggestion is made with reference to Antoine-Yves Goguet. In his 1758 treatise, *De l'origine des loix, des arts, et des sciences; et de leurs progrès chez les anciens peuples* (1758, On the origin of the laws, the arts, and the sciences; and their progress among past civilizations), Goguet suggests there must be a law in order to keep the mutual attraction between the sexes within certain limits. "Le penchant mutuel qui porte les deux sexes à se rechercher est le 'principe qui perpétue et maintient la société; mais ce penchant, s'il n'est pas contenu dans de certaines bornes, est la source de bien des maux" Goguet, *De l'origine des loix*, (1809) 1:56. Goguet's argument for marriage as a way to contain human desires (especially of females) continues over the following two pages with examples drawn from myths and history of antiquity.
95. "For Boehme and the Gnostics, God is an androgynous unity. His self-propagation continues through the three principles of His manifestation; the first principle (anger, wrath, and darkness) is masculine, the second (light and love) is feminine and the third principle, that of the world in its ideal or magic state, is a fusion of the two. The medieval Cabbala insisted that, as Adam kadmon (the Gnostic Anthropos) was created in God's

image, then he must also be androgynous." Furness, "The Androgynous Ideal," 59.

96. The relationship is one of supplementarity and, in its structure, has something in common with the model of subjectivity discussed in the context of Kant and Sömmering.

Bibliography

Adelung, Johann Christian. *Grammatisch-kritisches Wörterbuch der Hochdeutschen Mundart, mit beständiger Vergleichung der übrigen Mundarten, besonders aber der Oberdeutschen.* 4 vols. Wien: B. Ph. Bauer, 1811.
Altner, Günter. "Gestaltwandel der Welt—Zur Morphologie Goethes." In *Goethe und die Natur,* edited by Horst Albert Glaser. Frankfurt: Peter Lang, 1986.
Amrine, Frederick. "Metamorphosis of the Scientist." In *Goethe's Way of Science: Towards a Phenomenology of Nature,* edited by David Seamon and Arthur Zajonc. Albany: SUNY Press, 1998.
Aristotle. *On the Generation of Animals,* translated by Arthur Platt. In *The Works of Aristotle,* edited by J. A. Smith and W. D. Ross. 12 vols. Oxford: Clarendon Press, 1912.
Assman, Aleida. "Die Domestikation des Lesens. Drei historische Beispiele." *Zeitschrift für Literaturwissenschaft und Linguistik* 15.57/58 (1985): 95–110.
———. "Kultur als Lebenswelt und Monument." In *Kultur als Lebenswelt und Monument.* Edited by Aleida Assmann and Dietrich Harth. Frankfurt am Main: Fischer, 1991.
Assman, Jan. "Ancient Egypt and the Materiality of the Sign." In *Materialities of Communication,* edited by Hans Gumbrecht and K. Ludwig Pfeifer, translated by William Whobrey. Stanford: Stanford University Press, 1994.
von Baer, Karl Ernst. *Selbstbiographie von Dr. Karl Ernst von Baer.* Braunschweig: Verlag von Friedrich Vieweg und Sohn, 1886.
Bäumer, Gertrud. *Fichte und Sein Werk.* Berlin: F. A. Herbig, 1921.
Bark, Irene. *Steine in Potenzen.* Tübingen: Max Niemeyer, 1999.
Barnard, F.M. *Herder on Nationality, Humanity, and History.* Montreal: McGill-Queen's University Press, 2003.
Barnes, Jonathan. *The Presocratic Philosophers.* 2 vols. London: Routledge, 1982.
Bell, Matthew. *Goethe's Naturalistic Anthropology. Man and Other Plants.* Oxford: Oxford University Press, 1994.
Benn, Gottfried. *Goethe und die Naturwissenschaften.* Zürich: Arche, 1949.
Bennent, Heidemarie. *Galanterie und Verachtung. Eine philosophiegeschichtliche Untersuchung zur Stellung der Frau in Gesellschaft und Kultur.* Frankfurt: Campus Verlag, 1985.
Birrell, Gordon. *The Boundless Present.* Chapel Hill: University of North Carolina Press, 1979.
Blumenbach, Johann Friedrich. *Über den Bildungstrieb.* Göttingen: Johann Christian Dieterich, 1791.
Blumenberg, Hans. *Die Lesbarkeit der Welt.* Suhrkamp: Frankfurt am Main, 1981.
Brentano, Clemens. *Briefe,* edited by F. Seebaß. 2 vols. Nürnberg: Carl, 1951.

Brown, John. *The Elements of Medicine*, 2 vols. London: J. Johnson, 1795.
Brugmans, Anton. *Beobachtungen über die Verwandtschaften des Magnets; Philosophische Versuche über die magnetische Materie.* Hildesheim, Zürich, New York: Olms-Weidmann, 2004. Reprint of Leipzig: Crusius, 1781 and 1784.
Chaouli, Michel. *The Laboratory of Poetry: Chemistry and Poetics in the Work of Friedrich Schlegel.* Baltimore: Johns Hopkins University Press, 2002.
Daiber, Jürgen. *Experimentalphysik des Geistes. Novalis und das romantische Experiment.* Göttingen: Vandenhoeck & Ruprecht, 2001.
D'Alembert, Jean and Dénis Diderot. *Encyclopédie, ou Dictionnaire raisonné des sciences, des arts et des métiers, par une société des gens de lettres. Mis en ordre et publié par M. Diderot, et quant à la partie mathématique, par M. d'Alemebrt.* 17 vols. Paris: Chez Briasson, David, Le Breton, Durand, 1751–1765.
Deleuze, Gilles and Félix Guattari. *What is Philosophy?*, translated by Janis Tomlinson and Graham Burchell III. New York: Columbia University Press, 1996.
Descartes, René. *Meditations on First Philosophy*, translated by John Cottingham. Cambridge: Cambridge University Press, 1996.
Dictionnaire de l'Académie française, 5th edition. Paris: J.J. Smits, 1798.
Dieckmann, Liselotte. *Hieroglyphics: The History of a Literary Symbol.* St. Louis: Washington University Press, 1970.
Dyck, Martin. *Novalis and Mathematics.* Chapel Hill: UNC Press, 1960.
von Engelhardt, Dietrich. "Naturforschung im Zeitalter der Romantik." In *'Fessellos durch die Systeme.' Frühromantisches Naturdenken im Umfeld von Arnim, Ritter und Schelling*, edited by Walther Zimmerli, Klaus Stein, and Michael Gerten. Stuttgart-Bad Cannstatt: frommann-holzboog, 1997.
Euclid, *The Thirteen Books of Euclid's Elements*, translated by Sir Thomas Little Heath. New York: Dover, 1956.
Fichte, Johann Gottlieb. *Fichtes Sämmtliche Werke*, edited by I. H. Ficht. 8 vols. Berlin: Veit & Company, 1845–1846.
Foucault, Michel. *The History of Sexuality.* 3 vols. New York: Vintage, 1988–1990.
Förster, Eckart. "Die Bedeutung von § § 76, 77 der Kritik der Urteilskraft für die Entwicklung der nachkantischen Philosophie." [Part One]. *Zeitschrift für philosophische Forschung* 56.3 (2002): 169–190.
———. "Goethe and the 'Auge des Geistes.'" *Deutsches Vierteljahresschrift* 75 (2001): 87–101.
Frank, Manfred. *Das Problem 'Zeit' in der Deutschen Romantik.* Munich: Winkler, 1972.
———. *Der kommende Gott: Vorlesungen über die neue Mythologie.* Frankfurt: Suhrkamp, 1982.
———. *The Philosophical Foundations of Early German Romanticism.* Albany: SUNY Press, 2004.
———. and Gerhard Kurz. "Ordo Inversus. Zu einer Reflexionsfigur bei Novalis, Hölderlin, Kleist und Kafka." *Geist und Zeichen*, edited by Herbert Anton et al. Heidelberg: Carl Winter.
Frevert, Ute. *'Mann und Weib, und Weib und Mann': Geschlechterdifferenzen in der Moderne.* Munich: Beck, 1995.
Froebe, Hans A. "'Ulmbaum und Rebe.' Naturwissenschaft, Alchymie und Emblematik in Goethes Aufsatz 'Über die Spiraltendenz' (1830–1831)." In *Emblem und Emblematikrezeption. Vergleichende Studien zur Wirkungsgeschichte vom 16. bis 20. Jahrhundert*, edited by Sibylle Penkert. Darmstadt: Wissenschlaftliche Buchgesellschaft, 1978.
Fuchs, Thomas. *Die Mechanisierung des Herzens: Harvey und Descartes, der vitale und der mechanische Aspekt des Kreislaufs.* Frankfurt: Suhrkamp, 1992.
Furness, Raymond. "The Androgynous Ideal: Its Significance in German Literature." *The Modern Language review* 60.1 (Jan., 1965): 58–64.

Gaier, Ulrich. *Krumme Regel. Novalis' "Konstruktionslehre des schaffenden Geistes und ihre Tradition.* Tübingen: Niemeyer, 1970.
Gaine, Simon Francis. "Fruition, Freedom and Indifference: William of Ockham," in *Will There Be Free Will in Heaven?*" London: Continuum, 2003.
Gaventa, B. R. "Galatians 1 and 2: Autobiography as Paradigm." *Novum Testamentum* 28.4 (October 1986): 309–326.
Genette, Gérard: *Seuils.* Paris: Éditions du Seuil, 1987.
Gill. David H, "Through a Glass Darkly: A Note on 1 Corinthians 13,12." *The Catholic Bible Quarterly* 25 (4 October 1963): 427–429.
von Goethe, Johann Wolfgang. *Goethes Werke,* edited by Johann Ludwig Gustav von Loeper et al. Weimar: H Böhlau: 1887–1919. (Abbreviated in the text as WA.)
———. *Die Schriften zur Naturwissenschaft,* edited by Günther Schmid. 22 vols. in 2 parts. Weimar: Hermann Böhlaus Nachfolger, 1947-. (Abbreviated in the text as LA.)
———. *Sämtliche Werke, Briefe, Tagebücher und Gespräche,* edited by Dieter Borchmeyer et al. 40 vols. Frankfurt: Deutscher Klassiker Verlag, 1985f. (Abbreviated in the text as FA.)
———. *Sämtliche Werke nach Epochen seines Schaffens,* edited by Karl Richter, Herbert G. Göpfert, Norbert Miller and Gerhard Sauder. 33 vols. Munich: Carl Hanser, 1986. Paperback edition Munich: Random House, 2006. (Abbreviated in the text as MA.)
———. *The Metamorphosis of Plants: Goethe's "Botany" (1790) and Tobler's "Ode to Nature" (1782),* translated by Agnes Arber. Waltham: Chronica Botanica, 1946.
———. *Selected Poems,* translated and edited by Michael Hamburger et al. Princeton: Princeton University Press, 1994.
———. *Goethe's Collected Works.* 12 vols. New York: Suhrkamp, 1983–1989.
———. *Conversations with Eckermann,* translated by John Oxenford. San Francisco: North Point, 1984.
Goguet, Antoine-Yves. *De l'origine des lois, des arts et des sciences, et de leurs progrès chez les anciens peuples.* Paris: L'Haussmann et d'Hautel, 1809.
Gould, Stephen Jay. *Ontogeny and Phylogeny.* Cambridge: Belknap Press, 1977.
———. *Ever Since Darwin: Reflections in Natural History.* New York: Norton, 1977.
Grew, Nehemiah. *The Anatomy of Plants.* London: W. Rawlins, 1682.
Grob, Karl. *Ursprung und Utopie. Aporien des Textes. Versuche zu Herder und Novalis.* Bonn: Bouvier, 1976.
Hadot, Pierre. *Le Voile d'Isis: Essai sur l'histoire de l'idée de Nature.* Paris: Éditions Gallimard, 2004.
Hamburger, Käte. "Novalis und die Mathematik." *Deutsche Vierteljahrsschrift* 16 (1929): 113–184.
von Hardenberg, Friedrich. *Schriften,* edited by Richard Samuel, Hans-Joachim Mähl, and Gerhard Schulz. 6 vols. Stuttgart: W. Kohlhammer, 1960.
Harvey, William. *On the Motion of the Heart,* translated by Robert Willis. London: Sydenham Society, 1847.
Haywood, Bruce. *Novalis: The Veil of Imagery.* 's Gravenhage: Mouton, 1959.
Heinz, Marion and Friederike Kuster. "'Vollkommene Vereinigung.' Fichtes Eherecht in der Perspektive feministischer Philosophie" *Deutsche Zeitschrift fur Philosophie* 46.5 (1998): 823–839.
Helfer, Martha. "The Male Muses of Romanticism: The Poetics of Gender in Novalis, E.T.A. Hoffmann, and Eichendorff" *The German Quarterly* 78.3 (Summer 2005): 299–319.
Hemsterhuis, François. *Philosophische Schriften,* edited by Julius Hilss. 2 vols. Karlsruhe: Dreililien-Verlag, 1912.

Henderson, Fergus. "Novalis, Ritter and 'Experiment': A Tradition of 'Active Empiricism.'" *The Third Culture: Literature and Science*, edited Elinor Schaffer. Berlin: Walter de Gruyter, 1998.
Henrich, Dietrich. *Between Kant and Hegel: Lectures on German Idealism.* Cambridge: Harvard University Press, 2003.
Herder, Johann Gottfried. *Werke in zehn Bänden*, edited by Martin Bollacher et al. 10 vols. Frankfurt am Main: Deutscher Klassiker Verlag, 1985.
Herz, Andreas. *Dunkler Spiegel—helles Dasein. Natur, Geschichte, Kunst im Werk Johann Gottfried Herders.* Heidelberg: Universitätsverlag C. Winter, 1996.
Hoesch, Monica Birth. *"I Am All That Is, That Was, and That Shall Be, and No Mortal Has Lifted My Veil": Kant, Novalis, Goethe, and the Veiled Goddess Isis.* Dissertation, Johns Hopkins University, 2006.
Holzhey, Christoph. "On the Emergence of Sexual Difference in the Eigtheenth Century: Economies of Pleasure in Herder's Liebe und Selbstheit." German Quarterly 79.1 (2006): 1–27.
Honegger, Claudia. *Die Ordnung der Geschlechter.* New York : Campus Verlag, 1991.
von Humboldt, Wilhelm. "Über den Geschlechtsunterschied und dessen Einfluss auf die organische Natur" (1794). First volume in *Wilhelm von Humboldts Werke*, edited by Albert Leitzmann. 7 vols. Berlin: B. Behr, 1903. Reprint Berlin: Walter de Gruyter, 1968.
Hume, David. *A Treatise of Human Nature: Being an Attempt to Introduce the Experimental Method of Reasoning into Moral Subjects.* London: John Noon, 1739–1740.
Ishihara, Aeka. *Makarie und das Weltall: Astronomie in Goethes 'Wanderjahren.'* Koln: Böhlau, 1998.
Jordanova, Ludmilla. *Sexual Visions: Images of Gender in Science and Medicine between the Eighteenth and Twentieth Centuries.* Madison: University of Wisconsin Press, 1989.
Just, Carl. "Nekrolog für Friedrich von Hardenberg." *Nekrolog der deutschen für das neunzehnte Jahrhundert* 4 (1805): 187–241.
Kant, Immanuel. *Werkausgabe*, edited by Wilhelm Weischedel, 12 vols. Frankfurt: Suhrkamp, 1981–1982.
———. *Critique of Judgment*, translated by J. H. Bernard. New York: Hafner, 1951.
———. *The Metaphysics of Morals*, translated and edited by Mary J. Gregor. Cambridge: Cambridge University Press, 1996.
von Kielmyer, Carl Friedrich. *Ueber die Verhältnisse der organischen Kräfte unter einander in der Reihe der verschiedenen Organisationen, die Geseze* [sic] *und Folgen dieser Verhältnisse.* A facsimile of the 1793 edition. Edited by Kai Torsten Kanz. Marburg an der Lahn: Basilisken Presse, 1993.
Kirchhoff, Alfred. *Die Idee der Pflanzen-Metamorphose bei Wolff und bei Goethe.* Berlin: Schade, 1867.
Kittler, Friedrich. *Aufschreibesysteme.* Munich: Fink, 1987.
———. *Discourse Networks 1800/1900*, introduction by David Wllbery. Stanford: Stanford University Press, 1990.
Koerner, Lisbeth. "Goethe's Botany: Lessons of a Feminine Science." *Isis* 84.3 (September 1993): 470–495.
Koptak, Paul E. "Rhetorical Identification In Paul's Autobiographical Narrative." *Journal for the Study of the New Testament* 40 (1990): 97–113.
Kreuzer, Ingrid. "Novalis: Die Lehrlinge zu Sais." *Jahrbuch der Schiller Gesellschaft* 23 (1979): 276–308.
Kuhn, Dorothea, "Typus und Metamorphose." In *Typus und Metamorphose*, edited by Renate Grumach and Dorothea Kuhn. Marbach: Deutsche Schillergesellschaft, 1988.

Kuzniar, Alice. "Reassessing Romantic Reflexivity—The Case of Novalis." *The Germanic Review* 63 (1988): 77–86.
Lacoste, Jean. *Goethe. Science et Philosophie*. Paris: Presses universitaires de France, 1997.
Lejeune, Philippe. *Je est un autre. L'autobiographie de la littérature aux médias*. Paris: Éditions du Seuil, 1980.
Lenoir, Timothy. "Kant, Blumenbach, and Vital Materialism in German Biology." *Isis*, 71.1 1 (Mar., 1980): 77–108.
———. "Teleology without Regrets: The Transformation of Physiology in Germany." *Studies in the History and Philosophy of Science* 12 (1981): 293–354.
Lepenies, Wolf. *Das Ende der Naturgeschichte: Wandel kultureller Selbstverständlichkeiten in den Wissenschaften des 18. und 19. Jahrhunderts*. Munich: C. Hanser, 1976.
Libavius, Andreas. *Die Gerätschaften der chemischen Kunst: der Traktat* De sceuastica artis *des Andreas Libavius von 1606: Übersetzung, Kommentierung und Wiederabdruck*, translated and edited by Bettina B. Meitzner. Stuttgart: Franz Steiner Verlag, 1995.
Lichtenberg, Georg Christoph. *Schriften und Briefe*, edited by Wolfgang Promies. 3 vols. Munich: Hanser, 1967 ff.
Liedtke, Ralf. *Das romantische Paradigma der Chemie: Friedrich von Hardenbergs Naturphilosophie zwischen Empirie und alchemistischer Spekulation*. Paderborn: Mentis, 2003.
Lötschert, Wilhelm. "Goethe und die Pflanze" *Jahrbuch des Freien Deutschen Hochstifts* (1982): 216–230.
Loheide, Bernward. *Fichte und Novalis: transzendentalphilosophisches Denken im romantisierenden Diskurs*. Amsterdam, Atlanta: Rodopi, 2000.
Luhmann, Niklas. *Liebe als Passion. Zur Codierung von Intimität*. Frankfurt am Main: Suhrkamp, 1983.
Mahoney, Dennis. *The Critical Fortunes of a Romantic Novel: Novalis's "Heinrich von Ofterdingen."* Columbia: Camden House, 1994.
Mautner, Franz. "Der Aphorismus als litterarische Gattung." In *Der Aphorismus. Zur Geschichte, zu den Formen und Möglichkeiten einer literarischen Gattung*, edited by Gerhard Neumann. Darmstadt: Wissenschaftliche Buchgesellschaft, 1976.
von Martius, Carl Friedrich. "Über die Architectonik der Blüthen." Part One (report of his lecture) *Isis* (1828): col. 522–529.
———. "Über die Architectonik der Blüthen." Part Two (report of his lecture) *Isis* (1829): col. 333–341.
von Marum, Martin. *Description d'une très grande machine électrique*. Haarlem: J. Enschedé, 1785.
Mayer, Paola. *Jena Romanticism and its Appropriation of Jakob Böhme: Theosophy, Hagiography, Literature*. Montreal, Ithaca: McGill-Queen's University Press, 1999.
Mehra, Marlis Helene. *Die Bedeutung der Formel 'Offenbares Geheimnis' in Goethe's Spätwerk*. Stuttgart: H.-D. Heinz, 1982.
Menke, Bettine. "Töne—Hören." In *Poetologien des Wissens*, edited by Joseph Vogl. Munich: Wilhelm Fink, 1998.
Menninghaus, Winfried. *Unendliche Verdopplung*. Frankfurt: Suhrkamp, 1987.
De la Mettrie, Offray. *Oeuvres Philosophiques*. 3 vols. Berlin: Etienne de Bourdeaux, 1751.
Moll, K. E. *Mitteilungen aus seinem Briefwechsel*. 4 vols. Augsburg: Self-published, 1829–1835.
von Molnár, Geza. *Novalis' "Fichte Studies. The Foundations of His Aesthetics*. The Hague: Mouton, 1970.

von Montgelas, Maximilian. *Konstitutions-Urkunde der königlichen Akademie der Wissenschaften.* Munich: Zängl, 1807.
von Mücke, Dorothea. "Goethe's Metamorphosis: Changing Forms in Nature, the Life Sciences, and Authorship." *Representations* 95 (Summer 2006): 27–53.
Müller, Lothar. "Die 'Feuerwissenschaft'. Romantische Naturwissenschaft und Anthropologie bei Johann Wilhelm Ritter." In *Der ganze Mensch: Anthropologie und Literatur im 18. Jahrhundert*, edited by Hans-Jürgen Schings (Stuttgart: Metzler, 1994).
Müller-Sievers, Helmut. *Self-generation: Biology, Philosophy, and Literature around 1800.* Stanford: Stanford University Press, 1997.
———. "'Belebte Schraube Ohne Ende,' Zur Vorgeschichte der Doppelhelix." *Trajekte* 16 (2008): 25–28.
Needham, Joseph. *A History of Embryology.* Cambridge: Cambridge University Press, 1959.
Neubauer, John. "Dr. John Brown and Early German Romanticism." *Journal of the History of Ideas* 28 (1967): 367–382.
———. *Bifocal Vision: Novalis Philosophy of Nature and Disease.* Chapel Hill: University of North Carolina Press, 1971.
———. "Organic Form in Romantic Theory: The Case of Goethe's Morphology." In *Romanticism Across the Disciplines*, edited by Larry H. Peer. Lanham: University Press of America, 1998.
Neumann, Gerhard. *Ideenparadiese. Untersuchungen zur Aphoristik von Lichtenberg, Novalis, Friedrich Schlegel and Goethe.* Munich: W. Fink, 1976.
———. "Introduction." *Der Aphorismus. Zur Geschichte, zu den Formen und Möglichkeiten einer literarischen Gattung*, edited by Gerhard Neumann. Darmstadt: Wissenschaftliche Buchgesellschaft, 1976.
O'Brien, William Arctander. *Novalis. Signs of Revolution.* Durham: Duke University Press, 1995.
Ørsted, Hans Christian. *Correspondance de H. C. Oersted avec divers savants*, edited by M. C. Harding. 2 vols. Copenhagen: H. Aschehoug, 1920.
Ostwald, Wilhelm. *Electrochemistry: History and Theory.* 2 vols. New Delhi: Amerind Publishing Co., 1980.
Outram, Dorinda. "Autobiography, Science and the French Revolution." In *Telling Lives in Science, Essays on Scientific Biography*, edited by Michael Shortland and Richard Yeo. Cambridge: Cambridge University Press, 1996.
Overbeck, Gertrud. "Goethes Lehre von der Metamorphose der Pflanzen und ihre Widerspiegelung in seiner Dichtung." *Publications of the English Goethe Society* 31 (1961): 38–59.
Palti, Elias. "The 'Metaphor of Life': Herder's Philosophy of History and Uneven Developments in Late Eighteenth-Century Natural Sciences." In *History and Theory* 38.3 (October 1999): 322–347.
Peters, Günter. *Die Kunst der Natur. Ästhetische Reflexion in Blumengedichten von Brockes, Goethe und Gautier.* Munich: Fink, 1993.
Pfaff, Peter. "Natur-Poesie. Zu den 'Lehrlingen zu Sais' des Novalis." In *Was aber bleibet stiften die Dichter? Zur Dichter-Theologie der Goethezeit*, edited by Gerhard vom Hofe, Peter Pfaff, and Hermann Timm. Munich: Fink, 1986.
Pfefferkorn, Kristin. *A Romantic's Theory of Language and Poetry.* New Haven: Yale University Press, 1988.
Pickstone, John V. *Ways of Knowing: A New History of Science, Technology and Medicine.* Manchester: Manchester University Press, 2000.
Pinto-Correia, Clara. *The Ovary of Eve: Egg and Sperm and Preformation.* Chicago: Chicago University Press, 1997.

Portmann, Adolf. "Goethe and the Concept of Metamorphosis." *Goethe and the Sciences*, edited by Frederick Amrine, Francis J. Zucker and Harvey Wheeler. Dordrecht, Boston: Reidel, 1987.
Prechtl, Peter and Franz-Peter Burkard. *Metzler Philosophie Lexikon. Begriffe und Definitionen*. Stuttgart: Metzler, 1996.
Quintilian. *Institutio Oratio*, translated by Harold Edgeworth Butler. Cambridge: Harvard University Press, 1976.
Rang, Bernhard. *Identität und Indifferenz. Eine Untersuchung zu Schellings Identitätsphilosophie*. Frankfurt: Klostermann, 2000.
Rauch, Angelika. *The Hieroglyph of Tradition: Freud, Benjamin, Gadamer, Novalis, Kant*. Madison, NJ: Fairleigh Dickinson University Press, 2000.
Rehm, Else. "Unbekannte Briefe J. W. Ritters aus den Jahren 1800–1803." *Jahrbuch des freien deutschen Hochstifts* (1971): 32–89.
Reil, Johann. "Über das polarische Auseinanderweichen der ursprünglichen Naturkräfte in der Gebärmutter zur Zeit der Schwangerschaft" *Archiv für Physiologie* 3 (1807): 402–501.
Rheinberger, H. J. *Towards a History of Epistemic Things*. Stanford: Stanford University Press, 1997.
Richards, Robert. *The Romantic Philosophy of Life: Science and Philosophy in the Age of Goethe*. Chicago: University of Chicago Press, 2002.
Richter, Karl. "Beziehungen von Dichtung und Morphologie in Goethes Werk." In *der Mitte zwischen Natur und Subjekt*, edited by Gunter Mann, Dieter Mollenhauer, and Stefan Peters. Frankfurt am Main: Waldemar Kramer, 1992.
Richter, Klaus. "Der Physiker Ritter und Johann Gottfried Herder." In *Impulse* 3 1981: 109–119.
———. *Das Leben des Physikers Johann Wilhelm Ritter*, Weimar: Hermann Böhlaus Nachfolger, 2003.
Ritter, Joachim, Rudolf Eisler, Gottfried Gabriel, and Karlfried Gründer, et al. *Historisches Wörterbuch der Philosophie*. Basel: Schwabe, 2004.
Ritter, Johann Wilhelm. *Beweis, daß ein beständiger Galvanismus den Lebensproceß in dem Thierreich begleite*. Weimar: Industrie-Comptoir, 1798.
———. *Beyträge zur nähern Kenntniss des Galvanismus*. 4 vols. Jena: Friedrich Fromann, 1800–1805.
———. *Die Physik als Kunst. Ein Versuch, die Tendenz der Physik aus ihrer Geschichte zu deuten*. Munich: Joseph Lindauer, 1806.
———. *Physisch-chemische Abhandlungen in chronologischer Folge*. 3 vols. Leipzig: C. H. Reclam, 1806.
———. "Versuch einer Geschichte der Schicksale der chemischen Theorie in den letzten Jahrhunderten." *Journal für die Chemie, Physik und Mineralogie* 7.1 (1808): 1–66.
———. *Fragmente aus dem Nachlass eines jungen Physikers. Ein Taschenbuch für Freunde der Natur*. A facsimile of the first edition (Heidelberg: bey Mohr und Zimmer, 1810), afterword by Heinrich Schipperges. Heidelberg: Lambert Schneider, 1969.
———. *Briefe eines Romantischen Physikers. Johann Wilhelm Ritter an Gotthilf Heinrich Schubert und an Karl von Hardenberg*, edited by Armin Hermann and Friedrich Klemm. München: H. Moos, 1966, 30.
Roder, Florian. *Menschwerdung des Menschen: der magische Idealismus im Werk des Novalis*. Stuttgart: J. M. Mayer, 1997.
Roe, Shirley. *The Natural Philosophy of Albrecht von Haller*. New York: Arno Press, 1981.
von Sachs, Julius. *History of Botany (1530–1860)*, translated by Henry Garnsey. Oxford: Clarendon, 1890.

"Sammelrezension zweier Werke über Galvanismus." *Allgemeine Literatur-Zeitung* 310–314, (28 November 30 November, 1805).
Schaffer, Simon "Self Evidence." *Critical Inquiry* 18.2 (Winter 1992): 327–362.
Schelling, Friedrich. *Ideen zu einer Philosophie der Natur* (1797), edited by Manfred Durner. Vol. 1, 5 of the *Historische-kritische Ausgabe*. Stuttgart: Frommann-Holzboog, 1997.

———. *Erster Entwurf eines Systems der Naturphilosophie* (1799), edited by Wilhelm G. Jacobs und Paul Ziche. Vol. 1,7 of the *Historische-kritische Ausgabe*. Stuttgart: Frommann-Holzboog, 2001.

———. *Von der Weltseele: eine Hypothese der höhern Physik zur Erklärung des allgemeinen Organismus*, edited by Jörg Jantzen. Vol. 1,6 of the *Historische-kritische Ausgabe*. Stuttgart: Frommann-Holzboog, 2000.
Schick, Edgar B. "Art and Science: Herder's Imagery and Eighteenth-Century Biology." *The German Quarterly* 41.3 (1968): 356–368.
Schiebinger, Londa. "The Private Life of Plants: Sexual Politics in Carl Linnaeus and Erasmus Darwin." In *Science and Sensibility: Gender and Scientific Inquiry 1780–1945*, edited by Marina Benjamin. Oxford: Basil Blackwell, 1991.

———. *Nature's Body: Gender in the Making of Modern Science*. Boston: Beacon Press, 1993.

———. "The Loves of the Plants." *Scientific American* (February 1996): 110–115.
Schieren, Jost. *Anschauende Urteilskraft: methodische und philosophische Grundlagen von Goethes naturwissenschaftlichem Erkennen*. Düsseldorf: Parerga, 1998.
Schiller, Friedrich. *Musen-Almanach für das Jahr 1799*. Reprint. Hildesheim: Olms, 1969.

———. "Über naïve und sentimentalische Dichtung." In vol. 20 of *Schillers Werke. Nationalausgabe*, edited by Julius Petersen, Gerhard Fricke, Lieselotte Blumenthal, and Benno von Wiese. 42 vols. Weimar: H. Böhlaus Nachfolger, 1943–.
Schlegel, Friedrich. *Kritische Friedrich-Schlegel Ausgabe*, edited by Ernst Behler, Jean Jacques Anstett, and Hans Eichner. 19 vols. Munich: F. Schöningh, 1900–.

———. *Theorie der Weiblichkeit*, afterword by Winfried Menninghaus. Frankfurt am Main: Insel, 1983.
Schulz, Gerhard. "Novalis' Erotik. Zur Geschichtlichkeit der Gefühle." In *Novalis und die Wissenschaften*, edited by Herbert Uerlings. Tübingen: M. Niemeyer, 1997.
Sellars, John. *Stoicism*. Berkeley: University of California Press, 2006.
Shapin, Steven. "The House of Experiment in Seventeenth-Century England." *Isis* 79.3 (September 1988): 373–404.
Snelders, Henricus A. M. "Hegel und der romantischer Physiker J. W. Ritter." In *Hegels Jenaer Naturphilosophie*, edited by Klaus Vieweg. Munich: Wilhem Fink, 1998.
von Sömmering, Samuel Thomas. *Über das Organ der Seele*. Königsberg: Friedrich Nicolovius, 1796.
Stadler, Ulrich. *Die theuren Dinge*. Bern: Francke Verlag, 1980.
Siegert, Bernhard. *Passage des Digitalen. Zeichenpraktiken der neuzeitlichen Wissenschaften 1500–1900*. Berlin: Brinkmann & Bose, 2003.
Stannard, Jerry. "Linnaeus, Nomenclator Historicusque Neoclassicus." In *Contemporary Perspectives on Linnaeus*, edited by J. Weinstock. Lanham, Md.: University Press of America.
Starobinski, Jean. "The Style of Autobiography," translated by Seymour Chatman. In *Autobiography: essays theoretical and critical*, edited by James Olney. Princeton: Princeton University Press, 1980.

Steffens, Henrich. *Was ich erlebte*. Munich: Winkler, 1956.
Steig, Reinhold. *Achim von Arnim und die ihm nahe standen*. 2 vols. Bern: Herbert Lang, 1970.
Stein, Klaus. *Naturphilosophie der Frühromantik*. Paderborn: Schöningh, 2004.
Stockhammer, Robert. "Spiraltendenzen der Sprache, Goethes *Amyntas* und seine Theorie des Symbols." *Poetica* (1993): 129–154.
Strack, Friedrich. "Novalis und Fichte. Zur bewußtseinstheoretischen und moralphilosophischen Rezeption Friedrich von Hardenbergs." In *Novalis und die Wissenschaften*, edited by Herbert Uerlings. Tübingen: M. Niemeyer, 1997.
Strickland, Stuart Walter. "The Ideology of Self-Knowledge and the Practice of Self-Experimentation." In *Eighteenth-Century Studies* 31.4 (1998): 453–471.
Tantillo, Astrida Orle. "Goethe's Botany and His Philosophy of Gender." In *Eighteenth-Century Life* 22.2 (1998): 123–138.
———. *The Will to Create. Goethe's Philosophy of Nature*. Pittsburgh: University of Pittsburgh Press, 2002.
Theisen, Bianca: "'Macroanthropos.' Friedrich von Hardenberg's Literary Anthropology." *The Yearbook of Research in English and American Literature* 12 (1996): 243–255.
Tschurenev, Eva-Maria. "Hegels Abwehr der Totalisierung des Galvanismus bei Ritter." In *Hegels Jenaer Naturphilosophie*, edited by Klaus Vieweg. Munich: Wilhem Fink, 1998.
Uerlings, Herbert. *Friedrich Von Hardenberg, Gennant Novalis: Werk und Forschung*. Stuttgart: J.B. Metzler, Stuttgart, 1991.
Marcus Vitruvius Pollio. *The Ten Books on Architecture*, translated by Morris Hicky Morgan. Cambridge: Harvard University Press, 1914.
Vogl, Joseph. "Nomos der Ökonomie. Steuerungen in Goethes *Wahlverwandtschaften*." *MLN* 114.3 (1999): 503–527.
Volta, Alessandro. "On the Electricity Excited by the Mere Contact of Conducting Substances of Different Kinds. In a Letter from Mr. Alexander Volta, F.R.S. Professor of Natural Philosphy in the University of Pavia, to the R. Hon. Sir Joseph Banks, Bart. K.B. P.R.S." *Philosophical Transactions of the Royal Society of London* 2 (1800): 403–431.
Weber, Marianne. *Ehefrau und Mutter in der Rechtsentwicklung*. Tübingen: J. C. B. Mohr, 1907.
Wellbery, David. *The Specular Moment*. Stanford: Stanford University Press, 1996.
———. "Kunst-Zeugung-Geburt, Überlegungen zu einer anthropologischen Grundfigur." In *Kunst-Zeugung-Geburt. Theorien und Metaphern ästhetischer Produktion in der Neuzeit*, edited by Christian Begemann and David Wellbery. Rombach: Freiburg im Breisgau, 2002.
Welsh, Caroline. *Hirnhöhlenpoetiken*. Freiburg im Breisgau: Rombach, 2003.
Wetzels, Walter D. *Johann Wilhelm Ritter: Physik im Wirkungsfeld der deutschen Romantik*. Berlin: Walter de Gruyter, 1973.
———. "Johann Wilhelm Ritter: Romantic Physics in Germany" In *Romanticism and the Sciences*. Edited by Andrew Cunningham and Nicholas Jardine. Cambridge: Cambridge University Press, 1990.
Winkler, Hartmut. "Discourses, Schemata, Technology, Monuments: Outline for a Theory of Cultural Continuity," translated by Geoffrey Winthrop-Young and Michael Wutz. *Configurations* 10 (2002): 91–109.
Wyder, Margrit. *Goethes Naturmodell: Die Scala Naturae and ihre Transformationen*. Cologne: Böhlau, 1998.
Winckelmann, Johann Joachim. *Anmerkungen über die Baukunst der Alten*. Leipzig, Johann Gottfried Dyck, 1762.
———. *Geschichte der Kunst des Alterthums*. Leipzig: Breitkopf, 1764

Zammito, John. *The Genesis of Kant's 'Critique of Judgment.'* Chicago: University of Chicago Press, 1992.
Zanucchi, Mario. *Novalis—Poesie und Geschichtlichkeit: die Poetik Friedrich von Hardenbergs* (Paderborn: Schöningh, 2006).
Zedler, Johann Heinrich and Carl Günther Ludovici. *Grosses vollständiges Universal-Lexikon aller Wissenschaften und Künste.* Halle und Leipzig: Johann Heinrich Zedler, 1732–1750.

Index

A
Anaxagoras, 51, 54, 180n122
Aristotle, 7, 8
artisan, 58, 85–86, 95, 98, 100
Assman, Aleida, 119, 130–1
Assman, Jan, 131–2
Augustine, 117

B
Becher, Johann Joachim, 150, 151
Bell, Matthew, 47, 178n92
Benn, Gottfried, 33–34
Berzelius, Jöns Jakob, 154
Blumenbach, Johann Friedrich, 2, 4–6, 8, 10–11, 15, 29, 66–67, 157
Blumenberg, Hans, 118
Böhme, Jakob 156
Bonnet, Charles 7, 69, 177
Brentano, Clemens, 195n11, 201n90
Brown, John, 69, 76, 78–79, 188n75
Brugmans, Anton, 136
de Buffon, Georges-Louis Leclerc, 7, 167, 177

C
Carlisle, Anthony, 142
Chaouli, Michel, 187n60
chemistry, 56, 72, 75–76, 80, 113, 134–5, 137, 143, 145–6, 149–50, 152, 160, 204n45
Chladni, Ernst, 128

D
Davy, Humphry, 154
Descartes, René, 136
Deiman, Jan Rudolf, 141

E
Eckermann, Johann Peter, 24

electricity, 11, 74, 79, 113–4, 134–5, 137, 141–2, 145, 148, 155, 188n76, 202n22, 204nn46–47, 207n90
elegy, 19, 21, 42–49, 54–55, 85, 102, 151–4, 156, 158–9, 163, 179n105, 179n107, 200n78
embryo, 7, 8, 24, 28, 139, 141, 145, 153, 167n39, 172n37
epigenesis, 1, 5–10, 14, 16, 58, 66–69, 72, 167n25, 177n82, 185n37
experiment, 4, 14–15, 17, 21–22, 30, 38–42, 44, 50, 55, 68, 75–76, 80, 85, 91, 113–7, 135–6, 142, 145–8, 154–5, 158, 176n72, 176n81, 177n82, 184n29, 195n15, 200n77, 203n28
evolution, 1, 5–6, 8, 67–8. *See also* preformation

F
fairy tale, 96–97, 100–107, 160, 191n28, 192n41, 192n47, 193n55
Fichte, Johann Gottlieb, 3, 9, 15, 17, 56, 58–67, 76, 85, 106, 108–110, 138, 159, 169n6, 182nn3–8, 183n19, 184n29, 186n50
Förster, Eckart, 39, 177n85
Foucault, Michel, 10, 16–17, 130
formative drive, 2, 11, 15, 29, 67, 166n23, 173n42
Frank, Manfred, 17, 58–59, 61, 64–65, 106, 182n3, 183n18, 184n30
Frevert, Ute 12

G
Gaier, Ulrich, 78, 193n52

Galvani, Luigi 114, 120
Gehlen, Adolph Ferdinand, 125, 150
Genette, Gérard, 116
von Goethe, Johann Wolfgang, 1, 3, 8, 10–11, 13–14, 16, 18, 19–55, 59, 67–68, 72, 85, 98, 102, 108, 113, 120, 136, 138, 149, 151–161, 163; "The Metamorphosis of Plants" (poem) 14, 20–23, 25, 28–29, 33–35, 39, 42–49, 54–55, 85, 98, 152, 158; *The Metamorphosis of Plants* (essay) 20–21, 26, 30, 32–42, 44–45, 47–49, 50, 53–55, 151; *Wilhelm Meister* novels 20, 51, 119–20, 122, 175
Gould, Stephen J., 6, 8, 186n47
von Haller, Albrecht 7, 167, 177, 185n37
von Hardenberg, Friedrich (Novalis), 2, 3, 13, 15, 16, 18, 29, 55, 56–112; *The Apprentices of Sais*, 16, 55–56, 58, 84, 87–89, 95, 97–100, 102–11, 190n, 191n, 192n, 193n, 194n; "Fichte Studies," 15, 58–61, 64–66, 76, 85, 106, 108–110, 119; *The General Draft (Das allgemeine Brouillon)*, 57, 67, 70, 76, 79–80, 88, 98, 100, 103, 182n6, 189n81; *Heinrich von Ofterdingen*, 13, 16, 56, 84, 86, 95–99, 102, 105, 110, 161, 190n11, 191n25

H

Harvey, William, 28, 172n37
Helfer, Martha, 12–13
von Herder, Johann Gottfried, 5, 24–26, 30, 33, 54, 82, 113, 117, 125–130, 151, 162, 171, 196n22, 198n59
hieroglyph, 93, 97, 115, 126–132, 145, 155, 161–2, 198n62, 199n67
Hippocrates, 29
Hisinger, Wilhelm, 154
Holzhey, Christoph, 82
von Humboldt, Wilhelm, 2, 3, 10, 16–17, 165n8

K

Kant, Immanuel, 2, 9, 15, 20, 41, 66–67, 69, 74, 86, 89, 92, 142–145
von Kielmeyer, Carl Friedrich, 4, 5, 8, 16, 93, 190n16

Kittler, Friedrich 12–13, 168n49
Körner, Gottfried, 20
Kreuzer, Ingrid, 102, 104
Kuzniar, Alice, 12, 13, 104

L

Lampadius, Wilhelm August, 72
Lavoisier, Antoine, 80, 146, 150, 160
Lejeune, Philippe, 116, 196
Lempe, Johann Friedrich, 72
Lenoir, Timothy, 14–15, 67, 166n23, 185n37
Lepenies, Wolf, 17, 167n27
Liedtke, Ralf, 75–76, 78
Lichtenberg, Georg Christoph, 29, 113, 115, 128, 195n15, 207n90
Linné, Charles, 19, 23–25, 27, 45–46, 152, 170n13
Luhmann, Niklas, 45
Luther, Martin, 117

M

macroanthropos, 87–89, 91–92, 109
magnetism, 3, 18, 74, 113, 120–2, 134–7, 139, 141, 149, 157, 161, 201n6, 202n19
Mahoney, Dennis, 98
mathematics, 41, 50, 56, 67, 69, 71–75, 82, 87, 89, 91, 135, 157, 159–60, 177n82, 186n48, 190n19
von Martius, Carl Friedrich, 50–51
Mautner, Franz, 173n43
Menke, Bettine, 129, 162, 199n75
Menninghaus, Winfried, 12, 139–140, 168n50, 188n77, 203n33
metamorphosis, 14, 16–22, 24, 26, 28–30, 32–36, 38–55, 68, 85, 92, 96, 98, 102, 136, 149, 151–2, 154, 156, 158–9, 163
microcosm, 83, 87–88, 108–109
microscope, 1, 10–11, 66
von Molnár, Geza, 78
von Montgelas, Maximilian, 150
monument, 18, 119, 127, 129–133, 145, 155, 161–162, 200n81
Moritz, Karl Philipp, 30, 173n49
Müller-Sievers, Helmut, 9, 13, 68, 167, 180n117

N

Neubauer, John, 102, 104, 172n, 188n75
Neuenhahn, Karl Christian Adolf, 42

Index 221

Neumann, Gerhard, 29–30, 103–104, 189n84
Nicholson, William, 142
Novalis. *See* von Hardenberg, Friedrich

O

O'Brien, William Arctander, 98, 193n59
Ockham, William of 136
Ørsted, Hans Christian, 115, 125, 151, 195n15, 206n, 207n
Outram, Dorinda, 115, 196n
oxygen 12, 80, 82, 141–142, 145–147, 160, 204n

P

Paul (Saint), 117, 118, 124, 196n
Peters, Günter, 42, 170n, 178n, 179n
pile (Voltaic), 18, 25, 134–6, 141–2, 145–9, 154, 162–3, 204n, 206n76
Pinto-Correia, Clara 7, 8, 70
Portmann, Adolf, 47, 174n55
Preformation, 5–11, 14, 16, 58, 66–72, 166n22, 167n39, 177n82, 186n37, 185n40
Priestley, Joseph, 150

R

Rehm, Else, 124
Reil, Johann, 137–8
reproduction, 46, 8, 10, 14, 22, 28, 32–33, 36–38, 40, 44, 47, 49, 52, 68, 93, 158, 165n8, 173n38, 175n65, 178n92, 190n16, 200n87
Rheinberger, Hans-Jörg, 150, 206n74
Richter, Klaus, 114, 195n6
Ritter, Johann Wilhelm, 1, 2, 3, 8, 11, 14, 17, 18, 29, 64, 74, 76, 83, 112–163; *Fragments from the Estate of a Young Physicist*, 1, 2, 14, 17–18, 113, 115–125, 128–143, 148–50, 153, 161–3
Roe, Shirley, 7, 167n28

S

Schiebinger, Londa, 171n14
Schiller, Friedrich, 20–21, 42, 48–49, 169n, 179n105

Schlegel, Friedrich, 57, 72, 76, 89, 98, 121, 135, 146
Schlichtgeroll, Friedrich, 56
Schubert, Gotthilf Heinrich, 23, 124–5
Shapin, Steven 200n77
Siegert, Bernhard, 128, 162
von Sömmering, Samuel Thomas, 142, 143, 204n50
spiral tendency 48, 50–55, 158, 175n63, 180n112
Stahl, Georg Ernst, 150–1
von Stein, Charlotte 19, 22, 44
Strickland, Stuart Walter, 114

T

Tantillo, Astrida, 13–14, 42, 47, 181n125
Theisen, Bianca, v, ix, 87, 92
Tieck, Ludwig, 57
von Troostwijk, Adriaan Paets, 141

V

Vitruvius, 130–131, 200n87
Vogl, Joseph, 206n71
Volta, Alessandro, 18, 114, 120, 134–5, 142, 147, 154–5, 188n76, 204n46
Vulpius, Christiane, 21, 42, 170n12, 177n88, 201n90

W

Wellbery, David, 59, 137–138, 168n49
Welsh, Caroline, 145, 162, 199n75
Werner, Abraham Gottlob, 72
Wetzels, Walter, 152
Willer, Stefan, 166n14
Winckelmann, Johann Joachim, 130–1
Wolff, Christian, 7–8, 38, 67, 167n39, 175n67
Workshop, 18, 86, 111, 129–130, 132, 133

Z

Zanucchi, Mario, 184n33
Zedler, Johann Heinrich, 12, 86, 189n4